More Advance Praise for *The Russian Revolution*

"This is a book that we have been waiting for. *The Russian Revolution* is an enormous subject, and to write a short and authoritative book on it is very difficult indeed. Sean McMeekin brings many gifts to the task, not the least of which is that he can describe crowd scenes with immediacy. It should count as a classic."

—NORMAN STONE, author of *The Eastern Front 1914–1917*

"In vivid colors, Sean McMeekin presents a provocative narrative of the 1917 Russian revolutions with an emphasis on the conspiracies, mutinies, and acts of treason behind the scenes of both revolutions. He shows how the revolutions were a direct result of Russia's involvement in World War I in new ways. It is a book that will generate much debate."

—ERIC LOHR, Susan Carmel Lehrman Chair of Russian History and Culture, American University

THE RUSSIAN REVOLUTION

THE RUSSIAN REVOLUTION

A New History

SEAN McMEEKIN

P

PROFILE BOOKS

First published in Great Britain in 2017 by
Profile Books Ltd
3 Holford Yard
Bevin Way
London
WC1X 9HD

www.profilebooks.com

First published in the United States of America by
Basic Books, an imprint of Perseus Books, LLC,
a subsidiary of Hachette Book Group, Inc.

10 9 8 7 6 5 4 3 2 1

Designed by Jeff Williams

Printed and bound in Great Britain by
Clays, Bungay, Suffolk

A CIP catalogue record for this book is available from the British Library.

ISBN 978 1 78125 902 3
eISBN 978 1 78283 379 6

FSC
www.fsc.org
MIX
Paper from
responsible sources
FSC® C018072

For Ayla and Errol

CONTENTS

A NOTE ON DATES,
NAMES, TRANSLATION, AND
TRANSLITERATION

The Russian Revolution, like both of the twentieth-century world wars, wrought havoc with place names as cities and entire regions changed hands between empires, from empires to nation states, and sometimes back to empires again. Moscow, mysteriously, escaped the nomenclature revolution, but this is one mercy among endless headaches. Because St. Petersburg was Petrograd (and not yet Leningrad) from 1914 to 1924, that is what it is for most of the book. With other cities I have used the contemporary form with modern usage in parentheses, thus Reval (Tallinn). In more politically sensitive cases, I have offered three versions on first usage, as in Lemberg (Lvov/ Lviv). Today's Istanbul was called Constantinople in the period covered in the book, even by Ottoman government officials, and so that is the name we use. Although the Republic of Turkey did not come into formal existence until 1923, I refer to Turkey and the Ottoman Empire interchangeably before that date, as many Turks and most Russians and Europeans did at the time.

Dates provide an especially vexing problem in modern Russian history, in that the Julian calendar the empire used was first twelve, then thirteen days, behind the Gregorian one used in the West, to which the Bolsheviks switched in January 1918, right in the middle of the Russian revolutionary drama. For dates prior to this important in both Russian and European history I have tried to give both dates with a slash, as in November 1/14, 1916, where *1* is the Julian and *14* the Gregorian date. In 1917, when dates start coming fast and furious and the specifically Russian context becomes paramount, I switch over to the Julian calendar owing to the importance of months in revolutionary terminology (*February* Revolution, *April* and *July* days, *October* Revolution), before following the Bolsheviks in switching to the Gregorian in mid-January 1918. To guide readers, signposts will be offered when these switches are made.

For Russian-language words, I have used the Library of Congress transliteration system, with a somewhat modified version for names. It has been my customary practice in the past to make exceptions only for standard spellings of famous surnames (e.g., Milyukov, not Miliukov). And yet this seems unfair to others. With apologies to Russian specialists, I have applied these changes broadly in the main text, starting Russian names with *Yu*, not *Iu* (Yusupov, not Iusopov) and *Ya*, not *Ia* (Yakov, not Iakov), which rule also eliminates double initials for first names and patronymics (*Iu* and *Ia* are two letters in Latin, one letter in Cyrillic). I have also ended names with -*y*, not –*ii* (Trotsky, not Trotskii) and -*x*, not –*ks* (Felix, not Feliks). I have done likewise with names where a close English rendering is common, such as Alexander (not Aleksandr) and Peter (not Petr/Pyotr). Mikhail and Nikolai are spelled and pronounced differently enough in Russian that I have left these alone, unless affixed to an Anglicized title, such as "Grand Duke Michael" or "Grand Duke Nicholas." In accordance with convention, I have also used *Izvestiya* not *Izvestiia* and *Novoe Vremya* not *Vremia* in the main text, although following Library of Congress spellings in the source notes. "Soft" and "hard" signs are left out of the main text, so as not to burden the reader. The goal is to make it as easy as possible to read Russian names, and to remember them. It is impossible to be consistent in all these things; may common sense prevail.

All translations from the French, German, Russian, and Turkish, unless I am citing another translated work or note otherwise, are my own.

Introduction:
The First Century of the
Russian Revolution

L ike 1789, when the French Revolution erupted, 1917 has entered the lexicon of world-historical dates all educated citizens are expected to know and remember. The meaning of 1917, however, remains much contested, not least because two very different revolutions took place in Russia that fateful year. The February Revolution toppled the Russian monarchy and ushered in a brief era of mixed liberal and socialist governance, only to be superseded by the more radical October Revolution, which saw Lenin's Bolshevik Party impose a Communist dictatorship and proclaim an open-ended world revolution against "capitalism" and "imperialism." Each of these developments was significant enough to merit serious historical study. Together they constitute one of the seminal events of modern history, which introduced Communism to the world and paved the way for decades of ideological conflict, culminating in the Cold War of 1945–1991.

Because the Bolsheviks were avowed Marxists, our understanding of the Russian Revolution has long been colored by Marxist language, from the idea of a class struggle between "proletarians" and the "capitalist" ruling classes, to the dialectical progression from a "bourgeois" to a socialist revolution. Even many non-Marxist historians tended, in the Cold War years, to accept the basic Marxist framework of discussion about the Russian Revolution, concentrating on such matters as Russia's economic backwardness vis-à-vis more advanced Western capitalist countries, the stages of her emergence from feudalism and her "belated" industrial development, inequality and Russia's lopsided social structure, and so on. As late as 1982, Sheila Fitzpatrick, in an influential college textbook titled *The Russian Revolution*, described Lenin's aim in the October Revolution unambiguously as "the overthrow of the bourgeoisie by the proletariat."[1]

This relatively uncritical approach to the Russian Revolution proved surprisingly resistant to revision over the decades, in part because the great anti-Communist writers of the Cold War years, from George Orwell to Alexander Solzhenitsyn to Robert Conquest, focused on Communism in its period of Stalinist "maturity" in the 1930s and 1940s, not on its origins in the Revolution. Serious new studies of the February Revolution did appear, such as George Katkov's *Russia 1917* (1967) and Tsuyoshi Hasegawa's *February Revolution* (1981). Not until Richard Pipes's *The Russian Revolution* (1990) however, was there a serious reappraisal of the revolutions of 1917 as a whole. What happened in Red October, Pipes asserted, was not a revolution, not a mass movement from below, but a top-down coup d'état, the "capture of governmental power by a small minority." Far from being a product of social evolution, class struggle, economic development, or other inexorable historical forces foreseen in Marxist theory, the Russian Revolution was made "by identifiable men pursuing their own advantages," and was therefore "properly subject to value judgment." Pipes's judgment of these men was withering.[2]

Coming out at a time when the Soviet Union was in the process of collapsing, Pipes's thoroughly revisionist study acted like a wrecking ball, demolishing any last claim the Russian Communist Party had to democratic, popular, or moral legitimacy. Pipes was even called as an expert witness in the Nuremberg-style trial of the party's crimes convened in 1992 (and then quickly abandoned) by Russian president Boris Yeltsin's post-Communist government. Although many Soviet specialists scoffed at Pipes's revisionist history as irretrievably biased (Pipes had worked as an adviser to the Reagan administration in 1981–1982), no one could ignore it. In the long-running debates about Communism between sympathizers and "Cold Warriors," it seemed that the sympathizers had been placed squarely on the defensive, if not routed for good.

A quarter-century later, there are signs that the political worm is turning again. Works such as Thomas Piketty's 2013 international best seller *Capital in the Twenty-First Century*, along with the popularity of openly avowed socialists, such as Bernie Sanders, with young voters in previously socialism-unfriendly America, suggest that Marx may be poised for a surprising comeback. For "millennial Marxists," as the *Nation* magazine has described the wave of young activists motivated by the "scourge of inequality," the financial crash of 2008 has more resonance than the fall of the Berlin Wall in 1989, which marked the end of Communism in eastern Europe, or the collapse of the USSR in 1991. By many measures (such as the "Gini coefficient"), social inequality is indeed rising sharply in Western countries, which lends ammunition to ever-broader indictments of capitalism. We can surely now expect counterrevisionist books on the history of Communism, as younger historians revive the old dream of social revolution.[3]

An event as consequential as the Russian Revolution will always be used and abused in political argument, as an epochal transformation that brought the oppressed workers and peasants of Russia either liberation ("peace, land, and bread") or enslavement, depending on one's political sympathies. Edifying as these parables may be, they bear only passing resemblance to the actual events of 1917, which historians, granted access to original documentary material only after the fall of the Soviet Union and the opening of Russian archives, are still struggling to reconstruct.

Now that the Cold War is mercifully over, it is possible to treat the revolution more dispassionately, as a concrete historical event—controversial and significant in its lasting impact on world politics, but also worth understanding on its own terms, unmediated by our current prejudices. Half-true anecdotes and stories about the revolution, smoothed into well-worn grooves as they were told and retold according to historians' evolving preoccupations over the decades, have come to replace the crooked timber of events in our memory. It is time to descend from the airy heights of ideological argument about 1917 and return to the solid ground of fact. By going back to the original sources, we can rediscover the revolution as it transpired in real time, from the perspective of key actors who did not know, as they acted, how the story would turn out.

The most important revelation from the Russian archives has been a simple one. The salient fact about Russia in 1917, judging from virtually all documentary sources of the time, is that it was a country at war. Somehow, in all the historical arguments about Russia's autocratic political tradition; about "Russian economic backwardness"; about peasants and the land question; about factory statistics, strikes, and labor; about Marxism, about Bolsheviks, Mensheviks, Socialist Revolutionaries, and their competing doctrines, this simple circumstance was obscured, pushed so far into the background that it had to be discovered anew.[4]

Fortunately for historians of the revolution, the years since 1991 have seen an explosion of research into Russia's military performance in World War I from 1914 to 1917—a subject that, owing to Lenin's ties to Germany and his controversial decision to solicit a separate peace from Berlin in November 1917, had been almost taboo in Soviet times. It turns out that the Russian armies were not as hopelessly outclassed by the Germans on the eastern front as we have been told. Military censors' reports, only now rediscovered, show that the idea of creeping dissatisfaction in the ranks in winter 1916–1917, which one encounters in nearly all histories of the revolution, are erroneous: morale was trending up, not least because Russian peasant soldiers were much better fed than their German opponents.

Economic data tell a similar story. Far from there being a generalized collapse culminating in the February Revolution, the evidence points instead to a stupendous (if inflationary) wartime boom. There was a crisis during Russia's "Great Retreat" of 1915, when it seemed that shell shortage would doom the Russian war effort, but this was brilliantly overcome in 1916, a year that saw all war-industrial production indices shoot ahead—and the Russian armies advancing on every front. The world-famous bread shortages of Petrograd in winter 1917 likewise turn out, on closer inspection, to be mostly mythical.

Even the names are changing, as political actors recede from the story of the revolution or reemerge, center stage. Many historians have pooh-poohed the importance of the legendary Rasputin, but it now appears that lurid rumors had some truth to them after all: plots to sideline or murder the tsar's influential peasant faith healer engaged not only scions of Russian high society and liberal politicians but Allied spies and senior officials. Mikhail Rodzianko, the president of the State Duma (parliament) who was the most famous politician in Russia at the dawn of 1917, saw his celebrity dwindle over the decades into a small bit part in the February Revolution, a mere mention in most history textbooks; it now appears that he was the key player in the drama after all. Trotsky and Stalin really were in the middle of the action during the revolutions of both 1905 and 1917, and deserve their renown. The exiled founder of the Bolshevik Party, Lenin, by contrast, was an afterthought in 1905 and barely worth the attention of tsarist police agents until his return to Russia in April 1917, after an absence of nearly two decades. Even then, an out-of-touch Lenin would have had little impact on the political scene had he not been furnished with German funds to propagandize the Russian army at a time when Russia was at war on fronts stretching from the Baltic Sea to the Caspian, with more than 7 million men under arms.

Lenin and the Bolsheviks played no role worth mentioning in the fall of the tsar, an unexpected gift of fate that, in mockery of Marxist pretensions of historical determinism, took them entirely by surprise. But they were the ultimate beneficiaries. Lenin's "Zimmerwald Left" program, worked out at wartime congresses of socialist exiles in Switzerland, which proposed to "turn the armies red" by infiltrating them with radical agitators, was a minority doctrine much mocked by Europe's mainstream socialist leaders, who preferred to focus on draft resistance and organizing antiwar demonstrations. After Lenin was given the chance to put his program into practice after the February Revolution, few were laughing anymore. It was Lenin's opportunistic exploitation of Russia's vulnerable strategic position in 1917, his conscious efforts to change the "imperialist war" into civil war by promoting mutinies and mass desertions of soldiers with their arms, which furnished the Bolshevik Party with the muscle it needed to triumph in the October Revolution and impose Communist rule on Russia.

The Bolsheviks' hostile takeover of the Russian army in 1917 was an audacious, chancy, and close-run affair that was nearly thwarted at many critical moments. Had the statesmen thrown up by the February Revolution, above all Socialist Revolutionary orator and would-be strongman Alexander Kerensky, shown more competence and fortitude in suppressing Leninist agitation in the armies, the Bolsheviks would be no more remembered today than Europe's other socialist minority parties. Lenin would merit, at most, a footnote in the history of Russia, and of socialism.

This is not to take anything away from Lenin's breathtaking accomplishments, although these were very different from the "proletarian overthrowing of the bourgeoisie" he is credited with in traditional accounts. Fueled by German subsidies and his own indomitable will to power, Lenin succeeded in breaking the Russian Imperial Army in 1917 and then reassembled its shards in 1918, with Trotsky's help, into a formidable Red Army. Just as Lenin had foretold in his Zimmerwald Left prophesy, the resulting civil war of 1918–1920, which the Bolsheviks fought against a world of foreign and domestic enemies, both real and imagined, turned out to be even bloodier than the "imperialist war" with the Central Powers had been, requiring ever-mounting levels of mass mobilization, state control, and secret-police surveillance and repression.

After the departure of the last foreign and foreign-supplied armies from Russia in 1920, the Russian Civil War devolved into an internal struggle against recalcitrant peasant "class enemies" who had been reduced to poverty and famine by the Communist regime's forcible grain requisitions and its suppression of market and all moneyed transactions, as the full-on Marxist program of abolishing private property was put into practice. In a tacit concession that the Communist future would take longer to arrive than Lenin hoped, he abandoned the draconian measures of War Communism (as the abolition of private economic activity was retroactively labeled) in 1921–1922, to revive the grain trade, unleash market forces, and bring goods back into the stores. But Lenin's climbdown in this "New Economic Policy" was never meant to be more than a tactical retreat. After fighting and winning one final battle against the Orthodox Church in 1922, the Bolsheviks succeeded in subduing all resistance across the territories of the former tsarist empire, erecting a new empire in its place known as the Union of Soviet Socialist

Republics (USSR). Lenin and his successors could then set their sights on world revolution, exporting Communism to every corner of the globe.

After a quarter-century of exhilarating discoveries from the archives, it is time to take stock of what we have learned. Russia in the last days of the tsars was a land of contradictions, of great wealth and extreme poverty and the myriad social and ethnic tensions of a vast multiethnic empire; but there was nothing inevitable about the collapse of the regime in 1917. Nearly torn asunder by the revolution of 1905, which came in the wake of a humiliating defeat in the Russo-Japanese War, the Russian Empire made a remarkable recovery over the following decade, owing to the tsar's concessions that allowed the creation of the Duma, the formation of labor unions, and the far-sighted land reforms of Peter Stolypin. The tragedy of Russian liberalism is that it was the country's most dedicated reformers and constitutionalists who, by embracing the fashionable ideas of pan-Slavism, convinced Nicholas II that he needed to mobilize in July 1914 to appease public opinion—and then spent the war plotting against him anyway, in spite of his foolish decision to follow their advice. It was the tsar's fateful decision to go to war, despite the pointed warnings of Rasputin and other conservative monarchist advisers he usually trusted more than the liberals, which brought an end to an era of great economic and social progress in Russia, and ultimately cost him his throne. In this way an empire founded on the autocratic principle foundered on the feeble will to power of its last autocrat, who lacked the courage of his own convictions. Once he had the upper hand, Lenin would not make the same mistake.

The Russian Empire
Circa 1900

Arctic

London

NORWAY

Oslo

SWEDEN

Murmansk

Barents
Sea

Novaia
Zemlia

GERMAN
EMPIRE
Berlin

Stockholm

Finland

Helsinki

White Sea

Kara
Sea

East
Prussia

Reval (Tallinn)

Riga

St. Petersburg

Archangel

Vienna

Warsaw

Poland

Vilnius

Pskov

AUSTRIA-

Budapest

Brest-
Litovsk

Minsk

Vologda

HUNGARY

Austrian
Galicia

Smolensk

Moscow

SERBIA

Kiev

Briansk

Nizhny Novgorod

Ob

West

ROMANIA

Ukraine

Riazan

Sofia

Bucharest

Poltava

Perm

Siberia

BULG.

Odessa

Kharkov

Kazan

Ekaterinburg

Tobolsk

Constantinople

Sevastopol

Donetsk

Don

Volga

Saratov

Samara

Ufa

Ob

Ankara

Black Sea

Tsaritsyn

Orenburg

Omsk

Trans Siberian RR

Anatolia

Astrakhan

Orsk

Irtysh

Novonikolaevsk
(Novosibirsk)

Caucasus

Tiflis
(Tblisi)

Erivan

Aral
Sea

Turkestan

Semipalatinsk

Barnau

OTTOMAN

Baku

Caspian Sea

Syr Darya

EMPIRE

Azerbaijan
Persian

Amu Darya

Baghdad

Teheran

Askhabad

Bukhara

Tashkent

Samarkand

PERSIA

Fergana

Hindu Kush

Kabul

BRITISH
INDIA

AFGHANISTAN

- - - Railway under construction

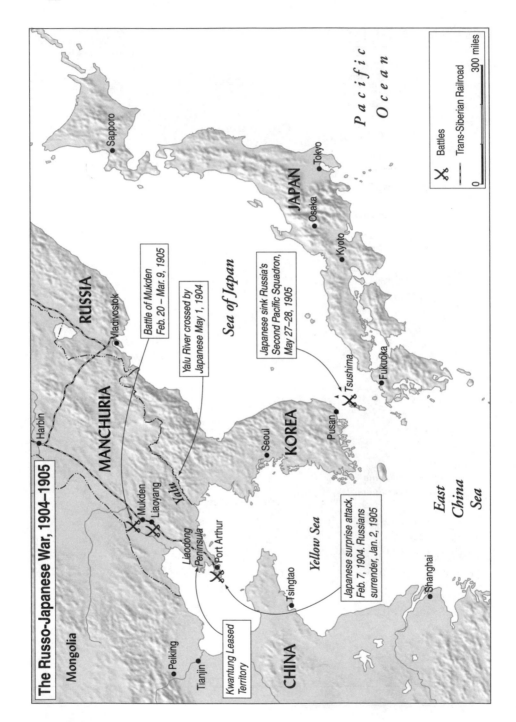

The Russo-Japanese War, 1904–1905

RUSSIA

Vladivostok

MANCHURIA

Harbin

Mongolia

Peiking

Tianjin

Mukden
Liaoyang

Battle of Mukden
Feb. 20 – Mar. 9, 1905

Yalu River crossed by
Japanese May 1, 1904

Yalu

Liaodong
Peninsula

Port Arthur

Kwantung Leased
Territory

CHINA

Tsingtao

Shanghai

Yellow Sea

Japanese surprise attack,
Feb. 7, 1904. Russians
surrender, Jan. 2, 1905

Seoul

KOREA

Pusan

Sea of Japan

Japanese sink Russia's
Second Pacific Squadron,
May 27–28, 1905

Tsushima

Fukuoka

*East
China
Sea*

JAPAN

Sapporo

Tokyo

Osaka

Kyoto

*Pacific
Ocean*

Battles

Trans-Siberian Railroad

0   300 miles

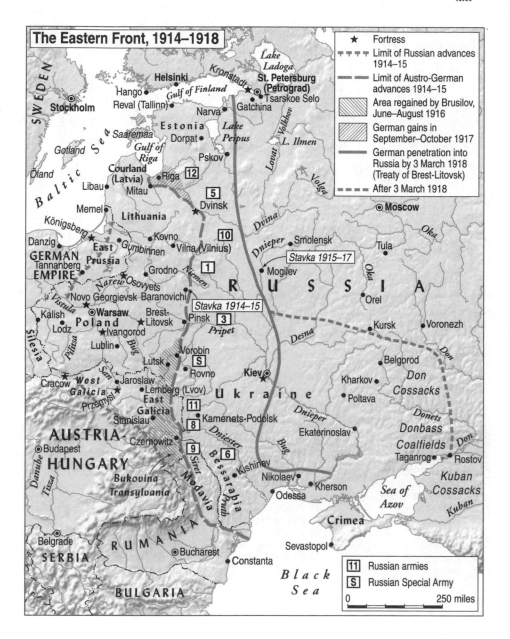

The Eastern Front, 1914–1918

★ Fortress

▼▼▼▼ Limit of Russian advances 1914–15

— — Limit of Austro-German advances 1914–15

Area regained by Brusilov, June–August 1916

German gains in September–October 1917

—— German penetration into Russia by 3 March 1918 (Treaty of Brest-Litovsk)

— — — After 3 March 1918

SWEDEN
Stockholm
Gotland
Öland
Baltic Sea
Königsberg
Danzig
GERMAN
Tannanberg
EMPIRE
East Prussia
Gumbinnen
Memel
Lithuania
Kovno
Vilna (Vilnius)
Grodno
Niemen
Narew
Osovyets
Novo Georgievsk
Baranovichi
Vistula
Kalish
Lodz
Warsaw
Poland
Ivangorod
Lublin
Silesia
Pilitsa
Bug
San
Cracow
West Galicia
Jaroslaw
Lemberg (Lvov)
East Galicia
Przemysl
Stanislau
Czernowitz
AUSTRIA-HUNGARY
Budapest
Danube
Tissa
Bukovina
Transylvania
Siret
Moldavia
Pruth
SERBIA
Belgrade
RUMANIA
Bucharest
BULGARIA
Constanta

Helsinki
Hango
Gulf of Finland
Reval (Tallinn)
Narva
Saaremaa
Estonia
Dorpat
Gulf of Riga
Courland (Latvia)
Riga
Libau
Mitau
Pskov
Lake Peipus
Lovat
L. Ilmen
Volkhov
Lake Ladoga
Kronstadt
St. Petersburg (Petrograd)
Tsarskoe Selo
Gatchina
12
5
Dvinsk
Dvina
10
1
Mogilev
Stavka 1915–17
Smolensk
Dnieper
Stavka 1914–15
Brest-Litovsk
Pinsk
3
Pripet
Vorobin
Lutsk
S
Rovno
Kiev
Kamenets-Podolsk
11
8
Dniester
9
6
Kishinev
Bessarabia
Nikolaev
Odessa
Kherson
Bug
Dnieper
Ekaterinoslav
Poltava
Kharkov
Ukraine
RUSSIA
Moscow
Oka
Oka
Orel
Tula
Volga
Kursk
Voronezh
Desna
Belgorod
Don Cossacks
Don
Donets
Donbass Coalfields
Taganrog
Rostov
Don
Kuban Cossacks
Kuban
Sea of Azov
Crimea
Sevastopol
Black Sea

11 Russian armies
S Russian Special Army

0   250 miles

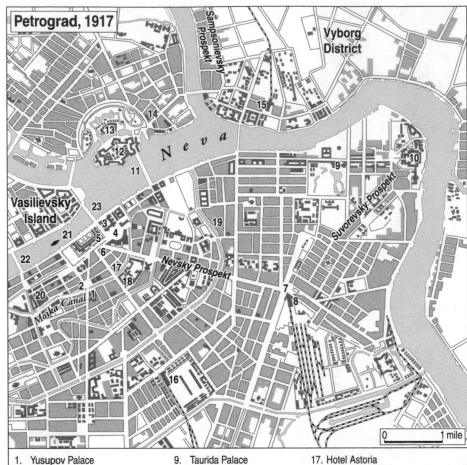

1. Yusupov Palace
2. Okhrana Headquarters
3. Winter Palace
4. Palace Square
5. Admiralty
6. War Ministry
7. Znamensky Square
8. Nikolaevsky (Moscow) Station
9. Taurida Palace
10. Smolny Institute
11. Troitsky Bridge
12. Peter and Paul Fortress
13. Arsenal
14. Kshesinskaya Mansion
15. Finland Station
16. Warsaw Station
17. Hotel Astoria
18. Marinsky Palace
19. Mikhailovsky (Engineering) Palace
20. Central Telegraph Office
21. Battleship Aurora
22. Nikoloevsky Bridge
23. Palace Bridge

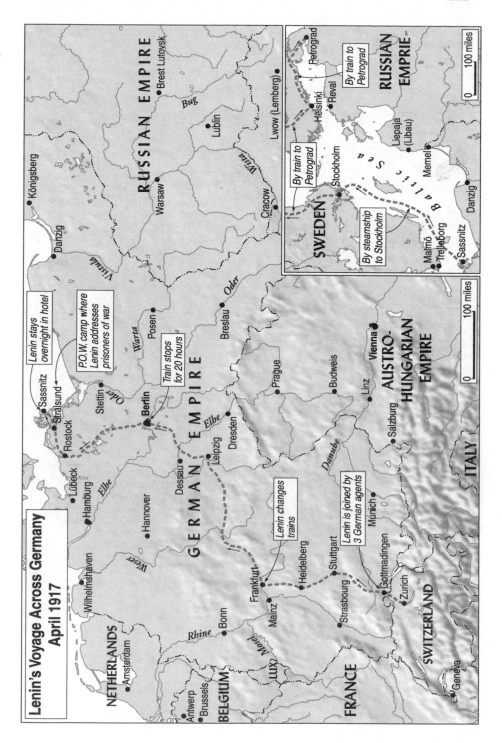

Lenin's Voyage Across Germany April 1917

Lenin stays overnight in hotel

P.O.W. camp where Lenin addresses prisoners of war

Train stops for 20 hours

Lenin changes trains

Lenin is joined by 3 German agents

By train to Petrograd

By train to Petrograd

By steamship to Stockholm

RUSSIAN EMPIRE

RUSSIAN EMPIRE

GERMAN EMPIRE

AUSTRO-HUNGARIAN EMPIRE

NETHERLANDS

BELGIUM

LUX.

FRANCE

SWITZERLAND

ITALY

SWEDEN

Baltic Sea

Brest Lutovsk

Lublin

Lwow (Lemberg)

Warsaw

Cracow

Königsberg

Danzig

Posen

Breslau

Prague

Budweis

Linz

Vienna

Salzburg

Munich

Gottmadingen

Zurich

Geneva

Strasbourg

Stuttgart

Heidelberg

Frankfurt

Mainz

Bonn

Antwerp

Brussels

Amsterdam

Wilhelmshaven

Hannover

Hamburg

Lübeck

Rostock

Stralsund

Sassnitz

Berlin

Stettin

Dessau

Leipzig

Dresden

Danube

Elbe

Oder

Warta

Vistula

Rhine

Moselle

Weser

Elbe

Bug

Vistula

Oder

Petrograd

Helsinki

Reval

Stockholm

Liepaja (Libau)

Memel

Danzig

Malmö

Trelleborg

Sassnitz

0   100 miles

0   100 miles

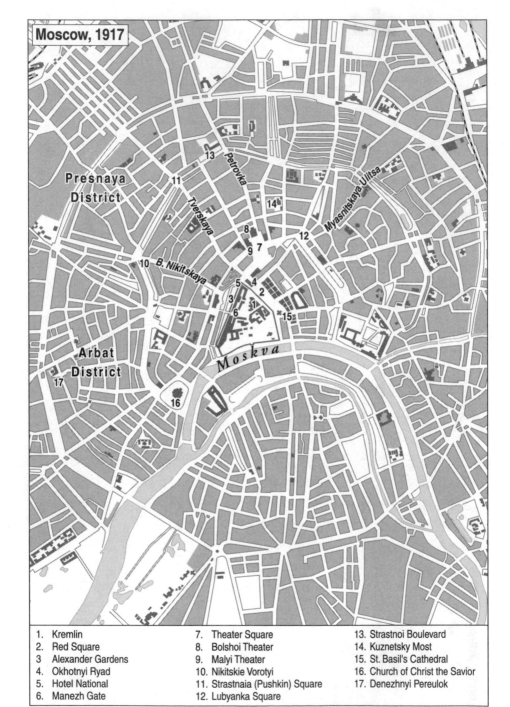

Moscow, 1917

Presnaya District

Arbat District

Moskva

1. Kremlin
2. Red Square
3. Alexander Gardens
4. Okhotnyi Ryad
5. Hotel National
6. Manezh Gate
7. Theater Square
8. Bolshoi Theater
9. Malyi Theater
10. Nikitskie Vorotyi
11. Strastnaia (Pushkin) Square
12. Lubyanka Square
13. Strastnoi Boulevard
14. Kuznetsky Most
15. St. Basil's Cathedral
16. Church of Christ the Savior
17. Denezhnyi Pereulok

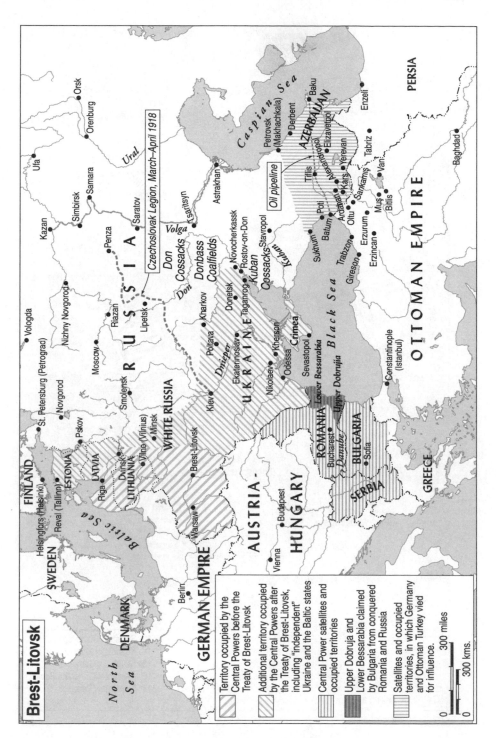

Brest-Litovsk

Czechoslovak Legion, March–April 1918

Oil pipeline

Territory occupied by the Central Powers before the Treaty of Brest-Litovsk

Additional territory occupied by the Central Powers after the Treaty of Brest-Litovsk, including "independent" Ukraine and the Baltic states

Central Power satellites and occupied territories

Upper Dobruja and Lower Bessarabia claimed by Bulgaria from conquered Romania and Russia

Satellites and occupied territories, in which Germany and Ottoman Turkey vied for influence.

0   300 miles
0   300 kms.

PERSIA

OTTOMAN EMPIRE

Baghdad

Enzeli

Tabriz

Van
Bitlis
Muş
Sarıkamış
Yerevan
Kars
Ardahan
Oltu
Erzincan
Erzurum
Giresun
Trabzon
Batum
Poti
Suknum
Tiflis
Alexandropol
Elizavetpol
AZERBAIJAN
Baku
Derbent
Petrovsk (Makhachkala)

Caspian Sea

Astrakhan

Orsk

Orenburg

Ufa

Ural

Samara

Simbirsk

Kazan

Penza

Saratov

Tsaritsyn

Volga

R U S S I A

Don Cossacks

Don

Donbass Coalfields

Novocherkassk
Rostov-on-Don
Taganrog
Kuban Cossacks
Kuban
Stavropol

Donetsk

Kharkov

Ekaterinoslav

Poltava

U K R A I N E

Dnieper

Kiev

Kherson

Nikolaev

Odessa

Crimea

Sevastopol

Black Sea

Lower Bessarabia

Upper Dobruja

Danube

ROMANIA

Bucharest

BULGARIA

Sofia

SERBIA

GREECE

Constantinople (Istanbul)

Lipetsk

Riazan

Moscow

Smolensk

Novgorod

St. Petersburg (Petrograd)

Nizhny Novgorod

Vologda

WHITE RUSSIA

Minsk

Vilno (Vilnius)

Dvinsk

Brest-Litovsk

Warsaw

LITHUANIA

LATVIA

Riga

ESTONIA

Pskov

Reval (Tallinn)

Helsingfors (Helsinki)

FINLAND

Baltic Sea

SWEDEN

DENMARK

Berlin

Vienna

Budapest

AUSTRIA-HUNGARY

GERMAN EMPIRE

North Sea

FINLAND Mannerheim
"White Finns"
L. Ladoga
Baltic Sea
Helsinki
Tallinin
Gatchina
Petrograd
ESTONIA Narva
Tsarskoe Selo
L. Peipus
NW (Yudenich)
Pskov
LATVIA
Riga
Vologda
Volga
RUSSIA
LITHUANIA Dvinsk
Kaunas
Vladimir
Nizhnii Novgorod
Vilno
Vitebsk
Moscow
Kazan
Smolensk
Oka
Minsk
Mogliev
Riazan
Furthest advance of Volunteers, Oct. 1919
Pinsk
Pripet
Gomel
Briansk
Tula
Mamontov's Raid, Aug.–Sept. 1919
POLES
Mozyr
Orel
Penza
Sam
Bug
Desna
Kursk
Tambov
Rovno
Kiev
Voronezh
Saratov
Berdychev
U k r i a n e
Don
Dneper
Kharkov
Don Cossacks (Krasnov)
Volga
Volunteers, Aug. 1919
Donets
Ekaterinoslav
Donbass Coalfields
Tsaritsyn
Kishinev
Makhno's Partisans
Novocherkassk
CA (Wrangel)
Odessa
Rostov
ROMANIA
Kherson
Astrakhan
French Landings
Wrangel 1920
Sea of Azov
Kuban Cossacks
Denikin's Volunteers, Mar. 1919
Sevastopol
Novorossisk
Kuban
Krasnodar
BULG.
B l a c k   S e a
Istanbul
GEORGIA
Batumi
Tbilisi
Ardahan
Ankara
Kars
Yerevan
ARMENIA
AZERBAIJA

CA Caucasian army
NW Northwest army
0   300 miles

TURKEY

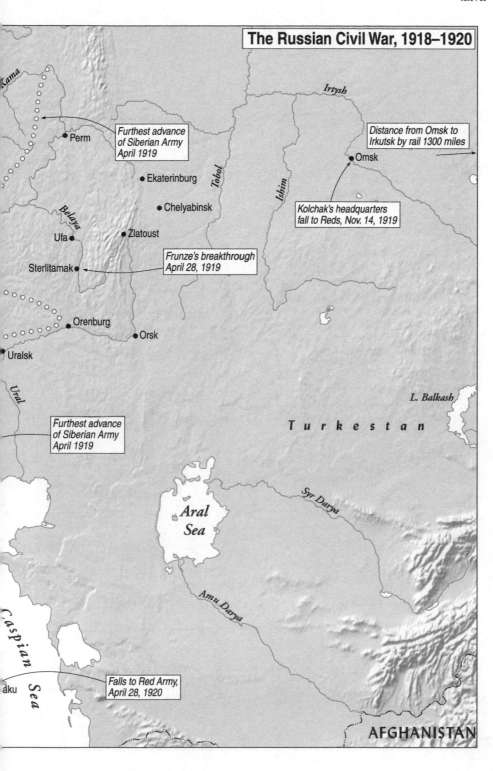

The Russian Civil War, 1918–1920

Irtysh

Kama

● Perm

Furthest advance
of Siberian Army
April 1919

Distance from Omsk to
Irkutsk by rail 1300 miles

● Ekaterinburg

Tobol

Ishim

● Omsk

● Chelyabinsk

Kolchak's headquarters
fall to Reds, Nov. 14, 1919

Belaya

● Zlatoust

Ufa ●

Frunze's breakthrough
April 28, 1919

Sterlitamak ●

● Orenburg

● Orsk

Uralsk

Ural

L. Balkash

Furthest advance
of Siberian Army
April 1919

T u r k e s t a n

*Aral
Sea*

Syr Darya

Amu Darya

Caspian Sea

aku

Falls to Red Army,
April 28, 1920

AFGHANISTAN

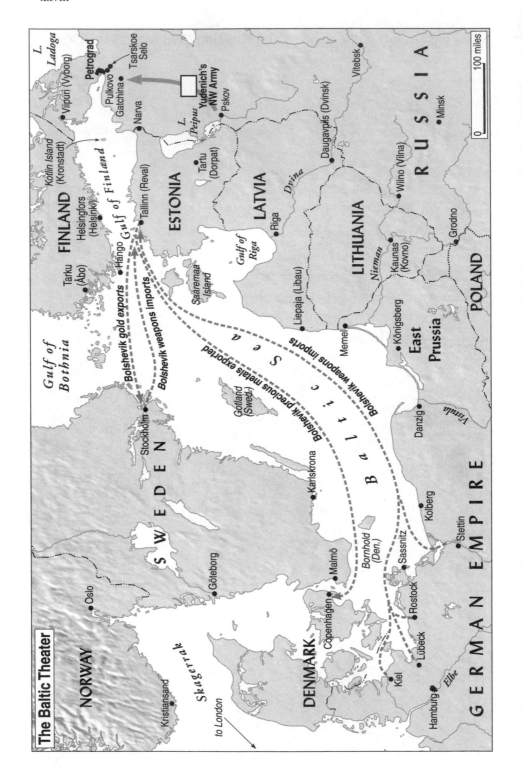

The Baltic Theater

The Polish–Soviet War, 1920

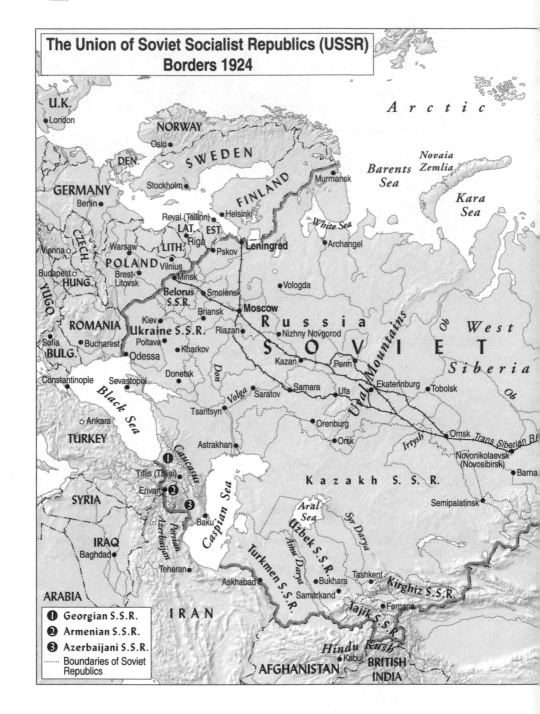

The Union of Soviet Socialist Republics (USSR) Borders 1924

U.K.
• London

NORWAY
Oslo •
DEN.
SWEDEN
Stockholm •
GERMANY
• Berlin
FINLAND
Helsinki •
Reval (Tallinn) •
LAT.
EST.
Vienna ○
CZECH
Warsaw •
Riga •
LITH.
Pskov •
Leningrad •
• Archangel
White Sea
Budapest ○
POLAND
Vilnius •
HUNG.
Brest-
Litovsk •
Minsk •
Belorus.
S.S.R.
Smolensk •
• Vologda
YUGO.
ROMANIA
Ukraine S.S.R.
Kiev •
Briansk •
Moscow •
R u s s i a
S O V I E T
West
Siberia
Ob
Ob
Riazan •
• Nizhny Novgorod
Ural Mountains
Sofia •
• Bucharest
BULG.
Poltava •
Odessa •
Kharkov •
Kazan •
Perm •
Ekaterinburg •
• Tobolsk
Constantinople •
Sevastopol •
Donetsk •
Don
Volga
Saratov •
Samara •
Ufa •
Tsaritsyn •
○ Ankara
Black Sea
Astrakhan •
Orenburg •
Orsk •
Omsk •
Trans Siberian R.
Irtysh
Novonikolaevsk
(Novosibirsk)
TURKEY
Caucasus
Tiflis (Tbilisi) •
❶
Erivan •
❷
❸
Caspian Sea
K a z a k h   S. S. R.
Barna •
SYRIA
Azerbaijan
Persia
Baku •
Aral
Sea
Syr Darya
Semipalatinsk •
IRAQ
Baghdad •
Amu Darya
Uzbek S.S.R.
ARABIA
Teheran •
Turkmen S.S.R.
Askhabad •
Samarkand •
Bukhara •
Tashkent •
Kirghiz S.S.R.
Fergana •
I R A N
Tajik S.S.R.
Hindu Kush
• Kabul
AFGHANISTAN
BRITISH
INDIA

Arctic
Barents
Sea
Murmansk •
Novaia
Zemlia
Kara
Sea

❶ Georgian S.S.R.
❷ Armenian S.S.R.
❸ Azerbaijani S.S.R.
.... Boundaries of Soviet
Republics

=== Prologue ===

THE BLOOD OF A PEASANT

With the Great War against Germany and the Central Powers entering its third terrible year, opposition to the autocratic rule of Tsar Nicholas II, who had assumed command of Russia's armed forces in 1915, deepened in Petrograd. Parliamentary leaders, itching to take a more active role in Russian political life, smelled blood. Pavel Milyukov, a distinguished historian who had founded the Liberal Kadet Party, worked the Duma into a frenzy on November 1/14, 1916, berating the tsar's latest chief minister, Boris Stürmer—with his unfortunately Germanic name—for his failures and asking acidly whether these were born of "stupidity or treason." The real traitors, Milyukov implied though he did not quite state, were the German-born tsarina, Alexandra ("Alix") of Hesse, and the "dark forces" surrounding her notorious faith healer, Grigory Rasputin, who had been ushered into her confidence owing to his mysterious ability to comfort her hemophiliac son and heir to the throne, Alexis. Coming from such a respected authority, which lent credence to popular rumors about Rasputin, Milyukov's incendiary speech confirmed the view of Petrograd society that, as one grandee put it, "the Empress and Stürmer were selling Russia out to Kaiser Wilhelm."[1]

What the Kadet leader insinuated, others stated openly. Vladimir Purishkevich, a reactionary deputy, distributed Milyukov's speech to frontline soldiers. Still unsatisfied, Purishkevich stood up in the Duma on November 6/19, 1916, and lambasted the tsar's ministers as "marionettes whose threads have been taken firmly in hand

1

by Rasputin and the Empress Alexandra Fyodorovna . . . who has remained a German on the Russian throne and alien to the country and its people." Purishkevich's real fury was aimed at the faith healer himself. "While Rasputin is alive," he argued, "we cannot win [the war]." Summoning Russia's leading politicians to enlist in a lynch mob, Purishkevich intoned ominously, "an obscure muzhik [peasant] shall govern Russia no longer!"[2]

These were not idle words. By month's end, Purishkevich had joined a burgeoning conspiracy of elites, fronted (if not necessarily masterminded) by Prince Felix Yusupov, to murder Rasputin. Yusupov, an Oxford-educated dandy who was sole heir to perhaps the richest family fortune in Russia—richer by most reckonings than the Romanovs'—was married to the tsar's niece, Princess Irina. Yusupov's mother, Princess Zinaida, was intimate with Romanov grand dukes and with the tsar's own family, and also a close friend of the wife of Mikhail Rodzianko, the president of the State Duma. Princess Zinaida's husband, another high-born count, had been sacked by the tsar from his post as governor-general of Moscow in 1915, and she blamed Rasputin and Tsarina Alexandra for his disgrace; her poisonous gossip was an important source of the mania in Petrograd high society about treasonous "dark forces." Princess Zinaida expressly instructed her son Felix to "educate" Rodzianko and the Duma about Rasputin. Another of her converts was Grand Duke Dimitry Pavlovich Romanov, a first cousin of the tsar, who became one of the principals of the assassination plot against Rasputin.[3]

The idea was simple. Yusupov would invite Rasputin over to his glittering palace on the Moika Canal on the pretext of meeting his beautiful wife, Irina. Princess Irina herself, who wanted nothing to do with the plot (although she knew of it), would not be home. Kept waiting downstairs, Rasputin would be offered cakes and wine, laced with potassium cyanide. In case the poison did not work, the conspirators would be supplied with pistols—and a rather transparent alibi concocted with a few phone calls. For added insurance, Grand Duke Dmitry Pavlovich would be present at the scene: as a Romanov he enjoyed absolute legal immunity from prosecution. At once baroque and sordid, the plot had one important factor working in its favor: the famous lust for new female conquests of a man the French ambassador called the "eroto-mystic-maniac of Pokrovskoye." Rasputin had never before declined an invitation to meet a princess.[4]

The Purishkevich-Yusupov plot was not the first of its kind. Alexei Khvostov, the minister of the interior appointed in September 1915 on Rasputin's recommendation, had turned against his benefactor only months later, offering to pay the secret-police officer in charge of Rasputin's security, Colonel Mikhail Komissarov, 200,000 rubles to murder the man he was tasked by the tsar with protecting—the man who, moreover, had given Khvostov his job. Implausible as this affair sounds, it was real enough that Colonel Komissarov tested out various poisons on Rasputin's cats (Khvostov, for his part, would have preferred to have the peasant strangled). Rumors about this bizarre plot broke in the press, which led to Khvostov's downfall when the tsar heard of it.

By 1916, Rasputin assassination fever was in the air. Rasputin himself received death threats in the mail, and was physically attacked on several occasions. The fever was so contagious that it spread well beyond Russia. Khvostov, having failed in his own plot, tried to recruit Rasputin's former sponsor from the Orthodox Church, the defrocked Archemandrite priest Sergei Trufanov (known in the West as Bishop Iliodor), then living in Norway. Trufanov was believed to have been behind the attempted murder of Rasputin in Pokrovskoye in July 1914 (stabbed in the abdomen by a woman screaming, "I have killed the Antichrist!" Rasputin had somehow survived). Although Trufanov refused, this time, to sully himself with murder, he carried the slander campaign to another level when he sailed for America and sold a juicy story ("Rasputin: the Holy Devil of Russia") to *Metropolitan Magazine* for $25,000, a front-page blockbuster advertised all summer. The Russian Consulate in New York squashed the story before it hit newsstands. Trufanov then sued the Russian government for damages. And so it came about that in November 1916, just as Milyukov and Purishkevich were lighting an anti-Rasputin fire under the Duma in Petrograd, Trufanov publicly testified in a New York City courtroom, of all places, that Grigory Rasputin "is strongly pro-German and has such influence over the Tsarina as to obtain her influence against the Allies . . . he is now engaged in a conspiracy to bring about a separate peace."[5]

British agents in New York were paying close attention to what Trufanov had to say. After testifying, he was called in to the British Consulate for an official debriefing. With little hope of a breakthrough on the western front—1916 was the year of bloody futility at Verdun and the Somme—fears in London were growing that Russia, giving up on her allies, was angling for a separate peace with Germany. To buck up the Russians, in June the floundering Liberal government of Prime Minister Herbert Henry Asquith had sent to Russia its most prestigious figure, Field Marshal Horatio Herbert Kitchener, on the express request of Tsar Nicholas II, only for Kitchener to die en route when his ship was sunk by a German mine. By fall 1916, British diplomats, spies, and cabinet officials interpreted every scrap of intelligence as indicative that the bottom was falling out of the Russian war effort.

From the British perspective, the tsar's controversial appointment of Alexander Protopopov as minister of the interior on September 18, 1916, was the last straw. From the reports of Ambassador Sir George Buchanan, the cabinet in London knew two things about Protopopov: that he had met with a well-connected German embassy official, Fritz Warburg (of the Warburg banking dynasty) in Stockholm in July 1916, ostensibly to discuss the possibility of a separate peace; and that he was a Rasputin protégé. After reading Buchanan's overheated reports, the secretary of state for war, David Lloyd George, sent a "confidential memorandum" on September 13/26, 1916, to Prime Minister Asquith, warning that "Germanophile influences have been considerably strengthened by recent changes. Our friends have disappeared one by one and there is no man now of any influence in the Russian Bureaucracy . . . favourable towards this country."[6]

Although the most libelous accusation against Rasputin—that he was a German spy—was untrue, there was enough truth in rumors of his outsized political influence to imbue his enemies with determination as they plotted his demise. It really was Rasputin who, together with the tsarina, convinced Nicholas II to take over the command of the Russian armies in August 1915; who, again together with the tsarina, arranged the appointment of Boris Stürmer, an elderly, retired political nonentity nearing age seventy, as chairman of the Council of Ministers in February 1916; who convinced the tsar to fire his long-standing minister of foreign affairs, Sergei

Sazonov, that July; and who pushed for Protopopov's appointment in September, despite the latter's reputation for being erratic and possibly insane (syphilis, contracted in his military days, was gradually eroding Protopopov's mental equilibrium). It was not Rasputin's advice alone that produced this politically damaging "ministerial leapfrog"—the tsar still made all the final decisions, and on several occasions went against the peasant's counsel—but Rasputin's sway over the tsarina was undeniable. With Nicholas II, away at the front, reliant on his wife's advice on political affairs in the capital, Rasputin was arguably the "third most powerful man in Russia" during a critical period in the First World War.[7]

No less true was the view of Rasputin's enemies that he was "soft" on the war (even if he was not really a pro-German traitor). The war was, ironically, the one subject on which Rasputin did *not* agree with the tsarina, as, despite her Germanic background (or rather because she came from a small but proud West German state, Hesse-Darmstadt, swallowed up by Bismarckian Prussia), she despised Kaiser Wilhelm II and his empire and wanted it destroyed. Rasputin, who had famously sent a special warning telegram to the tsar upon learning of Russian mobilization in July 1914, viewed the war as a pointless, tragic waste of life, and wished to bring it to an end as soon as possible.

By November 1916, it was an open secret in Petrograd that plans were afoot to murder Rasputin. Samuel Hoare, head of the British Secret Intelligence Service (SIS) in the city, later recalled that Purishkevich told him that "he would liquidate [Rasputin]." Neither Purishkevich nor Yusupov was discreet; both discussed their plans openly with family and friends, perhaps to reassure themselves that they were doing the right thing. So far as we know, no one actually disapproved, with the partial exception of Yusupov's wife, Irina, who warned her husband, on learning of the plot while vacationing in the Crimea, that he should not "stick his nose into this dirty business." There is some evidence that one British SIS officer, Oswald Rayner, who had known Yusupov since his Oxford days, was in on the plot, or at least was following it very closely, as so many British officials wanted Rasputin out of the way. As Yusupov himself explained the plotters' thinking: Tsarina Alexandra's "spiritual balance depends entirely on Rasputin: the instant he is gone, it will disintegrate. And once [the tsar] has been freed of his wife's and Rasputin's influence, everything will change: he will turn into a good constitutional monarch"—and, presumably, rededicate himself to winning the war.[8]

The weather was brisk and well below freezing on the night of December 16–17 (29–30), 1916, following a day when snow had blanketed the city. Over the preceding days, Yusupov and his fellow plotters had scoured the city's canals and rivers for possible dumping places for a dead body (they had purchased heavy chains to weigh down the corpse and make it sink), only to find the water nearly everywhere already frozen. The best spot was on the "Old Neva" outside the city limits, near a bridge to the islands where Rasputin frequently liked to "visit the gypsies," offering a possible alibi. It was also favorable in that the conspirators did not want the body to be discovered right away near the site of the murder. Still, they wanted to make sure it *would* be discovered, to scotch possible rumors that Rasputin was alive.[9]

The chosen site for the murder, Yusupov's grandiose palace on the Moika Canal (nos. 92 to 94), had its own problems. The Interior Ministry, and the adjoining police station, stood almost directly opposite the palace on the other side of the canal, only 50 or 60 yards away, which meant that any gunshots heard would bring unwanted police attention. As one of the best-appointed palaces in all Russia, which to this day draws tourists eager to ogle at what remains of its once glittering treasures, Yusupov's house was also swarming with liveried servants who might bear witness. While the high rank of Prince Yusupov and his Romanov coconspirator might stay the hand of any prospective witnesses, Purishkevich was taking no chances: he insisted that Yusupov dismiss the house help, leaving only two guards on duty. Improving the odds slightly, Yusupov had selected a vaulted storeroom at the bottom of the palace, surrounded by thick walls, which would deaden the sound of any gunshots. If Rasputin drank enough poisoned Madeira wine, of course, no one would hear a thing.[10]

Toward midnight on the fateful evening, Yusupov began arranging the scene of the crime. Cakes and wine had been laid out by servants before they were dismissed. A Dr. Lazavert, hired by Purishkevich, sprinkled cyanide crystals over the cakes, waiting until the last possible minute to dose the wine. At half past, the doctor drove Prince

Yusupov over to the back door of Rasputin's house on Gorokhovaya ulitsa, where they found him smartly turned out and smelling of cheap soap. Apparently taken in by the ruse about Princess Irina, a well-scrubbed Rasputin appeared more "clean and tidy" than Yusupov had ever seen him before. So far, the plan was working perfectly.[11]

As Yusupov ushered his guest downstairs into the vaulted storeroom of the Moika Palace via a back door, with the strains of "Yankee Doodle Dandy" faintly audible from a gramophone upstairs, Rasputin betrayed no signs of suspicion. Nor did he refuse Yusupov's invitation to have a drink while he waited (the peasant's passion for Madeira was second only to that for society ladies). But Rasputin refused to try the cakes, and much of the poison had evaporated in the wine. Aside from a bit of moaning, there were no signs that the cyanide was having any effect. At around two a.m., the accounts of the principals diverge, fueling an industry of theories and fables. All we know for certain is that two gunshots entered Rasputin's body between two and six a.m.; that he was also stabbed in the torso; that flesh wounds on the upper body and face suggest he was beaten; and that a third shot was fired into Rasputin's forehead, killing him instantly. (Contrary to an enduring myth that Rasputin was still alive when thrown into the icy river, the autopsy showed nothing more than that some water had entered into his lungs, signifying nothing. It was almost certainly the head shot which did him in.)[12]

Whatever the truth about the exact doing of the principals, it is clear beyond a reasonable doubt that the murder of Grigory Rasputin was premeditated; that high-born members of the Russian aristocracy were involved in the murder plot, including both Prince Yusupov and Grand Duke Dmitry Pavlovich; and that, owing to this circumstance peculiar to Russia's autocratic regime, despite a wide-ranging investigation, no one was ever charged with the crime (although Yusupov was banished from Petrograd, and Dmitry Pavlovich was exiled to a military post in Persia). So, far from being prosecuted or hanged, the murderers were feted in Petrograd society as heroes: they had felled the foul-smelling muzhik satyr whose machinations had brought the monarchy into disrepute. Surely, the denizens of liberal Russia believed, the tsar would now come to his senses and listen to their own enlightened counsel, and not that of the depraved Rasputin.

The celebration was premature. Rather than enlighten the tsar, the brutal murder of one of his trusted confidants, of a pious (though flawed) faith healer on whom he and his wife relied for the treatment of a beloved son afflicted with hemophilia, horrified him. To the dismay of Petrograd society, Nicholas declared that he was "ashamed before Russia that the hands of my relatives should be smeared with the blood of this peasant."[13]

In this way a misguided plot conceived by Yusupov's circle of well-born Russian elites to bridge the gap between the tsar and liberal Russia, instead widened that gap still further. Alone, bewildered, and betrayed by his own kin, Nicholas II hunkered down at military headquarters in Mogilev, where he hoped to shut out the incessant cacophony of politicians and their intrigues. His refuge would not remain quiet for long.

PART I

Twilight of the Romanovs

Russia has been strong thanks to autocracy.

—CONSTANTINE PETROVICH POBEDONOSTSEV, procurator of the
Holy Synod and adviser to Tsar Alexander III and Tsar Nicholas II

The revolutionary enters the world of the State, of the
privileged classes, of the so-called civilization, and he lives
in this world only for the purpose of bringing about its
speedy and total destruction.

—SERGEI NECHAEV,
Catechism of a Revolutionary (1869)

═ I ═

THE OLD REGIME, AND ITS ENEMIES

The Russian Empire at the turn of the twentieth century was enormous. In land surface area, the British Empire was larger, but it was strewn in noncontiguous bits and pieces across the globe. The tsar's domain stood as one, long and wide, stretching 6,000 miles from Russian Poland to the Pacific Ocean, from the frigid waters of the Arctic to the baking steppes of Central Asia. As a journalist observed, "The United States could be dropped into [Russia] and leave room to spare for China and India."[1]

Just looking at the map was enough to induce terror in Russia's neighbors. Relentlessly, as if impelled by some unshakable law of expansion, the tsarist empire had grown by 55 square miles a day—by 20,000 a year—since the seventeenth century. True, the extension of the borders left the tsar's armies with ever more territory to defend, but it also gave the empire strategic depth, as Napoleon had learned in 1812. Projecting trends forward, it was easy to imagine a future map on which Russia had swallowed chunks of China, Afghanistan, Persia, the Ottoman Empire, Austrian Galicia, and East Prussia. Compounding the sense of menace the empire posed to its enemies, Russia's population had quadrupled in the nineteenth century to 150 million (it would leap again after 1900, reaching nearly 175 million by 1914). The Russian economy, although still only the fifth-largest in the world (behind Britain, France, Germany, and the United States), was by the first decade of the twentieth century growing at nearly

10 percent annually, turning heads just as dramatically as a surging China has in the early twenty-first.[2]

Knowing how the story of the tsars turns out, many historians have suggested that the Russian colossus must always have had feet of clay. But surely this is hindsight. Despite growing pains, uneven economic development, and stirrings of revolutionary fervor, imperial Russia in 1900 was a going concern, its very size and power a source of pride to most if not all of the tsar's subjects. Only in retrospect have scholars discovered fatal weaknesses in an empire that, at the time, aroused fear in foreign enemies, even as its formidable (if underfunded) police apparatus, beefed up following the assassination of Tsar Alexander II in 1881, intimidated its sundry domestic opponents. Perhaps the best measure of any country's vitality lies in the numbers of migrants and investors who flock there. Russia in the early twentieth century was a substantial net importer of both people and capital: a telling fact that, since the revolution, has never been true again.

A foreign visitor descending on the Russian capital of St. Petersburg from the West, circa 1900, would have been struck by the city's European flavor—society spoke French, not Russian—and by the jaw-dropping wealth and glamor of high society. The Renaissance-style palaces lining the canals, built by Italian architects, gave it the air of a "Venice of the North." Located at 60 degrees latitude, at a level with Alaska just outside the Arctic Circle, St. Petersburg's social rhythm was enriched by the long winter nights, which embellished one of the grandest "seasons" of Europe, a round of parties and concerts lasting from New Year's Eve until Lent; and by the "White Nights" of early summer, when everyone took to the streets. Our visitor would have taken in the Imperial Ballet at the Mariinsky Theater, listened to a concert featuring the best work of Glinka, Mussorgsky, Rimsky-Korsakov, or Tchaikovsky, and perhaps attended a ball where, in the words of one biographer of the last imperial family, "the passion of Russian women for jewels was displayed on every head, neck, ear, wrist, finger and waist."[3]

Had our tourist continued on to Moscow, capital of old Russia before Peter the Great founded his window to the West on the Neva in 1703, he would have found a city less decadent and decidedly more Russian. Although the imperial bureaucracy had decamped to Petersburg, Moscow remained the spiritual heart of the empire, where every tsar was still crowned in the Uspensky Cathedral inside the redbrick walls of the Kremlin, on the Diamond Throne of Tsar Alexis. Moscow, city of "forty times forty churches," was the Third Rome of the Orthodox faithful (after Rome and Byzantine Constantinople, whence came the Russian church), a sacred city of ritual and tradition. Her elaborate and sensual Orthodox rite brought together peasants and princesses, all holding candles as they listened to enchanting hymns and breathed in smoky incense. Moscow was also a city of commerce, where Russia's historic trade routes—and her growing rail network—converged. It was a city of extremes, of stifling heat and humidity in summer, contrasted with some of the coldest winters anywhere. The city's industrialists and traders, more interested in money and deals than the socialites of Petersburg, were heavy drinkers. After cleansing his soul in one of the churches, our visitor would have toasted vodka in the bars and inns of Moscow, chased with the pickled cucumbers, herring, smoked sturgeon, and caviar that still comprise the Russian drinking diet today.

If our traveler was intrepid enough to venture beyond the great capitals, he might have visited the medieval cities of the Golden Ring northeast of Moscow (Kostroma, Suzdal, Vladimir, or Yaroslavl), taken the train north to Tver or Novgorod, east to the Siberian boom town of Irkutsk, south to Crimea or the spas and mineral baths of the north Caucasus and the mountainous wine country of Georgia, or maybe traveled the Volga on a steamer. The trains, running on cheaply built tracks not quite up to Western standards (the rails on most lines were half the weight of the US norm), still traveled slowly, which would have allowed our tourist plenty of time to take in the passing scene. Outside the big cities and a few pockets of industrialization in Ukraine and western Siberia, he would have noticed, interspersed amid forests of birch, small villages of unpainted peasant *izbas* (log huts), crowned in the better towns by onion-shaped church domes. In summer, he would have seen men and women hard at work in the fields, planting and harvesting grain during the short growing season. If visiting in winter, our tourist would have had the chance to ride in a troika (horse-pulled sleigh), which made overland travel easier in snow-covered Russia in winter than in the muds of spring and fall, or the dust-choked tracks of summer (the country as yet had few macadamized all-weather roads). While he might have shivered as his troika was buffeted by frigid winds, our traveler would still have marveled at the ethereal white beauty of the Russian winter.

Of course, there is a great deal our traveler would not have seen, confined as he likely was to the nicer neighborhoods in the big cities and towns, the well-trafficked arteries and provincial capitals, and if he ever ventured farther afield, the better country inns. Although a tourist primer might have made passing mention of the "peasant problem," it would have taken an inquisitive soul to scratch below the surface of Russian rural life, in a country where peasants still composed 80 percent of the population. By Western standards, agriculture was woefully inefficient, with yield per acre less than half the European norm and as little as one seventh that attained in England. Surplus margins were small enough that bad harvest years could bring famine, as in 1892, when nearly half a million peasants died, mostly of cholera.

Some of this poor performance owed to the short Russian growing season and the poor quality of the soil everywhere except the "Black Earth" belt of southern European Russia and Ukraine. But it also had to do with social organization. The serfs had been freed, on paper at least, all the way back in 1861, and yet for many "liberation" had been a booby prize. Rather than fulfill their obligation to the local lord with compulsory labor, as in the bad old days, freed serfs had been invited to redeem the land "given" to them by paying in installments, in effect paying down a mortgage—not an easy task in a near-cashless economy where many villagers still made their own boots and tools. Making the new system still more complicated, the redemptions were paid not individually but collectively, by way of the mir, a kind of rural commune, which caused endless headaches over who owed what to whom. In this way the liberation, rather than turning the peasantry into property-owning smallholders, had paradoxically strengthened the traditional Russian communes, into whose control most of the redeemed land had fallen by 1900. It was said that there was only one man in Russia who really understood the peasant question, the economist A. V. Chayanov. After devoting his life to studying the subject, Chayanov had concluded that

Russian peasant agriculture was impervious to reform, and advised government administrators to leave well enough alone. This was not popular advice.[4]

If our traveler came to Russia in the last decade of the nineteenth century, he would have been struck by telltale signs of an industrialization boom around the larger cities of European Russia, the Urals, and Ukraine. As in the United States, the impetus came largely from railroads built to conquer the vastness of the country, which stimulated colossal demand for iron ore, steel, and energy. The era was dominated by Sergei Witte, director of railway affairs from 1889 to 1891, who launched construction on the great Trans-Siberian Railway before being promoted to minister of ways and means and then minister of finance, which critical post he held until 1903. Under Witte's able leadership, Russia adopted the gold standard and pioneered the state capitalism still practiced in many emerging markets today, with government officials directing capital flows into infrastructure and heavy industry and encouraging foreign investment in technology, while striving to harmonize trade policy with domestic needs. Private property was respected, although most banks were government-owned or operated, and the state retained a monopoly over certain commodities (such as, in Russia, vodka). Whatever Witte's formula, it seemed to work: by 1900 the economy was growing at 8 percent annually. Mining, metalworking, and energy all surged ahead. Such ports as Riga, on the Baltic Sea, and Odessa, on the Black Sea, nearly quintupled in size during the Witte years, while boomtowns sprang up everywhere from western Siberia to the Caspian Sea, where filthy, oil-saturated Baku was transformed almost overnight into one of the richest cities in the world, producing, among other fortunes, that of the Nobel family, which still pays for the prizes today.

Alongside the outsized wealth of Russia's oil barons and industrialists, the Witte boom spawned a large and growing industrial proletariat. According to the government's own estimates, there were 2.5 million factory wage laborers by the late Witte years, and nearly 3 million by 1914, although these figures may be low, as the factory inspectors responsible for them were understaffed and came nowhere near investigating all manufacturing enterprises, particularly smaller ones. Wages were low for the unskilled, especially women (paid less than men, who were seen as breadwinners), but they ramped up quickly for workers skilled in textile spinning, metallurgy, or machinery. Factory conditions were often rough. The urban flophouses most workers lived in were cramped and crowded, as were the public soup kitchens where they ate. Nonetheless, certain aspects of traditional Russian culture softened the worst excesses of industrialization, such as the generous holidays of the Orthodox calendar (nearly 90 every year, with all Sundays off and Saturday hours curtailed). Russia had nothing like the German system of accident insurance and old age pensions pioneered under Bismarck in the 1880s, leaving most workers unprotected against the cruel whims of fate. Still, religious charities did provide some medical care for the injured. The patriarchal nature of Russian social life also imposed limitations on the kind of work children and women were allowed to do, in a way the more egalitarian ethos of northern European culture had not done (most famously in England, with the exploitation of child chimney sweeps, or of women in textile sweatshops). The Russian laborer's lot was tough, but not necessarily tougher than that of other workers in Europe at the time.

If Russia's industrialists were no more exploitative than their European counterparts, her political protestors were more radical. The strength and also the weakness of autocracy was that there were few intermediary institutions between the tsar and his subjects to absorb and dampen popular frustrations. Labor unions were illegal. There was no national parliament to focus the government's attention on social problems. In the brief era of liberal concessions that had followed Russia's humiliating defeat in the Crimean War (1853–1856), Tsar Alexander II had allowed the creation of small provincial assemblies known as zemstvos in 1864, but their power had been substantially curtailed by his more conservative successor, Alexander III, in 1890, when the zemstvo councils were subordinated to regional governors appointed by the tsar. The members of the Russian state bureaucracy that really governed the country, assembled hierarchically in an ornate table of ranks that reflected each official's noble status, service, and longevity (rather than merit), answered directly to the tsar, who appointed all government ministers and other top state officers personally. In the barren political soil of autocracy, it was not surprising that labor and peasant agitators, denied legal recourse or other means of redress, often resorted to violence.

Long before Russia had much of an industrial proletariat, she had already disgorged world-famous revolutionaries, such as Alexander Herzen (1812–1870), editor of the influential socialist periodical *Kolokol* (The Bell), and Mikhail Bakunin (1814–1876), who almost single-handedly created the "anarcho-syndicalist" philosophy of direct industrial action that came to dominate the labor movements in France and Italy. What set Bakunin apart from European rivals was his Russian panache, which lent him a glamor on the European Left that not even Karl Marx could match (Bakunin's defection from Marx's First Working-man's International Association after the fractious Hague Congress of 1872 led to that organization's demise four years later).

Russian radicalism was a world unto itself, which had emerged, in many ways, sui generis. Just as there was only one Bakunin, there was no real European equivalent of Sergei Nechaev and his nihilist-populist Narodniki (People's Will) movement, the progenitor of modern political terrorism. "The revolutionary," Nechaev wrote in his influential *Catechism* (1869), "is a doomed man. He has no personal interests, no business affairs, no emotions, no attachments, no property, and no name. Everything in him is wholly absorbed in the single thought and the single passion for revolution."[5] The killing of Alexander II, the "Tsar-Liberator," by the Narodniki in 1881, inspired a wave of copycat assassinations across Europe and North America that took the lives of six heads of states and dozens of lesser officials over the next two decades.

To snuff out the Narodniki, the reactionary regime of Tsar Alexander III (1881–1894) developed the *okhrannoe otdelenie* (Okhrana), a sophisticated network of police informers and double agents, which likewise had no equivalent in the Europe of the time. Over the years, the Okhrana and the revolutionary underground evolved in tandem, each studying and learning from the other, cultivating a ubiquitous air of conspiracy and paranoia. Usually the Okhrana was a step ahead of its opponents, but not always. In the Degaev affair of the 1880s, a colonel in the Petersburg Okhrana penetrated the upper reaches of the Narodniki, only to be murdered by his own source (the assassin then disappeared, and was not discovered until decades later, while teaching mathematics at the University of North Dakota). Another notorious double agent, Evano Azef, furnished the Okhrana with valuable information between 1902 and 1905—though arguably not as valuable as the lives of the two interior ministers and the Romanov grand duke he allegedly had assassinated to show his revolutionary bona fides.[6]

Still, despite occasional miscues, in most years the tsarist regime seemed to have the measure of its opponents. Unless he were unlucky enough to witness the odd terrorist bomb blast, our foreign visitor would have been more impressed with the spit and polish of the tsar's gendarmes, sharply turned out in blue-and-white uniforms with tall black leather boots, than with the scruffy bohemians of the revolutionary underworld. It is true that the Okhrana, like the tsarist bureaucracy more generally, was underfunded and undermanned. The police as a whole in 1900 employed all of 6,874 constables and 1,852 sergeants, with perhaps another thousand working in the political sections comprising the Okhrana—this in a country of 150 million people sprawling across the better part of two continents. Compared to the jumped-up Soviet Cheka, which employed hundreds of thousands, the Okhrana was thin on the ground, which speaks well of its efficiency. Even the Narodniki were largely domesticated after the turn of the century, with most of its leaders joining the Socialist Revolutionary (SR) Party, founded in 1901 to advocate for land reform along (more or less) legal lines. The SR Party was, in many ways, the quintessential Russian political party, a populist movement advocating for the interests of the peasants who comprised the vast majority of the tsar's subjects.[7]

Meanwhile a new, European-style Marxist party had emerged in Russia, largely defined by its opposition to the less disciplined romanticism of the Narodniki. This was the Russian Social Democratic Labour Party (RSDRP), formed in March 1898 as an affiliated national "section" of the Second Workingman's International Association, a.k.a. the Second International (1889–1914), an organization created to standardize the principles of Marxism after Marx's death in 1883. Owing to the explicitly revolutionary nature of the RSDRP program, the party was immediately placed under Okhrana surveillance; indeed its very formation was sparked by the suppression of earlier, less organized Russian Marxist leagues formed over the preceding years. The RSDRP was, almost from its inception, a party of exiles. Two of its leaders, Vladimir Ulyanov (Lenin) and Julius Tsederbaum (Martov), were in exile in Siberia during its founding congress; a third, Georgy Plekhanov, had lived in Switzerland since 1880. The second RSDRP Congress was held only five years later, not in Russia, but in Belgium.

Despite a reputation for Russian police thuggishness going back to the days of Nicholas I (1825–1855), the regime's methods of repression were not without subtlety. Only the absolute worst offenders, such as convicted or confessed political assassins, were given the death penalty. A more common punishment for political offenders was *katorga* (hard penal labor), and yet even this was rarely handed down unless the offense was heinous. The default punishment, for which Russia was famous, was "administrative exile" for periods up to five years, which usually meant Siberia. While the Siberian climate (especially in winter) could be harsh, conditions imposed on internal exiles were otherwise lenient, astonishingly so compared to later conditions in the Soviet Gulag: exiles even received an annual living allowance from the tsar for clothes, food, and rent. Some well-off exiles, like Lenin (whose father was a hereditary noble state councilor, fourth class in the table of ranks) traveled first class to Siberia: Lenin brought along his mother and his wife and even hired a maid to keep house. So, far from being imprisoned, exiles could do what they liked, as long as they stayed in Siberia. While policemen did patrol rail stations for escapees, it did little good, as thousands escaped anyway with false papers that were easy to procure on the black market. One energetic Georgian seminarian turned revolutionary, Yosif Djugashvili (Stalin), exiled for his role in organizing a violent March 1902 demonstration in Batum in which thirteen people were killed and fifty-four wounded, later boasted of escaping from Siberia six times (the true number may have been eight).[8]

Once back in European Russia, hundreds of escaped exiles continued west into Europe, where they became part of the furniture of European radicalism. The German Social Democratic Party (SPD) was a second home for Russian socialists plotting the demise of a regime foolish enough to let them escape. For the period between the Decembrist revolt of 1825, the first serious political unrest among the elites of the empire, and 1917, the supposedly fearsome tsarist regime executed only 6,321 people for all offenses combined (including criminal ones, such as first-degree murder), or less than seventy per year. Lenin, living comfortably abroad after his relaxing and well-catered holiday of Siberian exile of 1897–1900, was not among them.

Histories of the Russian Revolution tend to emphasize obvious antecedents of 1917, lavishing great attention, for example, on the famous split in the RSDRP at the Brussels Congress in July 1903 into "majority" (Bolshevik) and "minority" (Menshevik) factions. But at the time, the politicking of exiles interested few Russians other than the police agents paid to keep tabs on them, who were often bored by the task. A typical Okhrana report on Lenin spilled more ink on his looks ("2 *arshins* 5 1/2 *vershki* tall . . . his overall appearance makes a pleasant impression, hazel eyes, high raised forehead, round face, round chin, reddish beard . . . ") than on his political beliefs, and scarcely mentioned the Menshevik-Bolshevik split. It was only years later, after Lenin had become famous, that such arcane developments were ascribed with world-historical significance.[9]

Far more important, at the time, was the struggle between the tsarist regime and its domestic critics, particularly student protestors. The years at the turn of the century saw an upsurge in radicalism in the universities of St. Petersburg, Moscow, Warsaw, and Kiev, owing to a government decree passed in July 1899 that lifted military deferments for students found guilty of political misconduct. Predictably, many students who protested this decree were impressed into the army. In February 1901, a student at St. Petersburg University murdered the education minister, N. P. Bogolepov, marking a critical escalation. Although Tsar Nicholas II appointed his inoffensive octogenarian war minister, General Vannovski, to replace Bogolepov, Vannovski's efforts to appease the students enflamed the radicals further. The following year, in April, another student assassinated the interior minister, as if to reject the tsar's olive branch. Nicholas II got the message, appointing a strongman, Viacheslav Plehve, with sweeping new powers.[10]

Plehve's strategy combined direct repression with efforts to co-opt the more useful elements of the opposition. While he had little tolerance for student radicals, the new interior minister was more subtle in his approach to the Russian labor movement, believing that the working masses, if isolated from student agitators and given some economic carrots, could be won over to at least passive acceptance of the regime. Working closely with the head of the Moscow Okhrana, S. P. Zubatov, Plehve penetrated illegal Russian underground labor organizations and created new ones controlled by the police. Less successful was Plehve's ploy to neutralize the zemstvo councils by absorbing them directly into the Interior Ministry. This heavy-handed maneuver only annoyed Russian liberals, who saw the zemstvos as a stepping stone to a proper national parliament. More heavy-handed still was Plehve's "Russification" campaign, especially in Finland and Poland, which had long been hotbeds of national-separatist sentiment.

Despite considerable grumbling from the opposition, Plehve's reforms seemed, at first, to breathe new life into the regime, improving the morale of the bureaucracy at a time when many officials believed their lives to be in danger. Given time to work out the kinks with the zemstvos, labor, and student protestors, Plehve might well have succeeded in restoring the government's prestige with the public. But his reforms were rapidly subsumed by controversy after an anti-Semitic pogrom erupted in Kishinev on Easter Sunday 1903, which saw thirty-eight Jews (and four gentiles) killed, and some 1,350 (mostly Jewish) homes sacked.

In the historical literature, the Kishinev pogrom is usually invoked as a point of no return in relations between tsarist Russia and its Jewish subjects. The pogrom inspired the anti-Semitic forgery *Protocols of the Elders of Zion* and kicked off a massive wave of out-migration of Russian Jews from the Pale of Settlement, the area of western Russia where Jewish residency was allowed and beyond which it was mostly prohibited, particularly to the United States. All this is true enough, but in Russian terms, it is only part of the story. What appeared, to Western eyes, to be a black-and-white drama pitting Jews against Christian anti-Semites was perceived very differently by Plehve and millions of Russians. 1903 was a year of violent explosions across Russia, with strikes breaking out in all the great industrial cities, many put down by the army (in Zlatoust alone, the butcher's bill was 45 killed and 83 wounded). By summer, chaotic peasant uprisings (*bunts*) were sweeping the countryside, with fifty-four manor estates burned to the ground. The horrendous Kishinev pogrom in April was part of a national wave of unrest that claimed some 174 civilian casualties—and 162 in the army. By July 1903, many police agents paid by the Okhrana had gone over to the strikers, prompting Plehve to fire Zubatov, whom he blamed for the disaster. In a months-long struggle between the regime and its enemies, Kishinev was merely an episode.[11]

Still, the Kishinev pogrom marked a watershed in Russian political history, and not a happy one. To Russian conservatives, there was an elemental connection between Jews and radicalism: Plehve estimated that 40 percent of Russian revolutionaries were of Jewish origin. His figure was probably high, but it is undeniable that huge numbers of educated Jews had joined the socialist movement, mostly via their own Jewish-Marxist organization, the General Jewish Workers Union of Lithuania, Poland, and Russia (Bund), formed in 1895. The Bund actually predated the RSDRP and, with nearly thirty-five thousand members, outnumbered it four to one. The founding of the "gentile" Marxist party in March 1898, indeed, owed much to an Okhrana crackdown on the Jewish-Marxist Bund earlier that month, which had seen 500 Jewish revolutionaries jailed, including 175 in Kiev alone. These details mattered little in Kishinev in April 1903. But the pogrom's well-publicized aftermath saw a hardening of attitudes, with many moderate Jews abandoning assimilation for revolutionary politics, which lent further ammunition to anti-Semites. Less intellectual Jews, meanwhile, joined armed self-defense organizations.[12]

The foregrounding of the Jewish question by Kishinev indelibly marked the history of Russian socialism. Contrary to the common belief, expounded in most history books, that the famous Bolshevik-Menshevik split of July 1903 occurred because Lenin's advocacy of a professional cadre of elites (sometimes called vanguardism), outlined in his 1902 pamphlet *What Is To Be Done?*, was opposed by Mensheviks who wanted mass worker participation in the party, the real fireworks at the Brussels Congress surrounded the Jewish question. Party organization was not even discussed until the fourteenth plenary session. Lenin's main goal in Brussels was to defeat the Bund—that is, Jewish—autonomy inside the party. His winning argument was that Jews were not really a nation, as they shared neither a common language nor a common national territory. Martov, the founder of the Bund, took great umbrage at this, and walked out in protest to form the new Menshevik (minority) faction. He was followed by nearly all Jewish Socialists, including, notably, Lev Bronstein (Trotsky), a young intellectual from Kherson, in southern Ukraine, who had studied at a German school in cosmopolitan Odessa, which helped prime him for the appeal of European Marxism. With Lenin all but mirroring the arguments of Russian anti-Semites, it is not hard to see why Martov, Trotsky, and other Jews joined the opposition. Paradoxically, the merging of the Bund with the new Menshevik faction of the RSDRP—though confirming, for Okhrana agents, the tautology that Russian Jews were socialists—may actually have weakened the Jewish character of Russian Marxism, now that Lenin's gentile-led Bolshevik—"majority"—faction stood in pole position (even if it was, confusingly, much smaller in numbers than the Menshevik faction and the Bund). In effect, Lenin had rejected Jewish socialist internationalism—the cosmopolitan faith of such intellectuals as Trotsky—for Russia's native revolutionary tradition, grafting his own, ruthless version of Narodniki-style populism onto Marxism. Bolshevism, like its founder, was Russian to the core.[13]

Still, we should be wary of reading too much into the celebrated convulsions of the Brussels Congress. Jews and Marxists alike remained tiny minorities in the tsarist empire, and neither group enjoyed support in Russia outside the ranks of the radical intelligentsia. In the only post-Kishinev violence pitting Christians against Jews in 1903, a far less publicized clash that erupted in Gomel in late August, casualties were counted in single digits. Owing to the formation of Jewish self-defense organizations, this time more Christians died (five) than Jews (four), although once again it was Jews who lost the most, with 250 Jewish-owned homes sacked. Whatever produced the horrible violence in Kishinev and Gomel, there was an interesting parallel between the two cases that, contrary to the ferociously anti-tsarist chorus of the foreign press, arguably spoke well of the regime (if not all its servants). Although the local police in these towns of the old Jewish Pale of Settlement had failed abysmally to prevent the pogroms, peace was rapidly restored after the regular army arrived.[14]

So long as the Russian army remained disciplined, there was no reason that the empire could not survive periodic outbreaks of industrial strikes and pogroms. The cat-and-mouse struggle between revolutionaries and the Okhrana was as remote from the lives of most ordinary Russians as the Petersburg balls attended by aristocratic debutantes. However one reckoned the strength of what might loosely be called the opposition, the combined number of socialists, populists, national separatists, Jewish radicals and self-defense organizations, and even Russian gentry liberals, was dwarfed by the predominantly peasant army, which even in peacetime counted over a million soldiers by the early twentieth century, most of them loyal to the tsar they served. Maintaining social order had long been an important part of the brief of the Russian Imperial Army. According to statutes "Determining the Method for the Call of Troops to Aid the Civil Power," in legal force from 1877 to 1906, civil authorities had the right to summon the army for a bewildering variety of purposes: "to keep order during church services, fairs, and public assemblies . . . protect state property . . . prevent smuggling . . . to serve as guards or help execute judicial sentences . . . capture bandits and robbers," even to "extinguish forest fires . . . [and] help during floods." The army was perpetually on call in case regional governors or city officials wished "to prevent or stop popular disorders." Understandably, many officers—and their men—resented being called upon to suppress internal dissent. Nevertheless, they did so, and successfully, too, judging by the minimal casualty figures recorded in domestic operations—until the sharp uptick in 1903.[15]

Despite some grumbling about police duties, morale in the Russian Imperial Army was generally robust as the twentieth century dawned. And why not? The Witte boom brought a doubling of tax revenue in the 1890s. Although military spending did not rise quite this fast, the annual army budget still increased by 60 percent from 1890 to 1900, which made possible a generational leap as the Russian army adopted the new Mosin three-line rifle and its first quick-firing field artillery piece, a 3-inch gun. At any rate, the Russian army was far stronger than revolutionaries and bandits foolish enough to challenge it. Its domestic record was unbeaten, even if not morally unblemished.[16]

As regarded foreign opponents, the picture was similarly positive. Although the Crimean War of the 1850s had not gone well, it had been fought, after all, against the two greatest powers of the day (France and Britain), as well as the Ottoman Empire and Piedmont-Sardinia. Russia's last war, fought against the Ottomans alone in 1877–1878, had been a triumph, with her Caucasian Army seizing three provinces of eastern Turkey (Kars, Ardahan, and Batum) even while the main thrust, through the Balkans, had reached as far as San Stefano (site of today's Atatürk Airport outside Istanbul). True, after Britain dispatched her fleet, Russia's peace terms had been watered down at the Congress of Berlin in 1878. Still, the morale of an army is usually linked to its performance in the last war, and Russia's army, in 1900, was a winner.[17]

There were lingering concerns about the army's cohesion, of course, drawn as it was from the population of a sprawling empire comprising nearly a hundred nationalities—even more than in the famously multiethnic dual monarchy of Austria-Hungary. The census of 1897, the first and only conducted in tsarist times, had recorded 125 million souls (almost certainly an undercount), of which only 55,667,469 million, or 44 percent were Great Russians. Another 22 million "Little Russians" (Ukrainians, as we call them today) and 6 million "White Russians" (Belorussians) rounded out a kind of Eastern Slavic–Orthodox super-majority of 87 million, although there remained huge non-Russian, non-Orthodox–Christian minorities, such as predominantly Catholic Poles (nearly 8 million) and mostly Protestant Finns (3.5 million), as well as an imposing Muslim Turco-Tatar population of 13.7 million. Jews numbered some 5.2 million (by religious affiliation), or a bit over 5 million if defined ethnically as Yiddish speakers. Most of the other groups—Armenians, Germans, Georgians, Latvians, Lithuanians, Romanians—numbered under 2 million, although they were all concentrated heavily in the areas in which they lived, rendering them vulnerable to the lure of national separatism.[18]

Still, the tsarist army reflected, to an impressive degree, the multiethnic composition of the imperial population, though with significant exceptions. The core of the army was "Eastern Slavic," with nearly 75 percent of its units composed of Great Russians, Ukrainians, and Belorussians. Despite well-founded concerns about the loyalties of Poles in a Russian-dominated empire, Poles served in the army in numbers more or less proportional to their share of the population, although they were deliberately scattered about the empire so as to keep their numbers below 20 percent in each unit. Virtually no Poles were allowed to serve in Russian Poland itself, a critical border region thrusting out, like a salient, between German East Prussia and Austro-Hungarian Galicia. The Polish model was used for smaller minorities, too, the general idea being to keep minority soldiers away from their coethnics, so as to frustrate any effort to form nationalist militias. An exception was made for Finns, who were allowed to serve in their own formations as part of the agreement under which Finland had been absorbed into the empire in 1809 (Finns were also seen as less obstreperously nationalist than Poles). The cases with Germans and Muslims were varied. On the one hand, Baltic Germans were heavily represented in the officer corps (this was even more true in the navy, especially in the Baltic Fleet). But the German Mennonites living in the Volga region, encouraged to immigrate to Russia by Catherine the Great, had been given perpetual immunity from military service. In a similar manner, the Turkic nomads of Central Asia were generally left alone by tsarist draft boards, while the settled Muslims of the Caucasus and Crimea were prized for their martial qualities, much as Punjabi Muslims were valued by the British Indian Army.[19]

The Cossacks formed a category unto themselves. Although predominantly Eastern Slavic Orthodox, they were less an ethno-religious group than a calling. The self-governing Don, Kuban, and Terek Cossack "hosts" had been military vassals of the Romanov tsars since the seventeenth century, defending and often expanding Russia's southern border regions, while also serving as mounted auxiliaries in Russia's great power wars. By the late nineteenth century, the tsarist regime had begun to lean heavily on the Cossacks for help with internal policing, with their heavy rawhide whip (*knut*, usually mistranscribed into English as "knout"), used in crowd control, a notorious symbol of Russian repression. Because of this, and their periodic participation in anti-Semitic pogroms, the Cossacks acquired, and endure to this day, a terrible reputation in the West. It is therefore well to recall that, before 1905 at least, they were highly valued by the tsarist army and widely admired by patriotic Russians for their loyal service to the country. Tolstoy wrote an inspired novella, *The Cossacks*, contrasting their selfless courage and élan to the drab, colorless Russian officers who were nominally their superiors. Vilified in Soviet times as loyal tools of the Old Regime, since 1991 the Cossacks have returned to favor, with popular histories chronicling their heroic deeds.[20]

Compared to her German rival, the tsarist Russian army was less advanced. The literacy rate of draftees fluctuated between 30 and 40 percent, compared to almost 90 percent in the German empire. Russian peasants made for sturdy infantrymen, but it was hard to get them to master the rudiments of modern warfare, from artillery targeting to machine-gunning and radio communications. Better schooling and literacy, whether in Germany, a possible opponent since Russia had signed a defensive alliance with France in 1894, or in Russia's ally France, also cultivated a sense of national identity, of shared references and common purpose, which was largely absent from the tsarist army. The very size of Russia's population made it difficult to mobilize as large a fraction of manpower as could her continental rivals. Scarcely more than 20 percent of eligible young men were called up into the army. Russia's military potential was enormous, but her social and political limitations made it difficult for her to realize it fully.[21]

Nonetheless, the tsarist army remained formidable as the twentieth century dawned. The peasant soldiers (muzhiks) may not all have been able to speak the same language, or read, but they were decently trained, well equipped, and well armed. Above all, muzhiks were well fed. The meat consumption of conscript soldiers, 2 pounds per week, was four times higher than that of the typical peasant. Being enlisted into the army was, for most Russians, a step up in life, and most seized it happily. In the officer corps, the army was an engine of social mobility, providing a glaring exception to the rule of tsarist Russia's reputation as a class-riven society of grotesque inequality. Something like two fifths of officers below the rank of colonel were of peasant or lower-class social stock. Even among officers of aristocratic origin, who made up an imposing but not overwhelming 40 percent of service academy graduates, most were landless: indeed, these nobles were pursuing a military career because they needed the income. It was a sign of the egalitarian ethos of the tsarist army that most officers traveled third class on the railways, until the government was shamed into allowing them to travel second class for the third-class fare. Although bastions of traditional elitism remained (as in the Guard Corps), the army was meritocratic enough that men of humble origins, in some cases only a generation removed from serfdom, could rise to the rank of general and above. For these reasons, morale throughout the ranks was generally robust, and relations between officers and men were far better than those between Russian landlords and peasants, or between wealthy urban industrialists and their employees.[22]

So long as the army remained loyal, revolutionary schemes to topple the tsar remained little more than fanciful wish-dreams. On their own, populist-Narodniki assassins, student radicals, socialists, Jews, Poles, Finns, and other disgruntled minorities had little hope of breaching the regime's formidable defenses. Even the liberation of the serfs and the organization of zemstvos under Alexander II had only been possible because of the regime's loss of prestige in the Crimean War, which had undone decades of political quiescence under Nicholas I. In the end the only real danger to the regime came from such mistakes in the international arena. Unfortunately for Nicholas II, who had enjoyed a decade of peace upon assuming the throne in 1894, a foreign policy disaster was brewing in Asia, owing to the greed and incompetence of his own officials.

2

1905: SHOCK TO THE SYSTEM

The reign of Tsar Nicholas II began under a cloud of ill omen. Legally speaking, he became sovereign upon the sudden and unexpected death of his father, Alexander III, on October 20 (November 1), 1894, in itself a misfortune, as the fallen tsar had scarcely begun training his son in the awesome responsibilities of autocracy. But Nicholas's formal reign did not truly begin until his inauguration in the Moscow Kremlin on May 14/26, 1896. By tradition, the day following the coronation was devoted to the common people of Moscow, who were all invited to an open-air feast with the new tsar at the Khodynka meadow. Nicholas II had spared no expense, ordering up "hundreds of barrels of free beer" along with "cartloads of enameled cups" to consume it in, each souvenir mug stamped with the Romanov seal. Nearly 100,000 Muscovites had camped out overnight. Toward dawn, a rumor went round that there would not be enough beer, which caused a stampede. Horrendous scenes ensued, as hundreds of Muscovites, including women and children, were trampled underfoot. In a superstitious country, such omens were taken seriously, and they bode poorly for Nicholas's reign.[1]

Considering the poor beginning, the first decade of the tsar's reign did not proceed too badly. While student and labor unrest were on the rise, and the Kishinev pogrom damaged Russia's international reputation, the economy continued to hum along. So, far from being isolated in the wake of Kishinev, in fact Tsar Nicholas II took the lead in European mediation efforts during a Macedonian crisis later that year, signing off on an Ottoman reform program at Mürzsteg in October

1903 with Habsburg emperor Franz Josef I. Russia and Austria-Hungary, diplomatic enemies since the Crimean War, had buried the hatchet. Russia's position in Europe had never been stronger.[2]

In the Far East, the strategic picture was less favorable. The presence of serious rivals to the west—Germany and Austria-Hungary, the core members of the "Triple Alliance" (alongside a semialoof Italy) since 1882—had imposed discipline on tsarist foreign policy in Europe, a sense of limits that must not be crossed. In Asia, Russia had long had her way against weaker neighbors, from the Muslim warriors of the Caucasus conquered in the 1850s to the emirs and khans of Central Asia she had overwhelmed in the 1860s and 1870s, to China, which Russia (alongside the other European powers, the United States, and Japan) humiliated in 1900 by crushing the Boxer Rebellion.

Although this "Eight-Power Expedition" is remembered today for the German kaiser's impolitic remark that "for a thousand years no Chinaman will ever again dare to squint at a German," which epitomized the European racial prejudice of the era, the two largest contingents of troops were sent by Japan (20,840) and Russia (12,400), the nearest powers to China and the most directly interested in her affairs. In 1896, Witte had strong-armed China into allowing a shortcut in the Trans-Siberian Railway through northern Manchuria to Vladivostok, an ice-free port on the Pacific. Despite cynical assurances that Chinese sovereignty would be respected, Witte had turned Manchuria into a veritable Russian colony. In the era of high imperialism, Witte was, as an admirer said, "Russia's Cecil Rhodes," building an Asian empire in the name of the tsar.[3]

Russia's Japanese neighbor was less admiring. In the Sino-Japanese War of 1894–1895 (fought largely in and over Korea), Japan had seized Kwantung, the territory on the southern end of the Liaodong Peninsula—only for Germany, France, and Russia to pressure Tokyo into returning it to China. In an act of blithe contempt, the Russian navy had then invested Port Arthur, the peninsula's most critical port on the Sea of Japan, in December 1897. Meanwhile Russian companies began buying up mining and forestry concessions near the Yalu and Tumen Rivers in Korea, still closer to Japan—and viewed by Tokyo as Japan's natural sphere of influence on the Asian mainland.

Salted with the European racial prejudice of the era, these machinations infuriated Japanese leaders.

Although Japan and Russia were ostensibly on the same side in the Eight-Power Expedition, the crisis nakedly revealed the clash of interests between St. Petersburg and Tokyo. After the Boxer Rebellion was crushed, instead of withdrawing, the Russians sent in *more* troops, blanketing Manchuria with more than 100,000 soldiers. Owing to furious Japanese protests—endorsed by Great Britain, which signed an alliance treaty with Tokyo in February 1902—Russia agreed to recognize Chinese sovereignty over Manchuria and promised a gradual, phased withdrawal of Russian troops. Had this evacuation proceeded on schedule, the crisis might have stopped short of war.

Instead, the Russians went the other way. Urged on by Kaiser Wilhelm II, who mischievously saluted him as the "admiral of the Pacific," Nicholas II succumbed to the influence of rabble-rousing courtiers who insisted that backing down to a non-European power, such as Japan, would be shameful—an appeal well calculated to the tsar's own feelings. On a state visit to Japan in 1891 while still heir to the throne, he had nearly been killed by one of his Japanese police escorts, who lunged at him with his saber and left a 3 1/2-inch scar on the tsar's forehead that constantly reminded him of the painful incident. Against Witte's advice, Nicholas II declared a "new course" in Russia's Far Eastern policy in May 1903, disavowing the Manchurian withdrawal agreement. Witte, alarmed, resigned the Finance Ministry in August, in effect retiring from public service. A "Russian Timber Partnership" was created to shore up Russia's concessions in Korea. Russia, it appeared to officials in Tokyo, was clearing the decks for war.

Was it a bluff? Given the haphazard decision-making style of Nicholas II, it is hard to know whether there was method to the madness of provoking Japan. In June 1903, Nicholas II even dashed off a telegram to Port Arthur, informing his viceroy that he had resolved to allow Japan "to take full possession of Korea." But he did not press the point. In November 1903, Alexei Kuropatkin, the minister of war, advised Nicholas II that "a war with Japan would be extremely unpopular," allowing revolutionaries to "spread sedition" through the Russian army. At a time when "disorders of various sorts" were "increasing in frequency," any military setback in the Far East might prove fatal to the regime. Taking the opposite tack, the interior minister, Plehve, told Nicholas II that what he needed to quell domestic unrest was a "small victorious war." At a conference in December 1903, the tsar expressed misgivings about going to war with Japan, but then remarked, "All the same, it is a barbarous country." In the end, the tsar's prejudice won out. He dismissed demands for concessions as "impudent," and instructed his diplomats to warn Japan that "Russia is a big country" and that "there are limits to our patience."[4]

The Japanese got the message. Tokyo sent an ultimatum to St. Petersburg in January 1904, demanding that the tsar renounce all interest in Korea, in exchange for a Japanese pledge to recognize Russia's sphere of influence in Manchuria. Any further delay, Tokyo warned, would have "extremely serious" consequences. After no reply was forthcoming, on the night of January 25–26 (February 7–8), 1904, a force of ten Japanese torpedo boats slipped into Port Arthur and attacked the Russian Pacific squadron lying at anchor. Three hours *after* this surprise attack, Japan declared war on Russia, enraging Tsar Nicholas II, who now resolved, as he told an aide, to wage war "to the death."[5]

It was an inopportune choice of words. After a Russian advance guard in Korea was defeated at the Yalu River on April 18/May 1, 1904, the Japanese army entered Manchuria and closed on the Russian garrison at Mukden. Meanwhile the Japanese navy landed troops on the Liaodong Peninsula, who laid siege to the Russian garrison at Port Arthur. The Russians, under General Antony Stessel, were outnumbered two to one by the besieging force (80,000 to 40,000), and the Japanese blockade made reinforcement by sea impossible. Still, the Russians held on bravely and inflicted severe casualties on the enemy. In Kwantung, the Japanese lost ten thousand men capturing a single elevated position (203 Meter Hill) in late November. But the victory allowed them to mount heavy siege guns and "pulverize" the fortress in Port Arthur and what remained of the Russian fleet in harbor.[6]

Inspired by the heroism of his men holding out at Port Arthur against heavy odds, Tsar Nicholas II tried everything he could to relieve them. With the landward route cut off by the Japanese army, the only possibility was to send the Baltic Fleet to the Pacific, some

18,000 miles away. The Black Sea Fleet was closer, but according to the Treaty of Berlin (1878), Russia had no right to send warships through the Ottoman Straits, as London had just reminded St. Petersburg. With Britain and Japan now allies, London might even declare war on Russia if she violated the Straits Convention. And so, in October 1904, the tsar asked Admiral Zinovy Rozhdestvensky, commander of the Baltic Fleet, to relieve Port Arthur—by way of the North Sea, the Atlantic Ocean, the Mediterranean, the Suez Canal, the Red Sea, the Indian Ocean, and the South China Sea. In all, the journey would take upward of six months (as it turned out, nearly 8), capturing the attention of the world—while also ratcheting up pressure on Tsar Nicholas II, who had invested political capital in the relief of Port Arthur.

The voyage did not go well. Scarcely had the "Russian Second Pacific Squadron" entered the North Sea than it encountered British fishing trawlers, which a Russian captain mistook for Japanese warships. The Russians opened fire. Although only three British fishermen were killed, this "Dogger Bank Incident" could easily have served London as a casus belli, had the tsar not wisely agreed to issue an apology and compensate Britain for her losses with 66,000 pounds sterling. But the consequences were serious: Rozhdestvensky was forbidden by Britain from using the Suez Canal, and thus forced to circumnavigate Africa, which added over a month to his squadron's exhausting journey.

Before the Russians rounded the Cape of Good Hope, the point of their voyage was made moot when General Stessel, on December 20, 1904 (January 2, 1905), surrendered Port Arthur to General Nogi Maresuke, commander of the Japanese Third Army. Rozhdestvensky's Second Pacific Squadron was still crossing the Indian Ocean when the climactic battle for Manchuria commenced at Mukden on February 7/20, 1905, which saw the Russians lose more than 88,000 casualties in the largest land battle since the Napoleonic wars. So far, the Russians had lost 200,000 men and spent a billion rubles—and had not won a single engagement. The tsar had paid heavily for his hubris, and his prejudice.

Worse was to come. Although the distance between European Russia and the theater of war meant that news trickled into the capital slowly, the cumulative effect was hard to suppress. In July 1904, the reviled interior minister, Plehve, was killed by a terrorist bomb blast. In the fall, liberals and representatives of the regional zemstvo convened a series of "political banquets," which paved the way for the first all-Russian "Zemstvo Congress," which saw 103 delegates assemble in St. Petersburg in November 1904. A resolution was passed demanding the election of a constituent assembly by universal male suffrage. When the tsar heard this, he vowed that he would "never agree to the representative form of government," which would violate his oath of office. In a compromise, on December 12/25, 1904— one week before the surrender of Port Arthur—Nicholas II issued a decree that expanded the role of the zemstvos, strengthened the rule of law, and eased censorship, but denied the popular demand for a national parliament.[7]

The impact of these two events on public opinion in St. Petersburg was electric. The humiliation at Port Arthur dealt a crippling blow to the prestige of the regime, even as revolutionary agitators were enraged by the tsar's rejection of reform. In early January, a walkout at the Putilov [arms] Works, inspired by the dismissal of four employees, spread to other factories. Galvanized by a charismatic priest turned police-agent named Father George Gapon, who had gone over to the workers in his sympathies, tens of thousands of strikers took to the streets, soon joined by thousands more sympathizers. On Sunday, January 9/22, 1905, Father Gapon led nearly 150,000 people to the Winter Palace to present the tsar a petition demanding the convocation of a Russian constituent assembly, an eight-hour workday, living wages, and the release of political prisoners. Many held up icons or portraits of the tsar, while Father Gapon held up a crucifix, giving the march the air of a religious procession (although this did not necessarily bode well, as many marchers had written farewell letters, prepared for martyrdom). When Gapon's procession, winding its way down Nevsky Prospekt, reached the entrance to Palace Square, the demonstrators ran into a squadron of Cossack cavalry. Behind the Cossacks stood a line of Guard troops, with bayonets drawn. Several warning shots were fired into the air, but Gapon held his ground and the demonstrators did not disperse as ordered. For a moment the two sides stared each other down, in a critical test of strength for the tsarist regime.

The regime's defenders were the first to blink. No one knows for sure who fired the first shot and whether it was fired in panic, anger, accident, or error. But fire someone did, setting off a terrible chain reaction as demonstrators screamed and ran, and soldiers and Cossacks fired into the crowd. Similar scenes transpired elsewhere in the city, with dozens more people mown down by Cossack sabers or felled by indiscriminate rifle fire. At least 200 were killed and 800 wounded in the massacre of "Bloody Sunday," as revolutionaries christened the events. Father Gapon, who took refuge in the apartment of Maxim Gorky, a world-famous Russian novelist sympathetic to the strikers, penned a "public letter" proclaiming Nicholas II the "soul-murderer of the Russian empire" and calling on "all the social-ist parties of Russia" to launch an "armed uprising." It was now open war between the tsarist regime and its enemies.[8]

News of the massacre, in a country already on edge owing to the disastrous course of the Far Eastern war, radicalized the population. In Riga, some 15,000 Latvian protestors stood down the police, all but goading them into firing: which they did, killing 70 and wounding 200. In February, the tsar's uncle, Grand Duke Sergei Alexandrovich, governor-general of Moscow, was blown to bits by a terrorist bomb outside the Kremlin. Across the countryside, peasants picked up the rebellious spirit, some taking up the regime's invitation to submit petitions of grievances to the tsar (60,000 were filed in all), others burning and looting manor houses. The Pale of Settlement saw a new wave of pogroms. In Baku, a demonstration in February 1905 took a sinister turn when Armenians shot a Tatar (Azeri Turk) Muslim, lead-ing to retaliatory attacks against Armenian Christians, some carried out with the support or connivance of Cossacks and police agents who viewed Armenians, like Jews, as dangerous revolutionaries. Although less well known than Bloody Sunday, the clashes in Baku were far deadlier; at least two thousand died. "Thousands of dead lay in the streets," wrote one stunned eyewitness. "The odour of corpses stifled us. Everywhere women with mad eyes sought their children, and husbands were moving heaps of rotting flesh." The young Stalin, who formed a (mostly Muslim) "Bolshevik Battle Squad" to exploit the mayhem by extorting protection money from terrified Armenian merchants, was positively exhilarated by the violence.[9]

Despite the anarchy engulfing the country, the tsarist regime was not without reserves of strength. As early as February 1905, just as the Battle of Mukden was commencing in the Far East, the Interior Ministry summoned the army to form "flying detachments" in the countryside. In all, provincial officials called in the army on 1,390 occasions between January and mid-June 1905, mostly for "preventive" policing in villages and towns. Regular troops engaged demonstrators 240 times during these interventions, or about 20 percent of the time. Although many army leaders were starting to bristle at the way their men were being used and abused by hapless civilian politicians, so far the army had held together, allowing the regime to weather the political storm.[10]

The army could not do everything, however. The high command, desperate to reinforce Manchuria, had already stripped the western borderlands of 20 percent of the infantry and artillery that guarded Russia against the Central Powers, and units in most interior districts were busy suppressing domestic unrest. The financial picture was bleak, as the government had already taken out new loans for a half-billion rubles. After the fall of Port Arthur, bond buyers were demanding stiffer premiums. Even as the Battle of Mukden was raging, the Interior Ministry concluded that internal disturbances in 32 of the 50 provinces of European Russia ruled out further mobilization of troops for Manchuria. On February 22 (March 7), 1905, Nicholas II told his foreign minister that he was ready to sue Japan for peace as soon as Russia won one face-saving battle.[11]

The tsar would not be so lucky. Mukden fell two days later. Although Japan's losses (75,000) were nearly as heavy as Russia's in a brutal slog that foreshadowed, in essentials, the close-order carnage of the First World War on the western front, Mukden was a strategic triumph for Tokyo, which left the Liaodong Peninsula, Korea, and much of Manchuria in Japanese control. With the land battle lost, there seemed little remaining point to the epic voyage of Admiral Rozhdestvensky's fleet other than the tsar's desperate need for a morale-boosting victory. On May 14/27, 1905, Russia's

Second Pacific Squadron, after eight months at sea, at last encountered Admiral Togo's fleet in the Straits of Tsushima. Togo's crews were rested; his battleships were at full strength and could steam at speed (about 15 knots). By contrast, Rozhdestvensky's battle cruisers and destroyers had been "fouled" by the long voyage and could make nine knots at best, and his men were in wretched shape. Three of his battleships were knocked out of action by midafternoon. On board the flagship *Suvorov*, Rozhdestvensky himself was badly injured when the conning tower was hit. Toward dusk, Togo's nimble destroyers and torpedo boats finished off what remained of the dazed Russian squadron. By the time he raised the white flag of surrender on May 15/28, Rozhdestvensky had lost 11 of 12 battleships, 7 of 12 cruisers, and 6 of 9 destroyers. More than 5,000 Russian officers and men were killed, with another 6,106 taken prisoner, against only 700 Japanese casualties. In despair, Tsar Nicholas II sued Japan for peace.[12]

With Russia utterly defeated in war—and by an Asiatic power, which, after all the chauvinistic boasting in St. Petersburg, compounded the humiliation—it was now open season on anyone unfortunate enough to be serving the tsarist regime. "Terrorism," recalled one Bolshevik with relish, "assumed gigantic proportions. Almost every day there was a 'political killing' or an attack on some representative of the old regime." By the regime's own estimate, 3,600 imperial officials were killed or wounded in 1905.[13]

June 1905 saw mutiny reach the Russian armed forces. With two of Russia's battle fleets—the Pacific and the Baltic—at the bottom of the ocean or in enemy hands, morale in her third, in the Black Sea, began to chafe and crack. Sailors supporting the Social Democrats (some Bolshevik, some Menshevik) organized a *tsentralka* (revolutionary central committee), ready to proclaim a general mutiny. On June 14/27, crewmen aboard the battleship *Potemkin*, out at sea, were served their usual beef borscht, only to see maggots crawling in the meat. The ship's doctor had declared the soup safe to eat, but the men were not buying it. When their appointed spokesman, Grigory Vakilinchuk, complained, a melée ensued in which Vakilinchuk was killed by the ship's second in command, trying to protect the captain, Evgeny Golikov. Enraged, the crewmen killed seven of the ship's eighteen officers, including Golikov. A *soviet* (sailors' committee) was then formed, which raised the red flag and steamed toward Odessa, headquarters of the Black Sea Fleet, to seek out support from revolutionaries on shore.

The arrival of a mutinous vessel in harbor enflamed a dangerous situation in Odessa, where a general strike had just been proclaimed. On June 15/28, Tsar Nicholas II signed an *ukaz* (imperial edict) proclaiming martial law in Odessa, instructed the local commander, General Semion Kakhanov, to "take the most severe, resolute measures to suppress the revolts both on the *Potemkin* and among the population of the port," and summoned to Odessa "the entire squadron and every torpedo boat." But it would not be easy to sink the *Potemkin*, as she outgunned every other Russian vessel in theater.[14]

A tense standoff now ensued. Although a few of the *Potemkin* mutineers went ashore to stage a funeral procession for Vakilinchuk, most stayed on board. By the afternoon of June 16/29, the funeral procession had turned into a "riotous tempest," with ten thousand people jammed into the port area. That evening, looters ransacked warehouses and set fires. A stampede began to escape the spreading flames, only for protestors to run into Cossack cordons. At midnight, General Kakhanov ordered his troops to fire into the crowds and disperse them, so that fire crews could come to grips with the inferno. Looking on in horror as their comrades were butchered on shore, the *Potemkin* mutineers took to sea. After being denied victual in Russian ports, the *Potemkin*'s mutineers maneuvered her into the Romanian port of Constanza and negotiated a deal to give up the ship in exchange for political asylum in Romania.[15]*

Perceiving that the fate of his regime was at stake, Tsar Nicholas II wasted no time opening peace talks. Fortunately for the beleaguered Russians, the Japanese, too, were exhausted. President Theodore

---

*In one last flourish of revolutionary spirit, the *Potemkin* mutineers opened the ship's valves before disembarking, although engineers later refloated the ship. Renamed the *Panteleimon* to erase memory of the mutiny, the battleship saw action against Turkey in World War I, carrying out numerous raids on the Bosphorus. Captured by the Germans in May 1918, after the armistice she was taken by the British, who later wrecked her engines to prevent her from falling into the hands of the Bolsheviks. The *Potemkin* was finally stricken from the Russian naval list in November 1925—just days before Eisenstein's film *Battleship Potemkin* was released, immortalizing her.

Roosevelt of the United States, an emerging Pacific power, offered to mediate, inviting the two warring parties to Portsmouth, New Hampshire. Summoning Russia's greatest statesman, the tsar called Witte out of retirement to negotiate. Witte salvaged what he could. Although Russia had to evacuate Manchuria and concede a sphere of influence in Korea, Japan acquired only the southern half of the Liaodong Peninsula (Kwantung, including Port Arthur). Tokyo was denied any war indemnity.

Peace achieved, the tsar and his ministers could now focus on dousing the flames of unrest. In July 1905, the Council of Ministers had discussed a plan drawn up by the new interior minister, A. G. Bulygin, to convene a consultative "Imperial Assembly" (Duma), elected by popular vote (though with the franchise strictly limited to property owners). In August, the tsar approved its convocation no later than January 1906. On paper, the assembly was given considerable authority, from budgetary oversight to "legislative initiative," including the "independent elaboration of new laws." At the end of August, the Interior Ministry announced that university students would be allowed to hold public assemblies. Police agents were banned from university precincts.[16]

The timing of these concessions granted by the tsarist regime in August 1905, however, was not ideal. Coming after Bloody Sunday, the military humiliation at Mukden, and the naval debacle at Tsushima, the initiative smacked of desperation and insincerity. Liberals faulted the franchise restrictions, which, they claimed, would limit the voting rolls to less than one percent of the adult male population in many cities. Others noted that the statutes also explicitly reaffirmed the "inviolability of autocratic power." It did not help the regime's credibility that several moderate opponents, including the historian Pavel Milyukov, founder of the liberal Constitutional Democrat (Kadet) Party, were arrested that August after voicing rather mild criticism of the Bulygin Duma plan. Social Democrats, both Bolsheviks and Mensheviks, vowed to boycott elections to a "bourgeois" assembly in which most workers would not have the vote.[17]

Far from calming public opinion, the tsar's belated efforts at reform galvanized his radical opponents. The Bolsheviks established a "Military Organization" and pumped out mutinous propaganda aimed at Russian sailors and soldiers, including a regular newssheet called *Soldatskaia Zhizn'* (Soldier's Life). On September 17/30, 1905, print workers in Moscow walked out. The ensuing police crackdown attracted sympathy protestors (especially students) in what turned into a general wave of protest. Soon the strike had spread beyond Moscow, with print workers in St. Petersburg marching in solidarity. On October 6/19, the Moscow railroad workers' union joined the strike, followed by their brethren across the country, who shut down Russia's rail network, including the Trans-Siberian. By month's end, it seemed the entire country had gone on strike, including telegraph and telephone workers, which paralyzed communications. Although no single party organized the October walkouts, they entered Euro-pean political lore as the "general strike" of 1905, a model of revolu-tion for the member parties of the Second International (1889–1914), which began discussing how to coordinate an international general strike to stop the great powers from going to war.[18]

Curiously, most of Russia's revolutionary politicians were not even in Russia when the revolution exploded in early 1905. Milyukov, who would emerge as one of the leading voices of Russian liberalism, returned only in April, after spending most of the previous decade abroad. Viktor Chernov, editor of the main Socialist Revolutionary (SR) Party organ, *Revolutionary Russia*, returned only in the fall. Julius Martov, founder of the Bund who, after the 1903 split, led the Mensheviks, returned only in November, as did the Bolsheviks' standard-bearer Lenin, who spent much of the year in London: this was far too late for either man to exert any real influence on events. Meanwhile, the founder-in-exile of the Russian Social Democratic Labor Party, Georgy Plekhanov, never bothered returning to Russia at all in 1905, ensuring his own political eclipse.

In the absence of senior leadership, it was left to more vigorous Russian socialists to make their mark. In Chernov's absence, a young SR trial lawyer, Alexander Kerensky, made his name by defend-ing revolutionaries ensnared in the courts. A twenty-six-year old Menshevik, Lev Trotsky, founded the "Soviet [Council] of Workers' Deputies," a self-appointed body of revolutionaries who met in the St. Petersburg Technological Institute on October 13/26. Alexander Israel "Parvus" Helphand was another lesser known socialist who burst on the scene in 1905, assuming chairmanship of the Petersburg Soviet after Trotsky was arrested. By risking their skin while senior Marxist or SR leaders stayed out of the fray, Kerensky, Trotsky, and Parvus achieved lasting fame and influence in the Russian revolutionary movement. So, too, did Stalin, the only Social Democratic leader to wreak havoc from beginning to end in 1905, which gave him neck-risking authenticity even Trotsky and Parvus could not match. Another young Bolshevik Party activist, Lev Rozenfeld (Kamenev), fell somewhere in between, helping Stalin evade the police in Georgia and arriving in Petersburg in time to attend the Soviet, but otherwise doing little to stand out, unless one counts the marriage of his sister Olga to Trotsky, which gave Kamenev an unusual familial link to the Mensheviks.[19]

The critical moment for the revolution, and the regime, came in October 1905. On October 9/22, Witte, after being asked to intervene by the tsar's advisers, handed his sovereign a "brutally frank" memorandum, warning Nicholas II that, if he did not act quickly, "the Russian bunt, mindless and pitiless, will sweep everything, turn everything into dust." Attempts "to put into practice the ideals of theoretical socialism," he continued, "will fail but they will be made," and this program "will destroy the family, the expression of religious faith, property, all the foundations of law." To prevent the catastrophe, Witte proposed that Nicholas II either (1) appoint a military dictator to crush the revolution; or (2) embrace constitutionalism, convoking a genuinely representative Duma to split Russia's liberals off from her revolutionary socialists. Half-measures, Witte warned, would be fatal to the regime.[20]

For a superstitious man who had never believed himself prepared to rule yet saw it as his sacred duty, it was an agonizing dilemma. Although crushing the rebellion by force might allow the tsar to preserve his oath of office intact, this would surely lead to another popular explosion, "and that," he wrote to his mother, "would mean rivers of blood." And so the tsar agreed to allow Witte to draw up a liberal reform plan. "My only consolation," Nicholas II told his mother, "is that such is the will of God and this grave decision will lead my dear Russia out of the intolerable chaos she has been in for nearly a year."[21]

The resulting "October Manifesto," issued in the name of Nicholas II on October 17/30, 1905, marked a climbdown for autocracy, even if it fell short of a genuine "constitution" (this word appears nowhere in the document). In it, the tsar guaranteed Russians "fundamental civil freedoms," including "real personal inviolability, freedom of conscience, speech, assembly and association." A parliament would shortly be elected by "those classes of the population which are at present deprived of voting powers," and have legislative powers ("no law can come into force without its approval by the State Duma"). Expressing "great and profound sorrow" for the recent "outbreaks of disorder and violence," the tsar concluded by calling "on all true sons of Russia to remember the homeland, to help put a stop to this unprecedented unrest and, together with this, to devote all their strength to the restoration of peace to their native land."[22]

This was Witte's carrot. Now came the stick. To convince his pious sovereign to issue this pride-swallowing Manifesto, Witte had quietly assured the tsar that he had a plan to bring revolutionary violence under control. Appointed chairman of the Council of Ministers in November 1905, he was given the chance to do so. Faulting the army for its "indecisiveness" so far, Witte proposed to put the whole country under martial law. Rather than waiting for riots to spin out of control, troops would be enjoined to open fire as soon as violence threatened: and not to back down, either. As the tsar himself minuted on a report of a clash in the strategic Ukrainian port of Nikolaev (home to important Imperial Navy dockyards), "The troops are obliged to answer fire with fire and are to smash the feeblest appearance of armed resistance." With the backing of both Witte and Nicholas II, the Russian War Ministry sent out an order to all units, emphasizing that "any crowd using arms ought to be fired on without mercy."[23]

The revolution now reached its climax. As if following Witte's script, Trotsky and Parvus responded to the Manifesto by calling for a general strike to achieve an eight-hour workday. St. Petersburg's industrialists, assured of Witte's backing, locked out more than 100,000 workers. In early December 1905, the Interior Ministry, led by P. N. Durnovo, an unapologetic authoritarian in Witte's mold, began arresting members of the Soviet's Executive Committee. In retaliation,

Trotsky and Parvus issued their own Manifesto, asking Russians to stop paying taxes and to withdraw their savings from state banks, to destroy confidence in the ruble. The next day, Durnovo and Witte ordered the arrest of 260 more members of the Soviet, including Trotsky and Parvus. Curiously, Lenin and forty leading Bolsheviks, including Stalin, were at a secret party conference in Finland when the Petersburg Soviet was smashed, which did not enhance their reputation (although Stalin, at least, had already proven his bona fides).

The focus of the revolution now shifted to Moscow, where the city's Soviet called on workers, on December 6/19, 1905, to mount an armed insurrection with the aim of creating a republic. With the backing of Witte and the tsar, the regular army was called in, spearheaded by the Semenovsky Guard Regiment, which stormed the rebellious factory district of Presnaya. Once Presnaya was pacified, the Moscow Soviet was brutally crushed, with some one thousand revolutionaries and strikers losing their lives.[24]

Tiflis, a hotbed of revolutionary violence all year, was next in line. General Fyodor Griazanov, commander of the Army of the Caucasus, banned political meetings and authorized his men to shoot rebels on sight. On January 5/18, 1906, he sent the Cossacks into the rebellious worker districts. They did not miss their chance, killing some 60 rebels, wounding another 250, and arresting 280 as they snuffed out the revolutionary wave at last. Stalin, true to form, had raced back from Finland to get in on the action, although he succeeded only in organizing the assassination of General Griazanov on February 3/16, 1906, too late to affect the outcome on the ground.[25]

Buoyed by his successes so far, Witte convened a special conference to coordinate a national strategy between Durnovo's Interior Ministry and army leaders. With Witte's backing, Durnovo proposed a radical redeployment plan, asking that border districts send troops to pacify the interior of the country: the Warsaw district (Poland) alone would give up 179 of its 194 battalions. Although the generals were "aghast" at the idea of denuding defenses against the Central Powers, Witte insisted that the redeployment was necessary—and he promised that Germany and Austria-Hungary would not press their advantage. On March 12/25, 1906, Tsar Nicholas II approved the Witte-Durnovo plan, blanketing the country with regular troops. To pay for the near-permanent state of siege, Witte negotiated a new foreign loan of 844 million rubles, shoring up the regime's financial position. Although there was grumbling in the officer corps, the army did as it was told and was able, over the coming months and years, to curb (though not end) the worst revolutionary excesses. This last great task achieved, Witte resigned in April 1906, believing that he had lost the tsar's confidence.[26]

By restoring some modicum of law and order to the country, Witte had bought the regime time to sort out Russia's new, quasi-constitutional order, even if he was not able to see things through himself. The "Fundamental Laws," promulgated on April 26/May 9, 1906, reaffirmed the "Supreme Autocratic power" of the sovereign, who alone could appoint government ministers, and curtailed the prerogatives of the State Duma (lower house of the Russian parliament elected in April 1906), by granting veto power over new legislation to both an appointed (that is, unelected) upper chamber called the State Council, and to the tsar himself. Collective associations, including labor unions, could be formed, although only after notice was given to the government, which had two weeks to reject applications. Duma deputies had the right to question the tsar's ministers about their policies, but not to appoint them. Most disappointing of all to liberals was the right given to the tsar to dissolve the Duma if he was displeased. Finally, Article 87 allowed the tsar to rule by "emergency decrees" when the Duma was not in session. The autocratic powers of the "Emperor of all the Russias" were no more, but neither was Russia a constitutional monarchy.[27]

Coming on the heels of military defeat, the revolution of 1905 had shaken the Russian Empire to its foundations. The tsar was fortunate that Russia had produced a statesman courageous enough to chart the right course. He could only hope that a statesman of similar caliber could fill the hole left behind by Witte's abrupt second retirement.

= 3 =

THE FRAGILE GIANT:
TSARIST RUSSIA ON THE
PRECIPICE OF WAR

After the ordeal of 1905, the tsarist regime enjoyed a resurgence of domestic prestige just as surprising, to its supporters and opponents, as its brush with death during the Russo-Japanese War had been. But recovery did not come about all at once. While the political threat had been contained, terrorism was another matter. Even as the Mensheviks and Bolsheviks, after the crushing of the Moscow and St. Petersburg Soviets, faded from view, the Socialist Revolutionaries—heirs to the Narodniki tradition—launched an assassination campaign in 1906 that saw 827 armed assaults on Russian Interior Ministry officials. Some 288 policemen and gendarmes were killed, and 383 wounded. By 1907, a total of 4,500 tsarist officials had lost their lives since the beginning of the Russo-Japanese War in 1904, along with a similar number of civilians, whether terrorists or bystanders. In view of horrendous statistics like these, one can forgive Witte for departing the scene before he, too, was felled by a bomb blast.[1]

Fortunately for Tsar Nicholas II, the revolutionary vortex had coughed up a statesman even tougher than Witte. This was Peter Stolypin (1862–1911), a scion of the Russian rural nobility from Penza and Saratov provinces, whose family had served the Russian regime since before the Romanovs ascended to the throne in 1613. More significant, in the present circumstances, Stolypin had performed with aplomb since 1903 as governor of Saratov, a Socialist Revolutionary stronghold, throwing himself into the melée on numerous occasions and surviving several assassination attempts. Like Witte, Stolypin had faced the revolutionary gauntlet and demonstrated real courage.

He was also politically imaginative. During earlier stints in Kovno and Grodno, in the westernmost Polish-Lithuanian territory of the empire, Stolypin had come to appreciate the potential of European-style private landholdings—still lacking in much of central and southern Russia where communes prevailed—to turn peasants into loyal law-abiding subjects, rather than potential recruits for revolutionary agitators. In Kovno, Stolypin had already had success in consolidating communal strips into contiguous peasant landholdings. Promoted to interior minister in April 1906, and then chairman of the Council of Ministers (while still interior minister) in July 1906, Stolypin was given the chance to apply his ideas to Russia as a whole.[2]

Essential as land reform was to Stolypin's vision, law and order had to come first, especially after he narrowly survived a terrorist bomb during a public reception on August 12/25, 1906, which killed 30 people and injured 32 more, including his own children. Invoking Article 87 of the Fundamental Laws to put through security measures without recourse to the Duma, Stolypin expanded martial law, authorizing military commandants to try terrorists in military courts, convened on the spot, with no possibility of appeal. In force until April 1907, Stolypin's "field courts" carried out one thousand death sentences by hanging.[3]

Stolypin's ruthless methods were decried by liberals and socialists, who referred to the hangman's noose as "Stolypin's necktie." But they worked. Slowly, fitfully, revolutionary violence began to wane. Morale in the Marxist and Socialist Revolutionary ranks plunged, with the men of 1905, such as Parvus-Helphand and Trotsky (along with Lenin, who had made little splash), drifting back into foreign exile, even as the tsarist bureaucracy recovered its morale. Stolypin's carrot-and-stick methods disarmed even many intellectual critics of the regime. As P. B. Struve, one of Russia's leading liberal thinkers, remarked, "Thank God for the Tsar, who has saved us from the people." Nicholas II was no less grateful to Stolypin, writing privately to his mother that "I cannot tell you how much I have come to like and respect this man." The pragmatic new era was encapsulated in Stolypin's famous retort to socialist deputies on May 10/23, 1907: "You want a great upheaval. We want a great Russia!"[4]

Stolypin backed his words with action. In spring 1907, Stolypin muscled laws through the Second Duma that protected citizens from arbitrary arrest, enacted a progressive taxation system, and extended insurance benefits for state workers. He then rammed through new franchise restrictions to ensure that the Third Duma, elected in fall 1907 after Stolypin shut down the Second that June, would be more pliant. For added insurance, Stolypin put a number of influential journalists, and conservative deputies in the new Duma, on the imperial payroll. For the most part, it worked, although Stolypin did not always get his way. One of his more farsighted plans, which would have eliminated the Pale of Settlement and granted civil equality to Russian Jews and other minorities, was scotched owing to opposition from Tsar Nicholas II himself.[5]

The most important Stolypin initiatives were in the realm of land reform. A new law freed Russian peasants from obligations to local communes, allowing the enterprising ones to turn their communal strips into private holdings, with the Peasant Land Bank extending them credit on relatively easy terms. While not everyone was willing to branch out on their own, over the next decade 2.5 million peasants did, fully a fifth of the rural population of European Russia. The last legal restrictions on peasants' internal movements were also lifted, and incentives were offered to anyone willing to cultivate state-owned farmland in Siberia and Central Asia. Three million peasants responded positively to Stolypin's invitation, most of them setting off east in a great wave in 1908 and 1909. Creating millions of new landowners, Stolypin's agrarian reforms also expanded the acreage of cultivated land, along with agricultural productivity. By 1911, Russia had achieved an export surplus of 13.5 million tons of grain, a total exceeded in 1913 when an astonishing total of 20 million tons were shipped abroad. Grain exports, in turn, paid for the inputs and machinery needed in Russia's thriving factories.

Stolypin also revived state capitalism, ushering in an economic boom even more stupendous than the Witte one. The impetus, again, came from railway construction, with the pliant Third Duma, in April 1908, allocating 238 million rubles to finish the last section of the Trans-Siberian Railway. This stretch through the Trans-Baikal region included some of the most difficult engineering obstacles, such as Lake Baikal, the largest freshwater lake in the world, and the Amur River, which required a bridge at Khabarovsk of 8,500 feet, the longest in Russia. As Stolypin explained to skeptical Duma deputies, the railway would pay for itself, once the riches of Siberia—gold, timber, furs, and fish—could be shipped overland to European markets. The Amur Railway, as this last stretch came to be called, was also a tremendous jobs program, employing fifty-four thousand skilled workers—all Russian subjects, too, as Stolypin strictly forbade the use of foreign labor. By 1910, Russia's economy was humming along at an annual growth rate of nearly 10 percent. Like China in the early twenty-first century, Stolypin's Russia in the early twentieth was the economic story of its day, a colossus in the making.[6]

Could it last? Russia's economic potential was vast, and the more this was tapped, the more Stolypin believed her social tensions would resolve themselves. Peasants, turned into property-owners with something to lose, could become a bulwark of law and order in the countryside. In the cities, inequality might increase as industrialists prospered; but workers, too, could see their wages rise, along with a gradual but noticeable improvement in their living conditions. Building on the Orthodox tradition, in which state and church had always been more closely intertwined than in the Catholic or Protestant West, Stolypin even threw government funds into church construction, with more than 5,500 new churches built during his years in office (1906–1911), and the hiring of 100,000 new priests. In this way Stolypin's Russia fused together the paternalism of the tsar and the church, promoting throne and altar as conservative counterweights to "heartless" liberal industrialists who, greedy for profits, were doing too little to improve the lot of the common man.[7]

The Stolypin program depended on the maintenance of external peace. With both the tsar and the other members of the Council of Ministers, Stolypin maintained the need to avoid foreign entanglements so as to avoid another 1905. In February 1908, as Muslim-Christian tensions were rising in Ottoman Macedonia, Russia's minister of foreign affairs, Alexander Izvolsky, broached the idea of intervening in Turkey again (as Russia had in 1877) if the Balkans boiled over. Stolypin responded "categorically" that, due to the continuing social fallout from the 1905 revolution, "Russian mobilization was impossible at the present time, under any circumstances."[8]

The diplomatic crisis of 1908 provided a critical test of Stolypin's peace policy. After the "Young Turk" revolution of July nearly toppled Sultan Abdul Hamid II, Turkey's neighbors angled to take advantage of the turmoil. In September, Austria-Hungary's foreign minister, Baron Alois Lexa von Aehrenthal, offered Izvolsky an apparent quid pro quo. In exchange for Russian acquiescence in Austria's annexation of Bosnia-Herzegovina, a province with a large Serb population, Aehrenthal "offered" to revise the Treaty of Berlin to allow Russian warships free passage through the Ottoman Straits—a diplomatic gift not in his power to give. In October 1908, the annexation was announced, along with Aehrenthal's claim that Izvolsky had given Russia's blessing.

Caught off guard, Izvolsky was roundly denounced in Russian society and the press, where the cause of pan-Slavism, which saw Russia as protector and would-be unifier of Slavic peoples (Poles, Czechs, "Ruthenes" [Habsburg Ukrainians], Bulgarians, and above all, Serbs), was increasingly fashionable. *Russkoe Slovo*, the largest-circulation liberal newspaper in St. Petersburg, said that Izvolsky had "utterly buried Russian prestige in the Balkans." The senior correspondent of *Novoe Vremya*, a paper-of-record akin to the *New York Times*, told a Russian diplomat that "our purpose now is to destroy" Izvolsky. Stolypin was nearly as angry as the pan-Slavists, though for different reasons: he was concerned that Izvolsky's incompetence might plunge Russia into conflict before she was ready. With Izvolsky's critics baying for blood, Stolypin had to resort to outright censorship, banning public lectures by pan-Slavists. But he did not want Izvolsky to resign, either, as this would signal to Europe that "Russia is going on a path to war."[9]

Reluctantly, Nicholas II and his more belligerent ministers came around. After the German ambassador, Friedrich Pourtalès, delivered a stark warning that Berlin stood behind Vienna on March 9/22, 1909, the tsar followed Stolypin's advice and accepted the annexation. In this way the Bosnian crisis was resolved short of war, although the

Russians (and Serbs) were smarting from their humiliation. As Tsar Nicholas II wrote his mother, "The German[ ] . . . treatment of us was rude, and that we won't forget."[10]

Peace had been preserved, for now. Stolypin named his trusted brother-in-law, Sergei Sazonov, a mild-mannered loyalist of vaguely liberal inclinations, to succeed the disgraced Izvolsky as foreign minister. At a reconciliation summit between Kaiser Wilhelm II and Tsar Nicholas II in June 1909, Stolypin went out of his way to charm the German kaiser, as Austrian diplomats noted. Disturbed though his own pride may have been by Russia's humiliation in the Balkans, Stolypin remained adamant that war was simply not an option for the foreseeable future. Frustrated by the tub-thumping of the liberal press, he summoned a provincial reporter from *Volga* in October 1909 to give his own side of the story. While Petersburg society was preoccupied with foreign policy failures, Stolypin sensed a wave of positive energy coursing through the country at large. Noting the rise in agricultural and industrial productivity, Stolypin concluded with a note of optimism: "Give the state twenty years of peace, and you will not recognize present-day Russia."[11]

In the short run, Stolypin got his wish. In the spirit of rapprochement, he sent Sazonov to Berlin in October 1910 to propose a compromise. Russia would cease its opposition to the Berlin-to-Baghdad Railway, a favorite imperial project of the kaiser, in exchange for a German promise not to countenance "aggressive dispositions" by Austria-Hungary in the Balkans. To Sazonov's pleasant surprise, the German chancellor, Theobald von Bethmann Hollweg, agreed. Although it was nonbinding, a Russo-German agreement signed in August 1911 established the principle that Russia would not go to war against Germany unless her own vital interests, not those of her French ally, much less those of Britain (which had signed an accord with Russia over colonial questions in 1907, although it fell well short of a binding military alliance), were threatened.[12]

Stolypin's twenty years of peace were off to a good start at an even two. But the idyll was rudely interrupted by a terrible sequence of events in September 1911. In late August, Stolypin headed to Kiev for a ceremony in honor of Alexander II. It should have been a moment of triumph for the reformer who had done so much to further the work begun by the "Tsar-Liberator." But court politics had turned against Stolypin. In Kiev, he was ignored by the tsar and tsarina, a snub they would soon have cause to regret. On September 1/14, while attending a performance of Rimsky-Korsakov's *The Story of Tsar Saltan*, Stolypin was shot twice at close range by a young revolutionary (and paid Okhrana informer—although in this case he appears to have been acting as a free agent) named D. G. Bogrov. Four days later, Stolypin died of his wounds.[13]

The assassination had devastating consequences for Russian politics. Other than Witte, there was no one close to Stolypin's stature in St. Petersburg, and Witte remained on bad terms with the tsar. Stolypin's successor, Vladimir Kokovtsov, minister of finance since 1904, was known more as a penny-pinching bureaucrat than a man of action. Modest in stature, quiet and deferential, Kokovtsov was literally and figuratively a smaller man than his predecessors. (The same could be said of Tsar Nicholas II, who, at a slim 5 feet 6 inches, was dwarfed by his 6 foot 3 father Alexander III, a broad-shouldered man of legendary strength, who had often amused his children by bending silver plates with his bare hands.) Sazonov was more imaginative, and sympathetic to liberal ideas, but he was of similarly unimposing appearance (bald, with a receding hairline) and timid manners. It is a measure of the limited stature of these two men that most of the ambassadors in Petersburg now viewed Alexander Krivoshein, the agriculture minister overseeing Stolypin's land reforms, as Russia's leading statesman.

The declining stature of the tsar's ministers would not have mattered so much had Stolypin's "twenty years of peace" endured. The Stolypin land reforms were on autopilot by 1911, ably overseen by Krivoshein. Indeed, the Stolypin boom survived his death, as Russia's economy hummed along into 1912 and beyond. Sazonov was inexperienced, but he could learn on the job. Before his death, Stolypin had laid down, in a kind of last testament, a foreign policy line a child should have been able to follow: "War during the next years, especially for reasons the people will not understand, would be fatal for Russia and for the dynasty."[14]

It was a misfortune of timing that Russia was plunged into another diplomatic crisis within days of Stolypin's death. On September

16/29, 1911, Italy declared war on the Ottoman Empire and invaded Libya. With the overmatched Turkish fleet unable to contest the eastern Mediterranean, in April 1912 Ottoman naval commanders did the only thing they could to defend Constantinople, laying mines and stretching steel chains across the Dardanelles. The closure of the Turkish Straits, through which more than half of Russia's burgeoning export trade was routed to world markets, was a huge blow. The volume of Russian exports dropped by one third in 1912, and revenue plunged, eroding Russia's balance-of-payments surplus. Heavy industry in Ukraine, where factories depended on imports that came through the straits, nearly ground to a halt. The timing was particularly unfortunate, as April 1912 also saw the most serious Russian labor unrest since 1905–1906. A strike at the Lena goldworks in northeast Siberia came to a horrible end when the army fired into the crowd, killing 270 men and wounding 250.[15]

Already anxious over price competition from German wheat producers, Krivoshein now saw that Russia's critically important grain exports were at the mercy of the Sublime Porte (as diplomats referred to the Ottoman government) and by extension Turkey's main European sponsor, Germany. Once a foreign policy conservative in the Witte-Stolypin mold, Krivoshein now followed the drift of many Russian elites toward "liberal imperialism" and the Francophile "war party" hostile to Germany. By 1914, Krivoshein was viewed by French diplomats as the most reliably bellicose anti-German member of the Council of Ministers.[16]

Meanwhile the eastern crisis spiraled onward. When the opportunistic Balkan League of Bulgaria, Greece, Montenegro, and Serbia invaded the Ottoman Empire in October 1912, the Sublime Porte sued for peace with Italy and opened the straits. For Russia, it was out of the frying pan and into the fire: the advance of the Bulgarian army into Thrace turned the Dardanelles into a war zone once again (although Turkey, to prevent Russia from joining her enemies, kept the straits open this time). After Serbia conquered much of Ottoman Macedonia and Albania, Austria-Hungary mobilized three army corps in late November, leading to a war scare between Vienna and St. Petersburg. Sazonov took the side of the careful Kokovtsov, the former finance minister now chairman, against Krivoshein and the war party, convincing Tsar Nicholas II not to order partial mobilization. For his moderate line, the foreign minister was denounced at public banquets and on the floor of the Fourth Duma, elected in October 1912 amid pan-Slavist hysteria over the Balkan crisis.

The leading figures of the Fourth Duma came from the center-right "Octobrist" Party (the name reflected the party's commitment to fulfilling the Tsar's October Manifesto of 1905). The party's founder, Alexander Guchkov, came from an old Moscow merchant family of Old Believers, a group that practiced Russian Orthodox rites dating to before a Church reform promulgated in 1666. A kind of Russian superpatriot, Guchkov had actually fought as a volunteer in the Boer War of 1899–1902 against Britain (then still viewed by most Russians as their hereditary enemy). Guchkov, true to character, beat war drums all winter, this time against Austria-Hungary. Another Octobrist leader, Mikhail Rodzianko, a huge bear of a man weighing 280 pounds, recalled Witte in his physicality—though not his policy views, which tended more toward chauvinistic pan-Slavism. In April 1913, Rodzianko advised Tsar Nicholas II that the time had come for Russia to "take advantage of the general enthusiasm" and seize the Ottoman Straits. "War," Rodzianko advised his sovereign—on Easter weekend, of all times—"will be accepted with joy and will serve only to increase the prestige of the imperial power." The Octobrists wanted the hawkish, pan-Slavist Russian minister to Belgrade, Nikolai Hartwig, a man credited (if that is the right word) by most European diplomats as the architect of the Slavophile Balkan League that had launched the First Balkan War against Turkey, to replace Sazonov. To save a foreign minister whose cautious instincts he trusted, Tsar Nicholas II stepped in to ban further public protests, and issued an imperial rescript endorsing Sazonov's policy line in the Balkans.[17]

Sazonov's patient course had bought Russia another two years of peace, making an even four since Stolypin's prophecy. But the press attacks had wounded Sazonov's pride. Scarcely had Europe's chancelleries had a chance to rest after the Balkan Wars than a new crisis broke out in November 1913 over the appointment of a German general, Otto Liman von Sanders, to command the First Ottoman Army Corps, whose responsibilities included defense of the straits. To Sazonov, the Liman appointment was a slap in the face. After he had bent over backward, as he saw it, to appease Vienna and Berlin, the Germans had responded by threatening one of Russia's most vital interests. The timing of the announcement seemed like a deliberate insult, as Sazonov had visited Berlin in October, and the chancellor had not told him of the appointment. His blood now up, Sazonov resolved to fight the Liman appointment, telling the British chargé d'affaires that it would "put the value of the Triple Entente"—as he referred to the still-nebulous quasi-alliance between Britain, France, and Russia—"to the test."[18]

Although Britain remained somewhat aloof from both France (with whom she had signed an entente cordiale over colonial questions in 1904) and Russia, Europe's core military alliance blocs of Germany–Austria-Hungary and France-Russia were hardening. By extending the required length of service from two years, France's "Three-Year Service Law," promulgated in August 1913, added 170,000 soldiers to her peacetime army, reaching a total of 827,000 at near parity with the Germans', at 890,000. Russia's own "Great Program," finalized in October 1913, envisioned a peacetime army of 2.2 million, nearly triple the size of Germany's. Although it was not expected to take full effect until 1917 or 1918, the well-publicized Russian army reform put pressure on German war planners, such as Helmuth von Moltke "the Younger," chief of the general staff, who had already begun talking openly about the idea of starting a *Präventivkrieg* (preemptive war), before Russia grew too strong.[19]

Sazonov, too, was growing more belligerent. On December 24/January 6, 1914, he proposed to Tsar Nicholas II that the Entente powers, to contest Liman's appointment, land troops in the Ottoman Empire, the British at Smyrna (Izmir), France at Beirut, and the Russians at the Black Sea port of Trabzon. At a meeting of the Council of Ministers a week later, Sazonov's strong line was backed by Krivoshein; by the war minister, Vladimir Sukhomlinov, and the army chief of staff, Yakov Zhilinsky; and by the naval minister, I. K. Grigorevich. Stunned that his colleagues were courting European war, Chairman Kokovtsov asked: "Is the war with Germany desirable and can Russia wage it?" Sukhomlinov and Zhilinsky replied that "Russia was perfectly prepared for a duel with Germany, not to speak of one with Austria." Sazonov claimed that France's ambassador had assured him that "France will go as far as Russia wishes." Still, he was unable to guarantee British support, and so Kokovtsov convinced everyone to back down. Sazonov accepted a compromise that saw Liman promoted, rendering him "overqualified" to command the straits defenses.[20]

Peace had been preserved again, by a whisker. But the Russian war party was growing in strength. Kokovtsov was forced to resign in February 1914, after being subject to withering attacks from Krivoshein and Sukhomlinov. Although both men had other reasons for resenting the parsimonious chairman—Sukhomlinov thought Kokovtsov was slighting the army, and Krivoshein opposed Kokovtsov's reliance on the vodka sales monopoly for state revenue, which he believed led to rampant peasant drunkenness—Kokovtsov's opposition during the two recent war scares was clearly a factor, too. The new chairman, Ivan Goremykin, was a conservative of sorts, but at an old seventy-four, he was someone Krivoshein hoped to control. A more important new appointment was the new minister of finance, Peter Bark, a liberal Krivoshein protégé who was friendly to the war party and unlikely to oppose new military spending. After Kokovtsov's fall, Sazonov convened a "top secret" military planning conference on February 8/21, 1914, at which Russia's leaders formulated an aggressive new posture against Turkey, including the expansion of the Caucasian rail lines to the Ottoman border, the construction of four Black Sea dreadnoughts, and a more ambitious operational scheme for amphibious operations against Constantinople.[21]

Not everyone shared the belligerent mood of Sazonov, Krivoshein, and the service chiefs. Catching wind of the war plans underfoot, P. N. Durnovo, the former interior minister who had been instrumental in suppressing the revolutionary disturbances of 1905–1906, submitted a long memorandum to the tsar on February 14/27, 1914, warning of the dangers posed by the drift of Russian foreign policy into aggressive pan-Slavism in the Balkans and Near East, and toward an ever-closer alliance with France and Britain. For Durnovo, the final straw was Kokovtsov's resignation, which removed the last roadblock to war in the Council of Ministers.

Arguing that "the vital interests of Russia and Germany do not conflict," Durnovo condemned the policies that had nearly plunged Russia into armed conflict twice in the last two years. Somehow, autocratic Russia had lined herself up alongside demotic-democratic France and liberal England against conservative-authoritarian Germany, which should have been her natural ally. War between Germany and Russia, Durnovo believed, would destroy the social order in both countries, although the damage to Russia would be greater, owing to the inchoate radicalism of her working and peasant masses, who all professed, even if "unconsciously, the principles of Socialism." In a war with Germany, he warned, both battlefield reverses and the inevitable "shortcomings in . . . supply" owing to Russia's inadequate rail network would be "given an exaggerated importance" in society, "and all blame will be laid on the Government." Liberal and center-right politicians and intellectuals would try to exploit the regime's weakness to seize power, only to learn that they "have no popular support." Revolutionary slogans would then be "scattered far and wide among the populace," and Russia would once more be "flung into anarchy, such as she suffered in the ever-memorable period of troubles in 1905–1906."[22]

It was a timely warning. But there is no evidence that the memorandum had an impact on policymakers. Durnovo was out of power, his only official position a seat in Russia's State Council, the upper chamber that reviewed Duma laws. The Durnovo memorandum was distributed to the Council of Ministers, although as it sharply rebuked their policies, it cannot have been read with much sympathy. Durnovo, like Witte, was now a virtual outcast in Petersburg society, with the pair's Germanophile views on foreign policy as far out of fashion in 1914 as was their conservatism in domestic affairs.[23]

Russian public opinion—among the elites of the capital, at least—was trending strongly toward the war party. When, on June 15/28, 1914, Archduke Franz Ferdinand, heir to the Habsburg throne of Austria-Hungary, was assassinated in Sarajevo by a young terrorist named Gavrilo Princip with shadowy (but easily established) ties to

Serbia, the Austrians were therefore unlikely to find much sympathy in St. Petersburg.

The question of European war and peace now depended largely, although not exclusively, on the Russian foreign minister. Having endured Austro-German bullying, as he saw it, during both the First Balkan War of 1912–1913 (when Austria-Hungary had mobilized against Serbia) and the Liman crisis of winter 1913–1914 (when he had been forced to back down), Sazonov was not about to let Russia's enemies have their way yet again. Within an hour of receiving news of Vienna's 48-hour ultimatum to Serbia at ten a.m. on July 24, 1914, Sazonov instructed Russia's new chief of the general staff, Nikolai Yanushkevitch, to make "all arrangements for putting the army on a war footing." Sazonov's *chef de cabinet*, Baron Maurice Schilling, then instructed Bark, the finance minister, to repatriate all Russian treasury funds deposited in Berlin (100 million rubles). That afternoon, the Council of Ministers convened at Tsarskoe Selo, the summer palace 15 miles south of St. Petersburg, where the tsar spent much of the year. Sazonov, taking a hard line, argued that if, "at this critical juncture, the Serbs were abandoned to their fate, Russian prestige in the Balkans would collapse utterly." Krivoshein spoke next, summarizing the consensus of Russia's elites that "public and parliamentary opinion would fail to understand why, at this critical moment involving Russia's vital interests, the Imperial Government was reluctant to act boldly." With not a single voice raised in opposition to the war party, Tsar Nicholas II had little choice but to sign into law the measures recommended by Sazonov and Krivoshein, including the inauguration of Russia's "Period Preparatory to War," and the issuing of a stern warning to Vienna that Serbia's fate "could not leave Russia indifferent."[24]

Was there anyone left, among the men advising Tsar Nicholas II, willing to speak up for the old Stolypin peace policy? Curiously enough, one of the tsar's advisers was firmly opposed to the war party, although he held no official rank or title. This was Grigory Rasputin, the Siberian faith healer who had won the confidence of the tsar and tsarina owing to his mysterious ability, first displayed during a visit to Alexander Palace in April 1907, to alleviate the pain of the hemophiliac heir to the throne, Alexis, whenever the unfortunate boy was injured. The most recent bleeding episode, at Spala in October 1912, had been so serious that the government was forced to reveal to the public for the first time that the heir was gravely ill (although the nature of Alexis's ailment remained a state secret, as it was feared no one would have confidence in an autocrat-to-be whose blood was unable to clot after minor scrapes and bruises). The "miracle at Spala" also revived Rasputin's influence at a time when this was being deplored in St. Petersburg society. Rodzianko had opened a formal investigation into his activities, which had been debated on the floor of the Duma, where his fellow Octobrist, Guchkov, roundly denounced the Siberian starets, incurring the enmity of the tsar. At a time when elite opinion in the capital was moving toward the war party, Rasputin's political recovery was potentially significant. During the Balkan Wars, Rasputin had denounced the aggression of Russia's fellow-Slav "little brothers," which, he said, had "destroyed Christ's teachings." In fall 1913, Rasputin told the *St. Petersburg Gazette* that Russia should "not encourage discord and hostility." He told another journalist, "as long as I live, I will not permit war."[25]

Had Rasputin been at court in July 1914, it is not hard to imagine the advice he would have given the tsar. And yet when the news from Sarajevo broke, the faith healer was in his home town of Pokrovskoye, in distant Siberia. Tsarina Alexandra did send him an urgent telegram on June 29/July 12, warning that "it was a serious moment, they are threatening war." Just as Rasputin was leaving his house to dictate a reply, he was stabbed in the stomach. Bleeding profusely, Rasputin survived the assault, but he was confined to a hospital bed for the rest of July.[26]

In this way the last influential voice for peace was silenced, and the tsar was surrounded by a unanimous chorus of belligerence as he navigated the ultimatum crisis. The critical steps were taken on July 12–13 (25–26), when Russia urged Serbia to reject the Austrian ultimatum, and inaugurated her Period Preparatory to War. Shortly after nine p.m. on Wednesday, July 16/29, Tsar Nicholas II ordered general mobilization against the Central Powers, only to change his mind after receiving an urgent telegram from Kaiser Wilhelm II, who had backed Austria-Hungary's hard line against Serbia earlier in July with his so-called blank check but was now having second thoughts. In a sign of how desperate he was for reasoned counsel, the tsar refused to see either his war minister or his chief of staff the next day, as he knew they would tell him to mobilize immediately. Nor would he meet with Krivoshein, whose hawkish views he knew well, nor with the belligerent Duma president, Rodzianko. The only adviser he was willing to receive was Sazonov, whom he believed, incorrectly, to be uncommitted. Instead Sazonov pressed the case for mobilization. At four p.m. on Thursday, July 17/30, Tsar Nicholas II ordered general mobilization. The countdown to war had begun, with the only remaining question being when the Germans would mobilize themselves—two days later, it turned out, after the tsar rejected a German ultimatum to rescind Russian mobilization.[27]

Stolypin's two decades of peace had expired just short of the five-year mark. In view of the near-constant diplomatic crises of the previous half-decade, it is not surprising that the one born in Sarajevo proved to be one European crisis too many. But it is well to be reminded of the warnings of Stolypin, Witte, Durnovo, and Rasputin—who, upon learning that mobilization had been declared, tore off his bandages and dictated an urgent telegram to Tsar Nicholas II, which reached him too late to be heeded. If Russia went to war, Rasputin warned the tsar and tsarina, "it would mean the end of Russia and yourselves."[28] The coming years would put this prophecy to the test.

= 4 =

RUSSIA'S WAR, 1914–1916

Despite all the prewar handwringing about her logistical short-comings and the possibility of labor unrest, Russia's mobilization proceeded relatively smoothly. In St. Petersburg as in the other belligerent capitals, the onset of war was greeted with a wave of patriotic demonstrations. On July 20/August 2, 1914, from the balcony of the Winter Palace, Tsar Nicholas II appealed to his subjects to fight against the common enemy, vowing like Alexander I against Napoleon that he would never make peace as long as a "single enemy soldier" remained on Russian soil. The crowd, according to eyewitnesses, saluted their sovereign with "tumultuous cheers." Duma politicians put aside their differences, issuing, on July 26/August 8, a resolution of solidarity with the tsar's government as it went to war. The military command was given to Grand Duke Nicholas Nikolaevich, a dashing Romanov prince of towering height, with a broad popular following. Although draft riots were recorded in seventeen of European Russia's fifty provinces and there were a few anti-Jewish and anti-German pogroms, for the most part "Russia's conscripts," David Stone writes in an authoritative new survey of Russia's war, "marched to their assembly points in good order with surprisingly little desertion."[1]

Contrary to German hopes that Russia would be slow enough off the mark to enable France to be knocked out of the war before she invaded East Prussia in strength, the Russian First Army, commanded by Pavel Rennenkampf, crossed over onto German soil as early as August 4/17, and won its first engagement, at Gumbinnen, on August 7/20. On the Russian left flank, General Alexander Samsonov's

Second Army, advancing northward from Poland, entered German soil on August 7/20 and crossed the Narev River. Terrified that the "pillaging horsemen" of German nightmares would soon roll into Berlin, General Maximilian von Prittwitz, commander of German Eighth Army, advised a retreat behind the Vistula River (though he was overruled by Moltke, who fired him). So ominous was Russia's advance that Moltke pulled back two corps from the western front, weakening the German right wing just as it approached Paris.

The Russians ironically suffered their first reverse on the Austro-Hungarian front, where their numerical superiority was greater. In the early flush of confidence, the Habsburg chief of staff, Conrad von Hötzendorf, had ordered his First Army to launch an immediate offensive northward into Galicia. On August 10/23, Austrian First Army collided with the Russian Fourth at Krasnik, just east of the San River, pushing the Russians back though suffering positively gruesome casualties: the Austrians' pike gray uniforms made them easier targets than the dirt-colored tunics worn by Russian muzhiks. But Russian Third, Fifth, Eighth, Ninth, and Eleventh armies were massing to the east, which forced Conrad to pull back. In a harbinger of things to come, the capital of Habsburg Galicia, Lemberg (Lvov to Russians, Lviv in Ukraine today), fell to the Russians on August 20/September 2. The rout was on.[2]

Had the war in eastern Europe continued on like this, it is likely that Austria-Hungary would have collapsed by winter 1914–1915, forcing the Germans to come to terms before the full might of the tsar's armies were brought to bear on East Prussia. The assembly of Russia's armies was, by late August 1914, nearing completion, with 3 million soldiers added to her peacetime strength of 1.3 million. Had even half of this force been sent against German forces in East Prussia numbering (even after Moltke sent two corps east to reinforce it) under 200,000, the outcome would not have been in doubt.

Instead, fate intervened at Allenstein, an East Prussian town located in what is now Poland. After Samsonov's Second Army crossed the German frontier on August 7/20, General Yakov Zhilinsky, commander of the northwestern front, informed Samsonov that Rennenkampf's First Army had beaten the Germans and ordered him to "cut off the German retreat to the Vistula." Samsonov pushed his men to the limits of their endurance in the August heat, force-marching them through a countryside devoid of fodder and food, put to the torch by the Germans. For the next five days, things proceeded as planned, with the Russians, winning a series of short, bloody engagements, pitching the German XX Corps into headlong retreat.[3]

Unfortunately for Samsonov, he was not the only one making haste. After Prittwitz was cashiered, Moltke gave the East Prussian command to Field Marshal Paul von Hindenburg and his brilliant staff officer Erich Ludendorff. Well informed about enemy dispositions because of aerial reconnaissance and the intercepting of unencrypted Russian radio messages, Ludendorff rerouted the German Eighth Army southwest by rail. Rather than four corps to one, Samsonov would meet a force roughly equal to his own, which enjoyed the element of surprise. By August 13/26, the trap was set, and Samsonov walked right into it, stubbornly pushing forward in the center, without realizing that his VI Corps, on the right, and I Corps, on his left, were crumbling under a German onslaught behind him. By August 15/28, Samsonov realized his mistake and ordered a retreat. It was too late: the German pincers had closed behind him, cutting off the last avenue of escape. Toward midnight on August 17/30, Samsonov, overcome with shame, said a prayer, cocked his revolver, and shot himself.[4]

Memorable as it was owing to Samsonov's suicide, the strategic importance of Tannenberg (as the Germans christened the battle, to honor a nearby engagement of Teutonic knights in 1410) was limited. Although the Russians lost 70,000 casualties and 92,000 prisoners, Second Army was not entirely destroyed. I and VI Corps, though beaten, survived and staked out solid defensive positions in western Poland on the Narev River. On the far right wing of Second Army, II Corps escaped northward to join Rennenkampf's First Army, which was further strengthened by the arrival of more recruits, even as an entirely new Tenth Russian Army was assembling in the gap between First and what remained of Second Army. Although Rennenkampf retreated to the Russian border, the First Army went back on the offensive as early as September 15/28, pitching the Germans back in a seesaw struggle that came to be called the Battle of the Masurian Lakes, which cost the German Eighth Army nearly 100,000 casualties.

Meanwhile the remorseless Russian advance into Austrian Galicia continued. By mid-September 1914, a general Austro-Hungarian retreat was under way, with Conrad's armies driven back 150 miles to the Carpathian Mountains, having lost 100,000 dead, 250,000 wounded, and 100,000 prisoners to the Russians. To the extent that Tannenberg allowed the Germans to regain the initiative, it was an important victory. But the Russians, although losing some 250,000 casualties on the northwestern front, had held the line against the Germans and were decisively beating the Austrians.

After a confusing series of engagements near Lodz in November, the eastern front had stabilized by December 1914. The Russians held a front stretching in virtually a straight line south from the Vistula to Gorlice-Tarnow, in the Carpathian foothills. Reflecting the strategic pattern so far, the line lay mostly east of the original German frontier but west of the Austro-Hungarian one. The Habsburg armies had suffered terribly, but so, too, had the Russians, who had endured an average casualty rate of nearly 40 percent from August to December, while losing nearly a million prisoners of war. The "burn rate" for the Russian army so far, according to some estimates, was something like 300,000 losses of all kinds per month. No matter how many millions of peasants could still be mobilized, no country, no army, could maintain such a pace forever.[5]

Doubts were beginning to seep in about Russia's chances of winning the war in Petrograd (as the tsar had renamed the Germanic-sounding St. Petersburg), as well as at Russian military headquarters (Stavka) in Baranovichi, near Brest-Litovsk in what is now Belorussia. As in the other belligerent countries, most Russians had expected a short, victorious war, not a long slog of attrition. Perhaps the best evidence of this "short war illusion" was the decree issued by Nicholas II on September 5, 1914, forbidding the sale of alcohol for the duration of the conflict. In the early flush of patriotic sacrifice, the generals at Stavka had gone the tsar one better by foregoing not only drink but female company, banning women from the staff compound and conducting daily religious services. By December 1914, reality had set in: women were seen at Stavka, and wine and vodka were being served, in ever increasing quantities.[6]

Drinking aside, there were serious grounds for concern in the Russian high command. To be sure, none of the belligerents had attained their objectives in 1914. But Germany's failure to knock France out of the war was qualified by the fact that she was occupying huge swathes of French and Belgian territory, and that she had survived the Russian invasion of East Prussia when she was most vulnerable. Russia, by contrast, had been given a grace period against the Central Powers while Germany focused on France. Now that the western front was settling down into a kind of equilibrium, the Germans could redeploy as many men as they dared to the eastern front. Russia's moment of opportunity had come and gone, and all that her armies had achieved was stalemate.

In material terms, too, Russia's advantage had dissipated. Prewar stocks of ammunition and shell were virtually exhausted by December 1914, and Russia's factories would be hard pressed to replace them. Before the war, Sukhomlinov's War Ministry had unwisely come to rely on British, American, French, and even German firms to supply everything from light machine guns to heavy artillery and shell, gun carriages, and fuses. But the Germans were now blockading the Baltic, and the Ottoman Empire had closed the straits in September 1914, effectively cutting Russia off from her suppliers. Russia's Pacific port at Vladivostok was still open, but it was too far from both Entente suppliers, and the Russian front lines, to work as a practical option. While the great Putilov Works of Petrograd had been turned over to war production, and the arms factories of Tula were cranking out arms and ammunition at full capacity, increased domestic production was not yet sufficient to make up the shortfall in imports. By 1915 "shell shortage" was a universal lament, which served either, at Stavka, as an excuse for battlefield reverses or, in Petrograd, as a cudgel with which opposition politicians could browbeat the government for its incompetence.[7]

The first signs of political trouble came in February–March 1915, after yet another debacle in East Prussia. Russian Tenth Army, commanded by Faddei Sivers, which Stavka believed faced a mere defensive screen at Gumbinnen, was in fact up against an entirely new German army, quietly fanning out around the Masurian Lakes. Owing to a blizzard, Ludendorff's planned envelopment did not quite come off, and Sivers was able to retreat in time. Even so, an entire Russian corps, XX, was cut off in the Augustów Forest. Although the men fought bravely, on February 8–9 (21–22) the last four division commanders of XX Corps surrendered to the Germans. Russian Tenth Army lost 110,000 prisoners and 100,000 casualties. In that three of Sivers's four corps had escaped the closing German net, the Battle of Masuria was no catastrophe. The Germans lost 80,000 men themselves, and failed to envelop Tenth Army. No new legends were created in the snowy wastes of Masuria to match those of Tannenberg.[8]

Nonetheless, the fallout from Masuria on the Russian side was more serious than that from Tannenberg. In a curious way, Samsonov's suicide had dampened the political impact of his encirclement: he was his own scapegoat. Because it occurred while the fate of France still hung in the balance, Tannenberg had even acquired a backhanded prestige, as a gallant gesture by the Russians to draw German pressure off their Gallic allies. The concurrent successes on the Austrian front in August 1914 had also provided political cover, giving the press victories to celebrate. But there was no silver lining in the Augustów Forest. Any Russian hope of conquering East Prussia now looked hopeless.

Compounding the political impact was an espionage scandal known as the Myasoedov affair. Colonel S. N. Myasoedov (the name translates as "Meat Eater") was an intelligence officer attached to the staff of Tenth Army. His low rank was misleading, as Myasoedov was a Sukhomlinov protégé who had worked high up at the War Ministry before being disgraced by accusations that he was an Austrian spy. These accusations had been made by the Octobrist leader, Alexander Guchkov, which prompted Myasoedov to challenge Guchkov to a famous duel in April 1912 (both men survived). Guchkov's real target had been Sukhomlinov, whom he was trying to topple from the War Ministry, to install his friend, A. A. Polivanov, a favorite of Duma liberals. The tsar had stuck with Sukhomlinov, although he dismissed Myasoedov, who was thereafter a household name in Russian society and military circles, associated with allegations of treason.

Myasoedov, demoted to a support position in staff intelligence in Tenth Army, was thus a perfect scapegoat for the disaster that befell that army in February 1915, even though military investigators could turn up no evidence of any treasonous contact with the enemy before or during the Masurian Battle. At what amounted to a show trial, convened in a special military tribunal in Warsaw on March 18/31, the only crimes prosecutors actually cited were Guchkov's stale old prewar charge and the relatively trivial offense of *maroderstvo* (the looting of enemy property; Myasoedov had allegedly pilfered two terra-cotta figurines). For these "crimes," the unfortunate intelligence officer was sentenced to death by hanging, that very night.[9]

Most scholars now agree that the Myasoedov "trial" was a travesty of justice, designed to find a scapegoat for Russia's Masurian disaster. The more serious initial charges, relating to acts of treason during the war, were actually dropped. The chief military procurator later admitted that the court had turned up no factual evidence. So, who was behind it? Guchkov was an obvious suspect. Still, though his military contacts were many, as a civilian he had no authority to convene an army tribunal. The critical decisions appear to have been taken by the very generals involved in the Masurian defeat, who had ordered Myasoedov's arrest. The final coup de grace was delivered by the army chief of staff, Yanushkevitch, who wrote to Sukhomlinov shortly before the trial with a hint of menace—Myasoedov, we should recall, was a Sukhomlinov protégé—that the traitor should be hanged quickly "to appease public opinion before the [Easter] holiday."[10]

The Myasoedov affair seriously disturbed Russian politics. Kerensky, the young Socialist Revolutionary firebrand, demanded an emergency session of the Duma. In a "private" letter to Duma president Rodzianko—which was reproduced for public distribution—Kerensky alleged that "in the bowels of the Ministry of Foreign Affairs a tight organization of real traitors has been calmly and confidently at work." Rodzianko vowed to root out Germans employed in the Russian war industry who, he claimed, enjoyed protection from sympathizers at court. A wave of Germanophobia descended on Petrograd, culminating in a great pogrom on May 29/June 11, 1915, which saw the looting of nearly five hundred stores, offices, and factories and mob beatings of Germans. Among the victims was Sukhomlinov, sacked by Tsar Nicholas II in June. The previous October, Yanushkevitch had written ominously to the chairman of the Council of Ministers, Goremykin, that "a very difficult struggle with Judentum lies in store for us." With Sukhomlinov out of the way, Yanushkevitch indulged his inner anti-Semite, dragging hundreds of Jews in to Stavka as suspected spies, and convincing Grand Duke Nicholas to sign off on the expulsion of Jews and Germans living in the zone of military administration behind the front lines. More than 500,000 Jews and 250,000 Germans were expelled from their homes.[11]

Meanwhile, the story at the front went from bad to worse. Although the Austro-Hungarian fortress at Przemysl fell to the Russians on March 9/22, 1915, all this did was to convince the German high command to get serious about propping up the Austrians. Erich von Falkenhayn, who had replaced Moltke as German chief of staff after the latter's nerves broke, found a general of genius, August von Mackensen, to command the new Eleventh Army, facing the Russian Third. Choosing a vulnerable spot in Russian lines southeast of Cracow, between Tarnow and Gorlice, Mackensen amassed significant local preponderance in men (2 to 1) and crushing superiority in firepower (700 guns and mortars, with huge reserves of shell). On the night of April 18–19/May 1–2, 1915, Mackensen's assault began with a devastating artillery barrage. By April 21/May 4, Russian resistance began to crumble, owing to ammunition shortages, and Mackensen urged his men into the gaps. Three days later, the Germans breached the last defensive perimeter on the river Wislok. Soon the four Austro-Hungarian armies on Mackensen's right joined in, and a general Russian retreat was under way. On May 21/June 2, Przemysl, scene of Russia's only victory in 1915, was evacuated. On June 9/22, Lemberg, scene of Russia's greatest victory in 1914, fell to the Germans. In less than two months, Mackensen pushed the Russians back 150 miles and inflicted 250,000 casualties, while taking a similar number of prisoners. It was arguably the greatest victory of the war so far, and inarguably the greatest defeat.[12]

Russia's Great Retreat was not over. After pausing for breath, Mackensen resumed the offensive in July, hitting the Russians hard on the left, Prusso-Polish sector. On July 23/August 5, the Germans marched into Warsaw. In mid-August, the Germans crossed the Bug River, and the Russians abandoned Brest-Litovsk and Kovno.

Farther north, a new German "Army of the Niemen" was advancing into the Baltic region, capturing Vilna (Vilnius) on September 3/16. The German offensive then ran out of steam, owing to Russian scorched-earth tactics, which made it difficult for Mackensen to feed his men the farther east (and north) they pushed. This was little consolation to the Russians, who had lost Galicia and Poland and seen the front pushed back between 100 and 200 miles along its entire axis from north to south (though on the bright side, the front was now shortened to about 800 miles).[13]

The political ructions from the Great Retreat followed the Durnovo prophecy perfectly, with "all blame laid on the government" for the disaster. In August 1915, Rodzianko united the liberal factions in the Duma, including Milyukov's Kadets and Guchkov's Left Octobrists, into a "Progressive Bloc" with a solid voting majority. The Progressive Bloc demanded reforms on minority rights, an amnesty for political prisoners, religious toleration, and a national unity government composed of "persons enjoying the confidence of the public." Although it stopped short of a government *answerable* to the Duma, the Progressive Bloc program was still a thorough repudiation of the government. Goremykin called a crisis meeting of the Council of Ministers.[14]

For the first time, there was serious dissension inside the council. Krivoshein and Sazonov, who were both closely in tune with liberal opinion, wanted to work together with Rodzianko and the Duma. Sazonov argued that spurning "the most active nonrevolutionary forces of the country" would be a "colossal political error." The government, he warned, "cannot live in a vacuum and rely exclusively on the police." He concluded, "The sovereign is not god, he can make errors." Krivoshein suggested that the tsar appoint "a person having the sympathy of the public and entrust him with the formation of a government." But Goremykin refused to budge. "As long as I live," the chairman told an aide after the fractious meeting, "I shall fight for the integrity of the tsar's power. Strength lies in the monarchy alone. Otherwise, everything will go topsy-turvy, and all will be lost. Our first task is to carry on the war to the end and not to indulge in reforms. The time for this will come when we have beaten the Germans."[15]

In a similar spirit, Nicholas II responded to these intrigues by assuming the army command. On August 22/September 4, after listening patiently to the objections of his ministers (excepting Goremykin), the tsar set off for Stavka—now relocated farther east at Mogilev, Baranovichi having fallen to the Germans—to replace Grand Duke Nicholas as commander in chief. As a sop, the grand duke was given the command in the Caucasus, where the Russians had done well so far against the Turks. The northwestern front commander, General Mikhail Alekseev, a tradition-minded career soldier who had seen action in both the Russo-Turkish and Russo-Japanese Wars, took over as the tsar's chief of staff. On September 3/16, the tsar's verdict on the Progressive Bloc came down when Goremykin prorogued the Duma until further notice. Krivoshein, in protest, resigned. For good and for ill, political responsibility for success or failure in the war, for victory or defeat, now lay entirely with Nicholas II.

If the tsar hoped by proroguing the Duma to put a stop to political shenanigans, however, he was mistaken. In a manner recalling the "political banquets" of 1904 that had preceded Bloody Sunday, a kind of parallel government began to emerge in the shadows. In August, General A. A. Polivanov, Guchkov's man and Sukhomlinov's successor as war minister, had convened a "Special Conference for the Coordination of Measures for the Defense of the State," inviting bankers, industrialists, and leaders of "Voluntary Organizations" that helped out with military and medical logistics. If the special conference was a kind of shadow parliament, its shadow executive was the "War Industries Committee" (WIC), chaired by Guchkov, which placed army supply orders with Russian factories.[16]

It was no accident that the liberals' shadow government emerged after Sukhomlinov's fall. Guchkov and Polivanov, the leading lights of the WIC and Special Conference respectively, had been plotting against Sukhomlinov since 1912. Having killed their prey at last, they now had real power over military procurement and policy, although they had to be careful about meeting together, as the tsar despised Guchkov for what he called his "inordinate ambition" and specifically warned Polivanov not to associate with him. Aware of the tsar's suspicions, Guchkov assembled the machinery of his proto-government in Moscow, out of sight of the tsar at Stavka, and out of reach of the

Council of Ministers in Petrograd. In Moscow, Guchkov had excellent contacts in industry, with the labor unions (which also sent delegates to the WIC), with Zemgor (the All-Russian Union of Zemtsvos and Municipal Councils), and in the Red Cross. The other members of Guchkov's Moscow group included the Kadet grandee Prince G. E. Lvov, chairman of Zemgor; the mayor of Moscow, M. V. Chelnokov, who headed the Union of Municipalities; and A. I. Konovalov, a rich Moscow industrialist who hosted most of Guchkov's meetings in his home. Owing to Okhrana surveillance, these meetings were known to the government, although the high rank of the principals, and their role in supplying the army, gave Guchkov's men a kind of immunity from arrest.

The emergence of Guchkov's shadow government in fall 1915, reluctantly tolerated by the tsar and his ministers, was significant. The closure of the Duma on September 3/16 left few other outlets for the frustrated energies of Russian elites, shunting political conversation into an underground world of secret meetings and handshakes, a hothouse environment driven by innuendo and rumor. In this world, the tsar's firing of Grand Duke Nicholas, a Francophile widely admired by Russian liberals, and Krivoshein's resignation, were interpreted in the direst terms, as victories for an imagined pro-German "Black Bloc" at court (the tsar was still seen, at this point, more as sinned against than sinner). Now that Sukhomlinov was gone, the key figures were alleged to be Goremykin (who had thwarted Sazonov and Krivoshein's efforts to reach out to the Duma) and the reactionary interior minister, A. N. Khvostov, appointed on the advice of Rasputin and the German-born tsarina. The "basic aim" of the Black Bloc, the plotters stated at Mayor Chelnokov's house on September 6/19, 1915, (according to police agents) was "the conclusion of a separate peace" with Kaiser Wilhelm II, to further the "strengthening of the autocratic principle in Russia." Out of these secretive Moscow gatherings grew the peculiar but invigorating belief among Russia's elite liberals that (1) the tsarist government was desperate to end the war against Germany to preserve autocracy, and (2) only by rooting out "traitors" at the top and intensifying the war could true representative government come to Russia.[17]

A good deal of mystery still surrounds Guchkov's wartime intrigues.

Most of the men he met and plotted with belonged to a secret Masonic order called the Grand Orient of the Peoples of Russia. A document obtained by German intelligence in fall 1915 spoke of plans for a "dictatorial directorate for Russia to consist, among other people, of Mssrs. Guchkov, Lvov, and Kerensky." While Milyukov, the Kadet leader, was not named in this document as a principal, he later wrote cryptically in his memoirs that the *four* men who later dominated the provisional government formed in 1917 (including himself) shared "a kind of personal bond, not purely political, but of a politico-moral character." Other plotters included Konovalov, the Moscow host; Nikolai Nekrasov, a left-wing Kadet who was a "Venerable Master" (Masonic grandmaster), and Mikhail Tereshchenko, a shadowy figure with a background in theater administration, recently ennobled, who chaired the Ukrainian WIC in Kiev. Every one of these men would become a minister after the February Revolution.[18]

Whatever else may be said of these conspirators, they were hard-working and competent. Russia's war effort received a shot in the arm after they took matters in hand. Production in all critical war sectors surged ahead in 1916, from boots and uniforms to metallurgy to rolling stock to weapons and ammunition. The most dramatic turn-around was in shell: 28 million 3-inch rounds were produced in 1916, as against 11 million the previous year. The monthly totals show an even more dramatic increase, from 358,000 produced in January 1915 to 2.9 million in September 1916, an increase of nearly 900 percent. Although Russia still imported heavy guns and other specialized supplies from her allies, the vast bulk of war production was now domestic, as reflected in the huge boom in the Petrograd stock market, which saw over a thousand new corporations chartered. Shell shortage, the great lament of 1915, was a problem no more.[19]

No less ambitious was the exploitation of Russian manpower. Stretched nearly to the breaking point by the losses of 1914 and 1915, the War Ministry, under the direction of Guchkov's ally Polivanov, called up 2 million untrained *opolchenie*, men previously exempted on grounds of older age or poor physical fitness. Others were drafted "young," a year or two ahead of their conscription age. Less successful was the decision to recruit nomadic Muslims from Central Asia in summer 1916, which sparked riots and armed draft resistance in many areas. Nonetheless, the Russian army was refreshed by more than 2.5 million recruits in 1916, allowing it to outpace its admittedly horrendous losses.

The mobilization of resources on such a vast scale was accompanied, inevitably, by social and political friction. The surge in domestic war production meant windfall profits for a few and greased pockets for others, while the population as a whole suffered from the run-up in food and fuel prices in a great inflationary boom (Russia had abandoned the gold standard in 1914 and deployed the printing press with abandon). Owing to poor weather, the wheat harvest in 1916 was smaller than in 1915, which exacerbated the food inflation—as did the decision of peasants to withhold grain from the market, in anticipation of higher prices tomorrow. A perverse result of the tsar's wartime restriction on vodka sales was that peasants had still less incentive to sell their surplus for cash, which bought little worth having, and less of it all the time.[20]

Still, the food crisis in Russia was far *less* severe than that faced by her opponents. Germany, Austria-Hungary, and the Ottoman Empire, none of them self-sufficient in food production in pre-war times, were all denied the mercy of imports owing to an Allied (mostly) British blockade, and to the cutting off of Russian grain exports. The Ottoman Empire was further devastated by a locust plague that swept through Syria and Palestine in 1915, producing shortages in everything from grain and potatoes to vegetables and animal fodder. The want of grain in Central Europe was so severe by the end of 1916 that Germans endured their famous "turnip winter," which gave the German high command cause to push for the resumption of "unrestricted submarine warfare" (abandoned after the sinking of the *Lusitania* in May 1915 with 114 neutral Americans on board), so as to give the British a taste of their own medicine. On the Baltic front, German soldiers often ventured into no-man's-land, begging Russians for bread (for which they bartered cigarettes). Although the prewar Russian soldiers' ration of 2 pounds of meat per week was steadily reduced between 1914 and 1916 (and fresh meat gave way to salted), the Russian army, compared to the ones it was fighting, was still very well fed, even if—owing to the tsar's crackdown on vodka production—alcohol was harder to come by on the Russian side of the front than on the Austro-German.[21]

Nor did Russian soldiers lack another creature comfort: female company. In occupied Galicia, prostitutes were available to any officer with money. To the shock of Russian journalists on frontline tours who tut-tutted that "our soldiers are no better than the Germans," child prostitution was common. Some soldiers' letters, suppressed by censors and discovered a century later, even spoke of orgies. Those unable to afford prostitutes made do with erotic postcards and prints: French pornography did its part for Entente solidarity. So rampant was sexual license at the front that a special conference was convened at Stavka in May 1916 to figure out how to keep "working girls and women" out of the trenches. Decently fed and sexed, the life of the typical Russian frontline muzhik was far from ascetic.[22]

Material factors do not always determine military outcomes, but in view of these broad trends it is not surprising that Russia's battlefield performance improved in 1916. On the Ottoman fronts, the Caucasian Army, ably led by Nikolai Yudenich under the nominal command of Grand Duke Nicholas, rode from triumph to triumph. In January, the Russians broke through Turkish lines at Köprüköy and raced on toward the great fortress city of Erzurum, which fell on February 3/16. On the Black Sea coast, Russian amphibious forces seized Rize and Trabzon. Farther south, the Russians marched into Bitlis and Muş. With an expeditionary force led by General N. N. Baratov mopping up Turco-German resistance in northern Persia (Iran), the Russians now controlled most of Armenia and Kurdistan. The carving up of the Ottoman Empire was at hand. Sir Mark Sykes and François-Georges Picot, after negotiating potential British and French spheres of influence in the Middle East, arrived in Petrograd in March 1916 to finalize Ottoman partition terms with Sazonov inside the Russian Foreign Ministry. In addition to the areas she had already conquered, the notorious Sazonov-Sykes-Picot Agreement of May 1916 gave Russia Constantinople and the straits in case the Allies won the war, fulfilling the ambition of every emperor since Catherine the Great.[23]

On the eastern European fronts, the story was not as unambiguously triumphant, but 1916 was still a banner year for Russia after the *annus horribilis* of 1915. It did not start well. In late March, a poorly timed offensive at Lake Narotch, north of the Pripet Marshes near

Dvinsk (Daugavpils) in what is now Latvia, ran into mud once the spring rains arrived, costing First and Second Armies almost 78,000 casualties (as against 20,000 German) in exchange for moving the front forward a mile or two. Far more successful was the offensive in Galicia planned by the new southwestern front commander, General Alexei Brusilov, a decorated, half-Polish career soldier who had commanded Eighth Army to victories in the Galician offensives of 1914. Although Brusilov's advantage in manpower (about 5 to 4) was small, his offensive, launched on May 22/June 4, was brilliantly conceived and audaciously executed. By attacking Austro-Hungarian positions in four separate places with nearly equal weight in a kind of rapid-fire cascade, Brusilov made it difficult for the enemy to determine where to bring up reinforcements. On the right flank, Russian Eighth Army made the quickest breakthrough, reaching Lutsk, roughly 18 miles behind Austrian lines, in the first three days. Russian Ninth Army, on the left, broke through more decisively still, punching a hole nearly 30 miles deep by May 31/June 13. Progress thereafter slowed as German reinforcements stabilized Austro-Hungarian lines, with Brusilov's attacks achieving less each time, at mounting cost in lives. By September, Russia had lost a million casualties in Galicia, against perhaps a million and a half on the enemy side. Still, in a year notorious for the fruitless carnage of Verdun and the Somme on the western front, the Galician breakthrough, where the Russians conquered 15,000 square miles—an area larger than Belgium—was a big story. Brusilov's headquarters were deluged with congratulatory telegrams from Russia's allies. The Brusilov offensive, frontline attachés, and neutral observers agreed, "had an electrifying effect on Russian morale," and a devastating one on Austro-Hungarian, forcing Conrad to swallow his pride and turn his armies over to German command. If any multiethnic empire stood on the brink in 1917, it would surely be the tottering dual monarchy of Austria-Hungary, not Russia in the flush of victory.[24]

In retrospect, it seems clear that Brusilov should have called off his offensive in early summer 1916, declaring victory, conserving lives—by September, some four thousand wounded and sick men were being evacuated from Galicia every day—and consolidating a solid defensive line. His very success, meanwhile, had one unwelcome effect, helping convince Romania, on August 27, to join the war on Russia's side, an intervention that turned into a fiasco after the Germans and Bulgarians invaded, seizing the Black Sea port of Constanţa in late October and, by early December, the capital, Bucharest, along with the nearby oil fields of Ploieşti (although a team of British engineers had torched most of the wellheads). Still, the Russians were able to stabilize the front on the Siret River in Moldavia. Despite the Romanian distraction and the losses at Lake Narotch and Galicia, 1916 was Russia's best year yet in the war, and her prospects for 1917 appeared bright.[25]

The improvement of Russia's strategic position in 1916, by all political logic, should have cooled down tempers on the home front. In the immediate afterglow of Erzurum, Nicholas II had allowed the Duma to reconvene and personally visited the chamber on February 9/22, where he was met with "long and continuous cheers." But the honeymoon was short-lived owing to the onset of "ministerial leapfrog." The aging but loyal chairman of the Council of Ministers, Goremykin, was finally retired in February, replaced by Boris Stürmer. Stürmer was not a great success, but there seems to have been no better reason for the vilification campaign against him than his Germanic name (and the fact that he maintained contacts with Rasputin). The Khvostov plot to murder Rasputin, exposed in March 1916, put more pressure on Stürmer, who had to replace Khvostov at the Interior Ministry. As if wishing to assemble all scapegoats in one person, in July the tsar put Stürmer in charge of the Foreign Ministry, too, after sacking Sazonov in yet another intrigue attributed to Rasputin. The appointment of Alexander Protopopov—a bona fide Rasputin protégé—as interior minister in September must have come as a relief to poor Stürmer, as the political mob would soon have another target for its wrath.[26]

By late summer 1916 a veritable mania had descended on Petrograd, with the Rasputin murder plots only the most visible manifestation. Guchkov, running the WIC and his Moscow shadow government, was loaded for bear. On August 15/28, 1916, Guchkov fired off a letter to the chief of staff at Stavka, General Alekseev, after making copies for distribution among his political allies. "The home front," Guchkov told Alekseev, "is in a state of complete disintegration . . . the rot has set in at the roots of state power." With breathtaking recklessness, Guchkov denounced by name the minister of transport and communications (and future chairman of the Council of Ministers), A. F. Trepov; the ministry of industry, Prince D. I. Shakhovskoy; and the agriculture minister, Count A. A. Bobrinsky. Guchkov then laid into Stürmer as a man who "if not an actual traitor—is ready to commit treason."[27]

So explosive was Guchkov's letter (obtained immediately by the Okhrana) that Nicholas II called General Alekseev in for an explanation. Although Guchkov had referred to earlier correspondence with Alekseev, implying that the two were coconspirators, both the tsar and the tsarina gave Alekseev the benefit of the doubt, blaming Guchkov exclusively. Stürmer, too, was given the tsar's full backing, although this did not help his reputation in Petrograd. But the mischief was done. Alekseev, a competent (if unexciting) chief of staff whose logistical work had made General Brusilov's breakthrough possible, had little stomach for politics. In over his head, Alekseev took medical leave in November.[28]

Damaging as the Guchkov affair was to cohesion in the army command, its political impact was somewhat muted. Guchkov was a notorious hothead from whom everyone expected this sort of thing. By September, the police and the northern army command (because Petrograd fell within its purview) had moved on to more pressing concerns, such as food shortages. A curiosity of First World War logistics, by no means unique to Russia, was that frontline soldiers generally ate better than urbanites, whether because they were given priority or because they were garrisoned closer to food-growing areas. Supplying Petrograd was especially problematic: located at 60 degrees north latitude, the city was far from Russia's prime agricultural regions. The largest deficiency was in milk, which had "virtually disappeared from Petrograd," as General Nikolai Ruzsky, the northern front commander, reported to Stürmer on September 17/30, 1916. Meat, too, was dear. But there were shortages across the board, exacerbated by speculators. By October, the Okhrana was warning of "great turbulence" approaching, owing to "hunger, the unequal distribution of food and articles of prime necessity, and the monstrous rise in prices."[29]

Russia's problems, as the third winter of the Great War approached, were real. But they were made to seem worse than they actually were by ambitious politicians who claimed to have easy solutions for them. The opening session of the Duma, which reconvened again on November 1/14, 1916, was always going to be a dramatic occasion. In the increasingly paranoid atmosphere of the capital, the event turned into a sensation. After listening to President Rodzianko's opening address, Boris Stürmer ostentatiously left the chamber, followed by the British and French ambassadors, and then Rodzianko himself. Stürmer had been expected to give an address promising autonomy to postwar Poland, a gesture dear to liberals and keenly awaited in Paris and London, only to get stage fright (or he may not have wished to listen to the denunciations he knew were coming from the floor). Whatever Stürmer's reasons, his departure not only gravely disappointed the Entente ambassadors, but also suggested, for suspicious opposition deputies, that he was taking orders from the pro-German Black Bloc.

With the government's representatives gone (and Rodzianko having established plausible deniability by leaving), deputies could loosen their tongues. First blood was scored by young Socialist Revolutionary firebrand Alexander Kerensky. Pointing to the seats emptied by the departing ministers, Kerensky denounced them as "hired killers," as "betrayers of the country's interest," and "men suspected of treason, these fratricides and cowards." In an ominous touch, Kerensky fingered "Grisha Rasputin" as the regime's pro-German mastermind. So incendiary was Kerensky's speech that he was reprimanded by the acting chair and asked to sit down.[30]

The floor was now clear for the Kadet leader, Milyukov. Because of his reputation for moderation, compared to such known hotheads as Guchkov and Kerensky, the shock value was much greater when Milyukov began tearing into the government. His theme, which had been cleared by the Progressive Bloc beforehand, was that suspicious elements in the government had been intriguing for a separate peace with Germany. But Milyukov laced his critique with wild allegations. He denounced Protopopov for having met with a German businessman in Stockholm. He insinuated, based on a story in the *Berliner Tageblatt*, that Stürmer's private secretary was a German agent. Other German newspapers, Milyukov claimed, had celebrated

Stürmer's replacement of Sazonov. An Austrian newspaper, he said, had approvingly discussed the activities of a pro-German "clique said to gather round the Tsarina." In contravention of Duma rules forbidding the use of foreign languages from the tribune, Milyukov read this last phrase out in the original German, to heighten the implication of treason. Although he claimed only to be repeating allegations made by others, Milyukov invited everyone to judge for themselves whether the government's notorious blunders had resulted from "stupidity or treason?"[31]

Milyukov's speech electrified Russians, both in parliament and—after millions of copies were printed for publication—across the country. The "sinister rumors of treachery and treason" he alluded to in his Duma speech, of "occult forces fighting for the benefit of Germany," became real for thousands of people because he uttered these rumors aloud, with the authority of Russia's leading liberal politician. Milyukov had made treason talk respectable, as did Rodzianko when, to stave off a possible prosecution of the Kadet leader, he refused to turn over an unabridged copy of the speech to the government. The coast was clear for ever more libelous rhetoric in the Duma, as when the reactionary deputy Vladimir Purishkevich, in early December, encouraged his fellow deputies to murder Rasputin.[32]

The hysteria now engulfing Petrograd had many causes. At some level, the deteriorating food and fuel situation in the capital lay behind popular dissatisfaction with the government. But it was not milk and meat shortages that gave Milyukov's speech its incendiary power. Nor was it hunger that drove Purishkevich, Felix Yusupov, and Dmitri Romanov—three rich, comfortable men—to murder Rasputin in December. Kerensky and Guchkov's Moscow faction had showed their cards earlier; now Milyukov, too, was demonizing the government with malice aforethought. Like Guchkov and Kerensky, Milyukov attacked the government ostensibly to root out corruption and improve Russia's chances of winning the war, in reality to increase their own power and influence. They should have been more careful what they wished for.

PART II

1917: A False Dawn

Can I promise [Kerensky] that you will do your duty to the end, and if I order you to attack, will you attack?

—GENERAL ALEXEI BRUSILOV
to the men of the southwestern army, May 1917

= 5 =

FULL OF FIGHT

Winter descended even more savagely than usual in January 1917, with temperatures in northern European Russia dropping to –20 degrees Fahrenheit and staying well below zero for weeks. Blizzards blanketed the roads and railways with snow, disabling locomotives and causing supply bottlenecks of food, fodder, and fuel destined for the cities of the north. The fall grain harvest had yielded only 71 million tons, almost 25 percent below the figure reached in 1913. Although the fact that grain was no longer exported cushioned the impact in the countryside, the problems on the railways, coupled with the increase of the money supply (up from 1.6 billion to 9 billion rubles since 1914), sent food and fuel prices in Petrograd skyrocketing.

For Petrograd's shivering residents, the lasting image of the frigid holiday season was the hunt for Grigory Rasputin's body through the frozen canals. After a long search, a lookout at last glimpsed, near the Petrovsky Bridge, "a sleeve of a beaver-skin coat frozen into the ice." A team of policemen then "hacked away at the frozen crust of the river with spades, picks, and sledgehammers," to reveal Rasputin's petrified corpse. Liberal Russia rejoiced, but many commoners were just as horrified as the tsar by the murder. As one wounded soldier was overheard remarking in a Petrograd military hospital, "Yep, only one peasant managed to make his way to the Tsar, and so the nobles killed him."[1]

Compounding the mischief wrought by the assassination was the immediate political backstory: Rasputin's last intrigue. On October

12/25, 1916, shortly before the Duma had reconvened, Tsar Nicholas II had shocked liberal Petrograd by releasing Vladimir Sukhomlinov from the Peter and Paul Fortress prison. It was widely believed that Rasputin, by arranging a meeting between Sukhomlinov's wife, Ekaterina Viktorovna, and the tsarina's favorite lady-in-waiting, Anna Vyrubova, was behind the controversial decision to free the "traitor," a decision that had helped to fuel the treason talk of Alexander Kerensky, Pavel Milyukov, and finally Vladimir Purishkevich's borderline murderous speech in the Duma. Now that Rasputin had been removed from the tsar's inner circle, many politicians were baying for Sukhomlinov's head, too, and not quietly. In the anti-German spy mania of January 1917, Sukhomlinov and the German-born Tsarina Alexandra appeared to be, after Rasputin's death, the next targets in line. As liberal Russian law professor A. A. Pilenko recalled several months later to an American friend, "It was common talk in the best families, in the homes of generals, et al., that the Empress should be killed and gotten out of the way."[2]

The gulf between Tsar Nicholas II and Petrograd society widened into a chasm. The tsar was horrified to learn that his own nephew had been involved in the Rasputin murder plot. No less disturbing were the letters to Purishkevich, Prince Yusupov, and Princess Zinaida, passed on to Nicholas II by the Okhrana, in which prominent figures openly congratulated the assassins. Significantly, one of these came from the wife of Duma president Mikhail Rodzianko, Anna Nikolaevna. In a defiant though ineffectual gesture in the wake of Rasputin's murder, the tsar dismissed A. F. Trepov, Stürmer's hapless successor as chairman of the Council of Ministers, and appointed in his place the even more hapless Prince N. D. Golitsyn, an elderly figurehead serving as deputy chairman of one of the tsarina's charity commissions. An unambitious man who often fell asleep during meetings, Golitsyn declined the job but was enjoined by the tsar to take it anyway.

An unmistakable fatalism now set in at Tsarskoe Selo, where the imperial couple settled in for the long Russian winter. "The Empress and I know," Nicholas II told Golitsyn on January 5/18, 1917, "that all is in God's hands—His will be done." When an agitated Rodzianko visited Tsarskoe Selo two days later and tried to shake his sovereign from his lethargy, pleading that the tsar not "compel the people to choose between [him] and the good of the country," Nicholas II "pressed his head between his hands" and asked whether his entire twenty-two-year reign had been "a mistake."[3]

The tsar's passivity was infuriating to energetic politicians, such as Rodzianko and his fellow Octobrist Alexander Guchkov, who began plotting to depose him. Guchkov's plots were the most transparent. Although no evidence has emerged that Guchkov was involved in the Rasputin murder, he is known to have assembled a war chest of anti-Rasputin material with the help of Sergei Trufanov ("Bishop Iliodor"). Guchkov's famous August 1916 letter to General Mikhail Alekseev was one of dozens he sent to top-ranking generals that year, in some of which he openly discussed the prospect of some kind of military dictatorship or coup d'état. Other top officers importuned by this arch-conspirator included General A. M. Krymov, commander of the Third Cavalry Corps, Lieutenant General Anton Denikin, and Lieutenant General V. I. Gurko, who became acting chief of staff at Stavka after Alekseev took medical leave.[4]

Although much remains murky about Guchkov's plans, we know that a critical meeting took place in Moscow in early October 1916 at the home of the Moscow liberal M. M. Fedorov. Several prominent Duma deputies, including Milyukov and even President Rodzianko, were also present, although not everyone agreed with Guchkov's view that Russia's liberals should lead the way in toppling the tsarist regime, lest they cede ground to more radical elements. Russia, Guchkov argued, was too anarchic a country for her to follow the model of nineteenth-century European revolutions, like the French one of 1848, where street agitators faded from the scene once established political elites took a hand. Guchkov later recalled warning his liberal colleagues, "I fear that those who make the revolution will themselves head the revolution."[5]

Although he failed to sway Milyukov and Rodzianko, Guchkov received pledges of loyalty from the left-wing Kadet (and Masonic grandmaster) Nikolai Nekrasov, and the chairman of the War Industries Committee (WIC) in Kiev, Mikhail Tereshchenko. Together, this "troika" agreed that the best way to topple the regime was to arrest the tsar and force him to abdicate in favor of his son Alexis, with the tsar's brother, Grand Duke Michael, serving as regent until the boy came of age. The upshot would be a constitutional monarchy with a "government of public confidence" including the plotters, alongside experienced ministerial hands acceptable to liberals, such as Alexander Krivoshein and Sergei Sazonov. Concluding that security would be too tight at Stavka or Tsarskoe Selo, the troika planned to stop the imperial train en route between the two. Because Guchkov was under Okhrana surveillance, he brought in a low-profile Romanov prince serving in the Imperial Guard, D. L. Vyazemsky, and a First Cavalry Guards' captain, D. V. Kossikovsky, who promised to win over his regiment, stationed near Novgorod on the route between Mogilev and Tsarskoe Selo. Tereshchenko and Vyazemsky set off for Stavka to recruit officers. Among their converts, Guchkov claimed, were General Krymov and an up-and-comer, Lieutenant General Lavr Kornilov. At an Octobrist Party meeting in Moscow in mid-January, Guchkov openly revealed his plans to his party colleagues. If opinion in the army seemed favorable, Guchkov planned to strike in March or April 1917.[6]

It was indicative of the feverish political atmosphere of the time that another "palace coup" plot was being launched simultaneously by another elite faction, this one led by Prince Georgy Lvov, the head of Zemgor (the All-Russian Union of Zemtsvos and Municipal Councils). Lvov, descended from the ruling dynasty of Yaroslavl, was a gentry "class traitor" in the tradition of such highborn political radicals as Bakunin and Alexander Herzen. During the political crisis of fall 1915, Lvov had written an extraordinary letter to Nicholas II, which blended over-the-top obsequiousness ("Your Imperial Majesty, Russia looks to you in these fatal years for a sign") with imperiousness as he demanded that Russia's sovereign, to save the country from the "abyss," surrender his authority to a government of public confidence. The tsar did not deign to reply.

Failing to persuade Nicholas II to give in, Lvov resolved to force his hand. His own plot was bolder than Guchkov's, though it left more to chance. Like many gentry liberals, Lvov was an admirer of the Grand Duke Nicholas, whose removal from Stavka in 1915 he had taken as a sign of the malevolent, if not treasonous, influence of the German "Black Bloc" around the tsarina. The grand duke, in Tiflis commanding the victorious Army of the Caucasus, would be convinced to assume the throne. Once the military commanders—beginning with General Alekseev, who was apparently informed of the plot—had lined up behind the grand duke, the tsar would voluntarily abdicate; and the tsarina, to keep her quiet, would be exiled to Crimea. Enlisting the mayor of Tiflis, A. I. Khatisov, in his plans, Lvov was confident of success. At the New Year's Day reception in Tiflis on January 1/14, 1917, Khatisov cornered the commander and explained Lvov's plans for a bloodless palace coup. Grand Duke Nicholas protested that neither the army, nor the people, would support overthrowing Russia's sovereign in wartime. Disappointed, Khatisov sent Lvov the agreed-upon code: "The hospital cannot be opened."[7]

Less brazen than Guchkov and Lvov, but no less significant, was the shift of Duma president Rodzianko from a posture of disaffection with the regime toward one of open confrontation. At the October 1916 meeting at Fedorov's house in Moscow, Rodzianko had opposed Guchkov's "revolutionary" line, but this may have been because he had his own plans. Guchkov and Lvov both courted General Alekseev as a possible strongman behind the throne. Rodzianko had his own favorite general: Alexei Brusilov, the hero of Galicia (whom Guchkov correspondingly disdained, just as Rodzianko had turned against Alekseev). In late fall 1916, Rodzianko took the unorthodox step of writing directly to Brusilov to complain about the incompetence of the Russian high command, which "ignored . . . heavy losses" and "does not care as it should for the welfare of the soldiers." Brusilov forwarded Rodzianko's letter to Stavka, which did not endear the Duma president to Alekseev or the tsar. Despite this betrayal of his confidence, Rodzianko continued viewing Brusilov as the only front commander he could "rely on."[8]

Further poisoning relations between Rodzianko and the imperial couple was his refusal to punish Milyukov for his German-language insinuations against the tsarina in his incendiary Duma speech, and the reckless letter of support his wife, Anna Nikolaevna, wrote to Rasputin's assassins. A third provocation occurred at the New Year's Day reception at the Winter Palace in Petrograd on January 1/14, 1917, when Rodzianko ostentatiously snubbed Interior Minister Protopopov, his former deputy, when the latter came to shake his hand in holiday greeting, shouting (according to a witness), "Go away! Do not touch me." In the stylized world of Russian court etiquette, this was a virtual declaration of war on the government, and was soon "the talk of Petrograd."[9]

More was to come. According to Rodzianko's own recollection, General Krymov, one of Guchkov's key collaborators at Stavka, was invited over to Rodzianko's Petrograd apartment in mid-January 1917 along with "a large number of members of the Duma" and other high-ranking liberals, where the general quite openly confessed his revolutionary intentions. "The spirit of the army," Krymov informed Rodzianko's associates, "is such that the news of a coup d'état would be welcomed with joy . . . if you decide on such an extreme step, we will support you." Although Rodzianko later claimed to have firmly opposed Krymov's plans on the grounds that he had "taken an oath of allegiance" to the tsar, he stopped short of reporting Krymov's evidently treasonous remarks to the Interior Ministry, just as he had run interference for Milyukov after his November Duma speech.[10]

In his large, imposing, and yet fragile frame, Rodzianko embodied the anguish of liberal Russia, torn between loyalty to an emperor he believed was not up to the task of wartime leadership and his own growing sympathies with seditious elements plotting to depose him. In a private interview conducted in May 1917 after the February Revolution, and only recently rediscovered, Rodzianko said he had concluded, by winter 1916–1917, that "a political coup was the only way out" (he would flatly contradict these remarks in the better-known public deposition he gave later that year and in his memoirs). Strikingly, in view of the congratulatory letter Rodzianko's wife wrote to Rasputin's assassins, he told his May 1917 interviewer—a sympathetic historian who promised him, to ensure confidentiality, that the interview transcript would be sealed for fifty years—that "with the murder of Rasputin, we saw what can be achieved through a palace coup, but because of its spinelessness, it did not succeed." Far from disavowing the Guchkov and Lvov plots, Rodzianko chided his rivals for failing to recruit frontline troops or reliable commanders for them—such as General Brusilov.[11]

Most historians have agreed with Guchkov, Lvov, Rodzianko, and their Allied cheerleaders about the impotence and incompetence of the tsarist government at the dawn of 1917, if not also endorsing the plots they hatched. And yet the tsar's complacency, even if rooted in superstitious fatalism, accorded better with Russia's real military and strategic situation than did liberal and Allied hysteria. Morale in the Russian high command on the eve of spring campaigning was high, and for good reason. Intelligence shared at an inter-Allied conference in Petrograd in February 1917 confirmed that the Entente belligerents would enjoy crushing material superiority on every front over the Central Powers that year. Shell shortage, in eastern Europe, would now be an Austro-German problem, as Russia enjoyed an advantage of 60 percent in men and guns. On the Caucasian front, Russia's advantage over the Turks in manpower and matériel was more than two to one, with plans going ahead for a spring offensive targeting Sivas and Ankara. Fuel shortages in Constantinople, owing to a powerful Russian naval screen, had grounded the Ottoman fleet, which could no longer venture out to sea. In Odessa, the new commander of the Black Sea Fleet, A. V. Kolchak, was assembling an amphibious force to land at the Bosphorus in summer 1917. Kolchak, a talented officer who had distinguished himself in a rare naval victory during the Russo-Japanese War when he sunk a Japanese cruiser at Port Arthur, had ordered a blockade of the entire Turkish coastline from Trabzon to Constantinople. Surveying intelligence on Ottoman dispositions, Kolchak estimated that five divisions would suffice to seize Russia's great prize, spearheaded by a "Tsargradsky Regiment" he named himself (Russian chauvinists called Constantinople "Tsargrad"). With twenty-four new Russian divisions expected to buttress her armies by spring, it was small wonder that the Allied generals at the Petrograd conference reported that "Russia's generals were full of fight."[12]

The mood among frontline troops was no less robust. On the northern front—closest to Petrograd, where Russians faced Germans exclusively—there was little sign of defeatism. Among letters sent home by soldiers in the Fifth Army in the first two weeks of January 1917, military censors noted a "substantial rise in cheerful spirits" over the previous year. Although there was some grumbling about boredom and rising prices, the soldiers were well fed and clothed. Only 19 out of 151,963 letters from ordinary soldiers expressed dissatisfaction with food rations, and only 22 complained about the winter clothing they were issued. The most common sentiment over the New Year's holiday was that Russia would finally settle accounts with the Germans in 1917.[13]

More significant, in political terms, was opinion in the officer corps. Far from buying the argument of Russian liberals that change was desperately needed at the top, officers on the northern front were generally pleased with how things were going. Out of 16,512 letters sent home by Fifth Army officers and examined by military censors, only 17 criticized the conduct of the war in a serious way, and only 4 were critical of senior military leadership. It is possible that some officers, suspecting that their letters were being read, may have self-censored, or tempered their complaints. And yet other periods in the war had seen plenty of blunt, unambiguous criticism, and a few letters spoke in this vein even now. The mood of the soldiers had not merely improved: it was now positively ebullient. In the northern army overall, a military censors' report concluded in January 1917, "morale and the material situation is superlative."[14]

The most visible signs of defeatism in early 1917 were found on the Austro-German side of the lines. During the now-traditional Christmas lull in the fighting, Russian soldiers were struck by how many Germans came across, begging for food. Germans who deserted outright spoke almost unanimously of hunger as the reason they had left. On the Habsburg fronts, it was a common sight for Austrian soldiers to "emerge from their trenches, shouting, 'Russian, don't shoot! Soon there will be peace!'" Although some Russian soldiers traded their bread for cigarettes, the prevailing sentiment was less accommodating. On Christmas eve, a group of Germans on the northern front, waving a white flag as it entered no-man's-land, was mown down by Russian machine-gun fire. As one muzhik in the Fifth Army gloated, "now our roles have reversed. Last year we were retreating, but now the Germans are preparing to run away." A gunner in the Seventeenth Artillery Brigade wrote to his wife in February 1917, "We hear that on your side [i.e., among people in the rear] there is talk of peace, but among us we talk only of the upcoming offensive. When we win, beat the mighty Prussians, clear out Poland, and take Cracow and Berlin—then there will be peace."[15]

Such belligerent sentiments were by no means universal in the Russian army as 1917 began. Contrary to what we might expect given the relative success the Russians had enjoyed so far in the war in Galicia, morale was shakier on the southwestern than the northern front, likely owing to a lingering hangover from the bloody Brusilov offensive. On the Galician front, there had been thirty-five recorded soldier protests of various kinds in 1916, a 500 percent increase over 1915; but the upward trend then leveled off, with only seven demonstrations in the first two months of 1917. Whereas the tone of soldiers' letters from First Army (on the "western" front, also facing Germans) was similar to those sent home from Fifth Army, there was more grumbling in Third Army, below the Pripet Marshes. Third Army saw real action that winter, including a blistering (though short-lived) enemy attack on January 10/23. The Russians recovered, counterattacked, and captured a whole line of German trenches, where they discovered huge stocks of beer and cognac. It may have been true, one soldier wrote home, that the Germans were short of bread, but they did have pork sausage and plentiful booze. The muzhik's diet, by contrast, was made up of bread, kasha (a kind of porridge), lentils, and fish soup—nutritive, but bland. Still, the fact that it was Russian soldiers munching on German sausage and drinking German beer in German trenches, and not Germans downing kasha and fish in Russian ones, boded well for spring campaigning.[16]

In the navy, morale remained reasonably strong, although tensions simmered below the surface. The potential for mutiny was usually greater at sea than on land. In the Russian as in all navies, the social divide between blueblood officers and enlisted men "impressed" into service was acute. Naval conscripts also served longer terms—five years, as against three in the army. The fleet recruited most of its men from towns and cities, netting more factory workers or tradesmen than peasants, who manned the army. Because their urban families had to store-buy their food, sailors were more sensitive to inflation than peasant soldiers, whose rural families could always live off the land when times were tough. The rate of literacy was also higher among sailors than soldiers, as high as 84 percent in the Baltic Fleet, which helped insofar as it meant men could read instruction manuals, although it also meant they could read political pamphlets. During the political ructions of fall 1915, there had even been a mutiny in the Baltic Fleet on board the battleship *Gangut*, in the harbor of Helsingfors (Helsinki). Just as on the *Potemkin*, the mutiny had started with a protest against unpalatable food before it escalated into violence. Unlike in 1905, however, the *Gangut* mutineers, about ninety-five in all, were corralled quickly, surrendering as soon as submarines surrounded the ship.[17]

The other difference from 1905 was that the Black Sea Fleet, scene of the *Potemkin* mutiny, was in far better shape, morale-wise, than the Baltic one. Unlike in 1905, when the Black Sea Fleet had been confined to inactivity in the Far East owing to the Straits Convention, from 1914 to 1917 the Black Sea was an active naval theater, in which the Russians were now utterly dominant. In 1916, the Russians had sunk four German submarines, three Turkish torpedo boats, three Ottoman gunboats, and sixteen steam transports and tugs, along with three thousand sailing colliers. In conditions of constant, successful action, the discipline problems of 1905 were a distant memory.[18]

The Baltic theater, by contrast, was quiet in the world war, with most ships doing little more than standing guard in case the Germans tried to break through, which they had not yet done. The fleet literally "hibernated" during the long winter months from November through April, when the harbors froze. Idleness is never conducive to discipline in a large body of armed men, and this was especially true in Russia's Baltic Fleet. The most sensitive spot was the naval base at Kronstadt, on Kotlin Island, which guarded the entrance to the Gulf of Finland, 20 miles west of Petrograd. Over the years, Kronstadt had developed a reputation for radicalism, in part because it housed naval prisons along with a few factories, and also because it was so close to Petrograd, offering access for political agitators. Kronstadt's governor-general from 1909 to 1917, Admiral R. N. Viren, was a notorious disciplinarian whose strict enforcement of rules restricting sailors' access to bars and restaurants was widely resented. Also of note was the ethnic makeup of the officer corps, composed heavily of *ostzeiskie* (Baltic German noblemen) with such names as Körber, Keyserling, Grünewald, Stark, Graf. In view of the anti-German paranoia in the capital, such officers had reason to view their men warily. All these factors furnished ample "dry kindling" in the Baltic Fleet. But so far, aside from the *Gangut* mutiny, swiftly dealt with, there had been no spark.[19]

As the morale differences between the active Black Sea and dormant Baltic Fleets suggest, if there was potential for trouble, it lay not at the front but in inactive rearguard units—such as those in Petrograd, where thousands of recruits were jammed into overcrowded barracks for training. Like Kronstadt but on a much larger scale, Petrograd also housed hundreds of factories. Several of its working-class neighborhoods, in Vyborg and on Vasilievsky Island, were already bywords for radicalism.

Still, the image many of us have from popular histories—of a hungry working-class populace driven over the edge by spiraling bread prices—does not accord with the material facts. There were few signs of burgeoning labor unrest in Russia in early 1917. In May and June 1916, nearly 200,000 workers had walked out for an average of six and a half days. But there was only a fraction as many strikes in November and December, which saw about 30,000 laborers walk out for an average of two and a half days. Since 1905, there had been sympathy strikes in Petrograd nearly every year on the anniversary of Bloody Sunday, but the ones in January 1917 were smaller, by an order of magnitude, than those in 1916. Significantly, the German Foreign Office had subsidized the January 1916 strikes, spending a million rubles, but not the 1917 ones. The food picture in Petrograd was satisfactory and improving, if still far from perfect. At no time in January or February 1917 did the city's flour reserves dip below twelve days' worth.[20]

The fact is, no one had any inkling of what was about to transpire in Petrograd: not frontline soldiers, not the tsar or his advisers, not liberal society, not the Allied ambassadors, not the German agents provocateurs who had subsidized the strikes of January 1916, not Lenin in Switzerland, nor, judging by stable bond prices, the millions of foreigners who had invested in the tsarist regime in Paris, London, and New York. What most people in Petrograd were talking about in winter 1917 was not bread shortages, nor the prospect of popular street disturbances in a city so bitingly cold that few people ventured outdoors for long. Most political gossip, rather, centered on palace plots against the throne, observed warily by the Okhrana.

Nor was it apparent that any of these intrigues would succeed. The Lvov plot had fizzled out, and Guchkov's plans were well known to the police. The "worker groups" of WIC, which, in the absence of senior Bolshevik and Menshevik leaders exiled abroad, furnished the only real platform for socialist agitation against the regime, were fully penetrated by the Okhrana and held on a very short leash. It is true that the Menshevik leader of the Central Labor Group in Petrograd, K. A. Gvozdev, who had close ties with WIC, called, in late January 1917, for a demonstration in front of Taurida Palace when the Duma convened in February, and advocated "the decisive removal of the autocratic regime." But Gvozdev had promptly been arrested on Protopopov's orders, along with eight other (mostly Menshevik) leaders of the Labor Group. Although often seen as a critical mistake, we could just as easily conclude that Protopopov's decisive move showed that the supposedly moribund regime had the measure of its opponents in February 1917.[21]

In the ebb and flow of Russian politics during the war, it appeared that the worm had turned once again. With Russia's armies, along with those of her allies, poised for great spring offensives against the overmatched Central Powers, and with soldier morale on the upswing, the tsarist government appeared to be poised for another surprising recovery. This time, however, the tsar's luck had run out.

= 6 =

A Break in the Weather

What transformed the Russian political landscape in February 1917 was the most natural thing in the world, and the most unexpected: the weather turned. After nearly two months of bitter, unrelenting cold, on the day after the tsar left for the front on February 22/March 7, 1917, serenely unaware his throne was in danger,* the mercury suddenly rose sharply to well above freezing, reaching 46 degrees Fahrenheit. The sun came out, too, and the glorious weather would last another five days. Coincidentally, the spring weather broke out on the socialist-inspired International Women's Day (February 23), turning the demonstrations into a rolling street party, as thousands of city residents ventured outdoors to enjoy their first leisurely stroll in weeks.[1]

At first the mood was festive and relatively peaceful. Although large detachments of police and Cossack cavalrymen were on patrol, few of them wanted to molest crowds demonstrating primarily—it appeared—for cheaper bread, in which women were so prominent. While city officials were taken aback by the size of demonstrations on

---

* In a critical accident of timing, the tsar's children, including the hemophiliac tsarevich Alexis, came down with measles the morning after their father left for the front. Had this occurred 24 hours earlier, it is likely the tsar would have stayed in Tsarskoe Selo, in easy communication with his ministers over the critical days to follow.

At this point in the narrative, when the day-by-day timeline in Petrograd becomes critical and events outside Russia less so, we will revert to the "old calendar" dates of the Julian calendar, before following Russia's switch to the Gregorian early in 1918.

February 23—which, owing to an ongoing strike at the Putilov Works begun five days previously, attracted around 90,000 to 100,000 people—and by the reluctance of the Cossacks to intervene, there was no sense that the situation was violent or threatening. Frank Golder, an American historian who had just arrived in Petrograd, spent most of that day working in the archives, noting in his diary that night only that, owing to protests of "no bread or poor bread," there had been "disorder in the city and cars interrupted."[2]

The mood of the protestors took a darker turn on Friday, February 24, when more workers went on strike and rougher elements from Vyborg and Vasilievsky Island (where bread supplies were short, owing to a lack of fuel for the bakeries) joined the crowds on Nevsky Prospekt, which swelled to 160,000. When police and Cossacks, trying to stem the inflow across the Neva, blocked the bridges, people walked across the frozen river instead. A battle-hardened Socialist Revolutionary (SR) Party politician named Vladimir Zenzinov, who had been arrested in the 1905 revolution, observed "chains of soldiers stationed at many points; undoubtedly their duty was not to let the passersby go any farther, but they performed this duty poorly."[3]

There was little sign, at this point, of political direction of the burgeoning protest movement. While wandering the streets Friday afternoon Golder observed, "The crowd did not seem to be organized; it was a miscellaneous mob of men and women, students, boys, girls and workmen. One or two carried red flags." Golder noticed an interesting trend of Milyukov impersonators—the Kadet deputy was now, owing to his incendiary "stupidity or treason" speech, a national celebrity—going around "to stir the working man." Liberal Russia was not yet up in arms: *Novoe Vremya*, the Octobrist organ of Alexander Guchkov and his allies, published a directive that day from Lieutenant General Sergei Khabalov, commander of the Petrograd military district, reassuring the public that "flour exists in Petrograd in sufficient quantity, and shipments [into the city] proceed uninterruptedly." As Milyukov's Kadet paper, *Rech*, noted, "the reserves of flour which the city possessed have made it possible to live through the most acute period. . . . at the present time, the number of cars arriving at the capital with flour has increased to such a degree that . . . any apprehensions should be considered unfounded." Duma president Rodzianko, for his part, noted in his May 1917 interview that, according to his own multifarious "sources of information," in late February, "there were no perceptible shortages of food."[4]

The situation grew tenser on Saturday, February 25. By now workers at virtually every factory in the city had walked out in what amounted to a spontaneous general strike. The crowds swelled to an enormous size: the Interior Ministry estimated the number at 200,000. Even the newspapers were shut down by the strike, so that regular news reports ceased. Rumors ran rife: it was said that blood had been spilled overnight in various locations across the city, including the covered shopping bazaar known as Gostinyi Dvor, where three indeed had been killed and ten wounded. In Vyborg, the district chief of police was reportedly dragged from his horse and beaten "with sticks and an iron hook." Miraculously, he survived, and was taken to a military hospital. Near the Nikolaevsky railroad station, a police inspector was hacked to death by Cossacks, apparently in retaliation after he fired at them for disobeying his orders to disperse protestors. Nearly all eyewitnesses, including Golder, noted the reluctance of the Cossacks to engage protestors, which was so radically different from what everyone remembered from 1905 (the reasons why remain mysterious, although it is noteworthy that Cossack cavalry units, conscripted for frontline service, had not been issued the dreaded leather whips they had traditionally used in crowd control). Saturday evening, rioters in the Vyborg district set fire to a police station. Still, despite some ominous signs of radicalization and the curiously passive behavior of the Cossacks, there was little sense that authorities had lost control of the city. There were no barricades, no pitched battles or massacres, nothing close to the scale of Bloody Sunday.[5]

We can only surmise what the "real" motivations of the protestors may have been. Most eyewitness accounts agree that antiwar sentiments were not, at this stage, prominent. The basic line taken all winter by liberal critics from Milyukov to Guchkov to Rodzianko—a line adopted by the SR leader Kerensky, only a bit more shrilly— was, after all, that the regime was honeycombed by defeatists and pro-German traitors. This was a far cry from pacifism. While not everyone went along with the liberal prowar line, few opposed it unambiguously. According to the SR veteran of the 1905 revolution Vladimir Zenzinov, the raising of a "Down with the war" placard in Znamenskaya Square on Saturday afternoon "evoked protests from the crowd and it was withdrawn immediately." So out of touch was pacifism with the prevailing mood that Milyukov told Kerensky shortly after this that he believed that the printing of the "Down with the war" placards had been covertly financed by the Germans (a plausible allegation, although made without supporting evidence, against which Kerensky, defending the "honor" of the revolutionaries, objected vehemently). The political mood of the time was captured by a more commonly seen placard reading, "Down with the German woman!" (that is, Tsarina Alexandra, born in Hesse).[6]

Next day, the regime struck back. Although telegrams on the Petrograd disturbances sent to Mogilev by the district military commander, Khabalov, and the Interior Minister, Protopopov, had been sugarcoated so as not to alarm him, Tsar Nicholas II had received more disquieting reports from his wife (including a soon-infamous telegram in which she denounced protestors as "hooligans"), and from the palace commandant at Tsarskoe Selo. Whether based on these reports or his own intuition, the tsar sent Khabalov a telegram on Saturday evening "commanding" him to "put an end as from tomorrow to all disturbances in the streets of the capital, which are inadmissible at this difficult time when we are at war with Germany and Austria." Khabalov duly ordered his men to be ready at dawn to confront any aggressive crowds according to "standing rules," which mandated three warning signals before opening fire; smaller groups could be dispersed with simple cavalry charges.

Sunday morning, February 26, Khabalov's troops spread out across the city in combat gear. A hundred or so of the most notorious political agitators in the city were arrested, including the members of the Labor Group who had escaped Protopopov's net the last time. To prevent radical elements from Vyborg or Vasilievsky Island from reaching the city center, the Neva bridges were raised (although this did not stop intrepid souls from crossing the river ice, which, despite the warm temperatures, had still not melted). Around midday, scattered gunfire was heard on Nevsky Prospekt and a few other locations. It was the army, and not the police, that fired into the crowds, with much of the action involving the Pavlovsky Guard Regiment. The most serious clash transpired in Znamenskaya Square, where two inexperienced training companies of the Volynsky Guard Regiment fired into the crowd, killing about forty and wounding a similar number. By dusk, the city was calm again. Satisfied, Tsar Nicholas II authorized Prince Golitsyn to hand the decree dissolving the Duma to Rodzianko, who received it just before midnight. A police communiqué declared that "order has been restored."[7]

The announcement was premature. Although the streets were quiet, discontent was rumbling through the army garrison. The first stirrings of mutinous sentiment arose among men in those units deployed in crowd control on Sunday. Some protestors went over to the Pavlovsky barracks to remonstrate with off-duty soldiers about the behavior of the active companies, igniting a small demonstration by the men. Although no officers were killed, the men resolved not to obey any further orders to fire on demonstrators. Word was then spread to the nearby Preobrazhensky and Litovsky Guard Regiments, which resolved to do the same. More serious was the reaction of the Volynsky companies that had fired into the crowd at Znamenskaya Square. Many men recoiled at the bloodshed they had unleashed, and they blamed their commanding officer, Major Lashkevich, who was roundly abused that night. On Monday morning, February 27, a confrontation took place between Lashkevich and his men, one or several of whom shot him dead. Whatever the precise circumstances, the murder of a commanding officer, like the *Potemkin* lynching in 1905, heralded a mutiny. The logic was simple. Even if only a few were involved, the men knew they would be viewed as collectively guilty, and so they closed ranks behind the mutineers out of both solidarity and self-interest.[8]

The news spread like wildfire through the garrison, leading one unit after another (though not all of them) toward mutiny. There were good reasons why peasant soldiers, many only recently drafted and then stuffed like sardines into the makeshift barracks of the capital—160,000 soldiers were housed in facilities designed to hold 20,000—may have been primed for protest already. But the catalyst for the shift in most soldiers' loyalties on February 27, judging by the timing, was the lynching of Lashkevich—along with the ineffectual response of the Petrograd army command. Instead of court-martialing mutineers in the Pavlovsky and Volynsky Regiments, Khabalov hesitated in a critical loss of nerve, and even briefly disappeared from sight. His deputy, General M. I. Zankevich, mustered loyal troops at the Winter Palace and gave a rousing speech— but then gave no orders to the men, leaving them free to return to barracks, or not to. One brave commander of a cyclist battalion, Colonel Balkashin, put together a loyal guard around his barracks on Sampsonievsky Prospekt and sent emissaries to military headquarters asking for instructions, but they never returned. At dawn on Tuesday, the Sampsonievsky barracks was surrounded by mutineers. Balkashin addressed them, vouching that his men had not fired on protestors; his reward was a bullet in the heart.[9]

The mutiny crashed on. Not all units went over at the same time, or for the same reasons, but the story everywhere in Petrograd on Monday, February 27, was broadly similar. In a kind of mass peer pressure, helped along by the presence of pretty young women, more soldiers every hour abandoned (or sold) their weapons, adorned themselves with red ribbons, and joined the milling crowds. Frank Golder recalled the scene on Nevsky in his diary: "Girl students were talking to the soldiers and offering them food and teaching them to sing the Marseillaise . . . in one automobile a hooligan with a sword sat astride the engine, about two dozen soldiers with a girl student in their midst stood up . . . and all waved the red flag. There is some shooting in the air."[10]

The fragile order achieved by loyal soldiers at a painful human cost on Sunday now gave way to an exhilarating anarchy on Monday, which turned out to be even bloodier. Police stations were overwhelmed and torched; uniformed policemen were lynched; shops and markets were looted; the arsenal and the Central Artillery Administration were stormed for weapons. Dozens of revolutionaries were killed, too, many in firearms accidents as the streets were flooded with discarded weapons from deserting soldiers. The freeing of some eight thousand inmates from the city's prisons did not help, as most were hardened criminals who had been put there for good reason. For obvious reasons, such men took particular relish in looting and burning police stations; others looted liquor stores, or broke into homes of the city's well-to-do, robbing and raping. A retired professor who had supported radical causes for decades came onto the streets to celebrate the revolution, only to have his glasses smashed and his gold watch stolen. The most significant triumph of the revolutionary mob was the storming of the Okhrana headquarters on the Moika Canal late Monday afternoon, which produced a great bonfire of secret-police files (suspected Okhrana informers were the likely culprits). As night descended on Monday, February 27, the director of the Hermitage museum wrote in his diary, "The city reverberates with the most terrifying noises: broken glass, screams, and gunshots." With red flags flying over the Interior Ministry and the Okhrana, the collapse of the tsarist regime, in Petrograd at least, was plain to see.[11]

Who now controlled the city was more difficult to ascertain. Owing to the press strike, there were no news reports or announcements of an official kind. The last action taken by the government had been the Duma dissolution decree handed to Rodzianko late Sunday night, February 26. But Rodzianko had already fired a shot across the government's bow by sending his own message to the tsar earlier Sunday evening, warning that Petrograd was "in a state of anarchy," with "wild shooting on the streets" and "troops firing at each other." Rodzianko's advice, that Nicholas II immediately appoint a "government of public confidence," was predictable, and predictably ignored by the tsar, who told an aide that "fat Rodzianko has again written me all kinds of nonsense which I shan't even bother to answer." By Monday afternoon, however, when the tsar began hearing from other sources that mobs were raging out of control, "fat" Rodzianko had begun to sound like a prophet, as much (or as little) in charge of the situation as anyone else. When the Council of Ministers finally assembled at four p.m. on Monday, February 27, in the Mariinsky Palace to discuss the crisis, there was no one willing to take charge. Protopopov offered to commit suicide as a sop to the protestors. His offer was declined. Golitsyn offered to resign, but no one wanted to take his place.[12]

Into the breach stepped Rodzianko. Still untainted by overtly seditious actions of the kind taken by the Guchkov and Lvov plotters, Rodzianko was the only credible opposition figure trusted, to some extent, by the tsar. As the face of the "people's house," whose robust figure and majestic bass voice were known to all who attended its sessions, Rodzianko had a higher profile than Lvov, Milyukov, or Guchkov. For this reason he was an ideal candidate to head a government of public confidence, if Russia's sovereign could be persuaded to accept one. On Sunday, February 26, the tsar refused. By Monday afternoon, the situation was different, and Rodzianko had good reason to believe that his moment had come. In a new telegram to Mogilev he warned Nicholas II, "Tomorrow will be too late. The last hour has struck, when the fate of the country and dynasty is being decided."[13]

While Rodzianko waited for word from the Emperor on Monday, with chaos engulfing the streets, the Duma's senior party leaders convened a *senioren convent* (meeting of the elders) in a semicircular hall adjoining the main chamber in Taurida Palace. As the tsar had dissolved the Duma overnight, the situation was analogous to the famous "tennis court oath" of 1789 during the French Revolution, when the doors of the meeting hall at Versailles had been locked—but only up to a point. No one had ordered the doors shut, as there was no functioning government left to do so. The reason the party leaders met furtively, rather than openly, was that most of them remained wary of being caught out in an act of insubordination against the tsar. Several leaders of left-wing parties, including Kerensky and A. A. Bublikov, head of the Progressive Party, wanted to go "public" and embrace the revolution, but they were argued down by Milyukov, Lvov, and Rodzianko. Toward midnight on Monday evening, February 27, the "elders" agreed to form a temporary Duma committee tasked with "the re-establishment of order in the capital and for contacts with institutions and individuals."[14]

In Mogilev, Nicholas II faced a terrible decision. By Monday afternoon, February 27, General Alekseev had learned, from both Rodzianko and the war minister, Belyaev, that the mutiny in Petrograd had spiraled out of control. Monday evening, Alekseev received a desperate wire from Khabalov, who confessed that he had lost control of the garrison, and requested that reliable troops be sent from the front. The last message the tsar had received from Prince Golitsyn, wired from the Mariinsky Palace at two p.m. that day, had endorsed Rodzianko's suggestion that the Council of Ministers resign in favor of a parliamentary ministry of "public confidence" and appoint a popular general military dictator of Petrograd, with authority to put down the street disorders by force.

Although the tsar was unwilling to appoint a Duma ministry, he responded more favorably to Golitsyn's second proposal. Between ten and eleven o'clock on Monday night, Nicholas II and General Alekseev agreed to dispatch to Petrograd two cavalry and two infantry regiments from both the western and northern fronts. To command the critical mission the tsar chose N. I. Ivanov, a charismatic and popular general who had made his name on the Galician front, and who had also, notably, put down a soldiers' mutiny during the 1905 revolution. Ivanov, at the head of the "St. George" battalion, furnished with machine guns, was to proceed to the capital by way of Tsarskoe Selo, where he would post a guard to ensure the safety of the imperial family. Because his children, sick with measles, were unable to travel, the tsar proposed to travel to Tsarskoe Selo himself. At five a.m. on Tuesday, February 28, his imperial suite left Mogilev, preceded by an armed escort train, en route for Tsarskoe Selo by a circuitous eastward route via Smolensk, to avoid the direct line from Mogilev to Tsarskoe Selo (via Vitebsk) reserved for Ivanov and his troop train, which departed at eleven a.m.[15]

In view of the bewildering sequence of events unfolding in Petrograd, the decision to delay the tsar's arrival in Tsarskoe Selo had baleful consequences. Had he traveled home on the direct route (the one used by Ivanov, who arrived without incident 22 hours after departure), Russia's sovereign would have arrived by three o'clock Wednesday morning, March 1, into the fervent embrace of his adoring children and his affectionate—and stubborn—wife, Alexandra, who would have put steel into him. Instead the most important man in Russia wasted away a critical day on a meandering train journey, out of touch with his wife, the generals in Mogilev, and the politicians in Petrograd (although Nicholas II was briefed at stations the train stopped in by local authorities). Unbeknownst to the tsar, both the generals and the politicians, hedging their bets between the throne and the revolutionaries in Petrograd, were conspiring behind his back.

The president of the State Duma was the man of the hour. All day Monday, while he tried to restrain the Duma elders from taking any irreversible actions against the throne, Rodzianko had plotted secretly with Prince Golitsyn to dethrone Nicholas II and impose a regency headed by the tsar's brother, Grand Duke Michael (who was conveniently in Petrograd), until Tsarevich Alexis came of age. By Monday evening, the Grand Duke had reluctantly agreed, but only on condition that the tsar give his consent first. At half past ten on Monday night, Michael Romanov telephoned General Alekseev at Stavka and stated his terms for assuming a regency, which Alekseev passed on to Nicholas II. While the tsar was thinking things over, another telegram came in from Prince Golitsyn, reiterating Rodzianko's suggestion that he appoint a government of "public confidence." Alekseev, who had been hearing bad news from Petrograd all day, was despondent. Barely able to stand owing to a high temperature, Alekseev begged his sovereign, "on his knees," to agree to Golitsyn's proposal to appoint a Duma ministry, if not also Grand Duke Michael's proposal that he abdicate his throne. Unable to reconcile either act with his conscience or his oath of office, the tsar declined and resolved to travel to Tsarskoe Selo to master the situation.[16]

In view of the collapse of the regime's sworn defenders in Petrograd, it is hard to fault Nicholas II's decision to go see for himself—and to send reliable troops to the city. Khabalov, at eight a.m. on Tuesday, February 28, wired to Alekseev that he could count on only five hundred reliable infantrymen and six hundred cavalrymen. Protopopov's one constructive idea was to kill himself. Grand Duke Michael, the would-be heir to the throne, was so unsure of himself that, after leaving the Mariinsky Palace after the terminal meeting of the Council of Ministers, he tried to leave the city for his dacha that night, only to find that the last train had left. Far from throwing in with his coplotter Rodzianko (who remained at Taurida, headquarters of the burgeoning revolution), toward midnight Grand Duke Michael went over to the Winter Palace and summoned General Khabalov and the war minister, General Belyaev, only to tell them that he did not want their troops to open fire on anyone "from the house of the Romanovs," which put a damper on palace security. The only safe-house left was the Admiralty building, where Khabalov's loyal troops were told to leave their weapons. If this was the end for the tsarist regime, it was an inglorious one.[17]

Even as the regime was wilting away, Rodzianko and the other revolutionaries at the Taurida Palace, surrounded by fractious mutineers of uncertain loyalty, were terrified that loyal troops were about to come and arrest them. In view of what was going on inside the building, any such troops would have had ample justification for doing so. Alongside the senioren convent of the Duma, a more radical body styling itself, after the 1905 precedent, the Provisional Executive Committee of the Petrograd Soviet of Workers' Deputies, was assembling in rooms 12 and 13 of Taurida Palace under the chairmanship of two Menshevik Duma deputies, N. S. Chkheidze and M. I. Skobelev. Monday afternoon, this Soviet was further radicalized by the arrival of Gvozdev, the Labor Group leader sprung from prison, Menshevik lawyer N. D. Sokolov, and a vigorous Bolshevik underground organizer, Alexander Shliapnikov. Together with the Socialist Revolutionary (SR) Duma firebrand Kerensky, who was appointed to a three-man presidium, Chkheidze and Skobelev began issuing Soviet decrees. The most important was the appointment of a military commission headed by Colonel S. D. Mstislav-Maslovsky, an old SR warhorse popular with the men of the Petrograd garrison—who, as former peasants, favored the SRs almost to the man.

Although an appeal was sent to factories and military units to "elect" deputies to this new Soviet, the "executive committee" that ran the thing was, in truth, a self-appointed revolutionary body, created essentially sui generis. Its formation put terrible pressure on Rodzianko and the elders. Upstaged by the Mensheviks—and by Kerensky, who, confusingly, retained his seat in the elders' council even while assuming leadership of the Soviet—by Monday night the elders had been literally pushed to the back of the building, into rooms 41 and 42, adjoining the office of the left Kadet deputy (and Masonic grandmaster), Nikolai Nekrasov. After spending much of the day conspiring on the wires, just before midnight Rodzianko made a sudden appearance in room 41, announcing the creation of a new "executive committee of the State Duma," presumably superseding the "committee for the reestablishment of order in the capital and for contacts with institutions and individuals" announced earlier. To wrest control over the Petrograd garrison from the Soviet, Rodzianko announced that the

Centre Party deputy, B. A. Engelhardt, a retired colonel on leave from Stavka who was one of the Duma's leading military experts, would now command the Petrograd military district. In a dramatic scene, Menshevik lawyer N. D. Sokolov, who had been sent by the Soviet to room 41 to keep an eye on the elders, declared defiantly that Mstislav-Mstislavsky had already been elected and that his "staff has already been formed and is operating." "No gentlemen, really!" Rodzianko replied: "As you have forced us to intervene in this business, will you kindly obey." Although Mstislav-Mstislavsky accepted Engelhardt's appointment as head of the Military Commission and promised to work with him, Sokolov walked out, as if daring Rodzianko to challenge the Soviet's authority.[18]

The Duma president was up to the challenge. At two a.m. on February 28, Rodzianko published (in *Izvestiya*, a kind of running chronicle of the revolution printed in Taurida by sympathetic journalists) his first decree, appealing to "the inhabitants of Petrograd" to protect "the telegraphs, water-supply stations, electric-power houses, street railways, and Government office-buildings." Another decree, issued in Rodzianko's name several hours later, declared that a "Provisional Committee of the State Duma" (a new coinage) "found itself compelled under the difficult conditions of internal chaos brought on by the old Government, to take into its own hands the restoration of State and public order." There were inconsistencies in these announcements, but one connecting tissue: they were all made in the name of "The President of the State Duma, Mikhail Rodzianko."[19]

Just as the Soviet was sui generis, no existing statute in Russia's basic laws of 1906, nor in the statutes of the Fourth Duma elected in 1912 that he headed, gave Rodzianko the authority to issue government decrees, however "provisionally." Like Chkheidze & Co. in the Soviet, he was making things up as he went along. Few of Rodzianko's telegrams sent to Alekseev at Stavka on February 28 have survived, but we can glean their contents from Alekseev's own wire to the head of the St. George's Battalion, General Ivanov, sent Tuesday night, requesting that Ivanov postpone punitive military action on the grounds that, "according to private information (e.g., from Rodzianko), Petrograd became completely calm on February 28; the troops who had rallied behind the Provisional Government are being brought to order. The Provisional Government, *under the chairmanship of Rodzianko*, is meeting in the State Duma; it has invited the commanders of the military units to come and receive instructions for the maintenance of order."

Significantly, Alekseev told Ivanov that Rodzianko's appeal to the population had emphasized "the necessity of maintaining the monarchical principle in Russia," although none of Rodzianko's public communiqués in *Izvestiya* mentioned any such thing.[20]

Rodzianko was only getting started. Even while reassuring Alekseev privately that he remained a loyal monarchist, he appointed A. A. Bublikov, the radical leader of the Progressive Party, minister of transportation, with responsibility for the railways (including the telegraph lines that ran along them)—a critical post in wartime, and even more critical now that the tsar's and Ivanov's trains were converging on Tsarskoe Selo from different directions. At four o'clock on Tuesday afternoon, February 28, Nicholas II was informed that railway orders were now being issued by Bublikov from the Transportation Ministry, over Rodzianko's signature. This was shortly confirmed when Rodzianko ordered that the tsar's train be routed directly to Petrograd, avoiding Tsarskoe Selo. In another wire sent Tuesday to Chelnokov, the mayor of Moscow, Rodzianko declared: "The Old Government no longer exists. Interior Minister arrested. Power now resides in a committee of the State Duma under my chairmanship." Reassuring Chelnokov that the soldiers of Petrograd had accepted this new authority and that order had been restored, Rodzianko asked that the mayor instruct General I. I. Mrozovsky, commander of the Moscow military district, to inform his men that he was loyal to Rodzianko's Duma committee, to prevent "the shedding of blood" (that is, Mrozovsky's). For good measure, Rodzianko then fired off another telegram directly to General Mrozovsky, repeating this warning and demanding that he brief the Duma committee on the situation in Moscow.[21]

Considering that the tsar had not yet abdicated, there was an element of presumption in Rodzianko's actions on February 28. To the generals at Mogilev, Rodzianko presented himself as the only man capable of restoring order in Petrograd—in fact he was claiming, dubiously in view of the emergence of the Soviet and the chaos at

Taurida Palace, to have done this already. To the mayor of Moscow, a man he knew was in touch with liberal rivals such as Guchkov and Lvov, and to the military commander there, Rodzianko claimed to have full control of Russia's new Duma-committee government, whatever exactly it was called. In effect, Rodzianko was inaugurating a new government himself, and demanding loyalty from Moscow and the army command.

Remarkably, in view of the loyalty oaths they had all pledged to their sovereign, most of Russia's top generals threw in with Rodzianko. Alekseev was the earliest and most significant convert. Together, he and Rodzianko agreed, in the course of Tuesday, February 28, on the terms of an abdication manifesto in which Tsar Nicholas II would pass the throne to his son under his brother's regency, while instructing Rodzianko to form a government responsible to the Duma. To strengthen Rodzianko's hand with the Taurida radicals, Alekseev agreed to call off Ivanov's punitive mission while Rodzianko and the generals worked on the tsar, trying to convince him to abdicate. The problem concerned who would do the convincing, and where. Alekseev expected General Ruzsky, commander of the northern front nearest to Petrograd, to carry out the task when Nicholas II's train (on its original route) pulled into Pskov, where Ruzsky had his headquarters. Rodzianko, fearful that the tsar might be able to rally loyal troops in Pskov, wanted to go meet the tsar himself at a station along the main Moscow-Petrograd line, which is why he had ordered the train rerouted.[22]

We can only guess what Rodzianko would have said to Russia's nominal sovereign, for the meeting never happened. Awoken just after midnight between Bologoe and the village of Malaya Vishera, Tsar Nicholas II was informed that his train would shortly pass through an area in the hands of disloyal troops. Although the report was inaccurate and would soon be contradicted, the tsar was taking no chances: he ordered the train to turn around and take the branch line to Pskov, where he hoped to find refuge with Ruzsky and the northern army—and a secure telephone line to Tsarskoe Selo so that he could speak with his wife and children. By the time he reached Pskov, the empire ruled by the "tsar and autocrat of all the Russias" had changed beyond recognition.

= 7 =

ARMY IN THE BALANCE

Outside Petrograd, the revolution's impact was muted at first. Not even in Moscow, the unofficial capital of liberal political intrigue in 1915–1916, was there so much as a sympathy demonstration until February 28. The Rodzianko-Bublikov coup at the Transportation Ministry that day, and General Alekseev's failure to contest it, was therefore a decisive step. Not only could Rodzianko now route and reroute trains; he could shape public opinion across the country through the telegraph wires. As soon as the news about the revolution went national, the revolution could go national, too.

Even so, a basic rule of geography still applied, at least in the armed forces that, in the middle of a world war with 7 million active-duty personnel at the front and several million more reserves in the rear, formed the primary audience for politicians auditioning for national leadership. The closer military units were to Petrograd, the sooner the men learned of the revolution. The first serious disturbance outside the capital occurred, predictably, in the naval squadron on Kronstadt, where the sailors (and soldiers; the island housed several army regiments, too) could literally see the fires raging in Petrograd, only 20 miles away. "Disorders" were reported at Kronstadt as early as Tuesday, February 28, with dockyard workers going on strike and sailors abandoning their training courses. By Tuesday night, a full-bore mutiny was under way, with almost the entire garrison on the streets, and a regimental band playing "La Marseillaise." At least one naval officer was lynched that night, and several more arrested. Next day, in a simulacrum of events in Petrograd, the Kronstadt headquarters of the Okhrana was stormed. A revolutionary tribunal was set up in Anchor Square, with death sentences pronounced on 24 officers, and another 162 sentenced to detention by their men. The violence reached its apogee on Wednesday afternoon, March 1, when the hated Admiral Viren was bayoneted to death.[1]

That same day, the Kronstadt mutiny spread through the Baltic Fleet, to Reval (Tallinn), and then to Helsinki, home of Fleet headquarters. All through the day, the commander in chief of the Baltic Fleet, Admiral Adrian Nepenin, sent frantic telegrams to the Admiralty, begging that Rodzianko, Kerensky, or some other authority from Petrograd visit Kronstadt to calm down the men. All Nepenin was able to secure was a telegram from Rodzianko assuring him that the Duma committee had taken power, which Nepenin promptly forwarded to his officers and men, effectively recognizing the new government as legitimate. It did not help. The mutiny raged on. In Kronstadt, Reval, and Helsinki, hundreds of officers, mostly unfortunate Baltic German ostzeiskie with obvious German names, were hunted down and lynched.[2]

A similar geographic dynamic was at play in the army, where Ruzsky's northern army, nearest to Petrograd, was the first to be infected by the revolution. In Russian Fifth Army, in which censors had just reported morale to have been "superlative," things changed quickly when the men learned of the revolution in Petrograd. The officers were "gloomy," complaining that troops no longer obeyed their orders. Among the men, the gung-ho mood of January–February collapsed in days (six days, to be precise, between March 1 and 7), with everyone suddenly weary of the war and talking of peace.[3]

Russian First Army, a bit farther south on the "western" front below the Pripet Marshes, was less infected. Here, the prevailing reaction, once the men learned of political changes in Petrograd, was one of relief that traitors had been purged, allowing the army to do its job unimpeded. "Now that the pro-German ministers have been removed," an engineer in the Thirty-Seventh Engineering Regiment wrote home, "our valiant army thirsts for battle with enthusiasm. I hope we will destroy the enemy." Far from an isolated view, no less than 75 percent of letters sent home from First Army in March 1917 expressed similar sentiments of renewed belligerence in the wake of the revolution.[4]

In Galicia, the impact of the revolution was muted almost entirely. Because this was such an active theater, the men were too busy to pay much attention to political developments in Petrograd. In Lutsk, a more pressing concern was the offensive the Austro-Germans, buttressed by an Ottoman expeditionary force, were expected to mount any day—especially now that "news of the serious disorders in Petrograd will have reached the enemy," as Alekseev wired from Mogilev on March 1. It was a prescient warning. At ten o'clock that evening, the First Turkish Army Corps opened an artillery barrage against the Russians at Maly Porsk, just west of the Styr River. Toward eleven p.m., Turkish infantrymen dropped hand grenades into Russian trenches, killing 15 and wounding 45. The following night, the same unit felled 38 Russian soldiers and wounded 60. By March 5, a real battle was raging in Galicia, with German units bringing up heavy artillery to buttress the Turks, including mortar and poison gas shells. In one fierce engagement on March 7, the Russian Thirty-Ninth Army Corps fought off a German company that had invaded its trenches, taking six prisoners while losing not a single man.[5]

The same theme was visible on the Ottoman fronts, where the Russians had been unambiguously victorious in 1916—and were planning still greater triumphs for 1917. In Lazistan, on the Turkish Black Sea coast, Russian engineers were hard at work building a rail line from Batum to Trabzon. In Odessa, revolution or no revolution, Admiral Kolchak was readying his precious "Tsargradsky Regiment" for the amphibious descent on the Bosphorus that, weather permitting, he hoped to launch in June 1917.[6]

It is important to keep the strategic picture in mind when we evaluate the decisions taken in the high command in the early days of the revolution, when Russia's political fate was being decided. General Alekseev's first priority was plain: to keep frontline troops from being infected by politics. But he was not thinking about mere survival: he genuinely believed that Russia was primed to win the war. Only if we understand this can we make sense of the blind trust Alekseev placed in Rodzianko on February 28. Believing that the Duma president had the situation under control, Alekseev called off the punitive expedition to Petrograd, informing General Ivanov that "negotiations will lead to pacification, so that the shameful civil strife for which our enemy longs will be avoided." Early on March 1, with the tsar en route for Pskov, Alekseev wired General Ruzsky to expect Rodzianko, too. "Information received," he told Ruzsky, "gives us reason to hope that the Duma deputies, led by Rodzianko, will still be able to halt the general disintegration, and that it will be possible to work with them." Any delay in reaching a settlement, however, might "open the door for the seizure of power by extreme leftist elements."[7]

Both of Alekseev's assumptions proved erroneous. Without bothering to inform Alekseev or Ruzsky, Rodzianko decided not to go to Pskov. When he finally did speak to Ruzsky on the phone at 2:30 a.m. on March 2, Rodzianko offered a self-serving excuse, claiming that "the unbridled passions of the popular masses must not be left without my personal control, because I am still the only one who is trusted and whose orders are carried out." Undermining his own excuse, Rodzianko confessed that he was "far from having succeeded" in taming the "people's passions"; that "the troops are completely demoralized"; and that news of "the dispatch of General Ivanov with the St. George battalion has only added fuel to the flames." The tsar, he told Ruzsky, must "stop sending troops—they will not take action against the people." Only hours later, Rodzianko sent off a panicked wire to Alekseev, pleading that "to rescue the capital from anarchy it is imperative that you appoint to the Petrograd military district a popular fighting general to impress the public with his authority." For this task, Rodzianko informed Alekseev, the Duma committee "has chosen the hero known across Russia as the gallant commander of the Twenty-fifth Army Corps, Lieutenant General [Lavr] Kornilov."[8]

Rodzianko had already begun ceding control to the "leftist elements" Alekseev feared. In one of the decisive encounters of the night of February 27–28, Rodzianko had demanded that members of the Duma committee follow his instructions—only to be publicly rebuked by Kerensky, who was rapidly emerging as radical tribune of the Soviet, the self-appointed body of radical socialists meeting in rooms 12 and 13 of Taurida Palace. The Socialist Revolutionary (SR) orator had developed a popular rapport with the soldiers outside

Taurida, whom he harangued with great effect, addressing them not as mutineers but as heroes whom he asked to "defend your freedom, the revolution, defend the State Duma."[9]

And Kerensky, who made a point of protecting many tsarist officials from mob lynchings by "arresting" them in Taurida, was far from the most radical member of the Soviet. Parallel to the *Izvestiya* printed in Taurida by volunteer journalists, which published Rodzianko's communiqués, the Soviet began publishing its own newssheet also called, confusingly, *Izvestiya*. Contrary to what we might expect from a body dominated by Mensheviks and Socialist Revolutionaries, the Soviet *Izvestiya* was tinged with Bolshevik influence from the outset, because it was edited by a close friend of Lenin's, Vladimir Bonch-Bruevich. Bonch-Bruevich, brother of a prominent general of the same name who was chief of staff of the Sixth Army responsible for counterespionage, was the best connected Bolshevik in the capital, with contacts in army intelligence, among the Kuban Cossacks, and even (until his death) Rasputin. As early as February 27, Bonch-Bruevich seized control of a printing press previously used by a low-brow popular daily newspaper and offered its use to the Soviet. It was Bonch-Bruevich who published in *Izvestiya* on March 1 the instructions from the Soviet to the Petrograd army garrison, written up the previous day mostly by Menshevik lawyer N. D. Sokolov, which became known to history as Order No. 1.[10]

Although the flood of subsequent editions makes it difficult to determine exactly what the original version of the order stated, the first two clauses were clear enough, instructing soldiers in Petrograd to elect committees and send deputies to the Petrograd Soviet. To forestall a counterrevolutionary push by officers against mutineers, the new soldiers' committees were instructed to seize control of weapons and ammunition. Officers were also forbidden to address their men with the informal "you" (*tyi* instead of *vyi*), while men would no longer be required to salute their superiors. Politically speaking, the most important clauses were 3 and 4, which stipulated that the garrison was now subordinate to the Soviet, and that any orders issued by the Military Commission of the State Duma "should be carried out with the exception of those cases where they contradict orders and decisions of the Soviet of Workers' and Soldiers' Deputies" (this clause was later amended in a still more radical direction, to read that orders from the Duma Military Commission "are to be carried out *only* in those cases in which they do not contradict the orders and decisions of the Soviet").[11]

Order No. 1 was addressed specifically and meant to apply only to the Petrograd garrison, not to the Russian armed forces as a whole—and certainly not to frontline troops. But news of it was immediately sent out over the telegraph wires. By March 2, thousands of copies had been printed for distribution across the country. Subtleties of wording and jurisdiction aside, a radical sailor present at Taurida Palace when it was being hashed out captured its likely impact when he remarked, "Educated folk will read it differently. But we understood it straight: disarm the officers."[12]

Events in Petrograd were now moving at a bewildering pace. Monday, February 27 had seen the creation of the Soviet and Rodzianko's provisional Duma committee. Just since the tsar had left Mogilev early Tuesday morning, the last bastions of the old regime in Petrograd had fallen. Rodzianko had begun issuing decrees on behalf of an entirely new government; even as Kerensky was openly contesting Rodzianko's authority, the Soviet was asserting its control over the Petrograd garrison, and a ferocious mutiny was breaking out in Kronstadt. A number of army training units stationed near the capital, including the First and Second Machine Gun Regiments in Oranienbaum and the Second Artillery Division in Strelna, had left their barracks and marched to Petrograd to join the revolution. By the time the tsar arrived in Pskov on Wednesday afternoon, March 1, Order No. 1 had been promulgated, although it had not yet reached frontline troops, and Moscow was following the capital into revolution, with a general strike in the factories and mutiny in the garrison.[13]

In Mogilev, Alekseev was more on top of events than Nicholas II, but he was still struggling to keep up. Around three p.m. on Wednesday, March 1, Alekseev composed a message to his sovereign, although it did not reach the latter in Pskov until nearly eleven p.m. In it, Alekseev warned the tsar that "disorders in the rear will produce the same result among the armed forces. It is impossible to ask the army calmly to wage war while a revolution is in progress in the rear." To "halt the general collapse" and "reestablish order," Alekseev informed Nicholas II that a draft manifesto had been prepared for him by the tsar's diplomatic aide-de-camp at Stavka, Nicholas de Basily, announcing that, to calm the public and "solidify all the forces of the nation," the tsar "consider[ed] it his duty to appoint a ministry responsible to the representatives of the people, and to entrust the president of the Duma, Rodzianko, to form it with the help of persons possessing the confidence of all Russia."[14]

The effect of Alekseev's message on Tsar Nicholas II must have been shattering. Compounding the effect, three more wires reached Pskov in support of Alekseev's line, one from the tsar's first cousin, Grand Duke Sergei Mikhailovich, who was inspector of artillery, one from General Brusilov, hero of the Galician offensive of 1916, and a third from Admiral Nepenin in Helsinki, who all but begged their sovereign to salvage what remained of military discipline through the "supreme act" of abdication. According to General Ruzsky's recollection of his conversation with Nicholas II in Pskov that evening, it was Alekseev's telegram that broke down the tsar's resistance, once he realized that the high command had turned against him. In one final act of imperial stubbornness, the tsar at first insisted that Rodzianko (as opposed to the Duma as such) name the members of the cabinet, so that its legal authority would still derive from the sovereign's will, delegated via the Duma president. But Ruzsky broke him down on this point as well, and the tsar signed Basily's draft manifesto, unedited, just before midnight. Bowing to what appeared to be a united front between Rodzianko and the army command, at 12:20 a.m. on March 2 Nicholas II sent off a wire to Tsarskoe Selo, demanding that General Ivanov, commander of the St. George's Battalion, "take no measures whatever before my arrival." By calling off Ivanov's punitive military expedition, the tsar forfeited his last chance of restoring his authority in Petrograd.[15]

It was a fateful decision, which might easily have gone the other way. In another critical accident of timing, Ruzsky and Alekseev convinced the tsar to surrender his authority to Rodzianko at midnight on March 1–2, 1917, several hours before Rodzianko, in phone conversation with Ruzsky, confessed his own inability to rule Taurida Palace, let alone Petrograd and Russia. Had Ruzsky spoken to Rodzianko earlier that evening, it is possible that he would have advised his sovereign very differently after realizing that the entire premise of the Alekseev-Basily manifesto was mistaken. The revelation about the impotence of "fat Rodzianko" would not have surprised Nicholas II, who had initially refused to sign, according to Ruzsky, because of his low opinion of "the people who claimed to enjoy the nation's confidence."[16]

Still, it was not too late to head off disaster. Although the tsar had agreed to let Rodzianko form a government, he had not yet given up his throne. Once he learned more of the true situation in Petrograd, he might even change his mind about the Basily manifesto, which had not yet been made public. The Duma president was so unsure of himself that, when Ruzsky asked him, at seven a.m. on March 2, whether the high command should publish the manifesto in which the tsar had entrusted him with forming a new parliamentary government, Rodzianko could only mumble, "I really don't know what to say; everything depends on events, which are developing at hair-raising speed."[17]

With the tsar bowing out and Rodzianko falling apart in Petrograd, General Alekseev took matters into his own hands. At 10:15 a.m. on March 2, the acting commander in chief wired to all army and navy front commanders that

> the war can be continued to a victorious end only if requests for the Emperor's abdication in his son's favour, with [Grand Duke] Michael serving as regent, are satisfied. The situation apparently does not permit of any alternative solution . . . the army must fight the external enemy with all its strength, while the decision on internal affairs will spare it the temptation to play a part in the *coup d'état*, which will be less painful if effected from above.[18]

In this extraordinary telegram, Alekseev outsmarted himself. By advocating Rodzianko's old plan for the tsar's abdication, he made a decisive political intervention on behalf of the armed forces. By demanding "unity of thought and purpose among the highest commanders of the armies" in a telegram he knew Nicholas II would read, he was pressuring the tsar to abdicate his throne out of patriotism—while disingenuously avowing that the army must remain above politics. Like Rodzianko, Alekseev wanted a political solution without the burden of political responsibility. In effect, he was asking the tsar to sacrifice himself so as to save the army from sullying itself in politics.

It was fitting that, on the same day Alekseev demanded his abdication, Nicholas II was visited by Alekseev's old political muse: Octobrist archplotter Alexander Guchkov. As Rodzianko refused to go to Pskov, the task was left to the old conspirator, who asked for a volunteer to accompany him. As the other Duma men were no more enthusiastic than Rodzianko, Guchkov was accompanied by an obscure deputy from Kiev named V. V. Shulgin. Just before three p.m. on March 2, the two men boarded a train for Pskov, arriving at nine o'clock that night. Although Ruzsky had requested to see the Duma deputies before they met the tsar, it was already so late that everyone simply gathered in Nicholas II's train suite in Pskov station and got on with it.[19]

If any politician seemed poised to seize the moment, it was Guchkov. For two years, he had been plotting the tsar's downfall, and now he was handed the opportunity to finish him off in person. And yet the truth was that the old Octobrist, no less than the sovereign he despised, had been overtaken by events outside his control. Guchkov had played little role in the Petrograd street disturbances. Whatever else he was, he was no mutineer, and he was genuinely shocked by the bloodshed. While Guchkov addressed troops earlier that morning, one of his closest friends, a Preobrazhensky Guards officer, had been shot dead standing right next to him. Clearly shaken, Guchkov declined to take over the War Ministry. He arrived in Pskov unshaved, disheveled, and out of sorts. He pleaded with the tsar, more in sorrow than in anger, to help stop the spread of anarchy. "All the workers and soldiers who took part in the riots," Guchkov explained, "are firmly convinced that the retention (*vodvorenie*) of the old regime would mean summary justice for them, and this is why we need a radical change." What was needed, Guchkov argued, was a "crack on the whip of public imagination"—not only the tsar's abdication, but the appointment of a government headed by Prince Lvov, the head of Zemgor and a fellow Masonic plotter (not, that is, by Rodzianko, to whom the tsar had delegated authority).[20]

Stubborn to the end, Nicholas II deprived his enemy of the satisfaction he craved. Calmly, he informed Guchkov that he had earlier decided to abdicate in favor of his son, Alexis, with Grand Duke Michael as regent; he had now changed his mind and would *not* do so, instead passing on the throne directly to Michael, so he could remain with his son (after consulting with a doctor, Nicholas II had been informed just hours previously that Alexis's hemophilia was incurable). Although there was no precedent for this in Russian law, and Guchkov complained that it would therefore be unacceptable to the Duma committee, the tsar insisted, and Guchkov, reluctantly, agreed. In the final act of abdication, signed at 11:50 p.m. on March 2 but backdated to 3:05 p.m. to make it seem that it had not been coerced, Nicholas II passed the Romanov throne to his brother Michael, "in agreement with the State Duma." Significantly, the abdication was addressed not to Guchkov or Rodzianko as representatives of the Duma, but to General Alekseev—that is, to the army. In an accompanying declaration, the tsar appointed Grand Duke Nicholas commander in chief. The only concession Guchkov was able to wring out of him was the naming of Lvov (not Rodzianko) as chairman of the Council of Ministers, a curious appointment in that this body no longer existed.[21]

In spite of the anticlimactic atmosphere in Pskov, the abdication was a momentous event in Russian history. But its consequences were far from those desired by the men who argued for it. Guchkov had been onto something when he suggested that bringing a formal end to the old regime would reassure mutinous soldiers afraid of "summary justice." But the awarding of immunity to mutineers, as he should have realized, was no recipe for restoring military discipline. Alekseev had second thoughts almost immediately. Rather than help Alekseev restore discipline in the armies, the abdication would make that task virtually impossible. Every officer, every soldier, every sailor in Russia—all 9 million plus military personnel, including reserves and training units—had sworn allegiance to Nicholas II. Now that Russia's sovereign was no more, to what or whom would they swear an oath?

The most obvious answer was Michael Romanov, the man to whom Nicholas II had abdicated. But the tsar's brother came down with cold feet almost immediately. If anyone was responsible for putting his name forward in the first place, it was Rodzianko, a man who no longer inspired confidence. As soon as Rodzianko learned of the tsar's abdication at five a.m. on March 3, he called General Ruzsky in Pskov and demanded that the abdication manifesto *not* be published. The crowds at Taurida, he claimed, might "perhaps reconcile themselves to the regency of the Grand Duke . . . but his accession as emperor would be completely unacceptable." Once again painting himself, dubiously, as the only bulwark of order amid revolutionary chaos, Rodzianko warned that "the proclamation of Grand Duke Michael Aleksandrovich as Emperor would pour oil onto the fire and a merciless extermination of everything that can be exterminated would start. We will lose from our hands all authority and no one will remain to appease the popular unrest."[22]

When Ruzsky forwarded Rodzianko's remarks to Mogilev, Alekseev finally lost patience with the Duma president. According to the quartermaster-general, A. S. Lukomsky, Alekseev told him, "I shall never forgive myself for having believed in the sincerity of certain people [e.g., Rodzianko], for having followed them, and for having sent the telegram about the Emperor's abdication to the commanders-in-chief." At seven a.m. on March 3, Alekseev warned front commanders not to trust further instructions from Rodzianko, whose messages from Petrograd, owing to "very strong pressure being exerted . . . by parties of the left and the Workers' Deputies . . . lacked sincerity and candor." He warned that the Petrograd garrison "had been completely propagandized" by the Soviet, and had become "harmful and dangerous elements for everyone." In view of the critical situation in Petrograd, Alekseev summoned army and navy front commanders to Mogilev for a conference "to establish unanimity in all circumstances and in any eventuality." Having called off Ivanov's expedition to restore order in Petrograd under what appeared to be false pretenses, Alekseev was now desperate to avert civil war.[23]

Into this political cauldron Grand Duke Michael was now hurled. A shy and retiring man who had never expected or wanted to rule, he had suddenly become the most important man in Russia, guarded, in his temporary quarters in Princess Putyatin's Petrograd apartment at 12, Millionaya ulitsa, by a detachment of officers-in-training (there being no actual officers willing to risk their own skins). At ten a.m. on March 3, a Duma delegation arrived, headed by Rodzianko, Lvov,

Milyukov, and Kerensky (Guchkov had been delayed at the railway station). According to Milyukov's account, Rodzianko was "in a blue funk," and the others, too, were all "frightened by what was happening." But everyone bowed to Rodzianko's rank, and they left him alone with the grand duke. Convincing Michael to decline the throne was not difficult.[24]

In his own act of abdication, dated March 3, 1917, Grand Duke Michael stated that he had been asked to assume the "heavy burden" of the "Imperial Throne of All the Russias at a time of unprecedented warfare and popular disturbances."* Gamely, he declared himself willing to assume "supreme power"—but only "in the event that such is the will of our great people, upon whom it devolves by a general vote, through their representatives in the Constituent Assembly, to determine the form of government and the new fundamental laws of the Russian State." Until then, Michael asked "all citizens of the Russian State to pay allegiance to the Provisional Government, which has come into being at the initiative of the State Duma and which is endowed with full power."[25]

Whether or not Russian troops would obey this mysterious new "Provisional Government" referred to by Grand Duke Michael was an open question. For whom, if not an emperor, would the men fight? For the Grand Duke Nicholas—a man who, whatever his popularity with liberals and other virtues, was no less a Romanov than the two men who had just renounced the throne? (This alone likely disqualified him: the Petrograd Soviet had ordered all members of the imperial dynasty arrested on March 3.) Many generals, such as Alekseev, Brusilov, and Kornilov, were popular with the men. But then Alekseev, to forestall civil war, had foresworn army intervention in politics—even while asking the tsar to abdicate, summoning front commanders to Mogilev, and issuing a new order on March 3 (no. 1925) warning officers not to allow "revolutionary gangs" from Petrograd to infect their units with defeatism. Order No. 1 was a

---

* While Michael was huddling with Rodzianko, Nicholas II, suddenly realizing that he had not bothered to inform his brother he was abdicating the throne to him, composed a wire asking him to "forgive me if it grieves you and also for no warning—there was no time." The telegram, dispatched at 2:56 p.m. on March 3, 1917, was returned "address unknown."

dagger aimed at the officer corps, at Stavka itself. Surely the army could not ask its men to swear allegiance to the Soviet that had issued it. Should the new oath be to the Duma committee, then? If so, then to Rodzianko as Duma president, or to Lvov, as chairman? Or perhaps to Guchkov, the man still expected (despite his own fear of the mob) to take over the War Ministry?[26]

In the middle of a world war, these were not academic questions. On March 2, an order had been sent from Stavka asking front commanders to obey their new commander in chief, Grand Duke Nicholas, but this was complicated by the announcement of Grand Duke Michael's abdication on March 3, forwarded to front commanders at two a.m. on March 4, which asked soldiers to transfer their allegiance to the "Provisional Government." Not until March 5 did most frontline troops learn of the second and final Romanov abdication. Meanwhile, Grand Duke Nicholas, named commander in chief by a sovereign now twice removed from power, was on a train en route to Mogilev that very day when a vigorous protest erupted in the Petrograd Soviet over his appointment.[27]

Control of the Russian armed forces was up for grabs. At Mogilev, Alekseev was still acting commander in chief (at least of the troops in the field, if not of the Petrograd garrison that obeyed the Soviet) until Grand Duke Nicholas arrived, but no one knew to what political authority he himself answered. On March 4, Guchkov, having recovered his nerve and assumed the dual titles of war minister and naval minister of the Provisional Government, issued an order to the army and fleet to unite behind this new regime and "break the resistance of the enemy."[28] On March 5, Alekseev's chief of staff, General Danilov, passed on another order in the name of "War Minister Guchkov," which enunciated some of the less explosive clauses of Order No. 1, relating to the proper form of address for enlisted men (the formal *vyi*, with the term *nizhnyi chin* [lower ranks] abolished in favor of *soldat* [soldier]). Officers were allowed to retain their rank, but would no longer be addressed as *gospodin* [master].[29] Next day, Rodzianko issued an order demanding obedience to the "Provisional Committee of the Members of the State Duma," insisting that "each soldier, officer, and sailor calmly does his duty."[30] Forwarding this message to all front commanders on March 6, Alekseev and Danilov issued a signed order (no. 1998) that appeared to affirm the authority of the "President of the State Duma, Rodzianko"—until, that is, they received a formal loyalty oath for their men on March 7, signed by "Prince Lvov" on behalf of the "Council of Ministers of the Provisional Government," a formulation blending together the defunct Tsarist Council with this new "Provisional Government" everyone was talking about, even if no one knew exactly what it was.[31]

In this tripartite battle of political wills, it was perhaps inevitable that the first two men to team up against the other would prevail. The critical day was March 7, when Guchkov and Lvov began cosigning orders to the army and navy as ministers of the "Provisional Government," even as Kerensky (visiting Moscow) made a public vow that Grand Duke Nicholas would not assume the army command.[32] On March 11, Lvov formally deprived the Grand Duke of the command, which was given to Alekseev. On March 13, a new loyalty oath was issued for army officers, demanding allegiance to the "Provisional Government"—and to a Constituent Assembly to be elected later in 1917.[33] Even so, confusion reigned at the front, where, as a number officers reported to Stavka, soldiers kept "asking the question, whether they are serving the Provisional Committee of the State Duma headed by Rodzianko, or the Council of Ministers headed by Prince Lvov." Asked by General Alekseev on March 26 to resolve the matter, Guchkov (who now controlled communications between Petrograd and Stavka) answered: neither of the two. Soldiers, rather, must "swear an oath to the Provisional Government"—whatever exactly this was.[34]

While the politicians sorted out who was in charge, frontline soldiers began forming their own committees along the lines of Order No. 1. Although a follow-up Order No. 2, cosigned by Guchkov (for the "Provisional Government") and Skobelev (for the Soviet), wired to Stavka on March 5, clarified that Order No. 1 was only meant to apply to the rearguard Petrograd garrison, Order No. 1 was so much more widely publicized than the retraction that Order No. 2, as Alekseev soon complained, may as well never have existed.[35]

Order No. 2 certainly did not come through soon enough for Admiral Nepenin in Helsinki. At 1:30 a.m. on March 4, Nepenin wired one final report to the Admiralty on the lynching of five more officers, including two admirals, before he was himself lynched in gruesome fashion less than twelve hours later. Nor did the clarification of relations between men and officers arrive in time for Admiral Viren or the hundred-odd officers lynched in Helsinki, Kronstadt, and Reval. By the second week of March 1917, the mutinous blood-lust in the Baltic Fleet had finally been spent. Officers with German names, mercifully, were less numerous in the Black Sea Fleet, where "only" twenty were killed in the first month after the revolution.[36]

In Petrograd, a kind of modus vivendi was worked out between the self-declared Soviet and the self-declared Provisional Government, partly out of a shared hostility to Duma president Rodzianko, whose communiqués were now being ignored by almost everyone. The man of the hour was Kerensky, the only man permitted (by acclamation of the Soviet after a rousing speech on March 2) to serve both of the embryonic governments in Taurida Palace, as justice minister of the Provisional Government and as a member of the Soviet's three-man Presidium. Kerensky had become an all-purpose troubleshooter, now protecting "old regime" officials from mob lynchings; now haranguing the garrison into obedience; now calming mutineers in Moscow and Helsinki; now signing, on March 12, a decree abolishing the death penalty, to appease the Soviet. On March 15, Petrograd's archives were reopened, a small but significant sign that daily life was returning to normal.[37]

At the front, too, things were slowly settling down. Lynchings in the army were happily less common than in the navy, although many officers were "arrested" by their men. Most of the fifty-odd army officer victims of February and March 1917 were killed in Petrograd and environs, not at the front. There was a noticeable uptick in desertions, with Stavka estimating that frontline divisions lost an average of five to seven men per day in March 1917, amounting to more than 100,000 in all—a substantial number, but hardly fatal in a frontline army of 7 million being replenished daily by new recruits. In the southwestern army in Galicia, where heavy fighting was under way in March against the Austro-Germans and Turks, desertion was minimal, picking up only in late April, after the battle quieted down. In the Caucasian Army, still poised for a historic victory over the Turks, desertion was almost nonexistent.[38]

Despite, or perhaps because of, the rivers of blood spilled in mutinies in army barracks and on naval bases in Petrograd, Kronstadt, Helsinki, and Reval—indeed, the vast majority of the casualties of the February Revolution (about 1,300 to 1,400, of which 169 were deaths) were incurred inside military units in the Baltic region—the Russian armed forces had survived the revolution more or less intact. This was all to the good, for there was a war on, and the German enemy was moving in for the kill.[39]

— 8 —

THE GERMAN GAMBIT

N ews of the February Revolution in Russia traveled quickly
around the world after the Nicholas II's abdication, although
many details were lost in translation. In London and Paris,
where consular reports composed of Russian liberal talking points
had prejudiced opinion against the tsar, the reaction was euphoric.
The *Westminster Gazette* celebrated the tsar's fall as "the removal of a
heavy load," a "dramatic stroke" that brought autocratic Russia "into
line with the faith and practice of its partners." *Le Matin* celebrated
the February Revolution as "a victory for the Entente," predicting
that "the emancipation of Russia will ruin the diplomatic plans of our
enemies."[1]

Nowhere was news greeted with more enthusiasm than in Washington, DC, where President Woodrow Wilson faced a suddenly
urgent battle to convince Congress—and the American public—of
the case for war against Germany. In November 1916, Wilson had
won reelection largely on the boast that "he kept us out of the war,"
only to be shocked by a series of German outrages. Reckoning on
possible US intervention after the resumption of unrestricted submarine warfare on February 1, 1917, the Wilhelmstrasse made this more
likely by dispatching the soon infamous "Zimmermann telegram" to
the German ambassador in Mexico City—via a US diplomatic cable.
In this explosive document, Berlin promised to support a Mexican
reconquista of the American southwest (Texas, New Mexico, and Ari-
zona) if Mexico declared war on the United States. First deciphered
by British cryptographers, who carefully shared the bombshell with

Washington, the Zimmermann telegram was released to the press on February 15/28, 1917, just days before the Russian Revolution broke out in Petrograd.[2]

The effect of the revolution on American public opinion was electric. Although the Wilson administration had already severed diplomatic relations with Berlin in early February after the resumption of unrestricted submarine warfare, this fell short of a declaration of war. Wilson, a liberal academic idealist who subscribed to the creed of "American exceptionalism," would never have been comfortable plunging the United States into war for traditional reasons of state. Not even the Zimmermann telegram pushed Wilson beyond a stance of "armed neutrality." Only after Russia had joined the "liberal democratic" camp did Wilson find his inspiration, declaring before a joint session of Congress on March 20/April 2, 1917, that "the world must be made safe for democracy," and "peace must be planted upon the tested foundations of political liberty."[3]

Wilson saw what he wanted to see in the February Revolution. The lofty ideals he expressed were the luxury of powers, such as the United States and (to a lesser extent) Great Britain, which faced no existential threat to their security beyond German U-boat raiders on the high seas. In France, where the Germans held a salient at Noyon just 65 miles from Paris, the elation over Russian democracy aborning was overwhelmed by practical concerns about the impact of the revolution on Russia's spring offensives, expected to draw off German strength from France. By the end of March, *Le Matin* was warning about the "extremists" of the Petrograd Soviet. In a veiled allusion to Order No. 1—a decree so explosive it was still not being reported by Allied correspondents—*Le Matin* complained, "Decisions were being reached by the 1,600 delegates in Taurida Palace of which the least that could be said is that they were reached in confusion."[4]

In Berlin, patriotic journalists tended to emphasize the disorders thrown up by the revolution in Petrograd, while downplaying positive news. The *Berliner Lokal-Anzeiger* ran a banner headline, "The Socialist Flood and the Coming Anarchy." The *Berliner Tageblatt* noted with approval that German war prisoners in Russia were being sent home via Stockholm. A Copenhagen correspondent from the *Tageblatt* published a gory account of "The Spread of the Bloody

Revolution to Finland." From the German point of view, the more chaotic the revolution became, the better.[5]

While Entente observers succumbed to wishful thinking about the impact of the revolution on Russia's war-fighting capacity, the darker German accounts, though tinged with their own bias, hewed closer to the truth. Mutinies *were* spreading through Russia's army and navy (although not with equal effect on all fronts), and anarchy was spreading across the land. Moreover, the Germans, who had agents on the ground in Petrograd and excellent contacts with Russian revolutionary circles abroad, were ideally positioned to exploit the chaos in Russia—and to exacerbate it. It was time to play the Lenin card.

The Bolshevik Party leader had had a quiet war so far, although not for lack of trying. The outbreak of hostilities in August 1914 found Lenin in Poronino, near Cracow in Austrian Galicia close to the Russian border, agitating among local Ukrainians. The Cracow police arrested him as an enemy alien, until an Austrian socialist leader vouched that Lenin was not a tsarist spy but a "bitter enemy of Russia." It helped Lenin's case that a search of his flat turned up just the sort of dry economic research that might obsess a bona fide Marxist agitator. Interviews conducted by Austrian officials confirmed that Lenin was a revolutionary fanatic who had publicly endorsed Ukrainian separatism—a central war aim of the Central Powers. Lenin was released in early September by special order of the Habsburg War Ministry and dispatched on a military mail train—accompanied by his wife, Nadezhda Krupskaya, and his loyal Bolshevik aide-de-camp, Grigory Zinoviev—to Switzerland, where he would spend the war conspiring against the tsar.[6]

Lenin, already on Austrian radar, came to the attention of the German Foreign Office in 1915, from two independent sources. The first, Alexander "Parvus" Helphand, we have already met, stirring up trouble in Petrograd in 1905. After escaping from Siberian exile, Parvus had lived a rich and interesting life abroad in Germany and then Turkey. The outbreak of the war found him running a political salon on the Bosphorus for Ukrainian separatists, Armenian and Georgian socialists, and other tsarist exiles, in which capacity he requested an audience, in January 1915, with the German ambassador to the Ottoman Empire, Baron Hans von Wangenheim. "The interests of the German Imperial Government," Parvus told Wangenheim, "are identical with those of the Russian revolutionaries."[7]

The second intermediary, Alexander Kesküla, was no less colorful. An Estonian Bolshevik who, like Parvus, was a hardened veteran of the 1905 revolution, Kesküla had more recently embraced full-throttled Estonian nationalism (asked, by a Finnish friend, what his plans for Petrograd were after Estonia conquered it, Kesküla replied that its palaces would make an excellent "stone quarry"). Kesküla's motivation for going to work for German intelligence in September 1914, as he later recalled, was simple: "hatred of Russia." In September 1915, Kesküla informed the German consul in Bern, Gisbert von Romberg, of Lenin's views and ideological outlook. Romberg thereafter paid Kesküla 20,000 marks a month to distribute to Lenin and other Bolsheviks.[8]

In view of Lenin's position on the war, which he outlined at socialist exile congresses at Zimmerwald (1915) and Kienthal (1916), it is not hard to see why the German Foreign Office cultivated him. Whereas the majority at these gatherings supported the resolutions penned by Trotsky (still a Menshevik) and others, which opposed the war and urged that workers refuse to work or fight on the old "general strike" principle, Lenin formulated the minority doctrine of "revolutionary defeatism." Socialists, he argued, should work to bring about the defeat of their own country—he meant this literally—and thereby "turn the imperialist war into civil war." Rather than counsel draft resistance, socialists should encourage workers to join the military and turn the armies "red" by promoting mutinies. Although these views were seen as divisive by the Marxist majority at Zimmerwald, Lenin was hewing more closely to the spirit of Eugène Pottier's socialist anthem, "The Internationale," which endorsed army mutiny:

> *The kings intoxicate us with gunsmoke,*
> *Peace between ourselves, war on the tyrants.*
> *Let us bring the strike to the armies,*
> *Fire into the air and break ranks!*
> *If they insist, these cannibals,*

On making us into heroes,
They'll know soon enough that our bullets
Are for our own generals! [9]

So explosive was Lenin's "Zimmerwald Left" doctrine that, when Consul Romberg explained it to Berlin, the German Foreign Office intervened to quash publication of Lenin's program, lest the Okhrana use it to justify mass arrests of socialists in Russia.[10]

In the months before the February Revolution, Lenin had fallen off the German radar somewhat. Parvus concentrated his own efforts on industrial sabotage in Russia, while Kesküla cooled on Lenin owing to the latter's indifference to the Estonian question (the Germans reciprocated, cutting Kesküla off in October 1916). Lenin himself had begun to lose touch with Russian affairs, about which he was despondent. In the Zurich Volkshaus on January 9/22, 1917, Lenin told a youth-socialist gathering that "we old-timers may not live to see the decisive battles of the coming revolution."[11]

Lenin first learned of the revolution from an Austrian comrade on March 1/14, 1917. Elated, he wished to return to Petrograd at once, although to avoid the western and eastern fronts, the shortest and safest path from Switzerland to Russia required crossing Germany, which might look suspicious to Russians back home. Romberg, the German consul in Bern, was eager to help, but both he and Lenin needed to proceed carefully. A Swiss socialist, Fritz Platten, acted as middleman, handling all negotiations between Lenin and the Swiss and German governments, purchasing all tickets, and acting as official "host" and spokesman while the train crossed Germany, so that no Russians would have to speak with German officials. For added camouflage, Platten also stipulated that Lenin and his nineteen Bolshevik associates—including Zinoviev, Lenin's wife, Nadezhda, and his mistress, Inessa Armand; and a chain-smoking Polish-Jewish journalist, Karl Radek—be accompanied on the train by Julius Martov, the old Menshevik leader, and six non-Bolshevik members of the Jewish Bund. Platten also tried, but failed, to enlist Socialist Revolutionary (SR) exiles: none of these more patriotic Russians wished to be associated with Lenin. The most important condition related to "extraterritoriality," with the story put out on press wires that Lenin's train car was "sealed" and would not open its doors while crossing Germany. On March 23/April 5, 1917, the German government appropriated 5 million gold marks for revolutionizing Russia, and four days later, Lenin was sent on his way.[12]

Try though everyone did to sell the idea of the sealed train car, the story sprang leaks almost immediately. The Russians had to switch trains after crossing the Swiss frontier, meaning that they *did* set foot on German soil, at Gottmadingen. Once aboard the new German train, they were accompanied by two German army officers, Captain von Planetz and Lieutenant von Buhring, who both answered directly to General Erich Ludendorff at the German high command (Buhring had been chosen because he was fluent in Russian). A third German, a trade union official named Wilhelm Jansson, answering to Parvus, also joined the Russians at Gottmadingen. We also know, from German records, that the Russian delegation "missed its connection in Frankfurt," necessitating a long stopover there in between trains; that a fourth German "officer in civilian clothes" visited Lenin's train car while it passed through Berlin; that the train stopped there for twenty hours and was resupplied with food and fresh milk; and that this second delay later forced the Russians to spend an entire night in a German hotel in Sassnitz, while waiting for the next ferry to Denmark.[13]

According to the sworn testimony of Russian prisoners of war repatriated from Germany after the revolution, the reasons that Lenin's train car stopped in Germany were not so innocuous. One of these, Senior Under Officer F. P. Zinenko, testified that Lenin's acceptance of aid from the Germans, along with Lenin's support for Ukrainian separatism, were openly discussed in his prisoner-of-war camp. Another witness, Captain E. A. Tishkin, reported that in his camp, at Stralsund, on the Baltic coast, "Everyone suddenly began talking about Lenin" in April 1917, not surprising in that Lenin's train passed Stralsund, en route for nearby Sassnitz, where he spent the night on March 29/April 11, 1917. It was common knowledge in the Stralsund camp, Tishkin testified under oath, that Lenin got off the train while crossing through Germany to give political speeches.[14]

Whatever the truth of these specific allegations, the thrust of Germany's Russia policy in 1917 was unmistakable. Socialist exiles of all stripes (except prowar SR "defensists," who sought help from the Allies instead) were dispatched, at German expense, into Russia to exacerbate tensions between the Soviet and the Provisional Government. Tsarist prisoners of war of Ukrainian, Finnish, Polish, or Estonian extraction were sent home to agitate for independence. In this flood of discontented humanity pouring into revolutionary Russia, Lenin was but a single individual. But in the extremity of his views on the war, and his opportunistic embrace of Ukrainian separatism, Lenin was the critical catalyst of chaos, a one-man demolition crew sent to wreck Russia's war effort. As Parvus himself explained to the German minister in Copenhagen in late March, to prevent a revival of Russian fighting morale under the new Provisional Government, the "extreme revolutionary movement will have to be supported, in order to intensify anarchy." Or as Parvus explained to the German Socialist leader Philip Scheidemann, then visiting Copenhagen, Lenin was "much more raving mad" than the rest of Russia's socialists.[15]

The German investment in Lenin paid immediate dividends. After a brief stopover in Stockholm, where Lenin's friend Karl Radek set up a Bolshevik Foreign Mission to handle communications with Lenin in Petrograd, the Russian exiles traveled on by train, arriving at Petrograd's Finland Station just past eleven p.m. on April 3, 1917, in a train car later encased in glass to commemorate the historic moment (it remains there today). Whisked away to Bolshevik Party headquarters, Lenin launched into a fiery two-hour speech denouncing the "piratical imperialist war," along with party backsliders who had offered support to the Provisional Government still fighting it. The program Lenin proposed was so extreme that the Party organ, *Pravda*, initially refused to print it. These "April Theses" are best remembered today for the slogan "All power to the Soviets," but they were equally extreme on foreign policy, disavowing any support for the war and advocating the abolition of the Russian army. Within hours Lenin's "extreme radical and pacifist" program was the talk of Petrograd, as Frank Golder recorded in his diary, along with the rumor that Germany had sent him to Petrograd so that "he and his party might preach pacifism and bring about a demoralization." Small wonder German army intelligence in Stockholm reported the following day to the German high command: "Lenin's entry into Russia successful. He is working exactly as we would wish."[16]

As an exile who had scarcely set foot in Russia for seventeen years, Lenin had been free to devise a policy line unconstrained by concern for comity with fellow Russian socialists or other practical considerations. His perspective on the war thus differed from that of Bolsheviks who had stayed in Russia, such as Lev Kamenev and Josef Stalin, both amnestied from Siberian exile after the February Revolution. Kamenev, who was the editor of *Pravda* and a Bolshevik Duma deputy when the war broke out, had been arrested in January 1915. Stalin, sentenced to four years of internal exile in 1913, had spent the war in northeastern Siberia, near Turukhansk—his most isolated banishment to date; escape had proved impossible. Kamenev, who felt he had earned his leadership position by hard knocks during the war, insisted after Lenin's bombshell speech that the Bolshevik Central Committee would defend the current party platform, which offered qualified support for the Provisional Government and the war, "against the demoralizing influence of 'revolutionary defeatism' and against Comrade Lenin's criticism." Stalin, less polite, denounced Lenin's "Down with the war" slogan as "useless" in *Pravda*. In the Central Committee, Lenin's April Theses were voted down soundly on April 8, by 13 to 2.[17]

Lenin, however, had an ace to play: German money. For the first month after its inaugural postrevolutionary issue on March 12, 1917, *Pravda* had been publishing its editorials in limited runs out of a government-owned printing works on the Moika Canal. After Lenin's arrival, the Bolsheviks purchased a private printing press on Suvorovsky Prospekt for 250,000 rubles (equal to $125,000 then or some $12.5 million today) after promising the owner that they would retain the experienced staff at full pay (an expense of more than 30,000 rubles monthly, the current equivalent of $1.5 million, or $18 million per year). This last stipulation was critical to overcome the owner's reluctance, as he was suspicious as to how a shadowy group styling itself the "workers' printing collective" had that kind of ready cash on hand.[18]

The Bolsheviks could now print propaganda in virtually unlimited quantities. The circulation of *Pravda* quickly ratcheted up to eighty-five thousand. On April 15, the party launched a new broadsheet, *Soldatskaia Pravda*, addressed to soldiers in the Petrograd garrison. It had an initial circulation of 50,000, then 75,000. Editions aimed at frontline soldiers (*Okopnaia Pravda*) and sailors in the Baltic Fleet (*Golos Pravdy*) soon followed. Before long, the Bolsheviks' daily print run reaching frontline troops reached six figures. Special pamphlets were also printed in the hundreds of thousands. In light of this stunning publishing coup made possible by German subsidies, it is unsurprising that Lenin was ultimately allowed, despite the loud objections of Kamenev and Stalin, to publish his still unpopular anti-war platform in *Pravda*.[19]

Because so many files were later destroyed by the Soviet government, historians face a difficult task in tracing the money trail between the German government and the Bolsheviks in Petrograd. Lenin kept his own hands clean, except for a few suggestive telegrams to Radek in Stockholm, in one of which, on April 21, he acknowledged receiving 2,000 rubles. In another, Lenin requested "more materials."[20] Colonel B. V. Nikitin, who worked in counterespionage for the Provisional Government, reproduced several incriminating telegrams in his memoirs, in which he also claimed that a Bolshevik agent, Evgeniya Sumenson, confessed under interrogation to passing on money (which she laundered from a German import business) to a Polish lawyer named Miecyslaw Kozlovsky, who was a member of the Bolshevik Central Committee. After leaving Russia later in 1917, Kerensky debriefed Allied intelligence (and later wrote in memoir accounts) about documents he claimed to have seen, including a famous withdrawal of 750,000 rubles from Sumenson's account at Siberian Bank. Until now, most historians believed that these contentious matters, owing to the lack of corroborative evidence from the Russian archives, must remain obscure.[21]

Not all of the documents on Bolshevik-German ties uncovered by Provisional Government investigators, however, were destroyed. New evidence from the Communist Party Archives shows that Sumenson was indeed running a genuine, if unusual, import business out of a huge, fully furnished Petrograd apartment at Nadezhdinskaia ulitsa

36. (Her operation received considerable attention from neighbors curious why an unmarried, childless woman lived in a four-bedroom flat and received so many male visitors.) Sumenson sold German-made thermometers, medicines, stockings, pencils, and Nestlé food-stuffs, for cash. She had active accounts at Siberian Bank and also at the Russo-Asiatic and Azov-Don Banks, into all of which she deposited hundreds of thousands of rubles, accrued from her sales of these scarce German luxuries to well-off Russians. Multiple witnesses saw Sumenson hand cash to Kozlovsky personally, in regular installments of several thousand rubles.[22]

Sumenson also received direct wire transfers from banks in Stockholm and Copenhagen, usually from her cousin, Jakob Fürstenberg-Hanecki (revolutionary alias "Kuba"), one of Lenin's most trusted party comrades and a future Soviet finance minister. In one damning telegram, Kozlovsky requested that Kuba wire 100,000 rubles from Nya Banken in Stockholm to Sumenson in Petrograd: several days later, this exact amount was duly wired to her account at Russo-Asiatic Bank. Through such direct wire transfers, and also through the laundering of ruble profits from Sumenson's import business, the German government was able to transfer enormous sums to Lenin's party in Petrograd, ultimately amounting to 50 million gold marks, the equivalent of over $1 billion in current terms.[23]

After years of living hand-to-mouth in the Russian underground, the Bolsheviks were now flush, and they acted like it. After arriving at Finland Station, Lenin moved into the Kshesinskaya Mansion, one of the grandest residences in the city, built in art nouveau style in 1904–1906 for Mathilde Kshesinskaya—the most famous ballerina in Russia, mistress to Tsar Nicholas II and two Romanov grand dukes after him. The mansion, sited strategically opposite the Peter and Paul Fortress, was transformed, after Lenin's arrival, from an elegant ballerina's home into a fortified military compound, the nerve center of Bolshevism. (Renamed the Museum of the Revolution in Soviet times, it is today the Museum of Political History.)

Kshesinskaya's was a beehive of activity, hosting meetings of the party's Central Committee, the editorial offices of *Pravda* and *Soldatskaia Pravda*, and the headquarters of the Bolshevik "military organization," which sent commissars to convert army units to the antiwar cause. Downstairs there was an accounting office, along with "expensive printing equipment" later discovered by Nikitin's men, which churned out identity cards and automobile passes for trusted operatives and soldiers. Pamphlets, and propaganda littered the hallways; couriers scurried to and fro, carrying out instructions.[24]

At street level, the scene was even more striking. Kshesinskaya's was soon the meeting place for demonstrators from all over the city, who came for the excitement—and the protest signs. The Bolshevik skill for propaganda was real, and it was given a further shot in the arm by Lenin's no-holds-barred political program. Whereas Mensheviks and SRs in the Soviet had agreed, reluctantly, to collaborate in restoring discipline to the armies (as with Order No. 2), the Bolsheviks churned out placards proclaiming simply, "Down with the government." According to some witnesses, after Lenin's arrival, Bolshevik placards appeared stating: "The Germans are our brothers."[25]

With German armies on Russian soil, such slogans were explosive, if not treasonous. Rumors were already swirling that Lenin was a German agent. In such circumstances, it is remarkable that anyone would hold up such placards. Here, too, new evidence offers a clue. According to the sworn deposition of a Russian Red Cross nurse named Evgeniya Shelyakhovskaya, who had just returned to Petrograd from the front, several well-dressed men (whose features she described in detail) passed out antiwar and pro-German placards in late April 1917 in front of Kshesinskaya's, handing out 10-ruble notes to anyone willing to hold them up. This was real money, akin to $500 today. These Bolshevik bagmen, according to Shelyakhovskaya, would pass out cash until their satchels were empty, at which point they would reenter Kshesinskaya's and quickly reemerge with their satchels stuffed anew with 10-ruble notes. A second witness confirmed the essentials of Shelyakhovskaya's observation under oath.[26]

Adding spice to the nurse's story, according to Colonel Nikitin, these 10-ruble notes passed out in front of Kshesinskaya's were likely counterfeits printed by the German government, which had acquired the plates for 10-tsarist-ruble notes before the war. There was a distinct marking on these counterfeit bills, on which, according to

Nikitin, "the last two figures in the serial number were faintly under-lined." Many of these "German" notes were later discovered in the possession of arrested Bolshevik agitators.[27]

Lenin, and his German sponsors, were playing for keeps. The Provisional Government, under terrible pressure from the Allies to carry out the spring offensive Russia had promised to undertake before the revolution, even while locked in a bitter struggle with the Soviet over control of the army, now had another enemy to reckon with. It would not take long for the Bolsheviks to draw blood.

9

TWILIGHT OF THE LIBERALS

Considering that its leaders had been plotting the demise of the tsarist regime for years, the Provisional Government gave off a strange whiff of amateurism. Rodzianko had made a hash of things. Guchkov, the minister of war, had scarcely done better. It had taken Guchkov the better part of ten days to sideline Rodzianko, get the army loyalty oaths in order, and begin to clean out aristocratic "deadwood" in the army by sacking six front commanders and several dozen generals. Only on March 7 was the Provisional Government formally announced to the nation, in an equivocal declaration that its task was to "convoke the Constituent Assembly within the shortest time possible" so as to resolve Russia's political future.[1]

To be fair to Guchkov and Prince Lvov, the presiding "chairman" of the new Provisional Government (a curious office harking back to the old Council of Ministers, which no longer existed), the problems they inherited were formidable. It did not help that the obstreperous Soviet had hobbled the armed forces with Order No. 1 and assumed veto power over the Provisional Government, which prompted the latter to concede Taurida and decamp to the Mariinsky Palace. This awkward arrangement is usually called *dvoevlastie* (dual authority). But the Lvov government also had to reckon with Rodzianko, who continued to speak out publicly (and issue communiqués) as president of the now-defunct State Duma. As the only nationally elected body in Russia until the convening of the Constituent Assembly, the Duma retained a residual, ghostlike prestige, ignored in Petrograd but not in the country at large, where Rodzianko and the Duma had far greater name recognition than Lvov, the Provisional Government, or the Ispolkom (Executive Committee of the Soviet).*

For all these reasons, the Provisional Government was hesitant to tackle really important issues, such as land reform, which was simply shunted forward to the Constituent Assembly. Instead the ministers concentrated their energy on measures most liberals and socialists agreed on, such as a general amnesty for political prisoners from the old regime (March 7), the abolition of the death penalty (March 12), a ban on flogging in prisons (March 17), and an end to the detested tsarist punishment of deportation to Siberia (April 26). More consequentially, the Provisional Government proclaimed equal rights and legal status for all nationalities and religions on March 20, putting paid to the Jewish Pale of Settlement. A declaration granting unlimited freedom of the press and public assembly soon followed, making Russia, temporarily at least—as Kerensky later boasted—"the freest country in the world."[2]

Foreign policy was a tougher nut to crack. In peacetime, this might not have been the case. But in 1917, the question of war aims superseded all others. For what or for whom, after all, were the 7 million men currently mobilized on fronts stretching from the Baltic to the Black Sea, Anatolia and Persia, fighting, bleeding, and dying for?

On this critical question, the divide between the Provisional Government and the Soviet was fundamental. As Pavel Milyukov had made clear in his incendiary Duma speech of November 1916, Russia's liberals were patriots who objected to the tsarist regime not because it was fighting an unjust war, but because it was not committed fervently enough to winning it. In a sense, Russia's liberals had "owned" the war ever since July 1914, when they and their champions on the Council of Ministers (Krivoshein and Sazonov) had pushed a reluctant Tsar Nicholas II into mobilizing. Even Kerensky, though further left than the liberals on domestic issues, had been a tub-thumper on

*It is often asserted that the Provisional Government derived its authority from the Duma, but this is far from the truth. By the time it was formed on March 7, any organic connection to the Fourth Duma had been lost; indeed the fact that Rodzianko had been excluded was a repudiation of the Duma. Moreover several ministers, including the finance minister, M. I. Tereshchenko, were not even Duma deputies.

the war, bashing the traitors in high places alleged to be hindering the war effort. By contrast, for the Mensheviks who dominated the Soviet, and even for left-leaning Socialist Revolutionaries (SR) less patriotic than Kerensky, the legitimacy of Russia's war was an open question, even if few sympathized openly with Lenin's extreme anti-war position. Many of the most radical members of the Soviet had just been amnestied from tsarist prisons, and they disdained anything associated with the regime that had incarcerated them—such as "imperialist" war aims negotiated by the tsar's diplomats.

In this tense standoff, the liberals were the first to strike. In his new capacity as foreign minister, Milyukov issued a statement on March 5, 1917, that the Provisional Government would "remain mindful of the international engagements entered into by the fallen regime, and will honor Russia's word." Intended to reassure Britain and France (this was before the United States entered the war) that Russia was still game for her spring offensives, Milyukov's declaration was a shot across the bow of the Soviet. Although it took over a week for the fractious deputies to agree on their own foreign policy statement, the resulting "Call by the Petrograd Soviet to the Peoples of the World," published in *Izvestiya* on March 14, disowned Milyukov entirely. In this extraordinary declaration, the Soviet promised that Russian "workers and soldiers" would "resist the policy of conquest of its ruling classes"—that is, Milyukov's—and called upon their brethren in the other belligerent countries of Europe to "start a decisive struggle against the grasping ambitions of [their] governments." In a supplemental declaration published on March 18, the Soviet denounced "the secret diplomacy of Nicholas Romanov" and demanded that the new government "in the field of foreign policy, cut loose completely from the traditions of Izvolsky and Stürmer."[3]

At the center of the controversy stood the "secret treaties" negotiated between Russia, Britain, and France, above all the Sazonov-Sykes-Picot Agreement of 1916 dividing up the Ottoman Empire. While its terms remained secret, rumors were running hot. In December 1916, the then chairman of the Council of Ministers, A. F. Trepov, to quiet a mob of Duma hecklers, had revealed publicly that Britain and France had promised Russia Constantinople and the Ottoman Straits. Kerensky had rifled through the Foreign Ministry archives in early March for copies of these treaties, and reportedly ordered diplomats to "Hide them!" Suspecting that the Provisional Government was indeed hiding something, Bolshevik factory committees in Petrograd issued a series of resolutions demanding the publication of all wartime treaties entered into by the tsar. Ispolkom, for its part, had been perfectly clear in its repudiation of "secret diplomacy."[4]

The Bolsheviks were not wrong to be suspicious. Plans were under way at Stavka and the Admiralty for an amphibious strike at the Bosphorus in summer 1917. These plans were reaffirmed in late February, as revolution tore through Petrograd, precisely to "calm public opinion in Russia." In the Russian Foreign Ministry, the issue was important enough that Russian diplomats cajoled out of the French government, on February 27 (the very day the tsarist government lost control of Petrograd), a solemn reaffirmation of its pledge to "settl[e] at the end of the present war the question of Constantinople and the Straits in conformance with the age-old vows of Russia." All through March, even as the Baltic and (on a much smaller scale) Black Sea Fleets erupted in mutiny, preparations continued at the Admiralty for the Bosphorus operation, to be spearheaded by Kolchak's Tsargradsky Regiment. At the War Ministry, Guchkov put his old War Industries Committee (WIC) business contacts to use, procuring coal colliers and merchant vessels for Kolchak's planned descent on the Bosphorus. Meanwhile, Milyukov gave a hint of his own priorities when he told a Kadet friend, in confidence, that "it would be absurd and criminal to renounce the biggest prize of the war [e.g., Constantinople and the straits] . . . in the name of some humanitarian and cosmopolitan idea of international socialism."[5]

On March 22, 1917, the shadowy political struggle burst into the open when Milyukov outlined Russia's war aims in a press conference (though respecting secrecy in regard to those of her allies). With the United States poised to enter the war on Wilsonian principles, Milyukov took pains to justify Russia's territorial claims in liberal-nationalist terms. Thus he proposed that Russia would conquer Habsburg territory so as to create "an independent Czecho-Slovakian state" and bring about "the union of the Ukrainian people of the Austrian regions with the population of our own Ukrainian regions." The "question of Constantinople and the Straits," Milyukov stated forthrightly (though dubiously),

> cannot be considered as involving the interests of the Turkish nation, because the Turkish nation, in spite of five hundred years' domination, has not spread its roots deeply . . . the Turks remain an alien element there, resting exclusively on the right of the conqueror, the right of the strongest. The transfer of the Straits to us would in no way contradict the principles advanced by Woodrow Wilson . . . [6]

As if to emphasize Milyukov's point, even as he was speaking to the press in Petrograd on March 22, a Russian naval squadron arrived at the mouth of the Bosphorus, comprised of six destroyers, two battle cruisers, and three seaplane carriers. Although news of this Bosphorus reconnaissance probe was little reported in the Allied capitals, it was real: there were genuine dogfights in the air, as the Germans and Turks scrambled seaplanes into action to send Russian pilots back to their carriers before they could surveil the city's defenses. Even as a firestorm of controversy engulfed Petrograd over Milyukov's statement, on the very next day (March 23), the diplomatic liaison at Russian military headquarters reported to Milyukov that two divisions would be ready to sail for the Bosphorus by mid-May, and hopefully a third later that summer. More even than the Bolsheviks and other suspicious socialists knew, Milyukov was dead serious about conquering Constantinople.[7]

The leaders of the Soviet were just as dead set on stopping him. Under ferocious pressure from Ispolkom, which threatened to withhold support for a "Liberty Loan" he wanted to float to patriotic Russian bond buyers, Milyukov was forced to issue a revised "declaration of war aims" on March 27, which stated, "The purpose of free Russia is not domination over other nations, or the seizure of their national possessions or forcible occupation of foreign territories, but the establishment of stable peace on the basis of self-determination of peoples." But he also pledged that Russia would observe "all obligations assumed towards our Allies." In an interview with the *Manchester Guardian*, Milyukov hinted that Russia might be willing to renounce her claim on Constantinople as long as she retained "the right to close the Straits to foreign warships," which was "not possible unless she possesses the Straits and fortifies them." Milyukov's equivocations did not really satisfy his socialist critics, but they put the issue on ice—for now.[8]

Into this delicately poised struggle over the soul of Russian foreign policy, Lenin, after arriving on April 3, intervened, with the subtlety of a sledgehammer. Trying to square the circle of liberal imperialism, Milyukov announced, while visiting Moscow on April 11, that Russia remained committed to "the reunification of Armenia" (that is, the ongoing carving-up of Ottoman Asia Minor) and "the gratification of the national aspirations of the Austrian Slavs" (i.e., the Russian conquest of Habsburg Galicia). Lenin published this statement in *Pravda* and exhorted all Russian "comrades, workers and soldiers" to "read this statement of Milyukov at all your meetings! Make it understood that you do not wish to die for the sake of secret conventions concluded by Tsar Nicholas II, and which are still sacred to Milyukov!"[9]

Adding force to Lenin's critique was the return of exiled SR leader Viktor Chernov, who arrived in Petrograd on April 8, just five days after Lenin did. Although Chernov was no "defeatist" in the Zimmerwald Left sense, his contempt for imperialist war aims was just as keen. Chernov, railing against the "saturnalia of predatory appetites" expressed in the "secret treaties," called for Milyukov's immediate resignation.[10]

Chernov's return also shamed Kerensky into taking a stronger position against the liberal imperialists. Although Kerensky had emerged as a popular tribune of the revolution, Chernov was still his senior in the Socialist Revolutionary Party, and he had the "purist" prestige of the exile that Lenin enjoyed with the Bolsheviks. On April 13, Kerensky pressured Milyukov into handing the March 27 statement, now referred to popularly (if inaccurately) as the "peace without annexations" declaration, to Entente diplomats, in effect repudiating his earlier statement of March 5. Kerensky did allow Milyukov to insert an addendum reaffirming Russia's intention to stay in the war and "fully to carry out [her] obligations" to her allies. It is not clear whether Kerensky, in arranging this compromise, meant to save Milyukov or destroy him. On the morning of April 20,

1917, Milyukov's "notes to the allies" were published in the Petrograd newspapers.[11]

The news struck Soviet leaders like a thunderclap. Milyukov's re-affirmation of Russia's obligations to her allies, even if couched in diplomatic boilerplate, seemed like a repudiation of everything revolutionaries had fought for. Before the Soviet had crafted a response, armed protestors had already taken to the streets, in an eerie replay of the February Revolution. Fortunately for the members of Ispolkom at Taurida, the departure of the Provisional Government left them out of the line of fire as a menacing procession of soldiers, led by a radicalized Guards officer named Theodore Linde, headed for Mariinsky Square instead. It was Linde's misfortune that the government was not at Mariinsky Palace that day: to accommodate an ailing Guchkov, the ministers had gathered at the War Ministry (on Palace Square) instead. Taking advantage of this stroke of luck, the popular general Lavr Kornilov, who Guchkov had recently appointed as commander of the Petrograd military district, requested permission to disperse the burgeoning mutiny. In a momentous intervention, Kerensky—who, by authorizing Milyukov's note, bore some responsibility for the street disorders—refused to authorize the use of force. His decision was backed by the rest of the cabinet.[12]

With Kornilov and loyal troops kept under leash, the field was clear for action. After denouncing the Provisional Government as "thoroughly imperialist," Lenin authorized the issuance of placards not merely denouncing Milyukov, but demanding the overthrow of the government. Placards were printed up at Kshesinskaya's reading, "All power to the Soviets!" and "Down with the Provisional Government!" By daybreak on April 21, more radical slogans began to appear, such as "Down with the minister-capitalists" (e.g., Milyukov and Guchkov), "Death to the bourgeois," "Down with the war," and "Against the offensive." According to Golder, on Nevsky Prospekt there were many cries of "Kill Milyukov." N. I. Podvoisky, head of the Bolshevik Military Organization (which also operated out of Kshesinskaya's), summoned armed sailors from Kronstadt to the city. The stage was set for a Bolshevik putsch.[13]

Although the Bolsheviks later disavowed any intention of overthrowing the government in April 1917, the evidence we have strongly suggests the opposite. Even before the news broke about the "Milyukov note," Lenin (on April 18) had published a denunciation of the Provisional Government in *Pravda*, stating clearly the Bolshevik aim of "all the state power passing into the hands of the Soviets of Workers' and Soldiers' Deputies." Bolshevik-printed placards expressly advocated this. Podvoisky's summoning of Kronstadt sailors, already notorious for their love of brawling, demonstrates unmistakably violent intent. Shelyakhovskaya, the Red Cross nurse who witnessed bagmen passing out 10-ruble notes to protestors in front of Kshesinskaya's, asked one armed demonstrator what he was up to. She was told, "we are going to unleash a Bartholomew's night [massacre], we're going to cut up the bourgeois and the Ministers." On the afternoon of April 21, a column of armed Bolsheviks proceeding down Nevsky Prospekt ran into a counterdemonstration of loyalists chanting, "Long live the Provisional Government." When the column approached the Kazan Cathedral, shots were fired (to this day it is unknown by whom) and three people were killed before the loyalists finally beat off the Bolsheviks. In Moscow, similar scenes transpired on April 21, until government forces succeeded in winning back the streets.[14]

Once the failure of the putsch (if that is what it was) had become clear, the Bolshevik Central Committee disowned further agitation on April 22. Lenin stayed out of public sight, uncertain, as he put it in his own postmortem, "whether at that anxious moment the mass had shifted strongly to our side." The progovernment demonstrators had few doubts who was responsible, as their banners read "Down with Lenin!"[15]

Whatever his real intentions, Lenin made his position on the war clear during the April days, a position that went well beyond the mere distancing from imperialist war aims favored by Chernov, the Soviet, and the initial soldier-protestors (Linde, for example, appears to have been a conditionally prowar patriot of sorts). In a "draft resolution on the war" written on April 20 or 21, Lenin spoke approvingly of fraternization at the front. "By starting to fraternize," he wrote, "the Russian and German soldiers, the proletarians and peasants of both countries dressed in soldiers' uniforms, have proved to the whole world that intuitively the classes oppressed by the capitalists have discovered the right road to the cessation of the butchery of peoples." Among the placards held by Bolshevik agitators during the April Days were many reading, "The Germans are our brothers."[16]

Whether the riots amounted to a putsch or a mere "probe," they posed a serious challenge to the Lvov cabinet. It did not pass the test. On April 20, the ministers failed to give Kornilov the authorization he needed show the Bolsheviks—and the Soviet—that street rioting would no longer be tolerated, and then failed to issue so much as a peep to defend Milyukov against the mob. On April 21, Kornilov tried to take matters into his own hands, issuing orders to bring loyal troops into the city center, only to have his instructions expressly countermanded by the Soviet. The members of Ispolkom, who had only the day before denounced Milyukov's note ("revolutionary democracy will not permit the spilling of blood for . . . aggressive objectives"), repudiated the Bolsheviks, too, banning public meetings for forty-eight hours and denouncing as "a traitor to the revolution anyone who called for armed demonstrations or fired a shot even in the air."

Declaring neutrality in the political war between the liberals and the Bolsheviks, Ispolkom also asserted its own control over Kornilov and the Petrograd army garrison in a kind of addendum to Order No. 1. "Every order concerning the appearance of military units on the streets," an Ispolkom resolution dated April 21 stated, "must be issued on the blank of the Executive Committee, bear its seal and the signatures of at least two members of [Ispolkom]." Kornilov, disgusted, asked to be relieved of his command. For thus demonstrating his loyalty, however reluctantly, Kornilov was allowed to take over the Eighth Army in Galicia, an active command in the still-planned spring offensive.[17]

For the liberal imperialists in the Provisional Government, there was no such consolation prize. For all they had done to bring about the downfall of the old regime, the Kadet and Octobrist plotters had shown little stomach for the exercise of power. Milyukov, at least, had *tried* to formulate a foreign policy consistent with liberal, pan-Slavist principles, Russia's national interests, and her obligations to her wartime allies, only to be let down by Kerensky on April 20. Guchkov and Milyukov, whose policies had been repudiated by the Soviet, both wanted to resign, except that no one wanted to take their place.

Only after Kerensky threatened to resign himself did the socialists at Ispolkom finally vote, on May 1, 1917, to allow members of the Soviet to enter the cabinet and replace them. Chernov took over the Agriculture Ministry, and the prowar (but anti-imperialist) Georgian Menshevik leader Irakli Tsereteli became minister of post and telegraphs. The Foreign Ministry was entrusted to Tereshchenko, previously finance minister, who was a Kadet but closer to Kerensky's position on the war than to Milyukov's. Tereshchenko was also, significantly, a Freemason like Kerensky. The more important appointment was that of Kerensky himself, who took over the war and naval ministerial portfolios, while turning over the Ministry of Justice to his SR colleague Pavel Pereverzev. Lvov, a basically harmless front man, was kept on as chairman as a sop to the liberals. In a funereal coda, Milyukov and Guchkov were invited to address a rump session of the Duma in Taurida Palace. Rodzianko thanked them for their service on behalf of his ghost parliament, the deputies of which gave Milyukov a standing ovation.[18]

The new cabinet tried gamely to formulate war aims acceptable to the Soviet, vowing to "democratize the army" and denouncing imperialist war aims as outmoded. Tiptoeing gingerly around the Ottoman Straits issue, Kerensky and Tereshchenko tried, in a declaration on May 15, to reconcile Sazonov-Sykes-Picot with Ispolkom's "peace without annexations" principle. Showing that the ghosts of imperialism were not easily buried, this declaration referred to "provinces of Asiatic Turkey taken by right of war," then apologetically proposed that the formerly Ottoman provinces of Van, Bitlis, and Erzurum would remain "forever Armenian"—though administered by Russian officials. Here was a hot mess of contradictions that would be easy for Lenin to tear apart as sole authentic voice of opposition now that Chernov had joined the government.[19]

The April Days exposed the stubborn commitment of Russia's liberals to imperialist war aims that no longer enjoyed broad support— if, indeed, they ever had. It was now Kerensky's turn to save Russia's war effort against the Central Powers, or what was left of it.

10

KERENSKY'S MOMENT

Ll across Russia in spring 1917, furious and fractious debates were conducted over the war and whether to continue fighting it, over war aims and their meaning, and over Lenin and the Bolsheviks. The spread of soviets (councils) through the army and navy was remarkable and real, although we must be cautious in generalization, as there were dramatic differences from one front to another, or among different branches of service and units on individual fronts. In a letter sent to Chairman Lvov from Stavka on March 14, General Alekseev tried to summarize early reports "from the commanders in chief of the fronts and the commanders of the Caucasian Army and the Baltic and Black Fleets regarding the impression made on the troops by the change of the regime and by recent events." Far from celebrating the revolution, Alekseev said, most soldiers on the northern front had reacted to news reports with "calm and composure," and that many men "showed sadness and regret for the abdication of Emperor Nicholas II." In many other units, Alekseev noted, "Soldiers do not understand the [abdication] manifestos and cannot as yet find their way among the events that have occurred."[1]

The convening of soviets did not necessarily correlate with mutinous sentiment. In some units, men were heard demanding that a new tsar be elected as soon as possible, or demanding that a vote be held on whether Russia should really be a republic. In others, democracy brought anti-Semitic resentments into the open, as soldiers demanded that Jews no longer be allowed to be officers, or said things far nastier than this. Officers, too, were often allowed to speak out in the soviets, and many of them were unhappy about the course the revolution was taking, especially after the promulgation of Order No. 1, which had stripped them of much of their disciplinary authority over their men. In Russian First Army, on the western front facing the Germans, the prevailing view in the officer corps was that the Petrograd Soviet was "driving the country to anarchy," and that men now lived better than did officers, who were under constant threat of rhetorical abuse or lynching.[2]

Tensions were heightened still further in April by the decision of the Soviet's Executive Committee, Ispolkom, to send political "commissars" to the front. Although formally tasked with doing "everything in their power to remove the friction between officers and soldiers," most commissars, predictably, took the side of the men on disciplinary matters. After General Alekseev, hoping to counter the influence of Ispolkom, requested that the Provisional Government send its own "commissars," Defense Minister Guchkov began sending his own emissaries to the front, who, equally predictably, were lustily welcomed by the officers. In this way the uncomfortable balancing act of dvoevlastie (dual authority) was extended to the army.[3]

The eclipse of the liberals in May threatened to tip the balance at the front, too. In his first act as minister of war, Kerensky issued Order No. 8 on May 8, which reaffirmed the principles of Order No. 1 regarding soldiers' rights to express opinions and to respectful treatment from their officers, the abolition of mandatory saluting, freedom of movement on shore for off-duty sailors, and so on. Recognizing the need to restore at least some authority to the officers, Kerensky did stipulate (although not until Article 14) that, while "no serviceman may be subjected to punishment or penalty without trial" and no "degrading" corporal punishments would be allowed, a Russian officer still had "the right on his own responsibility to take all measures, down to applying armed force inclusive, against his subordinates who fail to carry out his orders." Likewise, the right to appoint or dismiss officers was reserved to commanders, not to the men voting in soviets. In this way Kerensky hoped to give officers just enough authority to restore discipline to the armies, while still requiring them to respect the dignity of serving men.[4]

Instead he created more confusion. It was hard enough already to figure out the chain of command in an army undergoing severe churn in the officer corps. Not fully trusting even the liberal-minded officers promoted by Guchkov, Kerensky accelerated the purges, dismissing another seven army commanders, five front commanders, twenty-six corps commanders, and sixty-nine division commanders—not to mention Alekseev himself, replaced as commander in chief by General Alexei Brusilov on May 22. Cleaning house at the top should have reinforced Kerensky's position in the army—except that Brusilov was seen more as Rodzianko's man than his own, such that many officers interpreted the move, confusingly, as a rehabilitation of the Duma president.[5]

The spread of Lenin's defeatist propaganda to the front further complicated Kerensky's task. In the northern army, Bolshevik antiwar placards were first seen on April 18 (May 1), just two days before the putsch in Petrograd (although this was a coincidence: the pretext for distribution that day was the "Western" May Day). Ominously, the arrival of Bolshevik defeatist propaganda from Petrograd coincided with the appearance of new Russian-language pamphlets urging fraternization, tossed over from German trenches. But the Bolshevik agitprop offensive at the front fizzled out just as badly as the simultaneous putsch in Petrograd, producing little more than a brief uptick in fraternization episodes and several boisterous May Day celebrations.[6]

More serious was the arrival at the front of mysterious "agitators" who seemed to have been authorized by neither the Provisional Government nor the Soviet. Only a few of these "comrades" openly avowed their Bolshevik sympathies, but the defeatist tone of their speeches often gave the game away. Military censors began to hear the name "Lenin" more and more often in May 1917, not always in approving terms, but frequently enough to be of political significance. Even as the pace of desertions slowed down after a wave in March and April, and episodes of fraternization in the northern army declined after briefly spiking on May Day, a more generalized paranoia began to overwhelm the officer corps. On May 12, a censor's report noted, "Masses of German spies and provocateurs are [at work] in the army." The April Days showdown over Milyukov's war aims, the censor noted, supplied a new line of argument for these agitators, who now demanded why men were being asked to "give their lives for England or France."[7]

Raising the stakes on the southwestern front was the fact that, in accordance with the inter-Allied agreements made prior to the February Revolution, Russia was expected to mount a major offensive in Galicia. While many of Russia's top admirals, generals, and now-retired politicians would have preferred a diversionary strike against the Bosphorus to rally the nation, the British and especially the French governments were adamant that only an attack on the European fronts would help. "In accordance with the decisions [at] Chantilly," France's commander in chief, General Robert Nivelle, wrote Alekseev in March, "I request the Russian army to render the greatest possible assistance in the operations that have already been begun by the Anglo-French armies." Compounding the diplomatic pressure on Kerensky, vast quantities of war matériel from Britain were pouring into Murmansk—paid for in Russian gold, which had been shipped to England. On the western front in France, following the failure of Nivelle's own offensive on the Aisnes sector, launched in mid-April 1917, the French armies began to crumble in the so-called Chemin des Dames mutinies, when soldiers refused orders to attack German lines (although most insisted they would still defend their own trenches). In a painful coincidence, the French mutinies began on April 20/May 3, the very day the Bolshevik putsch began in Petrograd. With France in danger of falling apart against the Germans, it is hard not to sympathize with Kerensky's acute dilemma, as he sought to balance Russia's own army morale problems against the strategic-moral imperative to do *something* to relieve the pressure on the western front.[8]

Kerensky was up for the challenge. The appointment of Brusilov on May 22 was a declaration of intent. Brusilov had been advocating for a renewed offensive all spring, only to run into fierce opposition from Alekseev, who had little faith in the capacity of the Russian armies for offensive action. On May 7, Alekseev had told a congress of officers at Stavka that "Russia is perishing; she is on the brink of the abyss; another push or two, and she will go over completely." On

May 18, Alekseev poured cold water on offensive plans in a letter to his successor. Brusilov and Kerensky had come up with the idea of sending "shock battalions composed of volunteers" to spearhead the Galician attack. "I do not share your hopes regarding the benefits of the projected measure," Alekseev wrote. Any new volunteer formations, he reminded Brusilov, "though perhaps full of enthusiasm, have to be indoctrinated and trained." All in all, Alekseev concluded by way of resigning his command, there was little hope of "general salvation."[9]

Brusilov, by contrast, was full of fight. Where Alekseev had accepted the revolution with reluctance and struggled to contain its impact at the front, Brusilov saw the eclipse of the liberals as a chance to build a new army imbued with revolutionary energy. Rather than oppose the influx of Soviet commissars, Brusilov welcomed them, so long as they were preaching a patriotic message. "The measures intended to create shock groups at the front of the armies," he reported to Kerensky on May 20, "are being carried on by me on a large scale and in close contact with the Front Congress of the armies' delegates; I have reason to count upon success." In accordance with Kerensky's wishes, Brusilov also vowed to recruit and assemble "special revolutionary shock battalions in the rear." With reinforcements expected to arrive shortly from Kolchak's Black Sea Division in Odessa, and other "volunteers from the Black Sea Fleet," Brusilov promised Kerensky that he would muster twelve fresh new battalions at the front.[10]

It was logical that Brusilov looked to the Ottoman fronts as a patriotic reserve. In Tiflis, headquarters of the Caucasian army that had dealt Turkey near-death blows in 1916, mutinous sentiment was virtually nonexistent. "The membership of the soldiers' committees," the new commander, Nikolai Yudenich, reported, was resolved "to conduct the war to a victorious end." In the Black Sea Fleet, morale was strong. "Of course there are extremists here as well," a British liaison officer reported from Sevastopol on April 29, 1917, "but the general feeling is that the war must be pushed on until the military power of the Central Powers is crushed." In mid-May, the sailors' soviet in Sevastopol debated whether to invite Lenin to town. The verdict was 342 to 20 against.[11]

To streamline the "commissar" system, Kerensky got Ispolkom to agree that, while the Soviet would supply candidates, the War Ministry (that is, Kerensky) would approve them, making it harder for the Bolsheviks to infect the frontline armies. But he still had to come up with his own positive message to rally the troops. Kerensky told a visiting delegation of Americans on May 1 that, while he could promise that "Russia will not sign [a] separate peace," he would still "endeavor to persuade the allies to revise war aims." Any peace treaty, he insisted, "must be based on humanity. New slogan: Freedom & Peace. Alsace-Lorraine, Belgium, Armenia will be regarded as conquered territory and each people will decide for itself."[12]

To preach this curious new gospel, Kerensky set off for a barn-storming tour of the front himself on May 12. One eyewitness compared Kerensky's passionate oratory to "a volcano hurling forth sheaves of all-consuming fire." Another observed, "Soldiers ran for miles after his motor car, trying to shake his hand or kiss the hem of his garment." At a soldiers' congress on the southwestern front at Kamenets-Podolsk, Kerensky asked the men whether they were willing to lay down their lives for the revolution. The answer came back: "We swear it! We will die!" Kerensky turned to Brusilov and told him, "Mr. Commander, set your mind at ease. These men will go wherever you command." Brusilov began touring with Kerensky, introducing the war minister as an "old revolutionary and tested fighter for the ideals of freedom, equality, and brotherhood." Brusilov would then ask the men, "Can I promise the War Minister that you will do your duty to the end, and if I order you to attack, will you attack?" Few dared say no.[13]

Kerensky's influence on the troops, however, dissipated almost as soon as he left the scene—and sometimes even beforehand. At Kamenets-Podolsk, a Bolshevik ensign from the Eleventh Army soviet, N. V. Krylenko, mounted the stage after Kerensky to inform the men about Lenin's critique of the "imperialist war." Although Krylenko's own resolution against the planned offensive was voted down 554 to 38, he had held his own against Kerensky and won respect for his courage, encouraging others to speak out, too. After one of Kerensky's speeches on the Galician front, a "simple soldier" raised his hand and asked, "What good are land and freedom to me if I'm dead?"[14]*

Not all area commanders were impressed with Kerensky. At Vorobin, on the northern edge of Galicia in "White Russia," where a new Special Army faced the Germans, General P. N. Baluev reported on May 18, that Kerensky had given a nice speech to the men that morning, although he doubted it would help. "If we do not restore discipline soon," Baluev warned Brusilov, "we will perish, and the whole world will despise not only us, but the idea of socialism." As if to prove his point, four of Baluev's soldiers deserted that afternoon, and another three the next day.[15]

Compounding the difficulty of Kerensky's task was the passivity of the enemy after a series of attacks along the Stokhod River in Galicia in March and April. The constant pressure in this sector had improved morale. On April 20, the day of the Bolshevik putsch in Petrograd, Russian gunners downed a German warplane near Vorobin, although not before the pilot dropped bombs, killing one Russian soldier and wounding two civilians, both women. Three days later, German artillery killed five and wounded thirty-two. Under this kind of fire, men tended to bond together against the enemy.[16]

For this very reason, the Germans chose to stand down in Galicia in May 1917. As Parvus had advised the German minister in Copenhagen shortly before Lenin returned to Russia, Germany should abstain from major offensives, so as to forestall the recovery of a Russian patriotic mood "for the defense of liberties now achieved." Instead the Germans should leave Lenin alone to do his worst, plunging the Russian war effort into "anarchy." Although it took a few weeks for Parvus's advice to reach General Ludendorff at the German high command and, through him, German front commanders on the eastern front, reach them it did. After the bombing at Vorobin on April 20, signs of enemy activity on the Stokhod River virtually ceased. As if to prove Parvus's point, desertions picked up

---

*According to Kerensky's later version of the episode, he put shame into this muzhik by releasing him from duty on the grounds that "we do not need cowards in the Russian Army," whereupon the soldier recanted and "turned into a model soldier." It is an inspiring tale, though unlikely to be entirely true.

again in May and early June, once the front was quiet and Russians had less obvious reason to fight on.[17]

From the perspective of Russian commanders, it was a terrible dilemma. Their men fought hard and defended their positions whenever the enemy attacked. Just as at Chemin des Dames in France, it was not defensive warfare the men objected to, but fruitless offensives into no-man's-land. But what if the enemy did *not* attack, for days, weeks, months on end? Desertions, running at one or two per day in most units, had not yet reached critical mass in Galicia. But the steady drip-drip effect might sunder fighting morale, were the men infected with defeatist propaganda from Petrograd.

The solution favored by Kerensky and Brusilov was simple: attack! There would have been little point to Kerensky's barnstorming tour of the front, after all, if the upshot was merely to tell the men to sit in their trenches and wait for the enemy to strike. Before Kerensky appointed him commander in chief, Brusilov had stated defiantly, after a tour of the southwestern front: "The army has its own opinion, and the opinion of Petrograd as to its state or morale cannot resolve the question . . . its real force is here, in the theater of war, and not in the rear." His conclusion, after canvassing both officers and men, was simple: "The armies wish to and can attack." If he was Rodzianko's man before, Brusilov was Kerensky's man now. It was their time to shine, or fail trying.

Brusilov's original plan was to launch the Galician offensive on June 10, just two weeks after Kerensky had finished his frontline tour. In view of the dissipation of the patriotic mood after he left the scene, this may have been several weeks too late. The attack was postponed further still by the convening of the first All-Russian Congress of Soviets in Petrograd, which body warned Kerensky not to strike before it gave the go-ahead, as it did (vaguely, reluctantly) on June 12. This put the launch back until June 16. Because Kerensky's Galician tour generated considerable publicity, its effect was akin to telegraphing a punch to the enemy—three weeks before the punch was made.[18]

In a sense, the offensive came two *months* too late. Nivelle's offensive in France, with which Russia's own was to be coordinated, had ground to a halt by late April (Russian style), after the Chemin des

Dames mutinies. May had seen only a few desultory British attacks in Flanders that had fizzled away long before the Russians were ready for their own offensive. The strategic upshot was clear. By mid-May 1917, intelligence reaching Stavka confirmed that no more German troop trains were heading west.[19]

Making the delay still more damaging, it was during the final six-day postponement in June that the first Bolshevik agitators from Petrograd reached the Galician front (this was not a coincidence: the discussion of the offensive in the All-Russian Congress of Soviets gave these agitators cause). When forty-five infantry companies (about 13,000 men) arrived in Vorobin in June 1917, two thirds of them fresh from training barracks in Petrograd, these were accompanied by, in the words of the commander of the First Guard Corps, Lieutenant General Ilkevich, "a not insignificant number of Bolshevik agitators, who carried out, sometimes openly, sometimes discreetly, propaganda pushing the idea of the illegitimacy of the Provisional Government, the War Minister [Kerensky], the necessity of ending the war and convening a peace conference, the need to distrust officers, and so on." According to Ilkevich, morale in Second Division had cracked, and First Division had been infected, too. On June 14, a mass meeting had been called, attended by twelve thousand guardsmen, which passed a "no-confidence" resolution in the Provisional Government and condemned the planned offensive as "contrary to the interests of the Revolution." "We are carrying on an intense struggle against these agitators," Ilkevich informed Brusilov on June 15—the day before the offensive was to begin!—"but it is extraordinarily difficult. It is of the utmost importance that experienced orators from competent institutions come to visit the front and stay on, ideally from the Soviet of Workers' and Soldiers' Deputies in Petrograd."[20]

The arrival of Bolshevik agitators in Galicia was the worst possible news for Stavka. Already officers were grumbling about "trench Bolshevism," a lack of fighting spirit some referred to, more sourly, as *shkurnyi bol'shevizm* (literally "skin Bolshevism," meaning that men feared for their skins). Then there were active-duty "front Bolsheviks" like Ensign Krylenko. But even Krylenko had been guarded in his critique of the war, stating that he would tell his men to obey orders to attack so long as these orders were given legitimacy by a democratic majority in the Soviet.

Bolshevik activists from Petrograd, by contrast, brought Lenin's anti-war message to the front in unvarnished purity, bypassing the need for such newspapers as *Soldatskaia Pravda* and *Okopnaia Pravda*, which still only reached garrisons near printing presses in Petrograd, Moscow, and Kiev. In Riga, General Radko-Dimitriev, commander of Twelfth Army, complained of the "strengthened agitation of the Bolsheviks, who have woven themselves into a firm nest." Every new recruit arriving from Petrograd, Radko-Dimitriev warned, needed to be vetted, as "a single agitator can set back on its heels an entire regiment with the propaganda of Bolshevik ideas." If Lenin's antiwar slogans reached Galicia, the Kerensky-Brusilov offensive would be doomed from the start.[21]

Coupled with the unfavorable strategic picture vis-à-vis the now inactive western front, news of the arrival of Bolshevik agitators in Galicia should have given Brusilov and Kerensky cause to call off, or at least postpone, the attack. As luck would have it, Kerensky was in Mogilev meeting with Brusilov on June 15, the very day Ilkevich's warning telegram arrived from the front (although it is unclear whether he or Brusilov read it this day). We do not know exactly what Kerensky and Brusilov said to each other, but we do know the result of their conversation, which was a wire from Kerensky to Lvov, confirming that the army was ready. Having received the blessing of the Provisional Government, Ispolkom, and the First All-Russian Congress of Soviets, Kerensky was not going to back down now. Russia would fight.[22]

PART III

Hostile Takeover

It is impossible to expel the main [Bolshevik] agitators [from the army], in view of the fact that they are armed.

—GENERAL BALUEV to GENERAL BRUSILOV,
June 23, 1917

II

LENIN SHOWS HIS HAND

A t dawn on June 16, 1917, Russian Seventh and Eleventh
Armies opened a furious artillery barrage along a 40-mile-
long sector of the southwestern front in Galicia. After stock-
piling shell all fall and winter, General Alexei Brusilov mounted the
most spectacular display of firepower yet seen on the eastern front.
Many Russian soldiers were themselves dazed by what one described
as a "devastating cacophony of whizzes, whines, roars, crashes, and
thuds of every conceivable kind of gun," even though it was the
enemy (mostly Austro-Hungarian IX Corps) who suffered. After a
two-day bombardment, Russian Seventh Army advanced into the
pulverized Austro-Hungarian trenches, moving the front forward
2 miles and capturing eighteen thousand prisoners and twenty-nine
guns, against minimal losses. The main thrust in the Zlota Lipa Valley
toward Lvov—where the Germans held the line—ran into heavier
resistance, with the Russians losing 15,000 casualties against 12,500
German. Nonetheless, the initial results were encouraging, prompting War Minister Alexander Kerensky to salute the "Regiments of
the 18th of June" and order victory banners sent to the front.[1]

Kerensky's congratulations were premature. The failure to beat
the Germans in the Zlota Lipa Valley bode poorly for any chance of
capturing Lvov. More damaging still, there were signs that the object
of the entire offensive—capturing "Lemberg" (as the Austrians
called Lvov)—had become controversial among the men, even (in
fact especially) in those units that had conquered enemy territory. A
soldier named Miroshkin, in Thirty-Fifth Division, after his unit had

captured some well-appointed Austrian trenches, convened a soviet and shouted, "Comrades! Whose land are we on anyhow? . . . Let's give the Austrians back their land and return to our own borders; then if they try to go further, over our dead bodies!" In a worrying sign for morale, the unit doctor pulled a copy of *Okopnaia Pravda* from his pocket and read out a Bolshevik "sermon" to the men. After a vigorous discussion, the men agreed on the resolution: "Ours we will not yield, but others' [lands] we do not seek."[2]

It was an elegant formula that made more sense than the muddled thinking of Kerensky about war aims. For why, after all, were Russian muzhiks now being asked to die for Austrian Lemberg, after the Soviet had sworn off annexations and fired liberal imperialists, such as Milyukov and Guchkov, to emphasize the point? In his call to arms, issued just before Russian guns opened fire in Galicia, Kerensky had told the men: "Warriors, Our Country is in Danger! Liberty and Revolution are threatened. The time has come for the army to do its duty." But the men were *already* doing their duty, defending their trenches against possible enemy attack. There were no signs of an impending Austro-German offensive; indeed the men were twitchy precisely because the enemy had become so passive, giving soldiers time to listen to speeches by Bolshevik agitators and debate the war. True, the truce in Galicia was an uneasy one. Two well-armed enemies were poised in close proximity, with sporadic fire across the lines keeping both sides honest. But it was a truce, of sorts. And the Russians had broken it. Why?[3]

Kerensky himself may not have known the answer. He was not, after all, a military man. In 1914, Vladimir Sukhomlinov and Nikolai Yanushkevitch had planned the conquest of Galicia to reach the Carpathian Mountains and close off the southern half of the "Polish salient," giving postwar Russia a defensible frontier. In 1916, Brusilov had reinvaded Galicia so as to break the Austro-Hungarian will to resist, only to fail on the cusp of success when German and Turkish reinforcements arrived. To the extent that the same general was stubbornly planning on doing more or less the same thing in June 1917, we might say that Kerensky had simply deferred to Brusilov on the matter.

If so, then the decision to attack represents a critical failure of imagination on Kerensky's part. In diplomatic-strategic terms, the obligation to mount a diversionary offensive to aid Russia's allies was nugatory in June 1917: those very allies had called off their own desultory attacks on the western front. Besides, a careful examination of Russia's wartime diplomacy reveals no great consistency in rendering support to her allies in times of genuine need, let alone a time of relative inactivity such as June 1917. During the Dardanelles campaign of 1915, Foreign Minister Sergei Sazonov and the generals at Stavka had pointedly refused to mount the diversionary strike at the Bosphorus that the British had requested as the price of Russia being promised Constantinople and the Ottoman Straits. Russia's crushing Erzurum offensive had been launched on January 10, 1916, literally *the day after* the last British soldier evacuated from Gallipoli. In Persia, General Baratov had not lifted a finger to help a British Indian expeditionary force of thirteen thousand men who were under Ottoman siege at Kut for five months in winter 1915–1916, despite repeated British requests for support lodged with Grand Duke Nicholas (the Brits all surrendered). Had Sazonov or the grand duke still been running things, they would have deflected Allied requests for an offensive in June 1917 on any grounds they chose—urgent necessity to strike elsewhere (such as at the Bosphorus), lack of compelling need, supply problems, signs of exhaustion or poor morale among the men. Self-excusing though such rationalizations may have been, they would have served Russian interests.

It is hard to see whose interests were served by Kerensky's offensive, targeting a region (Austrian Galicia) no longer figuring on anyone's list of Russian war aims. If the aim was to reinvigorate morale at the front—to show that Russia could still fight—then a mere demonstration might have done. The seizure of Austro-Hungarian trenches on June 18 would have proved the point: the men could have been told to dig in and hold the line for the rest of the summer. Many were already doing this, regardless of orders. On the northern end of the front, the bulk of Eleventh Army simply stopped moving forward after the first two days, as men saw little point in doing so. "In spite of the victory of 18 and 19 June," General Erdeli reported to Brusilov, "a conviction prevails that the [troops] have done their share and are not obliged to keep up an uninterrupted advance."[4]

Disregarding this and other warnings from the field, Brusilov ordered a series of follow-up attacks, each more futile than the last. In Second Division, the one infected by Bolshevik agitators in mid-June, a mutiny broke out among the grenadiers of I Guard Corps on June 20. The mutineers surrendered only after being surrounded by an entire cavalry division, two artillery batteries, and two armored cars. Significantly, only one hundred mutineers were tried in a military court; thrice as many were released and distributed to other units, which they infected in turn. After the mutineers had been cleared out, loyal guards units in Second Division renewed the offensive on June 23, only to be let down by the artillerists, who failed to knock out the barbed wire guarding the Austro-Hungarian trenches. The result was a horrible slaughter of advancing Russian infantrymen that killed off whatever fighting spirit had been regained by the expulsion of the Bolshevized mutineers.[5]

At Vorobin in White Russia, where General P. N. Baluev had sent a pointed warning about morale to Brusilov in late May after Kerensky's visit, Special Army was in turmoil. XXXIX Corps, which had been held in reserve during the first several days in case an opportunity opened up to descend on Lvov from the north, cracked even before going into action. Several divisions, General Baluev reported to Brusilov on June 23, were "entirely unwilling" to fight. In others, things broke down by unit: 216th Regiment was fully loyal; 209th and 212th, 75 percent battle-ready; and 210th, only 50 percent, with the men issuing a resolution that they would fight only on defense, and not go forward. In theory, morale could be improved by expelling Bolshevik troublemakers from the infected units. And yet, as General Baluev explained to Brusilov, "it is impossible to expel the main agitators, in view of the fact that they are armed." Just as he had vowed to do in Switzerland, Lenin had turned the armies red.[6]

The story was not everywhere this bad. After resigning his Petrograd command, General Kornilov had requested and been given a frontline command in Galicia, of Eighth Army, on the southern part of the front on the edge of the Carpathian Mountains. On June 23, Kornilov's army moved forward and broke through along nearly 20 miles of front, capturing an impressive haul of prisoners (7,000 men and 131 officers) and fifty guns. Making Kornilov's feat more impressive, his offensive was carried out in the teeth of Bolshevik agitation in four regiments of his XI Corps and two in XVI Corps. Almost uniquely in the difficult circumstances of June 1917, it seems that Kornilov knew how to motivate his men. Given the right leadership by a general they respected, Russian muzhiks could still fight bravely and well, even on the offensive.[7]

Such, at any rate, was Brusilov's hope, and he now put his faith in Kornilov, requesting that his Eighth Army swing north to relieve the beleaguered Seventh Army and agreeing to reinforce it. In the circumstances of June 1917, however, reinforcements were risky to rely on, as they often carried the infection of Bolshevism. By June 26, Kornilov's officers were complaining that "spirits . . . are now flagging, due to the agitation of Tsaritsyn replacements and 'yellow-bellies' claiming to be Bolsheviks . . . In the 15th Regiment, delegates from Petrograd infected with Bolshevism . . . passed out banners bearing the slogan 'Down with the war and the Provisional Government!'" On June 29, Twenty-third Division of XXXIII Corps tried to desert en masse, whereupon Kornilov ordered a "punitive unit consisting of machine-gunners and artillery to fire on the fleeing soldiers to bring them to a halt." Giving up on the offensive, Kornilov pulled back east of the Lomnitsa River to lick his wounds.[8]

By early July, the Kerensky-Brusilov offensive had ground to a halt. Russian losses, as of July 2, amounted to 1,200 officers and 37,500 men, a casualty rate of 14 percent. Although consistent with the horrendous standards of the war so far, it was a heavy price to pay for the tiny gains achieved. Kornilov had captured a salient south of the Dniestr, which at its greatest extent pushed out nearly 24 miles, but he had then retreated. Seventh Army, responsible for the main thrust on June 18, had achieved nothing except the exhaustion of its men. Its commander, General Selivachev, informed Brusilov on June 30 that "all corps of the army after the unsuccessful battles of June 18–20 are in the highest degree demoralized." Special Army, thrust into battle on the far right flank on June 22–23, had made a bit of progress but slowed down quickly, in part owing to Baluev's lack of faith in his men. Eleventh Army, inundated by Bolshevik agitators, had fared worst of all. Its Twentieth Finnish Rifle Regiment alone had hemorrhaged 346 deserters, who left with their arms. Twelfth Company, General Obruchev reported, "discarding all conscience and shame, not only willfully deserted the trenches on the night of June 19, but ridiculed those soldiers who remained in the trenches."[9]

Remarkably, in view of the slow-motion catastrophe unfolding in Galicia owing to the influx of Bolshevik agitators from Petrograd, Kerensky and Brusilov responded by ordering up reinforcements— from Petrograd! On June 20, the First Machine Gun Regiment, the largest unit in the Petrograd garrison with 11,340 men under arms, was ordered to send five hundred machine guns and their crews to Galicia. Billeted in Petrograd's radical Vyborg district, the regiment had been expressly targeted for months by leading Bolshevik orators, including Alexandra Kollontai, a fire-breathing antiwar activist who was one of Lenin's most trusted colleagues (like him, she had spent most of the war in exile, in Norway). Kollontai had first begun propagandizing the regiment in early April, even before Lenin's return, on the evils of the "imperialist war," openly encouraging its men to "fraternize with the Germans." Kollontai made a powerful impression on the men, several dozen of whom had joined the Bolshevik Military Organization by June 1917.[10]

Among Kollontai's converts was a young ensign named A. Y. Semashko, one of the Bolsheviks' best assets in the entire Russian army. After completing his training as a machine-gunner in March 1917, Semashko had been ordered to the front with Seventeenth Company in April, only to slip away and return to Petrograd. Technically, Semashko was a deserter, although this did not hurt his cause with other disaffected recruits. Semashko, recalled another ensign in the First Machine Gun regiment, "just kept coming back to the regiment," showing up at meetings of Ninth, Sixteenth, and Eighth Companies, in all of which he organized "Bolshevik collectives." Within days, Semashko, a Typhoid Mary of mutiny, had recruited some five hundred men into his Bolshevik collective from the First Machine Gun Regiment alone. As a deserter with no loyalty to his own regiment, Semashko was free to roam around Petrograd infecting other units, too, such as the Moscow Guard Reserves, which he invaded in mid-April. By month's end, Semashko had won over 750 men, who now encouraged their fellow soldiers to expel as a "provocateur" anyone who wished to continue the war. Before long, Semashko was running an underground army of mutineers from six different active companies (three in the First Machine Gun Regiment and three in the Moscow Guard Reserves), while maintaining regular contact with the Bolshevik Military Organization at Kshesinskaya's.[11]

What was Kerensky thinking when he ordered the First Machine Gun Regiment to the front? It was no secret that the regiment was infected with Bolshevik tendencies. Nor was the connection a secret between the Bolsheviks and their German paymasters, which was openly discussed in the city. On June 5, Frank Golder, who had just returned to Petrograd after touring the country, noted matter-of-factly in a letter sent home:

> German agents with pockets full of money have been working among the soldiers to disorganize the army and they have good success. Under the cloak of socialism they preach all damnable doctrines—incite lawlessness, plunder, strikes—until no one knows what tomorrow may bring forth. No one knows whether we have an army or a mob. Here in Petrograd we have no army but a lot of lazy, good for nothing soldiers who obey orders when it pleases them to do so.

Well aware of this, Kerensky apparently hoped, by dispatching the most infected regiment to Galicia, to rid Petrograd of troublesome agitators, perhaps even half-hoping that exposure to an active battlefront might cleanse the regiment of mutinous tendencies. As Kerensky wired Lvov from the front in early July, "I categorically insist on the decisive cessation of these traitorous demonstrations, the disarming of rebellious units, and the trial of all instigators and mutineers." Kerensky was fanning a bonfire of the mutinies in order to exorcise the army of Bolshevism.[12]

Foolhardy as it sounds, there was actually a certain political logic in awakening the Bolshevik beast. All through May and June, Russian military counterintelligence had been assembling files on Lenin's contacts with suspected German agents, helped along by a French intelligence officer, Captain Pierre Laurent, who turned over twenty-nine intercepted telegrams between Stockholm and Petrograd on June 21. On July 1, Colonel Nikitin, overseeing the investigation, met with the new commander of the Petrograd military district, General P. A. Polovtsov, who told him that "the position of the Provisional Government has become desperate; they [e.g., Kerensky] are asking when you will be able to unmask the Bolsheviks' high treason." Nikitin replied that he had "ample evidence," but he would not make a move before he was assured the army had "the troops we shall need to storm the Kshesinskaya Mansion, and the remaining thirty-odd Bolshevik strongholds scattered all over the city." Fatefully, Nikitin gave the date on which he planned to arrest twenty-eight leading Bolsheviks in Petrograd: July 7, 1917.[13]

By telegraphing his plans, Nikitin made what he later called a "grave error in judgment." The army command in Petrograd was in regular touch with city officials, the Provisional Government, and the Soviet. It could thus have been almost anyone who leaked news of the coming arrests to the Bolsheviks. Lenin may have been alerted by the placing of Evgeniya Sumenson under surveillance on June 29, or by Nikitin's visit to Siberian Bank the next day, when he learned that she had 180,000 rubles on deposit there (after withdrawing 800,000 rubles since April), or by the fact that "Kuba," presumably on a tip from Sumenson, had called off his trip from Stockholm, fearing arrest in Petrograd. However Lenin learned of the impending crackdown on his operations, he reacted swiftly, going into hiding in Finland between June 29 and July 4.[14]

The pressure to act was mounting in the Bolshevik camp. Rumors were swirling that the First Machine Gun Regiment, which had become such an asset to the party, was about to be dispersed and its men sent to the front. On June 30 and July 1, regimental representatives and agitators (including Semashko) convened a series of protest meetings. On July 2, Bolshevik leaders took a hand, inviting the regiment to the People's House for a concert, cover for a political assembly (although after the speeches the concert actually did proceed). With Lenin in Finland and his loyal aide-de-camp Zinoviev, Kamenev, and Kollontai—all likely fearing arrest owing to the ongoing investigation into Bolshevik finances—failing to appear, the floor was left to Trotsky, who, although still a Menshevik, had been converted to Lenin's antiwar cause after returning to Russia in early May. (Another Bolshevik, Anatoly Lunacharsky, the future Soviet minister of education, also appeared. But he made a much smaller splash than Trotsky.) With more than five thousand edgy soldiers from the First Machine Gun Regiment on hand at a critical moment in the war, it was an opportunity to make a lasting impression.

Trotsky did not miss his chance. Although no transcripts of the speech have ever been found, those who heard Trotsky's People's House address of July 2 would never forget it. The program he outlined was clear: the Galician offensive must be stopped immediately and all power vested in the Soviet. Some memoir accounts claimed that Trotsky was careful not to advocate overthrowing the government expressly, but a number of soldiers, deposed under oath that July, begged to differ. According to A. E. Zamykin, a second lieutenant in the First Machine Gun Regiment, Trotsky gave a "passionate, harsh, and heated speech" denouncing Kerensky as "no better than Kaiser Wilhelm II." In addition to standard Bolshevik epithets such as "Down with the minister-capitalists," Trotsky shouted out, in full war cry, "Down with Kerensky!" and even urged the men to "*kill* Kerensky." (A second witness confirmed that Trotsky indeed said this, and corroborated other key details independently.) The "entire purpose of [Trotsky's] speech," Zamykin recalled two weeks later, "was to convince us, that it was imperative to conduct an armed uprising against the government." Contrary to accounts that claim that the impetus for an uprising came from a regimental meeting held *after* the concert-speeches, Zamykin claimed that Trotsky urged the men of the First Machine Gun Regiment to forcibly overthrow the government, but the regimental committee, meeting later that night at barracks to discuss the idea, initially refused.[15]

It was then that Ensign Semashko, the one-man Bolshevik band, intervened. Witnesses who attended the meeting of the First Machine Gun Regiment on the night of July 2–3 all agree that Semashko played a key role in mobilizing the men and organizing a provisional revolutionary committee, with himself as chairman. Mutinous sentiment was not unanimous, but about half of the machine-gunners, some five thousand (roughly the number who had heard Trotsky speak), joined the uprising on July 3, "seized whatever automobiles came in their way, and called on the workers and soldiers to come out on the street." At five p.m., the Moscow Guard Reserves and the Pavlovsky and Grenadier Regiments joined in, followed by elements of the 1st, 3rd, 176th, and 180th Infantry Regiments. By nightfall on July 3, Frank Golder observed, the streets were "full of people and armed automobiles and sailors running up and down the streets." In front of the Mikhailovsky Theater, on the Griboyedov Canal, Golder heard machine-gun fire around 11:30 p.m.:

> The soldiers and the public ran for their life—the soldiers toward the Gostinyi Dvor. Most of the public dropped flat on the ground, scared to death. Then the soldiers began to shoot, and such shooting! . . . shooting lasted about 5 minutes. It was all dark. Went to Hotel d'Europe where the lights were turned out. After a bit started back on the Nevsky where the scared soldiers stood in groups. Some broke the front store windows and looted. . . . got back [home] 1 a.m. but could not sleep because of the renewed demonstration on the streets.[16]

All eyes now turned to the Kshesinskaya Mansion. With Lenin still in Finland, the Bolshevik chain of command was not clear. In view of the critical role of Semashko and the army, it was natural that N. I. Podvoisky and the Bolshevik Military Organization would take a leading role, and they did. At some point in the early morning hours of July 4, Podvoisky contacted his key collaborators in Kronstadt—naval ensign F. F. Raskolnikov and S. G. Roshal—and summoned their armed sailors to cross the Gulf of Finland, dock below the Nikolaevsky Bridge, and proceed to Taurida. Met at the pier, the sailors were told to proceed to Kshesinskaya's instead, where they arrived at ten a.m. on July 4. Raskolnikov's men—numbering around six thousand—would provide critical muscle as the Bolsheviks decided where to strike next.[17]

Almost simultaneously, Lenin returned from Finland, arriving at Kshesinskaya's just as the drama neared its climax. Curiously, he exhibited little stomach for the fight. Witnesses from Kshesinskaya's that day all say that Lenin looked unwell. Complaining of a mysterious ailment, he initially refused to address the crowd. Trotsky had had the chance to introduce himself to the public on July 2. This time it was the turn of Yakov Sverdlov, a hard-core Jewish Bolshevik underground organizer from Nizhny Novgorod who, like Stalin, had spent the war in Siberian exile (the two were arrested together in 1913, betrayed by the same Okhrana agent); Sverdlov had met Lenin for the first time in April 1917. Sverdlov mounted the balcony, unfurled a huge red banner on which was written "Central Committee of the Russian Social Democratic Party," and gave a short, forgettable speech praising Raskolnikov for his righteous devotion to the cause, before turning the floor over to Anatoly Lunacharsky, who said little memorable, either. Finally everyone convinced Lenin to speak. Whether owing to his illness or to fear of being caught out in an act of treason, the Bolshevik leader said only that he "was happy to see what was happening," and that it was good that the slogan "All power to the soviets" was "being translated into reality." As a call to arms, it was equivocal. Nonetheless, Lenin left little doubt that the Bolsheviks supported the armed uprising.[18]

The Bolshevik Central Committee worked out a careful plan for a putsch. According to Lunacharsky's recollection, "Lenin had in mind a concrete plan for a coup d'état," in which the Bolsheviks would seize power in the name of the Soviet. Only three ministers had been agreed on: Lenin, Lunacharsky, and, interestingly, the Menshevik Trotsky. They would immediately issue "decrees on peace and land, gaining in this manner the sympathy of millions in the capital and the provinces." After Taurida Palace was surrounded, the members of Ispolkom would be arrested, "whereupon Lenin would arrive at the scene of action and proclaim the new government."[19]

Raskolnikov's sailors, accompanied by a burgeoning train of armed soldiers and factory workers (many from the Putilov Works), now set off for Taurida Palace, carrying Bolshevik placards proclaiming "Down with the Provisional Government," "Down with the minister-capitalists," "Down with the war," and "Beat the bourgeois." Just as in April, 10-ruble notes were passed out by Bolshevik bagmen in front of Kshesinskaya's, and there was no shortage of either signs or agitators carrying them. According to the Red Cross nurse Shelyakhovskaya, who talked to a cross-section of men who took up arms for the Bolsheviks on July 3–4, they were paid 40 rubles a day (in most cases this amounted to 80 rubles, as the uprising lasted two days). Estimates of the size of Raskolnikov's force vary dramatically, but most agree that it numbered at least ten thousand, which suggests that the Bolshevik Central Committee spent nearly a million rubles (about $500,000 in 1917, worth $50 million today) on the July putsch.[20]

While the main Bolshevik strike force marched to Taurida, Red Guards surrounded other strongpoints, including the Peter and Paul Fortress, the Mariinsky Palace (seat of the Provisional Government, although few ministers were there), the Finland and Nikolaevsky railroad stations, and key intersections on Nevsky Prospekt. Teams of ten to fifteen armed men traveling about in cars and trucks, a journalist observed, "lorded it over the city" and seized whatever they felt like taking. Several anti-Bolshevik newspapers were forcibly shut down, including the printing offices of the liberal *Novoe Vremya*. An extraordinary drama took place at the Warsaw railway station. Catching wind of a rumor that Kerensky was fleeing the city to summon loyal troops from the front, six automobiles full with armed men hurried over to the station. The rumor was true, but Kerensky had left an hour and a half earlier.[21]

The most dramatic scene transpired as Raskolnikov's main column turned from Nevsky onto Liteinyi Prospekt, en route for Taurida. All of a sudden, shots rang out and hundreds of people hit the ground, in a moment captured by an amateur photographer that provides our only pictorial evidence of street violence in Petrograd in 1917. The casualties, according to *Izvestiya*, were mostly on the progovernment side, with six Cossacks killed and twenty-five wounded; twenty-nine horses were left "dead on the street." Shaken though victorious, Raskolnikov's sailors and a now-thinning cordon of soldiers, mostly from the First Machine Gun Regiment, carried on to Taurida.[22]

In the palace, there was a creeping sense of dread. The Petrograd Soviet, for so long the radical conscience of the revolution, was now a sitting target. The Provisional Government, fully under the thumb of Ispolkom since the fall of the liberals, had become an afterthought. "No one," Golder wrote in his diary on July 4, "pays attention to the government and it has apparently lost all power." Suddenly realizing the gravity of what the Soviet was up against, the Menshevik

Chkheidze, on behalf of Ispolkom, summoned General Polovtsov, commander of the Petrograd military district, to organize the Taurida Palace defenses. But Polovtsov, after canvassing his officers, realized he could count on only two thousand Cossacks and about a hundred men from the Preobrazhensky Guards in the entire garrison—a force smaller than the Bolsheviks' by a factor of five. Polovtsov decided to stay with the Cossacks to maintain his "freedom of action."[23]

Making the situation at Taurida still more desperate was the presence of many Bolshevik Soviet deputies *inside* the palace, a potential fifth column for the armed columns on the street, complete with car-mounted machine guns. After all, the Bolsheviks were ostensibly seizing power in the name of the Soviet, in theory by acclamation (in practice by coercion). And yet no one seemed to be in charge. According to Raskolnikov, Lenin himself slipped into Taurida late in the afternoon on July 4, although no one else saw him and he made no public speech. With the Bolsheviks scrambling to figure out who was in charge, Chkheidze came out first to address the crowd, bravely demanding, "Why have you come here armed? If you were needed [e.g., by the Soviet], I would welcome you myself, but why are you here now?"[24]

Viktor Chernov, the left-leaning Socialist Revolutionary (SR) agriculture minister, came out next to address the crowd, only to be accosted by hostile demonstrators who mistook him for Pavel Pereverzev, the more moderate, prowar SR justice minister. When Chernov's identity was confirmed, a cry rang out for him to "declare at once that the land is being turned over to the toilers and power to the soviets." According to Milyukov, one tall and imposing armed workman "raised his fist" to Chernov's face and shouted, "Take power, you s.o.b., when they give it to you!" It was then that several of Raskolnikov's sailors seized Chernov, "dragged him toward a car" and vowed "that they would not let him go until the Soviet took power." Only when Trotsky arrived did they free Chernov.[25]

It was now Trotsky's turn to speak. He made a better impression than Chkheidze or Chernov, but it was evident that he, too, was intimidated by the armed mob in front of him. Gone was the confident orator of the People's House. Carefully, Trotsky announced that "the Soviet of worker and soldier deputies has taken all power into its hands." With the battle already won, he let the men know that "they could now disperse." Losing heart, and with Lenin nowhere to be seen, Trotsky summoned Zinoviev. It was a chance for Lenin's loyal aide-de-camp, still little known to the general public, to introduce himself. According to Second Lieutenant Zamykin, who had been won over by Trotsky's earlier speech at the People's House, Zinoviev told the men in front of Taurida "not to enter the Soviet armed," and to use their "arms to fight only against unrighteous people, never righteous ones." In a not so subtle hint, Zinoviev pointed out that proletarians could "use their arms to pry away foodstuffs hidden by the bourgeoisie" rather than storming the Soviet. He then returned to the palace.[26]

Menacing as the armed column was even to the Bolsheviks who were paying them, it was hampered by a lack of discipline—and of leadership. Aside from the core muscle of Kronstadt sailors and a few diehards from the First Machine Gun Regiment, most of the other "Red Guards" were, in effect, hired Bolshevik mercenaries. The majority of the men, Colonel Nikitin observed, were "ordinary peasants incapable of loading a rifle." The very size of the crowd had turned into a hindrance, as communications among the men proved difficult and before long "their entire system of command broke down." Raskolnikov was a hardy soul, but he was no general. Nor was he a politician. With Lenin failing, for whatever reason, to take charge and give instructions, by nightfall on July 4 the armed Bolshevik columns had turned into a directionless rabble, with panic fire making the men as dangerous to themselves as to anyone inside the palace. After midnight, the men began at last to disperse, as Trotsky had asked them to hours earlier. Raskolnikov's armed sailors returned to Kshesinskaya's, along with many of the machine-gunners. Others returned to their units, or went home.[27]

Even as the Bolsheviks stood on the cusp of victory at Taurida, the political tide was turning against them elsewhere. At around five p.m. on July 4, Justice Minister Pavel Pereverzev summoned Colonel Nikitin, General Polovtsov, loyal officers, and a number of newspaper editors to military district headquarters. The very irrelevance of the Provisional Government had provided Pereverzev with a measure of safety, as no one had bothered to arrest him. Nikolai Nekrasov and Mikhail Tereshchenko, Kerensky's old Masonic colleagues, were there too. After Nikitin confirmed that he had enough evidence for a treason trial against the Bolsheviks, Tereshchenko ordered Nikitin to "proceed with their arrest." Pereverzev shared a brief summary of Nikitin's most damning findings—on Parvus and the Stockholm connection; on Kozlovsky, Sumenson, and the Siberian Bank account into which she had deposited at least 2 million rubles—with the editors and the army officers, who returned to their units to share the bombshell news with the men.[28]

The effect on the garrison was electric. Until news of Lenin's dealings with the Germans reached the men, the political struggle had been murky and difficult to follow. But treason and espionage were visceral themes, easily understood by all, which undermined the legitimacy of the entire uprising.

On the morning of July 5, *Zhivoe Slovo* ran the banner headline LENIN, GANETSKII & CO. SPIES in a broadsheet posted all over the city. The Bolsheviks were holed up at Kshesinskaya's, protected only by Raskolnikov and the Kronstadt sailors (the First Machine Gunners had by now given up the ghost). Another five hundred insurrectionists holding out in the nearby Peter and Paul Fortress surrendered personally to General Polovtsov on terms negotiated by Stalin (who had otherwise played little role in the uprising). "Now they are going to shoot us," Lenin told Trotsky, before shaving off his beard and slipping out of Kshesinskaya's. That afternoon, the *Pravda* printing press on Suvorovsky Prospekt, purchased in April for 250,000 rubles, was smashed. [29]

With loyal troops pouring in from the front—including the Fourteenth Cavalry Division, a battalion of armored cars, and an infantry regiment—the rout was on. At a cost of about eighteen casualties, most from the infantry regiment, the Bolshevik headquarters at Kshesinskaya's was stormed, giving Nikitin's intelligence officers access to a bounty of evidence for his treason investigation, including what one described as "an immense quantity of seditious literature," and six Bolshevik machine guns—these, fired from the roof, had been responsible for most of the army casualties. In all, some two thousand leading Bolsheviks were arrested, including Kamenev, Sumenson, Kozlovsky, and Lenin's wife, who screamed, "Gendarmes! Just like the Old Regime!"[30]

On July 6, the Provisional Government formally charged eleven Bolsheviks—including Parvus and Fürstenberg-Hanecki ("Ganetskii" from the headline, or Kuba) in absentia; Lenin, Zinoviev, Lunacharsky, and Alexandra Kollontai from the Central Committee; Kozlovsky and Sumenson; Raskolnikov and Roshal from Kronstadt; and Ensign Semashko of the First Machine Gun Regiment—with "high treason and organizing an armed uprising," pursuant to Articles 51, 100, and 108 of the Russian criminal code. Not all of the conspirators were in custody, and many of the key principals were in Finland or abroad. Shortly before its members were arrested, the Bolshevik Central Committee had even been able to publish, in a special two-page newssheet, a blanket denial of the "monstrous slander . . . made against Lenin that he apparently received or is receiving money from German sources for his propaganda." Trotsky, curiously in view of the role he had played in the uprising, in his incendiary speech on July 2 and in front of Taurida on July 4, was not initially charged, likely owing to his Menshevik origins and his connections with Chkheidze and the Soviet. Viewing this as an insult, Trotsky actually wrote to Chairman Lvov to complain that he had been excluded from the arrest warrant. Only when Trotsky formally joined the Bolshevik Party on July 23 was he apprehended.[31]

The charges, however, were serious. If the government made them stick in a public trial, the Bolsheviks would be finished in Russian politics. By ordering a controversial offensive and sending a Bolshevik-infected unit to the front, Kerensky had forced Lenin to show his hand. Now it was up to Kerensky to show his own.

12

ARMY ON THE BRINK

As the July putschists were being rounded up, a surge of patriotism shot through Petrograd. Frank Golder noted in his diary on July 6: "city quieting down. Troops brought from the front and the disturbers are cowed and quiet. Many of the ring leaders arrested." The Bolsheviks were exposed and on the run, with scores of witnesses coming forward to testify before the Petrograd Court of Appeals, where the public prosecutor, N. S. Karinsky, was cataloguing evidence for a treason trial. Many were soldiers from the First Machine Gun Regiment who had participated in demonstrations, only to recant after things went sour. Others were concerned civilians, such as Shelyakhovskaya, who had become suspicious about what was going on at Kshesinskaya's during the April Days, only to see her worst fears confirmed in July.

Among the witnesses deposed by Karinsky were former Okhrana agents who had lost their jobs after the February Revolution, only to return to favor now, owing to their hard-earned expertise on Bolshevism. S. V. Gagarin, an obscure ex-policeman, sixth class in the table of ranks, was surprised to find himself called in on July 11. A higher-ranking officer from the First Department (counterespionage), B. V. Lobachevsky, confirmed that Parvus had indeed been under surveillance as a German agent, and suggested that the prosecutor consult the First Department files at Okhrana headquarters (if they had not been destroyed). Another agent, V. V. Kurochkin, tasked with surveillance of the leading Bolsheviks before the war, spoke of Lenin's ideological outlook, but referred Karinsky to the First Department on his contacts with the Germans. Another agent, I. P. Vasiliev, confirmed that the Bolsheviks had targeted German prisoner-of-war camps for "anti-patriotic agitation," but he could not speak to the period since Lenin's return, as he had gone into hiding after the revolution.[1]

As the rehabilitation of the Okhrana suggests, the treason investigation had the potential to remake the Russian political landscape. Even Ispolkom was forced to issue a public statement in *Izvestiya*, on July 6, that Lenin and others had been "receiving money from an obscure German source" and announcing that it had "appointed a committee to investigate." On July 22, Karinsky released (in Milyukov's old liberal paper, *Rech*) a detailed summary of the "treasonous armed rebellion of July 3–5," based on eyewitness depositions:

> the revolt took place and continued according to the instructions of the Central Committee of the Social Democratic Party. All leading instructions emanated from the house of Kshesinskaya, called by witnesses the "headquarters of Lenin." . . . Forms of a military organization attached to the Central Committee . . . were discovered in the house of Kshesinskaya. These . . . forms [gave] written instructions on armed action distributed in the army units.

Further, Karinsky revealed the discovery, during the ransacking of Kshesinskaya's, of

> notes on the distribution of military units and "armed workers" according to regions; on the distribution among various persons of responsibilities on taking charge of armed forces, on reconnaissance, and outside watch; on contacts with units; on the Peter and Paul Fortress, on the military units comprising the Vyborg and Petrograd sections . . . and on establishing contacts with various regiments.

In conclusion, Karinsky declared, as "established" by "documentary data," the relation between the armed insurrection and the activity of the Central Committee of the S.D. Party, which maintained a military organization . . . [of] armed units which participated in the insurrection, both from the Petrograd garrison and from Kronstadt, proceeded to the house of Kshesinskaya, where they received instructions from Lenin and other persons . . . the data of the preliminary investigation *point directly to Lenin as a German agent* and indicate that, after entering into an agreement with Germany on action designed to aid Germany in her war with Russia, he arrived in Petrograd [where] with financial assistance from Germany, he began to act to achieve this aim.[2]

With Okhrana experts and scores of eyewitnesses aiding Karinsky's investigation, and Ispolkom putting up no objections, it looked like an open-and-shut case. Although Lenin later denounced the treason charges as "the despicable slandering of political opponents," he had so little hope of exoneration that he refused to stand trial. Convinced that the gig was up, he composed an ideological last testament, a book manuscript titled "Marxism and the State," and turned it over to Kamenev, whom he instructed to publish it if he were captured and executed. On the night of July 9–10, Lenin and Zinoviev, after disguising their appearance, boarded a train at the Finland station where the Bolshevik leader had made his dramatic return in April, and went into hiding indefinitely in the Finnish countryside. In this way the Bolshevik Party seemed consigned to oblivion by the cowardice of its founder. As Nikolai Sukhanov, a Menshevik member of Ispolkom who had friends in the Bolshevik Party, remarked, "The shepherd's flight could not but deliver a heavy blow to the sheep."[3]

Lenin, however, was fortunate in his enemies. Even as the Bolshevik Party apparatus was being smashed in Petrograd, fissures were appearing inside the Provisional Government in what should have been its moment of triumph. As early as July 5, tensions had emerged over Justice Minister Pavel Pereverzev's leaks to the press about German-Bolshevik ties, which had helped turn the political tide in the garrison, but may have undermined the government's legal case. Lvov, Tereshchenko, and Nekrasov, the last three Kadets left in the cabinet, protested Pereverzev's decision to go public before all the evidence had been finalized. Tsereteli, the Menshevik minister of post and telegraphs, objected for the opposite reason, demanding that newspapers not publish further "slanders" against Lenin. The justice minister who had crushed the Bolshevik uprising was fighting for his political life, fending off accusations from left and right.[4]

The man who should have stood up for Pereverzev was Kerensky. The embattled justice minister was a fellow Socialist Revolutionary (SR), appointed by Kerensky himself, who had stuck his neck out to save the government in Petrograd after the war minister had left for the front. If anyone was the target of the uprising of July 3–5, it was Kerensky: singled out for murderous abuse in Trotsky's incendiary speech at the People's House on July 2; universally blamed for the disastrous Galician offensive he had championed; and literally chased by the mob on July 4 to the Warsaw station, where, had he not departed just ninety minutes earlier, he would have been torn limb from limb. Whether or not Pereverzev's "premature" revelations had prejudiced the government's treason case, they had inarguably helped turn the troops against the Bolsheviks, saving Kerensky's skin. When he finally returned to Petrograd on the evening of July 6, by all rights Kerensky should have given Pereverzev a medal as a model patriot, as savior of the revolution.

Instead, he sacked him. Meeting with his colleagues on July 7, Kerensky claimed to have told Pereverzev to "publish[ ] the data on the activity of German agents" only "on condition that the press carry weighty charges and *that the accused could not escape.*" (This claim was contradicted by Kerensky's own wire sent from the front on July 4, in which he declared it "essential to accelerate the publication of the evidence.") Playing devil's advocate, Tereshchenko allowed the "desirability," in the critical hours of July 4–5, "of creating a decisive change of mood among certain strata of the population," but insisted that the justice minister still erred in going public before "the culprits were in our hands." Demonstrating the enduring influence of the prerevolutionary Masonic networks, Kerensky sided with the Kadets—Lvov, Nekrasov, and Tereshchenko—against his fellow SR party man, Pereverzev.[5]

This move might have made sense as part of a political realignment toward the "right," a reconciliation with the liberals. Pavel Milyukov, the former foreign minister, was still milling around Petrograd, and could easily have been called on to put steel into the government. But nothing of the sort happened. Part of the reason for the government's paralysis during the crisis of July 3–5 was that the ministers were already falling out over Ukraine. As with land reform, the Provisional Government had tried to punt the question of Ukraine's political future forward to the Constituent Assembly, only for frustrated nationalists in Kiev, who had formed a Rada (parliament), to publish a "manifesto" demanding autonomy, on June 24. On June 29, the Provisional Government had tried to massage the issue by publishing an "Appeal to Ukrainian Citizens," promising as an interim palliative, while the war continued, "temporary measures . . . to provide the Ukraine with local self-government in schools and courts." As this did not satisfy the Rada, Tereshchenko had gone to Kiev to negotiate a compromise. This pandering was too much for Lvov and the other Kadets, who (excepting Tereshchenko) submitted their resignations on July 3, only to be preempted by the Bolshevik uprising. And so it came about that, on July 7, 1917, Kerensky fired his embattled fellow SR justice minister to please the cabinet's Kadets—and then accepted the resignations of the very liberals he had appeased.[6]

In political terms, the cabinet reshuffle was nonsensical. A far-left uprising had just been crushed owing to a rallying of patriotic sentiment against Bolshevik treason. Counterintelligence officers and loyal troops were the heroes of the hour. On July 6, Kerensky issued a directive stipulating that soldiers who disobeyed legal military orders be "punished as traitors," and forbidding the distribution of Bolshevik newspapers at the front, naming *Pravda*, *Okopnaia Pravda*, and *Soldatskaia Pravda*. Why, in a moment of patriotic reaction, did Kerensky cleanse the cabinet of its last remaining moderates?[7]

In his resignation statement, Prince Lvov offered a clue. "I laid down the heavy burden," the outgoing prime minister wrote in *Russkoe Slovo*, "convinced that I am fulfilling my duty to the motherland" by appointing Kerensky as successor. To bury the Bolshevik threat to "the Russian people and the Russian army," Lvov argued,

strong government is needed. And to bring it about, a combination of elements of authority is needed such as are embodied in the person of Kerensky. In the army he is a recognized leader, in the country he is a symbol of the revolution . . . among the socialists he is perhaps the only man of action . . . he must have the greatest freedom of action . . . to rally everybody into one whole, in order to create that high spirit in the country which can alone save the motherland.

Composing a kind of last testament of liberal Russia, Lvov was inviting his successor—and fellow Freemason—to assume dictatorial powers.[8]

Never shy about his ambition, Kerensky celebrated his apotheosis as naval/war minister and minister-president of the new "Government of the Salvation of the Revolution" by moving into the Alexander III Suite at the Winter Palace, sleeping in the ex-tsar's bed, and traveling in the tsar's ornate train carriage. Shedding his man-of-the-people look, Kerensky began wearing elegant officer's tunics, and even took on a mistress, as if to conform to his new self-image as society grandee. (Kerensky's mistress, Lilya, was the cousin of his wife, Olga, which compounded the insult and finished off his marriage.) In two high-handed early moves, Kerensky ordered the removal of the Romanov crown jewels from Petrograd to the Moscow Kremlin, so as to prevent their capture by the Bolsheviks, and deported the Romanovs from Tsarskoe Selo, where Nicholas II and his family had been confined under house arrest since March, to Tobolsk in Siberia, for similar reasons.[9]

In his first order to the army, Kerensky declared any "willful withdrawal of units from their positions . . . tantamount to treason." He authorized officers to "apply artillery and machine-gun fire against such traitors," reassuring them that he would assume "entire responsibility for any casualties." On July 9, he introduced a resolution at Ispolkom requesting "unlimited powers to restore order and discipline in the army, and to struggle with all forms of anarchy and counterrevolution." Although the few Bolsheviks left at Ispolkom objected (along with several Mensheviks and left-leaning SRs), the resolution passed by a 5-to-1 margin. On July 12, the death penalty was reintroduced in the army, complete with "military-revolutionary courts" in each division, with guilt determined by a simple majority.

All units that had taken part in the July uprising were disbanded. Whether or not Russia needed a strongman, she now had one.[10]

In the armies, the results were mixed. In Galicia, the timing was tricky, as Kerensky's new disciplinary program was implemented just as the Russian offensive was going into reverse. By the end of July, the Russians had been expelled from Galicia, losing nearly 5,800 square miles to the Austro-Germans. Still, field reports from Vorobin, at the northern edge of Galicia, filed in mid-July 1917, suggest morale was holding strong in Special Army as the Russians assumed a defensive posture. Kornilov's Eighth Army also maintained good order in the retreat. By August, new trenches had been dug, and Russian lines were holding.[11]

On the less active fronts, there were positive signs. According to the commander of the Forty-Second Division of Second Army on the western front, "the introduction of the death penalty and other such orders . . . has made a very strong impression on the solders and left the so-called Bolsheviks thunderstruck." Tenth Army was strengthened by the arrival of the soon-legendary "Women's Death Battalion," created by Kerensky to shame male "skin Bolsheviks" into fighting. In Fifth Army, preparing for a joint offensive with Tenth Army against Vilnius, Kerensky put in a personal appearance on July 17, leading a mock frontal charge to put steel into the men.[12]

The surge of enthusiasm, alas, did not survive the offensive. On July 22, the Russian attack began after a three-day artillery barrage. By all reports, the Women's Death Battalion fought magnificently, advancing even when the men on their flanks refused to, seizing enemy trenches and taking nearly one hundred German prisoners. At the sight of this, the men in nearby units joined in and moved forward. But the first day's gains were erased when the Germans counterattacked on July 23. Within days this offensive, too, had petered out, with both sides returning to their original positions and digging in. General Anton Denikin, commander of the western front, gave a depressing postmortem. Although he thought artillerists had done "astounding work," and the Amazons had fought bravely, Denikin noted that most infantrymen had merely "carried out a ceremonial march through two or three lines of enemy trenches and [then] returned to their own lines."[13]

Could the army be saved? Kerensky certainly thought so. The reintroduction of the death penalty was a sign that he meant business. The measure had been demanded by General Lavr Kornilov, who was the leading candidate to replace Brusilov after the failure of the Galician offensive. Kornilov, having been undermined by the Soviet during the April Days, was not about to assume command without real reform. Insisting that he would answer only to "his conscience and the nation," Kornilov demanded, in addition to the restoration of disciplinary authority, an end to political interference with command and operational orders—in effect, the revocation of Order No. 1. When Kornilov's conditions were leaked and published in *Russkoe Slovo* on July 21, it forced Kerensky's hand. Three days later, Kornilov was appointed commander in chief of the Russian armies, with Kerensky's acceptance of his terms suggesting, for socialist critics at Ispolkom, that the two men had teamed up to erode Soviet authority over the army.[14]

They were not wrong to be suspicious. To broaden his political base, Kerensky announced on July 13 that an "All-Russian Conference" would be convened in Moscow in August, bringing together not just the Provisional Government and the Moscow and Petrograd Soviets, but also ex-Duma deputies (including Rodzianko), cooperatives and trade unions from the War Industries Committee (WIC), the provincial zemstvos, clergymen, retired commanders (including General Alekseev), and representatives of the Allied Armies—in all 2,400 notables. Although not quite a Constituent Assembly, the Moscow conference was meant to give political cover as Kerensky and Kornilov revamped the army.[15]

The conference convened on August 13 in the Bolshoi Theater. Outside, three columns of soldiers and cadet officers guarded the theater, flanked by policemen on horseback. Judging by the outbreak of strikes across Moscow to protest the conference—strikes called by the Bolsheviks—the guard was necessary. The atmosphere in the theater, wrote the correspondent from *Rech*, was "charged with alarm and nervous expectation."[16]

Rising to the occasion, Kerensky delivered a fiery opening speech. Alluding to the July Days, he vowed that any more Bolshevik putsches "against the people's government . . . will be stopped with iron and blood." More awkwardly, Kerensky reminded everyone that, as justice minister, he had abolished the death penalty in March, only to bring about its "partial restoration" as war minister—whereupon he was interrupted by "boisterous applause." In a revealing moment, he rebuked the audience, asking, "Who dares applaud when it is a question of capital punishment? Don't you know that at that moment, at that hour, a part of our human heart was killed?"[17]

Kornilov's appearance was no less dramatic. Arriving in Moscow for the conference's second day on August 14, the new commander in chief received an even more "triumphal reception" than Kerensky, who was there to witness it. When the general arrived in front of the Bolshoi at 11:15 a.m., reported *Izvestiya*, "flowers were showered upon him, until his automobile was filled with them." When he entered his opera box, "he was given a long and noisy ovation"—at least from the officers, liberal politicians, and "representatives of commerce and industry" seated on the right side of the hall, even as the worker and soldier soviet delegates on the left "sat quietly, without applauding." Kerensky and his fellow socialist ministers then walked out onstage, receiving an ovation from the left side of the hall, with shouts of "Long live Kerensky," while "the right was motionless." Before long, the house was in an "uproar." Remembering his manners, Kerensky quieted his supporters and asked them to "come to order and listen to the first soldier of the army, with the attention due him." Kornilov declared that "the army must be revived at all costs, for without a strong army there can be no free Russia." He noted that his recommendations for reforming the army had been approved by Kerensky and countersigned by the rest of his cabinet—including by two SR commissars attached by Ispolkom to the high command: Captain M. M. Filonenko, and Boris Savinkov, who was now acting war minister under Kerensky.[18]

In his brief speech, Kornilov had avoided politics, to the extent this was possible in Russia in 1917. Unfortunately, the speaker who followed him, a Cossack ataman general named A. M. Kaledin, who had commanded Eighth Army before Kornilov, did not do the same. Kaledin vigorously "protested against the accusation that Cossacks are counter-revolutionaries"—shortly before stating that "the soviets and army committees must be done away with," and that political authority should be vested not in Ispolkom but in the Constituent Assembly to be elected that fall. At this, the "right" cheered with approval, while shouts of "Never!" were heard on the other side of the hall, according to *Izvestiya*. Backtracking slightly, Kaledin allowed that soldier committees could perhaps still discuss "the question of supplies," but he flatly opposed the spirit of Order No. 1 by demanding that "the declaration of the rights of the soldiers should be revised and supplemented with a declaration on the *obligations* of the soldiers." Again shouts of acclamation and disgust were expressed on opposite sides of the theater. The argument was won, in effect, by the Menshevik Chkheidze, who rose to speak in the name of the Soviet, "notwithstanding the fact that the speaker who has just concluded demanded [its] immediate abolition."[19]

Kaledin had not really spoken for Kornilov, but for many on the left half of the theater, it seemed that he had. Like Kaledin, Kornilov was of Cossack stock, although Kornilov's ancestors were "Siberian Cossacks," who were more assimilated than the Don or Kuban Cossack hosts. Born in 1870 in Ust-Kamenogorsk, in what is now Kazakhstan, to a peasant-soldier father and a mother of mixed Polish-Altai (that is, Turkic) descent, Kornilov represented the Russian Imperial Army at its best, ascending from the humblest of origins to the top of the officer corps on talent alone. Kornilov spoke not only the Turkic dialects of Central Asia but also Chinese, which he learned while serving as Russian military attaché in Peking from 1907 to 1911. A far more cultivated, decorated, and subtler man than Kaledin, Kornilov nonetheless now found himself tainted by association with the idea of Cossack counterrevolution.

If this mistaken idea about Kornilov had been confined to Ispolkom and the Bolsheviks, it would not have been fatal. But in the wake of Kornilov's rapturous reception in Moscow, reinforced by glowing accounts in liberal-moderate organs of the "right," such as *Novoe Vremya*, Kerensky began to doubt the man he had just appointed commander in chief. "After the Moscow conference," he later recalled, "it was clear to me that the next attempt at a blow would come from the right, and not from the left." The documentary record (and Kerensky's subsequent behavior) leaves no doubt that he believed, by late August 1917, that a counterrevolutionary plot was brewing.[20]

Kornilov, for his part, wanted all hands on deck for the defense of Petrograd. For most of the year, the northern front had remained quiet, as the German high command, following Parvus's advice, had declined to give cause for a patriotic revival with an offensive, leaving the Bolsheviks free to wreak havoc in the rear. Now that Lenin was out of commission, things looked different. In early August, German Eighth Army, facing Russian Twelfth, began massing guns on the eastern bank of the Dvina River. On August 18, the Germans opened fire on the northern edge of the front, just west of Riga, in what turned out to be a feint. Next morning the real artillery barrage began farther south, with devastating effect. Toward nine a.m. on August 19, under cover of continuing shelling of the far bank, the Germans laid down pontoon bridges and a flotilla of wooden boats and crossed the Dvina in force, with nearly three entire divisions across by midday. By nightfall, German Eighth Army had a secure beachhead east of the Dvina, opening a clear path to Riga. Although isolated pockets of Russian troops continued resisting, on August 20–21 Russian Twelfth Army abandoned Riga and fell back 30 miles east. The Germans were now 300 miles from the Russian capital.[21]

By all political logic, the fall of Riga should have brought Kerensky and Kornilov, along with all patriotic (i.e., non-Bolshevik) socialists and liberals, closer together. There was every possibility the Germans would use Riga's excellent port facilities to launch naval operations into the Gulf of Finland, where the Russian defenses at Kronstadt were known to be unreliable, owing to the radicalism of the garrison. Other than Raskolnikov and Roshal, most of the Kronstadt insurrectionists had escaped Kerensky's net, and a local Bolshevik newspaper (*Proletarskoe Delo*) was still being printed on the island. On August 8, Kerensky approved a plan to remove Kronstadt's army garrison and transfer out its naval training detachments. If carried through, the plan would allow loyal sailors to do their jobs without political distractions, complicating any possible German landing and cutting the legs off from any future Bolshevik putsch.[22]

It was not to be. Just as they should have been teaming up to cleanse Kronstadt of Bolshevism and defend Petrograd against the Germans, Kerensky and his commander in chief crossed swords in an episode known to history as the Kornilov affair. Tensions between the two men had already arisen over the terms of Kornilov's appointment and at the Moscow conference. After returning to Mogilev, Kornilov was besieged by visiting officers and dignitaries, many of whom passed on, according to his chief of staff, General A. S. Lukomsky, "rumors of an intended rising of the Bolsheviks, which was to take place at the beginning of the next month." Whatever the truth of the rumors, such loose talk was foolish and, in the circumstances, dangerous. As Lukomsky later recalled, "Kornilov unfortunately spoke to many people who came to Stavka of his intention to deal a decisive blow to the Bolsheviks, and to [Ispolkom] . . . this intention had, in fact, ceased to be a secret, and part, if not all, of his plan had got to be known in Petrograd."[23]

It did not take long for Kerensky to pick up the scent. On August 23, he dispatched his acting war minister and fellow SR, Boris Savinkov, to Stavka. Next day, Savinkov met with Kornilov, ostensibly to discuss reforms in the army, in reality to ferret out information about the latter's intentions. Although there is no transcript of the meeting in Mogilev, Lukomsky and Savinkov left behind written accounts. According to Lukomsky, Kornilov and Savinkov clashed over the role of soldiers' committees and commissars in the army, which Savinkov, a former commissar himself, wanted to preserve (though with limits on their activity), whereas Kornilov insisted on their abolition. But the two men agreed on the need to reinforce the Petrograd garrison with "trustworthy cavalry units" that could be called on in the event of a Bolshevik uprising, expected to follow as soon as the strict new program on depoliticizing the army was announced.[24]

Savinkov, by contrast, had little recollection of the discussion of soldiers' committees and commissars, being struck instead by Kornilov's hostile attitude toward Kerensky. He found the commander in chief "in a very excited state of mind, heaping reproaches on the Government and declaring that he had no more faith in it, the country was going to the dogs, that he could no longer work with Kerensky, etc." Only after he reassured Kornilov that Kerensky had approved his army reform plan, Savinkov claimed in an interview conducted just days later, did Kornilov calm down. Nonetheless he noted that, in parting, Kornilov "bade me convey to Kerensky the expression of his satisfaction and the assurance of his perfect loyalty to the government."[25]

Recognizing the gravity of the situation, Savinkov and Kornilov had been able to overcome their mutual suspicions and reach a tentative agreement. Unfortunately, the next visitor to Stavka was not so careful. This was V. N. Lvov (no relation to the ex-chairman), an aristocratic dilettante and former Octobrist Duma deputy who had served as procurator of the Holy Synod before being fired by Kerensky in July. In his own mind, Lvov was a patriot trying to save the country. Hearing rumors of some kind of coup brewing at Stavka, he decided to sound out Kerensky (whom he met in Petrograd on August 22) and offer himself as intermediary. Lvov arrived at Mogilev on August 24 just after Savinkov left, entering Kornilov's office at ten p.m.

What transpired next could be played for farce, were the consequences not so catastrophic. Foolishly, Kornilov took his late-night visitor at his word as "an irreproachably honest man and a gentleman" when he claimed to be serving on an "important mission" for Kerensky. The two hit it off immediately, based on a shared antipathy to the Bolsheviks, who, Kornilov informed his guest, were planning to "overthrow the government, install themselves in its place, at once to conclude a separate peace . . . in order to demoralize the army and to deliver to Germany the Baltic fleet." Dubiously, Lvov claimed that Kerensky had authorized him to propose three courses of action to see off the Bolshevik threat: (1) a new government with Kerensky as dictator; (2) a small oligarchy of "three or four members" (including both Kerensky and Kornilov), to be "invested with unlimited powers"; or (3), a military dictatorship under Kornilov. Without asking his mystery guest for credentials, Kornilov took Lvov's proposals as genuine and stated a preference for option 3, so long as Kerensky and Savinkov remained on as ministers. Astonishingly, Kornilov had just advocated, in effect, the overthrow of the Provisional Government, even if under entirely false pretenses.[26]

Such was Kerensky's understandable conclusion after Lvov returned to Petrograd to brief him. Receiving his guest at the Winter Palace at six p.m. on August 26, Kerensky was shocked by Lvov's account of his conversation with Kornilov. Entirely omitting the context—that Kornilov believed himself to be responding to Kerensky's own proposals—Lvov informed Kerensky that "General Kornilov" had "invited [him] to urge the Provisional Government to transfer its powers that very day to the Generalissimo," with Savinkov and Kerensky traveling to Mogilev to assume the posts of minister of war and justice. So stunned was Kerensky on hearing this that he demanded that Lvov put Kornilov's supposed proposal in writing. This Lvov promptly did, adding, for good measure, that the "generalissimo" insisted "that martial law shall be proclaimed in Petrograd" and "that all Ministers, not excluding the Prime Minister, should resign." Here was written proof of Kornilov's treasonous intentions, although it came from the pen of an imposter, playing ventriloquist with the fate of millions.[27]

Kerensky did insist on speaking directly with Kornilov before taking action. But he did so under pretenses no less false than those under which Lvov had been operating. In part this was Lvov's own fault, as he left the Winter Palace to dine and failed to return in time for Kerensky's telegraphic hook-up, via the so-called Hughes apparatus, with Mogilev, scheduled for eight p.m. After keeping Kornilov waiting for a half-hour, Kerensky finally tapped out a message to military headquarters. Pretending to speak (actually typing) as "V. N. [Lvov]," Kerensky asked Kornilov "whether it is necessary to act on that definite decision which you asked me to communicate privately to Kerensky, as he is hesitating to give his full confidence without your personal confirmation." Falling right into Kerensky's trap, Kornilov confirmed to "Lvov" his "demand" that Kerensky "should come to Mogilev." This confirmed Kerensky's suspicions that Kornilov meant to arrest him at Stavka.

Believing that a right-wing military coup was imminent, Kerensky called an emergency cabinet meeting at midnight. Savinkov, to his immense credit, tried to talk him down, viewing the whole Kornilov business as a "fatal misunderstanding," not a conspiracy. But Kerensky was having none of it. He proclaimed melodramatically, according to Nikolai Nekrasov, "I will not let them have the revolution!" In a curious mirror imaging of what he claimed Kornilov was doing, Kerensky asked for and was granted dictatorial powers. His first action was to relieve Kornilov of his command, via a wire sent to Stavka at seven a.m., and summon him to Petrograd. Later on the morning of August 27, Kerensky released a radio-telegram addressed to "all the country," in which he accused Kornilov of demanding "the surrender of the Provisional Government" and placed Petrograd under martial law—just hours after Kornilov, in his last order as commander in chief, dispatched at 2:40 a.m., had proclaimed the same thing.[28]

When he received Kerensky's accusatory telegram, Kornilov was apoplectic. In his own radio-telegram reply to the country, he refuted the prime minister's "lie" by informing the country that Lvov had come to him as Kerensky's emissary, not the other way round, in what amounted to a "great provocation." Concluding, based on Kerensky's dishonorable accusation, that the government was "acting under [Bolshevik] pressure . . . in complete harmony with the plans of the German general staff," Kornilov accused his accuser of treason. "I, General Kornilov," he concluded his message, "son of a Cossack peasant, declare to all and sundry that I want nothing for myself, except the preservation of a Great Russia, and I vow to bring the people by means of victory over the enemy to the Constituent Assembly." Defiantly, Kornilov ordered the arrest of the SR commissar at Stavka, Captain Filonenko, and ordered a punitive detachment of four Cossack regiments, under General A. M. Krymov, to march on Petrograd. Here, incontrovertibly, was an order amounting to armed rebellion against Kerensky's government—even if Kornilov had been provoked into it by Kerensky's trumped-up accusations. In one last effort to heal the breach, Savinkov found a secure telephone line to Mogilev and asked Kornilov to call off Krymov's mission. Kornilov refused.[29]

The Kornilov affair, born in misunderstanding, was now poisoned by bad faith. After reading Kornilov's reply, Kerensky must have realized the mistake both men had made in trusting Lvov. Instead he doubled down, accusing Kornilov, in a follow-up communiqué, of "treachery" in withdrawing units from the front to threaten Petrograd—notwithstanding Kerensky's own request, issued a week previously, for reliable reinforcements from the front to garrison the capital. Kornilov, for his part, justified the Krymov mission on the grounds that "mercenary Bolsheviks" now "lord[ed] it over Petrograd," in all likelihood knowing perfectly well, as Krymov himself would soon ascertain, that no such Bolshevik uprising had taken place and that Kerensky was acting on his own volition. When Krymov arrived in Petrograd on August 31, having ordered his men to halt before the city, Kerensky relieved him of his command. Krymov, realizing he was finished, shot himself, becoming the first victim of the Kornilov affair.[30]

He would not be the last. Kornilov's short-lived rebellion was over by September 1, when General Alekseev arrived in Mogilev to accept his surrender. It would have been over sooner, except that, at first, Kerensky could not find anyone willing to take Kornilov's place. Kerensky's first choice, northern front commander General V. N. Klembovsky, politely demurred, wanting to avoid the political cross-fire. His second choice, Kornilov's chief of staff, General Lukomsky, declined less politely, warning Kerensky, in a telegram copied to all military front commanders at 1 p.m. on August 27, that the firing of Kornilov "will lead to horrors such as Russia has not yet experienced." Failing to find anyone willing to take over as commander in chief, Kerensky was forced to issue an amazing order to the effect that, although General Kornilov was guilty of treason, his orders were still to be obeyed until a suitable replacement could be found. Even Alekseev, though agreeing on August 30 to travel to Mogilev and take over the supreme command out of patriotic duty, did so only after speaking with Kornilov at length (over the Hughes apparatus), in what amounted more to a friendly debriefing on the state of the army than any kind of prosecution. By mutual agreement, Kornilov submitted to Alekseev without resisting, and was imprisoned in the nearby Bykhov Fortress, along with thirty other officers known to be loyal to him.[31]

The political fallout was dramatic. As early as August 27, a Menshevik motion tabled (and passed) at Ispolkom cited Kerensky's incendiary radio-telegram accusations against Kornilov as justification for inviting Bolshevik Party members to cooperate in forming a "Committee for the People's Struggle Against Counter-Revolution," with a view to "the arming of individual groups of workers" who might, "if the necessity arises . . . be placed under the command of the army." On August 31, the rehabilitation of the Bolsheviks was made quasi-official when *Izvestiya* announced the release, by the new

Tsarina Alexandra ("Alix of Hesse"), 1909.

Tsar Nicholas II and Tsarevich Alexis.

Stalin's police mug shot, c. 1911.

Lenin.

Grand Duke Nicholas, 1914.

Sergei Sazonov in 1916.

Grigory Rasputin in 1916.

General Mikhail Alekseev in 1917.

Tsarevich Alexis and Tatiana, 1917.

The Provisional Committee of the State Duma.
Seated on the right at the desk is Mikhail Rodzianko. Seated next to him is
Alexander Guchkov, and standing behind Rodzianko is Alexander Kerensky.
To Kerensky's right are Prince Georgy Lvov and Pavel Milyukov.

Alexander Kerensky, 1917.

Trotsky in full oratorical flight.

Siege of the Duma. Street Violence During the
Thwarted Bolshevik Putsch, July 4/17, 1917.

Taking Oath. The Women's Death Battalion, 1917.

Nicholas Romanov, the former tsar,
shoveling snow while under house arrest at Tsarskoe Selo.

Lev Kamenev arrives at Brest-Litovsk.

The Volunteer Army, 1918.

The Siberian Army, 1919.

Kolchak reviews Siberian Army Troops, 1919.

Red Army troops assault Kronstadt, March 1921.

Two Coffins. Scenes from the Volga Famine, 1921.

committee under the authority of Ispolkom, "of all those persons arrested in connection with the events of July 3–5 who have not been proved guilty of acts of a criminal nature." Here was a virtual amnesty for Bolsheviks arrested in July, excepting Lenin, who remained at large in Finland and was still wanted for questioning.[32]

To defeat a "Kornilov plot" he had largely conjured into existence himself, Kerensky decided to make his peace with Bolshevism. He could only hope the Bolsheviks would be as forgiving if they ever gained the upper hand over him.

13

RED OCTOBER

The Kornilov affair broke at the worst possible time for the Russian army. Relations between officers and men had slowly begun to mend after the July Days, as Kerensky and Kornilov had worked together to sideline Bolshevik agitators and restore the authority of officers. It had not been easy, and there remained plenty of grumbling among the men, but the trendline had been positive most of the summer. In Fifth Army, Major-General M. A. Svechin reported on July 28 that "planned political agitation" had ceased entirely owing to the crackdown on the Bolsheviks, with the voices of more patriotic Socialist Revolutionaries (SRs) now dominating soldiers' committees. In Special Army, on the northern edge of the Galician front, an operational report filed on August 12 noted that "soldiers and officers fought magnificently together."[1]

In a flash, the hard work of the summer was undone and the gaping wound reopened. Most (though not all) ranking officers took Kornilov's side in the standoff, blaming Kerensky for impugning his honor. On August 28, General Baluev, who had fought so hard against Bolshevik influence in Special Army before taking over as commander of Tenth Army—the one reinvigorated by the Women's Death Battalion—proclaimed in a telegram wired to all front commanders (but *not* to Kerensky) that he concurred completely with Kornilov on the measures he had ordered to "save the fighting capacity of the army," that Kornilov was "the only man in Russia capable of restoring order to the army through his iron will," and that Kornilov's sacking by Kerensky was tantamount to "the ruin of the army and of Russia." General Shcherbachev, commander of the Romanian front, sent a slightly more polite wire that day (polite enough to include Kerensky among the recipients), proclaiming that Kornilov's ouster "must inevitably have a disastrous impact on the army and the defense of Russia." General Lukomsky wired Kerensky that the fall of Kornilov would lead to "the final demoralization of the army" and possibly to "civil war." General Denikin, formerly chief of staff at Stavka and now southwestern front commander, revered Kornilov, whom he saw as a self-made man in his own mold: Denikin's father, born a serf in Saratov, had served twenty-two years in the army before becoming an officer. Denikin took a defiant tone with Kerensky. "I am a soldier and am not accustomed to playing games," he wrote, letting the minister-president know that, if the government ordered him to break with Kornilov, he could not "follow it along this path."[2]

Enlisted men saw things differently. In northern army, soldiers' letters from early September 1917 were shot through with hostile references to Kornilov, who was often described (inaccurately) as "bourgeois," a popular Bolshevik term of abuse. Many, with some justification, blamed Kornilov for diverting troops toward Petrograd, leaving trenchworks against the Germans undermanned. Several even claimed that Kornilov was taking "big money from the Germans." It was not that the men sided with Kerensky, exactly. As one soldier wrote on September 3, "The prevailing attitude of the army is loyalty to revolutionary democracy," not to any politician. One soldier, who had met Kornilov personally, wrote that he trusted him far more than the minister-president. But this was an exceptional view. A more common reaction was a fatalistic shrug of the shoulders, as men wondered, "Why should we fight now?" Summing up the feelings of many, one Muscovite enlistee declared, "This is not a war, this is the annihilation of the [Russian] nation."[3]

In Galicia, the mood was not quite so bleak. The best antidote to despair was the tonic of action, and the Austro-Germans obliged on the southwestern front in late August and early September, even as the Baltic front fell quiet after the fall of Riga. On the Russian right flank, Special Army saw off a series of attacks between September 4 and 6, engaging in fierce hand-to-hand combat and even taking German prisoners. On September 16, Russian XXXIX Corps actually went back on the offensive, raiding German trenches and capturing rifles and ammunition. Light skirmishing in this sector continued all month. So long as they were too busy fighting to indulge in politics, Russian muzhiks remained willing to defend their country from enemy attack.[4]

In the wake of the Kornilov affair, though, politics was difficult to ignore. On Kerensky's insistence, officers who had offered rhetorical support for Kornilov, such as Denikin, were arrested, along with their staff officers. Others, such as Generals Baluev and Shcherbachev, escaped the net by recanting their support after Kornilov's declaration of open rebellion (Baluev had also taken the precaution of not sending his pro-Kornilov telegram to Kerensky). Generals Yuri Danilov and D. P. Parsky, commanding Fifth and Twelfth Armies nearest to Petrograd, had avoided siding with Kornilov, whether out of loyalty to Kerensky or in the interest of self-preservation. Owing to its close proximity to the capital, the northern front was the most politicized in the entire Russian army.[5]

But for a brief interregnum after the July Days, the northern front had been inundated with Bolshevik propaganda ever since Lenin had returned to Russia in April. After the Kornilov affair, the Bolshevization of Fifth Army resumed in earnest. In the wake of Kerensky's communiqués accusing Kornilov of treason, a Bolshevik-inspired "committee for saving the revolution" had sprung up in the ranks. By the time Kornilov surrendered on September 1, Major-General Svechin reported, the "fighting capacity of the army" had been gravely undermined, not least by the desertion of 256 soldiers on the day of Kornilov's arrest. Bolshevik commissars had seized control of the telegraph apparatus and were now vetting all communications with Mogilev and Petrograd.[6]

In Twelfth Army, Bolshevization proceeded more slowly than in Fifth, but went deeper. General Parsky reported on September 28 that "there is absolutely no desire to fight in the soldiering masses." The reason was not hard to fathom. "On the grounds of Bolshevik propaganda," he explained, "commanding officers are, in the main, viewed as counterrevolutionaries." The officers, in turn, feared the men, whose monitoring of their every move for signs of counterrevolutionary sympathies left officers "feeling like they were oppressed."

Any attempt to "restore discipline and restore the desire to continue the war" was, in Parsky's view, "completely impossible."[7]

The situation on other fronts was less dire, but nowhere particularly promising. An army intelligence report prepared for Stavka in the last week of September 1917 noted a "general war weariness" on the western front, along with "an intense defeatist agitation accompanied by refusals to carry out orders, threats to the commanding personnel, and attempts to fraternize with the Germans." On the southwestern front, "defeatist agitation is increasing and the disintegration of the army is in full swing. The Bolshevik wave is growing steadily, owing to general disintegration in the rear." Politically speaking, it was the northern front that mattered most, and there Bolshevik influence was peaking: "Apart from the Bolsheviks, not a single political movement has any popularity. Those who read moderate newspapers are looked upon as . . . 'bourgeoisie' and 'counter-revolutionists.' An intensive agitation is being conducted in favor of an immediate cessation of military operations."[8]

Making the spread of Bolshevism in the Baltic region particularly ominous, it occurred just as the German threat to Petrograd was getting serious. On the night of September 29–30, the Germans launched amphibious Operation Albion against the archipelago where the Gulf of Riga meets the Gulf of Finland, guarded by three Russian regiments and shore batteries. The main island, Saaremaa, was captured by the Germans on October 15. Within a week it was all over, and the Germans were in control of the mouth of the Gulf of Finland, making possible landings behind Russian lines on either the Finnish or Russian coastline, if not a direct amphibious strike against Petrograd itself. Public opinion in Russian Finland, German spies reported gleefully to Berlin, was now "entirely pro-German." With Kronstadt and the Baltic Fleet succumbing to Bolshevik influence, it was hard to see what could stop the Germans now. On October 3, Stavka ordered the evacuation of Reval, the last major land fortress between Riga and Petrograd. The Germans were now 250 miles from the Russian capital. At a conference at Helsinki in mid-October, the admirals of the Russian Baltic Fleet concluded sadly that "the fate of Finland and the approaches to the capital depend primarily on the will of the enemy."[9]

The collapse of the Baltic Fleet and northern army put Petrograd in danger of falling either to the advancing Germans—or the Bolsheviks. And yet it is hard to see what else could have resulted from Kerensky's decision to break Kornilov, a man dedicated to restoring military discipline, and make peace with the Bolsheviks, who had made no secret of their desire to destroy this discipline. Even as Kornilov and dozens of Russia's most patriotic military officers were being thrown in jail, Trotsky was released from prison on September 3, after posting a bail of 3,000 rubles. On September 8, Kerensky abolished the counterintelligence department that had conducted the investigation into the Bolsheviks. On September 12, Ispolkom issued a resolution demanding protection of, and a "fair trial," for Lenin and Zinoviev—although Lenin, taking no chances, still refused to return to Petrograd from his Finnish hideaway.[10]

Making Kerensky's rehabilitation of the Bolsheviks in early September 1917 still more perplexing was the fact that the procurator's witness depositions on the events of July 3–5 had not yet been concluded. In fact, they were ramping up. On August 19, Viktor Chernov, who had been roughed up in front of Taurida on July 4, testified. Because Trotsky had intervened on his behalf, Chernov had little motivation to impugn him, and he had no inside knowledge of Lenin's role. But his was still damning testimony: Chernov was a cabinet member who had nearly been killed by paid political agitators. The events of July 4, Chernov concluded, "left me with little doubt that there had been some kind of attempt, planned beforehand by shadowy characters, to have me called out and arrested."[11]

More damning still was the testimony of M. N. Lebedev, the counterintelligence officer who had conducted the raid on Kshesinskaya's, who was called in on August 22, just before the Kornilov affair erupted. Lebedev reported, "On July 6, at ten a.m., I received a personal order from General Polovtsov to search through the Kshesinskaya Mansion, just seized by our troops, for documents, which I was to secure." Lebedev found papers with the inscription of the "Central Committee of the Russian Social Democratic Party," including operational orders marked with the "representative eagle of the First Machine Gun Regiment," on which the Bolshevik stamp had been applied. In a "filing cabinet, near the window," Lebedev found "a range of documents, prepared, apparently, in connection with the uprising," including "maps of armed operations" in Petrograd, a "list of regiments involved and orders pertaining to their cooperation, . . . list of names of persons authorized to enter the headquarters of each armed unit involved in the uprising . . . [and] permits for the use of automobiles, authorized by the central committee of the [Bolshevik] party." Downstairs, new treasures awaited: the editorial offices of *Pravda*, including account books; "expensive foreign equipment" used to print identification cards; and Bolshevik propaganda literature. Lebedev also confirmed, after reading Sumenson's account books, the way she had laundered money for Bolshevik operations by selling German-provided "thermometers, pencils, stockings, and medicine," and turning over ruble profits to Miecyslaw Kozlovsky, Sumenson's contact on the Bolshevik Central Committee. If evidence was required to go forward with a treason trial against the Bolsheviks, here it was.[12]

Just days after Lebedev's bombshell revelations, Kerensky decided to let the Bolsheviks off the hook so as to fight the phantom menace of "Kornilovism"—and then abolished the very Counterintelligence Department that had unearthed the evidence. Stunningly, Kerensky even allowed the Bolsheviks to rearm, ostensibly to help defend Petrograd against "Kornilovites," his idea being, apparently, that the Bolshevik Military Organization was the only experienced armed force available. The Bolsheviks promptly seized forty thousand rifles from a government arsenal.[13]

What on earth was Kerensky thinking? In September, Ispolkom convened a "Congress of All the Democratic Organizations in Russia" to meet in Petrograd on the fourteenth, in a curious sequel to the Moscow conference of August where Kerensky had clashed with Kornilov. After the rout of the "Kornilovites," the Petrograd Congress tilted left, so far left that the Kadets refused to participate. Kerensky, addressing this radical assembly of Mensheviks, Bolsheviks, and antiwar SRs (who now formally split off from the parent party to form a minority faction known as the Left SRs), gave a hint of the confused thought process behind his leftward lurch. Mostly he talked about Napoleon, to whom several of Kerensky's friends had told him he bore a resemblance, and about whose role in replacing

French revolutionary democracy with a military dictatorship he was now mulling over. It was not clear whether Kerensky saw himself as a Napoleonic figure, or as the man destined to save Russia from a Napoleonic figure (such as Kornilov). Kerensky stated that many Russians, at the time of his barnstorming tour of the front, had seen him as "practically the pretender to the title of Napoleon." But then the Bolsheviks, by inundating the armies with defeatist propaganda, had "destroy[ed] the solidarity and the strength of the troops" and in this way "prepar[ed] for the coming of a general on a white horse or a Napoleon"—meaning Kornilov. When Kerensky tried to take credit for thwarting the Napoleon-like threat of "Kornilovism," he was jeered by Bolsheviks in the audience as "the first general of Russia." When Kerensky defended the restoration of the death penalty at the front, cries of "shame" rang out all over the hall. Losing his temper, Kerensky warned the Bolsheviks that "anyone who dares . . . to stick his knife in the back of the Russian army, will learn the power of the revolutionary government." So far from being intimidated by this threat, the Bolshevik delegation (led by Kamenev) issued a resolution on September 21, demanding the abolition of capital punishment at the front, the "introduction of workers' control over production and distribution . . . [and] general arming of the workers and the organization of a red guard," the dissolution of the Provisional Government, and "the immediate release of all arrested revolutionists." By adopting a policy of no-enemies-to-the-left to defeat "Kornilovism," Kerensky had emboldened his Bolshevik enemies.[14]

In evaluating Kerensky's self-defeating behavior in fall 1917, we must keep in mind that the minister-president was still, despite his renown, only thirty-six years old and relatively inexperienced in politics. His Masonic connections had fueled his meteoric rise after the revolution, and his knack for oratory had served him well in February and at the front in May. But Kerensky had little sense of strategy, as the Galician offensive had painfully demonstrated. His record as minister-president since the July Days was worse, marked by the sacking of Pereverzev, the purge of "right" Kadets after they had just helped him defeat a left-wing putsch, and the histrionics of the Kornilov affair. The refusal of Generals Klembovsky and Lukomsky to replace Kornilov was a bad sign. General Alekseev, too, resigned on September 9, once he had ascertained the truth about the Kornilov affair. He left the command of the Russian armies to N. N. Dukhonin, quartermaster-general of the southwestern front—a virtual unknown. Kerensky was clearly operating above his pay grade.[15]

Worst of all was his decision to rehabilitate the Bolsheviks, who now returned from the political wilderness to take center stage. In September, Lenin's party recorded a stunning victory in elections to the Moscow municipal council, receiving just under 50 percent of the vote, more than four times their share (11.6%) in June. The SRs declined from 59 to 15 percent, in a neat illustration of Kerensky's political incompetence. On September 19, the Bolsheviks received a majority in the Moscow Soviet for the first time, and then repeated the feat in the Petrograd Soviet on September 25, winning thirteen out of twenty-two seats on the executive committee. The upshot was that Lev Trotsky—a man who, according to two eyewitnesses, had incited an armed mob to murder Kerensky—was elected chairman of Ispolkom on September 26. In August, the Soviet had moved from Taurida to the nearby Smolny Institute. With the party apparatus at Kshesinskaya's smashed, the Bolsheviks, exploiting their new majority in the Soviet, now took over the Smolny Institute, where they installed the headquarters of the revived Bolshevik Military Organization, which now operated under an ostensibly non-partisan mandate as the Petrograd Soviet's Milrevkom (military revolutionary committee).[16]

It was an extraordinary situation. With the Germans at the gates of Petrograd, the stronger half of Russia's "dual government" was now controlled by the Bolshevik Party, several of whose leaders (Lenin and Zinoviev) were still charged with treason. (Confusing things further, a new "Provisional Council of the Russian Republic," meant to supervise the upcoming elections to the Russian Constituent Assembly, convened in the Mariinsky Palace on October 7). Trotsky, fresh out of prison on bail, was chairing sessions of Ispolkom—when these were not chaired by his brother-in-law Lev Kamenev, also charged with treason. Lenin, not seen in Petrograd for three months, was a wanted man, with warrants for his arrest plastered all over the country—but his party was the dominant political force in Petrograd and Moscow.[17]

Nowhere were the consequences of the Bolshevik revival more serious than in the army. Controlling Ispolkom, the Bolsheviks could now
send agitators to front and rearguard units with the full sanction of the
Petrograd Soviet, in whose name they harassed any officers stubborn
enough to insist that men obey orders. Although the Bolshevization
of the troops remained slow in Galicia and Anatolia, on the western and northern fronts the Bolsheviks made rapid inroads. On
September 29, Second Army convened a full-on Bolshevik Party congress, registering some seventeen thousand supporters. At the Second
Regional Conference convened on October 4, the armies of the western front counted more than twenty-one thousand party members,
an increase of 450 percent since mid-September. More significantly,
a Bolshevik congress of the northern front convened on October 15
in the Latvian town of Tsesis (Cēsis), with representatives from the
rapidly Bolshevizing Fifth and Twelfth Armies, joined by Bolsheviks
from XVII Corps in Finland. The Latvian brigades of Twelfth Army,
who played a starring role at the conference, were emerging as a core
component of the Bolshevik Military Organization, whose men now
worked directly with Smolny headquarters.[18]

In the Russian armies closest to Petrograd, political battle lines
were being drawn. On one side stood Lenin's Bolsheviks, pushing
a program as sharp as it was clear: end the war now, all power to
the Soviets. On the other side stood—well, it was not clear exactly
who, just a loose coalition of anyone opposed to a hostile Bolshevik
takeover of what remained of Russia's government and armed forces.
Kerensky should have been the man to rally this coalition, but after
he had alienated the officer corps and everyone to the right of the
Mensheviks, he was a leader without followers. His threats might
have rallied Russian patriots against Lenin, except that everyone
knew they were hollow. For why should anyone believe Kerensky's
promise to unleash "the power of the revolutionary government" on
the Bolsheviks if they staged another putsch—considering that they
had *already* staged a putsch, and he had let them off scot-free?

In view of Kerensky's impotence, the only really surprising thing
about the course of events is how long it took the Bolsheviks to
act. In late September, Lenin issued a call to arms to the Central
Committee, declaring that the Bolsheviks were now strong enough

to "attack at once, suddenly, from three points: Petersburg, Moscow, and the Baltic Fleet," with "the chances a hundred to one that we would succeed with smaller sacrifices than [in July] . . . because the *troops will not move against a government of peace.*" But as Lenin, still in Finland, had failed to surface, his entreaties were ignored by the Central Committee, which asked him to return to Petrograd.[19]

In Lenin's continued absence, Trotsky was the man of the hour. Since February, the Petrograd Soviet had been the nerve center of the revolution, hampered only by the reluctance of its scrupulously principled members (Kerensky excepted) to take on the hard choices of governing in wartime. Dominated, until September, by the Mensheviks, Ispolkom had taken on the half-hearted character of this party, devoted to revolution in the abstract, but only in a longed-for future the party was in no hurry to rush into. The ascension of Trotsky, a former Menshevik convert, to the chairmanship was a critical development, marking the moment when the ineffectual, hand-wringing phase of Russian social democracy gave way to the unscrupulous will to power of the Bolsheviks. In a series of speeches at Smolny on September 21 and 23 that comprised a kind of audition for his election as chairman, Trotsky had proclaimed without apology, "All power to the Soviets!" When hecklers objected that the slogan "came from Germany" (i.e., that the Bolsheviks were German agents), Trotsky denounced his hecklers as "counterintelligence agents" and "old-regime reactionaries," to loud and sustained applause. Judging by the Soviet election of September 26, it was a winning argument.[20]

Once he was able to chair the plenary sessions, Trotsky doubled down on his attacks. On October 3, he opened discussion on an uprising in Tashkent that had begun in mid-September. In an adumbration of what Trotsky was proposing for Petrograd, Bolsheviks and other radicals in the local Soviet, mobilizing sympathetic soldiers from a training barracks, had seized on the Kornilov affair to arrest not only "Kornilovites" in the army, but also local members of the Provisional Government. When the commanding officer of the Tashkent garrison, General Cherkess, came to the Soviet to protest, he was pelted with bottles and pans; one smacked him in the head, knocking him out cold. Kerensky, outraged, ordered a punitive detachment to descend on Tashkent from Samara, only to be overruled by the

Samara Soviet. Trotsky proposed a resolution declaring "full solidarity" with the rebellious Tashkent Soviet as "representatives of revolutionary democracy." Kamenev denounced Kerensky as a "former Socialist Revolutionary" who had resorted to "the methods of Protopopov." It was "not the Bolsheviks," Kamenev declared, "who were calling for an armed offensive against the government . . . but rather the government which was driving the country into armed uprising [against it]."[21]

Here was a thinly veiled threat. It was no bluff. One week later, on October 10, the Bolshevik Central Committee convened at Nikolai Sukhanov's apartment on Vasilievsky Island. So critical was the discussion that Lenin made his first appearance in three months, after arriving in Petrograd incognito sometime between October 7 and 9. In view of the mounting German threat to Petrograd, he proclaimed that "the decisive moment is near." (In July, he claimed, "Decisive action on our part would have been defeated," but "the majority is now with us.") Dismissing the concerns of Kamenev and Zinoviev that seizing power before the November elections to the Constituent Assembly would be "a fatal step," Lenin argued that waiting was "senseless," as the Bolsheviks would never win a national election in which peasants, unlike in urban soviet-style elections, could vote. With an eye, perhaps, on the warrants for his arrest plastered all over Russia, he argued that the Bolsheviks should seize power *now*. To end the impasse, Trotsky proposed a compromise: the Bolsheviks would not wait until November, but seize power in the name of the Second Congress of the Soviets, which would meet on October 25. Trotsky's proposal carried, 10 to 2.[22]

A strange waiting game began. News of the impending coup leaked through the corridors of Smolny. *Rabochy Put*, a new Bolshevik broadsheet, proclaimed "All power to the Soviets" on October 13, leading a progovernment paper, *Delo Naroda*, to warn that "the Bolsheviks are getting ready for [armed] action." On October 16, a Menshevik, Fyodor Dan, asked Trotsky in the Soviet whether the Bolsheviks were planning a coup. Trotsky replied in mock indignation, "The Menshevik [wishes to know] whether the Bolsheviks are preparing an armed demonstration. In whose name has he asked this question: Kerensky, the counter-intelligence, the Secret Police?" On October

18, Trotsky announced mischievously, "We have still not decided on an insurrection."[23]

Kerensky knew the Bolsheviks were planning to depose him: it was the worst-kept secret in Petrograd. In July, he had encouraged Lenin's party to rise, confident that a putsch could be dispatched by loyal troops. This time, he was less sure. In a confidential message sent to London at the beginning of October, Kerensky warned that, barring some major diplomatic development, "when the cold weather comes I don't think I shall be able to keep the army in the trenches." Receiving no reply, Kerensky tried the direct approach, telling the British ambassador, Sir George Buchanan, that unless the Allies threw him a bone by "revising war aims with a view to opening armistice negotiations immediately," "Russia would be plunged into utter anarchy as soon as November." Unsure of the Baltic Fleet, Kerensky issued orders to rotate her crews out of their ships as soon as the ice froze. Doubtful of the army's ability to hold Petrograd, Kerensky proposed to the cabinet, on October 5, that the government be evacuated to Moscow, with critical industrial facilities being shipped east—a politically explosive decision that immediately leaked to the press.[24]

Relishing the turnabout, Trotsky and Lenin publicly accused Kerensky of planning to surrender the capital to the Germans. In a last roll of the dice, Kerensky visited Mogilev from October 14 to 16 to discuss plans with the new commander in chief, General Dukhonin, for assembling a "New Model Army" of volunteers, which he hoped would reverse the Bolshevization of the army. On Kerensky's return, General G. P. Polkovnikov, the commander of the Petrograd military district, increased the guard on public buildings, and alerted his troops that the Bolsheviks were planning to strike. On October 18, Kerensky's justice minister issued a new warrant for Lenin's arrest, although Lenin kept evading detection. On October 22, more bad news came in when Ambassador Buchanan informed Kerensky, after a "heated argument lasting over an hour . . . the Allies insisted on continuing the war." With more hope than conviction, Kerensky at last told Buchanan, "I only wish [the Bolsheviks] will come out, and I will then put them down."[25]

It was a foolhardy boast. The Bolshevik Military Organization already had thousands of adherents in the Petrograd garrison, in the Baltic Fleet, on Kronstadt, and in the Latvian rifles of Twelfth Army. Even so, Lenin, as cautious in military matters as he was bold in his rhetoric, was not satisfied. In a memorandum on October 8, he insisted on achieving a "gigantic preponderance" over progovernment forces, which he feared might number as high as 15,000 to 20,000, to "guarantee the success of the Russian and world revolutions." Upon being informed by the head of the Military Organization in the Baltic Fleet, P. E. Dybenko, that only 5,000 of his sailors could be relied on in a pinch, Lenin replied, "Not enough." Dybenko, with a better grasp of the mood of the men, replied, "Who would go against you from the front after [the] Kornilov [affair]?"[26]

Dybenko was right. Even if the pro-Bolshevik element in the Petrograd garrison was a minority (comprising some 4% of 160,000 men, about 5,000 to 6,000), and only another 5,000 or so reliable armed men were at Lenin's disposal in the Baltic Fleet, this still outnumbered by five to one the ever-dwindling ranks of Kerensky loyalists, which consisted of some 2,000 army cadets, 200 stalwarts from the Women's Death Battalion, "some Cossacks," and perhaps 134 officers. The northern army billeted in marching distance of the capital also counted tens of thousands of vaguely Bolshevized soldiers who lorded it over an impotent officer class, most of whom were as hostile to Kerensky as to Lenin. An idea of the true state of affairs is suggested by the open defiance of the "heavily Bolshevized" 128th Division, stationed near Helsinki, of Kerensky's orders, issued in mid-October, that it be transferred across the Baltic to the front. By the time Bolshevik coup preparations were being set in motion on October 23, Kerensky's urgent request for loyal troops to reinforce the capital, wired to northern front headquarters at Pskov, was simply ignored by the new front commander, General Cheremisov, who tossed the order over to his aide and said, "This is political and has nothing to do with me." In the looming struggle between the Bolsheviks and Kerensky's government, Russia's officers had no dog in the fight.[27]

On Monday, October 23, Kerensky abandoned his suite in the Winter Palace and moved into garrison military headquarters in the

Mikhailovsky Palace. At dawn on Tuesday, loyal cadets attacked the Bolshevik press that churned out *Rabochy Put*, while other detachments posted guards at the Winter Palace (where the Provisional Government, sans Kerensky, was meeting) and other choke points, and cut the phone connection to Smolny. Having learned the lesson of February, Kerensky raised the Neva bridges to cut off Vyborg and Vasilievsky Island, and canceled service on streetcar lines serving neighborhoods that were known Bolshevik strongholds. General Polkovnikov ordered the Petrograd garrison to "remove all commissars appointed by the Petrograd Soviet," and ordered the arrest of the members of the Bolshevik-dominated Milrevkom at Smolny, along with other Bolsheviks plotting against the government. Around noon, Kerensky arrived at the Mariinsky Palace to address the Provisional Council of the Russian Republic supervising the upcoming elections to the Constituent Assembly. Brandishing an intercepted order to the garrison, signed by the head of the Bolshevik Military Organization, N. I. Podvoisky, on behalf of Milrevkom, Kerensky stated that Petrograd was "in a state of insurrection," accused the Bolsheviks of "treason and betrayal of the Russian state," proposed "an immediate judicial investigation," and declared, "Let the populace of Petrograd know that [the Bolsheviks] will meet a resolute power." Government offices were closed early at 2:30 p.m., to allow employees to return home safely in daylight and to avoid crossfire in the streets. Kerensky had made his move.[28]

It was a weak one, however. None of the key Bolsheviks—Lenin, Trotsky, Kamenev, or the leader of the Military Organization, Podvoisky—had been arrested, although in Lenin's case there was a close call (according to legend, he escaped a picket near Taurida Palace by pretending to be drunk). While the phone lines to Smolny were cut, the building was not taken, which allowed the Bolsheviks to prepare a public reply to Kerensky's charges—and plot countermeasures. "The Kornilovists," Podvoisky declared in a Milrevkom resolution that night, "are mobilizing their forces to crush the All-Russian Congress of Soviets and to defeat the Constituent Assembly." In the name of the Petrograd Soviet, the Bolsheviks now assumed responsibility for "the defense of the revolutionary order against counter-revolution and pogroms," shorthand for a power seizure, although carefully camouflaged. Lenin put it more bluntly in his own instructions to the party that night: "delaying the uprising now really means death."[29]

Calculating that Kerensky's armed loyalists lacked enthusiasm, Trotsky and Podvoisky conceived an elegant plan. Just before dawn on Wednesday, October 25, armed Bolshevik "Red Guards" fanned out across the city under cover of darkness, walked up to cadets guarding key choke points, and simply told them that they were being relieved. With impressive insouciance, several Bolsheviks walked into the Central Telegraph Office and disconnected the telephone lines to the Winter Palace. From the Mikhailovsky Palace, Kerensky did send a wire to Pskov at 2:20 a.m., demanding that two reliable regiments of Cossacks from the Third Cavalry Corps be sent from the front—only to be disappointed when they failed to appear, hour after hour (the corps had been fiercely loyal to Kornilov and despised Kerensky). Now it was Kerensky's turn to adopt a disguise. After dictating a brief message to the Allied ambassadors urging them not to recognize the Bolsheviks, around 11:30 a.m. on October 25, Russia's minister-president slipped out of Petrograd in a car loaned to him by the US Embassy, to rally supporters at the front.[30]

While it is difficult to imagine that Kerensky's presence would have made a decisive difference, his departure did not help the government's cause in Petrograd. At 10:15 a.m. on October 25 General Polkovnikov wired Stavka, "The situation in Petrograd is menacing. There are no street disorders, but a systematic seizure of government buildings and railway stations is going on. None of my orders is obeyed. The cadets surrender their posts almost without resistance, and the Cossacks, who were repeatedly ordered to come out, refused to do so . . . There is no guaranty that the insurrectionists will not next attempt to arrest the Provisional Government."[31]

In an eerie echo of the February Revolution, the Cossacks had once more declared neutrality in a political fight between Russians, leaving the field clear for the Bolsheviks. "One has the feeling," Polkovnikov's aide wired to General Dukhonin at Stavka, "that the Provisional Government is in the capital of an enemy which has just completed mobilization but has not yet begun military operations." Kerensky's departure left the door wide open. The Bolsheviks did not even have to push, but simply to walk in.[32]

Even so, they nearly botched the job. In an appeal to "the citizens of Russia" released to the press at ten a.m., Lenin declared that "the Provisional Government has been deposed" and that "government authority has passed into the hands of the organ of the Petrograd Soviet, the Military-Revolutionary Committee." This was more than Lenin had been willing to do during the April or July Days. And yet his statement was not, strictly speaking, true. Although Red Guards had seized the bridges, the Mariinsky Palace, the Peter and Paul Fortress, and the telegraph office, they had not yet taken garrison headquarters at Mikhailovsky Palace. Moreover, at the hour Lenin declared it deposed, the government still sat, unmolested, in the Winter Palace. Toward two p.m., about five thousand ostensibly pro-Bolshevik sailors from Kronstadt docked on the Neva near the Troitsky Bridge, but they refused to join battle after they saw cadets, a few Cossacks, and the Women's Death Battalion guarding the Winter Palace. And so Milrevkom summoned a battle cruiser from the Baltic Fleet, the *Aurora*, and issued an ultimatum to the ministers in the Winter Palace at 6:30 p.m.: surrender power, or the *Aurora*'s guns would fire from the Neva, followed by the guns of the Peter and Paul Fortress.[33]

As the ministers of what remained of Russia's Provisional Government were still waiting for Kerensky to return at the head of loyal troops, no answer was given. Toward nine p.m., the *Aurora* opened fire, although, lacking any live shells on board, it fired only blanks. Bolshevik gunners then fired off thirty-five shells from the Peter and Paul Fortress, scoring two minor hits. Just past midnight, the tide of battle finally began to turn when cadets and Cossacks began abandoning their posts in front of the Winter Palace. The Women's Death Battalion, living up to its namesake, fought to the last, and paid the price. Several heroic women defenders were reportedly raped by Red Guards, as others swarmed into the palace, looting and vandalizing as they went. In the breakfast room, the ministers of the Provisional Government (minus Kerensky) could do little more but wait and hope for mercy. The minister of justice, P. N. Maliantovich—who had recently signed a new nationwide arrest warrant for Lenin—recalled his terror as the noise of the gathering mob "grew all the time, intensified, and swiftly, with a broad wave, rolled toward us . . . it penetrated and seized us with an unbearable fear, like the onslaught of poisoned air." Finally a small unit of Red Guards, commanded by the secretary of Milrevkom, V. A. Antonov-Ovseenko, burst in and arrested the ministers at 2:10 a.m. on October 26, 1917, as the clock in the room reads to this day.[34]

Many historians have remarked on the relatively bloodless nature of the October Revolution (or coup, as some now call it). As historian Richard Pipes writes, "the total casualties were five killed and several wounded, most of them victims of stray bullets"—causing fewer injuries than were sustained during the filming of the tenth-anniversary movie directed by Sergei Eisenstein in 1927. So unimpressive was the battle that life in the city—unlike in the February, April, or July Days—had been basically undisturbed. As *Delo Naroda* reported blandly on October 26 of the previous day's events, "streetcars ran almost as usual . . . there were few reports of disorders on the street in the course of the day." In Petrograd, the Kerensky government appears to have been so impotent by October 1917 that the Bolsheviks seized power while scarcely breaking a sweat.[35]

All this is true, but the ease with which the government was toppled in Petrograd masked a more dramatic upheaval under way across the empire. Kerensky had few defenders left for very good reason: the country he presumed to rule over as minister-president was falling apart at the seams. Far more than in February, in October 1917 critical economic and social indicators were flashing bright red. Coal production in the Donbass mines was 30 percent lower than the previous year, leading to shortages and forcing factories to scale back or close shop entirely. A report in *Rech* on October 12 noted that 568 factories in Petrograd had shut down since March, throwing 105,000 employees out of work, including 10,000 from the Putilov Works in September alone. Food prices were skyrocketing. In Petrograd, people were lining up at four a.m. at bread shops, and waiting until nearly midday. Inflation was raging: a small piece of meat cost 500 rubles (the prewar equivalent of $250, or $25,000 today); butter was a memory. Many Russians, according to a German intelligence officer, were overheard saying that they "hoped the Germans would come soon, to bring law and order, at least." This German report, filed shortly before the Bolshevik uprising, noted that "a thorough-going anarchy was raging across central and south Russia." "Disorders" had been observed in Minsk, Pskov, Moscow, Tver, Perm, Orenburg, Samara, Saratov, Kiev, Kherson, and Kharkov, with the only pockets of comparative calm found in "Siberia and the Transcaucasus." Far from registering surprise at the news from Petrograd, German intelligence reported on November 2 that "the Bolshevik uprising was completely expected" (although the agent predicted with equal confidence that the Bolsheviks would shortly be overthrown in turn).[36]

Outside the capital, Red October was not as peaceful as in Petrograd. A hint of things to come was provided in Moscow, where the pro-government forces were a bit stronger—strong enough to resist the power seizure proclaimed by the Moscow Milrevkom at ten p.m. on October 25. Catching the government by surprise, the Bolsheviks were able to secure the Kremlin on October 26 owing to the betrayal of a Bolshevik officer in the Fifty-Sixth Regiment charged with guarding it. But the entrances were soon surrounded by loyalist cadets, who recaptured the fortress in an early morning assault on October 28—the first victory of the counterrevolution. With the Provisional Government, represented by Moscow mayor V. V. Rudnev and the commander of the local military district, Colonel K. I. Riabtsev, holed up in the Kremlin, and the Manezh gate closed, and with most of the city center patrolled by loyal officer-cadets, the Bolsheviks were going to have to shed real blood to conquer Russia's second city.[37]

They did not hesitate to do so. For several days, the Bolsheviks, from a makeshift headquarters in the Hotel Dresden, recruited Red Guards from Moscow's industrial suburbs, looted arsenals, requisitioned cars and lorries, and generally prepared for armageddon. By October 31, Milrevkom had assembled a strike force of fifteen thousand men, which included an entire infantry regiment (the 193rd), along with ten machine guns and two mobile heavy artillery columns. The Bolshevik assault on the Kremlin would require a meticulously planned military operation, involving the capture not simply of choke points, as in Petrograd, but door-to-door fighting through some of the most famous buildings in Russia. A Milrevkom battle map drawn up on October 31 shows 150 Red Guards at Teatralnaya Ploshad (Theater Square), of which 50 stormed the Bolshoi Theater, 50 the Malyi Theater, and another 50 the Central Theater. Okhotnyi ryad, the strategic intersection where Tverskaya Boulevard meets Red Square, was taken by a hundred armed Bolsheviks. Fifty Red Guards fought their way into the Hotel National after it was battered with artillery fire. Other fierce battles took place at Strastnaia Square (including a firefight beneath the Pushkin statue), on Strastnoi Boulevard, on Lubyanka Square, and at the Nikitskie Gates. By October 31, fires were raging through the city center. Collateral damage was serious enough that Milrevkom issued a special warning to Bolshevik artillerists and machine-gunners to avoid the Swedish Consulate.[38]

The red brick walls of the Kremlin received no such consideration. After securing Okhotnyi ryad and the Hotel National, the Bolsheviks had a clear field of fire across the Alexander Gardens, and they used it. Late in the evening on October 31, the district headquarters of Milrevkom issued orders to assemble "all heavy guns in Moscow" for a final assault at dawn. Following a devastating artillery barrage, an elite strike force of five hundred Red Guards stormed the Manezh gate, covered by machine-gun fire, and deployed hand grenades to smoke out defenders behind the Kremlin walls. Other Red Guards stormed the rooftops of nearby buildings, where pro-government snipers held out. All through the day on November 1, a fierce battle raged for the Kremlin. The loyal cadet-officers fought bravely, but they were outnumbered. On the morning of November 2, Mayor Rudnev waved the white flag, turned over captured Red Guards, and surrendered. Showing mercy, which actually surprised the defenders, the Red commander, Commissar Davidovsky, allowed most of the loyalist cadets to leave unharmed, so long as they turned in their weapons and agreed not to oppose Soviet power. At nine p.m. on November 2, 1917, a Milrevkom decree announced the "end of combat operations in Moscow."[39]

Impressive though the victory was in military terms, the fact that the Kremlin had to be stormed was significant. While Kerensky had few supporters left, the shell holes in the Kremlin walls, and the fires still burning across Moscow, provided visible evidence that Lenin had legions of detractors, too. In the face of Bolshevik agitation at the front and near-universal war-weariness in the trenches, Russia's war against the Central Powers was beginning to wind down. But the war for Russia had only just begun.

⸺ 14 ⸺

GENERAL STRIKE

The Bolsheviks moved quickly to seize the reins of power in Petrograd. The first step was to neutralize the Second All-Russian Congress of Soviets, in whose name the revolution had ostensibly been carried out. At 10:40 p.m. on October 25, the congress opened in the Great Hall of the Smolny Institute. Although the body had been carefully stacked, the Bolsheviks, with 338 out of 650 seats, enjoyed only a precarious majority. The seizure of the Winter Palace later that night had the welcome effect of increasing the Bolshevik margin, after most of the Menshevik and Socialist Revolutionary (SR) Party deputies walked out to protest what one of them called Lenin's "criminal venture." "To those who have left," Trotsky announced to the rump congress in the wee hours of October 26, 1917, "we say: you are miserable bankrupts, your role is played out; go where you ought to go—into the dustbin of history."[1]

Once the opposition had left the building, the Bolsheviks were free to rubber-stamp their own revolution. The first resolution they passed on October 26 formally "transferred authority in the provinces to the Soviets," set free political prisoners, and declared that "the commissars who arrested them" (i.e., any officials of the Provisional Government who had imprisoned Bolshevik activists) were now themselves "subject to arrest." Another decree re-abolished capital punishment in the army, granted "fullest freedom of agitation" at the front, and demanded the liberation of Bolshevik soldier-agitators currently held by military authorities. A third decree "on peace" amounted to an open invitation, issued to "all warring peoples and their governments," to "begin at once negotiations leading to a just democratic peace."[2]

Getting into the spirit of things now, the Bolsheviks' next resolution declared grandly that "the right of private ownership of land is abolished forever." This much was consistent with Marxist doctrine. But a subsequent provision divided agricultural land "among the toilers in accordance with the consumption-labor standard"—the old rule of the rural communes. This was a shameless rip-off of the SR program; and in truth, neither land nor grain, at a time of terrible shortages in Petrograd, were really Lenin's to give. Still, the new Bolshevik trinity of "peace, land, and bread," coined by party propagandists, had genuine popular appeal.[3]

Having thus neutralized, they hoped, Russia's massive peasant population and the party that spoke for it, the Bolsheviks set about assembling the machinery of Soviet government. In the name of the rump congress of Soviets, a new "Provisional Workers' and Peasants' Government" was formed, "to be known as the Soviet of People's Commissars" (Sovnarkom). Trying to claim a broader mandate, Lenin invited a number of sympathetic Left SRs to join Sovnarkom, but none agreed to. And so every position in the new government was assumed by a Bolshevik, including Stalin (commissar for nationalities), Alexander Shliapnikov (labor), Anatoly Lunacharsky (education), Trotsky (foreign minister), and finally Lenin (after Trotsky insisted, over Lenin's objections) as chairman. The most interesting appointments were in the Commissariat of War. P. E. Dybenko, the head of the Bolshevik Military Organization in the Baltic Fleet, took over the Naval Ministry. V. A. Ovseenko, the former secretary of Milrevkom and conqueror of the Winter Palace, took over the War Ministry. The new commissar of war (in wartime, commander in chief) was N. V. Krylenko, the brave ensign from the Eleventh Army Soviet who had spoken out against Kerensky during the latter's barnstorming tour in May. The only institution to which Sovnarkom was answerable was Ispolkom, which was granted veto power over legislation and appointments. For added insurance, the Bolsheviks dissolved the current Ispolkom—even though Trotsky was already its chairman—and replaced it with a streamlined roll of 101 members, of whom 61 were Bolsheviks, 29 Left SRs, and only 6 Mensheviks.

Having turned Russia's government upside-down in one whirlwind day, at 5:15 a.m. on October 27, Lev Kamenev declared the Second Congress of Soviets closed.[4]

It would take time for the new government to set down solid roots in Russia. Kerensky had not yet been vanquished. After leaving Petrograd, the deposed minister-president passed through Tsarskoe Selo and reached Gatchina, 30 miles south of the capital, by the evening of October 25. Although he received no support from the local garrison there, Kerensky was allowed to continue safely on to northern front headquarters at Pskov, where he was able to link up with the Cossack Third Cavalry Corps, commanded by Peter Krasnov. Although Krasnov's men resented Kerensky for destroying Kornilov, about seven hundred mounted Cossacks did agree to accompany Krasnov and Kerensky back to Gatchina, where the overmatched garrison surrendered on October 27. Installing himself, in another tone-deaf gesture, in Gatchina Palace, Kerensky appointed Krasnov commander of the Petrograd military district and wired to Pskov for reinforcements. But the northern front commander, General Cheremisov, remained cool to Kerensky and refused to help. Cheremisov instructed commanders of First, Fifth, and Twelfth Armies to "keep out of the political struggle now going on in Petrograd."[5]

Lenin, having learned of Kerensky's presence at Gatchina, was taking no chances. On October 27, he wired Kronstadt and Helsinki for reinforcements. Once again, the thoroughly Bolshevized Baltic Fleet came through, dispatching another five thousand "bayonets," the battleship *Republic*, and two torpedo boats, within eighteen hours. It was none too soon, as even while this force was assembling, Kerensky and about 480 of Krasnov's mounted Cossacks marched from Gatchina to Tsarskoe Selo, just 15 miles from Petrograd, which they captured on the evening of October 28 "almost without resistance"—impressive considering that sixteen thousand troops were quartered there (although only two regiments offered any resistance).[6]

Meanwhile, in Petrograd itself, a burgeoning coalition of anti-Bolshevik forces, composed of elements from the Provisional Council of the Russian Republic overseeing the upcoming elections, of deposed Menshevik and "right" SR members of Ispolkom, and representatives from the main city unions (railway, post, and tele-graph) had emerged, styling itself the "All-Russian Committee to Save the Country and the Revolution." Meeting in the old city Duma on October 26, the committee began issuing its own decrees, order-ing "all military units" (in practice, mostly officer-cadets-in-training) to assemble at the Nikolaevsky Engineering School and await further orders. With General Polkovnikov, the former commander of the Petrograd military district, directing loyalist operations inside the city, and General Krasnov directing anti-Bolshevik operations with-out, there was a chance for a coordinated assault on Red Petrograd.[7]

Had Krasnov marched on Petrograd right away, it might even have worked. But the Bolsheviks got wind of the plot. On the morn-ing of Sunday, October 29, they sent Red Guards to Nikolaevsky to disarm the officer cadets, snuffing out the loyalist uprising before Krasnov's Cossacks got close to the city. With the reinforcements from Kronstadt, the Bolsheviks were able to dispatch a force of nearly six thousand Red Guards, soldiers, and sailors south toward Tsarskoe Selo. On October 30, in the hilly southern town of Pulkovo (site of today's Pulkovo Airport), they encountered Krasnov's Cossacks, who fought bravely but were overwhelmed and forced to retreat to Tsarskoe Selo—and then all the way to Gatchina. Although Kerensky sent more wires to Pskov and Mogilev requesting reinforcements, no one was listening anymore. On October 31, even Kerensky gave up and sent a wire to Petrograd informing the "Committee to Save the Country and Revolution" that he had "stopped all [troop] move-ments" and asked that everyone "take the necessary steps to stop the useless shedding of blood." With Kerensky bowing out, and the Moscow Kremlin stormed the following day, the immediate military threat to the Bolsheviks was neutralized.[8]

The battles for the Kremlin and Pulkovo gave a foretaste of an emerging civil war. Fortunately for bystanders, the early skirmishes were less violent in most provincial cities, because the numbers engaged were smaller. In Minsk, close to the front lines and home of western front headquarters, the "advent of Soviet power," as the Bolsheviks described their armed takeover of Russia, was mostly a matter of soldier committees, whose sympathies waxed and waned depending on events. Front commander General Baluev was arrested, then released. On October 27, a "Committee to Save the Revolution" was formed, but its influence with the men lasted only while hope remained alive in Moscow and Petrograd. After the rout of Krasnov and the fall of the Kremlin, the committee was disbanded. "Until a new power has become established in all of Russia and order is restored," General Baluev reported to Stavka on November 5, "I will conduct no political struggle and conduct no adventures."[9]

In cities farther from the front lines, the Bolshevik power seizure followed a different pattern, although soldiers were usually still involved. In Saratov, southeast of Moscow on the Volga, after learning of events in the capital the Bolsheviks staged a rump election in the Soviet at three a.m. on October 26, purging Mensheviks and Socialist Revolutionaries after they walked out in protest, just as the Central Committee had done in Ispolkom. The deposed deputies rallied a loyalist "army" in the City Duma, comprised of cadet officers, several machine-gunners, and many women and children. The loyalists then "set up," the Bolshevik commander recalled, "some rather pitiful barricades" made of "bags of quinces." As in Moscow, the Bolsheviks brought in artillery and, on the morning of October 28, shelled the enemy into submission, though they suffered nearly a dozen casualties themselves (mostly from machine-gun fire). There were a few tense moments while surrender terms were being negotiated, but by afternoon it was all over.[10]

In more distant cities, the Bolshevik revolution took place considerably later if at all, as there were few local party committees strong enough to act. In Viatka province in the Urals, the Bolsheviks had to send a commissar from Petrograd to effect the coup, and he did not arrive until November 23. In Perm province, a soldier-emissary named Deriabin arrived four days later still, only to discover that most of the locals had not yet heard the news from Petrograd. The only thing most of them had noticed was a wave of "drunken pogroms" in early November. When he told the story of Red October to peasants in the village of Otradnovo, they responded, "We know you Bolsheviks! In our city you robbed the poorest of peasants." Deriabin asked them to vote for the Bolsheviks in the Constituent Assembly elections, but he did not expect that they would. Farther east in Siberia, the Bolshevik revolution did not arrive until spring 1918.[11]

Part of the reason early armed clashes were limited in scale was that, following the failure of the counterrevolution in Petrograd and Moscow, most opposition forces began coalescing in the south, under protection of the Don and Kuban Cossacks in the Don River basin and the North Caucasus, respectively, where the Bolsheviks had made little headway. Generals Kornilov, Kaledin, and Alekseev were all en route for the safety of the Don region, but it would take months before they could muster a real army of resistance.[12]

With armed opposition subdued—for now—resistance to Bolshevik rule shifted onto new terrain. Despite wresting control of Ispolkom and its Soviet equivalents in most of the cities of European Russia, the Bolsheviks were unable to secure the loyalty of the civil servants who ran Russia's government, or what was left of it. Lenin's abolition of the aristocratic Table of Ranks on October 29, although supported by the Mensheviks and SRs, angered many state officials, who had worked their entire lives to achieve their positions. As early as October 28, the "All-Russian Union of State Employees" protested "the usurpation of power by the Bolshevik group in the Petrograd Soviet" and resolved that "work in all the administrative departments of the state shall cease immediately."[13]

This was no idle threat. On October 29, the Central Committee of the All-Russian Union of Railwaymen (Vikzhel) announced a "complete stoppage of all train movements" to begin at midnight, "if by that time fighting in Petrograd and Moscow has not ceased." While not supporting the Kerensky government either, Vikzhel denounced as "enemies of democracy and as traitors to the country all those who continue to settle internal quarrels by means of force." So critical were the railways to military logistics that Lenin was forced to dispatch Kamenev to negotiate a sort of laissez-passer with Vikzhel for a detachment of armed Baltic sailors sent to reinforce Moscow. It turned out to be a one-time concession, as Vikzhel returned to a posture of strict neutrality after the fall of the Kremlin. Not until January 1918 were the Bolsheviks able to break the Russian railway strike, after methodically packing Vikzhel with their own people.[14]

The railway strike was only the beginning. When Trotsky made his first visit to Chorister's Bridge on October 28 to introduce himself as the new minister of foreign affairs, he was met, according to a report in *Delo Naroda*, "with ironic laughter." Summoning his pride, Trotsky ordered everyone to return to work. Instead, six hundred employees packed up and went home. Employees at the Ministry of Agriculture struck next, followed by those at the Ministries of Education and Food. On November 7, telegraph and telephone workers walked out, followed by transport workers and school-teachers, and then Moscow municipal workers. On November 8, the "Union of Unions" called a general strike of government employees against Lenin's power seizure:

> The Bolsheviks, making use of brute force, have declared them-selves at the head of government. Both capitals are reddened with the blood of fratricidal war, the lives and freedom of citizens have been brutally violated, and holy places have been ruined. Now, the Bolsheviks are aiming to get control . . . of the entire machinery of government . . . we defy [their] threats, and refuse to offer our experience and knowledge.[15]

The world's first proletarian government was thus forced to devote its primary energies to strikebreaking.

The most stubborn resistance came from the banking community. For Lenin, a Marxist devoted to "maximalist socialism," banks were target number one for property nationalization. As he had written earlier in 1917, "The big banks are that 'state apparatus' which we *need* for the realization of Socialism." Ideologically, it seemed an open-and-shut case to Lenin, as the "actual work of bookkeeping, control, registration, accounting, and summation [in banks] is carried out by *employees*, most of whom are themselves in a proletarian or semi-proletarian position."[16]

The bank employees of Petrograd did not see things this way. Pri-vate banks shut their doors in protest of the Bolshevik power sei-zure on October 26. The State Bank and Russian Treasury remained open to honor obligations to soldiers and state employees, but they refused to release funds to the Bolsheviks. On October 31, Sovnar-kom issued a decree threatening the director of the State Bank, I. P. Shipov, with arrest if he did not authorize its withdrawals, but Shipov refused. On November 4, Shipov informed the public that the bank had authorized, in the week since the coup, 600 million rubles in withdrawals to employees and beneficiaries of Russia's "real" government, including charities and soup kitchens for the poor. To the Bolsheviks, he would give nothing.[17]

Lenin, however, was not easily deterred. On November 7, he dispatched his new "commissar of finance," Viacheslav Menzhinsky, accompanied by a battalion of armed sailors from the Baltic Fleet, to the State Bank, along with a small fleet of trucks to carry off what they hoped would be a great haul of gold and coin. The Bolshevik enforcers, a witness reported, then "began bawling and shaking their fists in the faces of their adversaries who consisted of the [bank] Directors, some Delegates from the Duma, the Peasants Soviet, and . . . the workmen employed by the Bank." For a time, as a British witness observed, "things looked nasty, but the Directors found their champion in a giant peasant, in soldiers uniform, who roared louder than any ten and had a larger fist."[18]

Lenin sent Menzhinsky back on November 11 with a larger force—and an ultimatum. Unless Shipov relented, all State Bank employees would be fired, lose their pensions, and those of military age would be drafted and sent to the front. At this threat Shipov gave himself up, but it did the Bolsheviks little good, as the employees walked out in protest, leaving no one in place to help Menzhinsky access the vaults. There was little to do but take hostages. And so on November 12, the Bolsheviks, according to Menzhensky's team leader, Valerian Obolensky-Osinsky, took into custody the branch manager, the head bookkeeper, and the guardian of the vaults, who surrendered the keys. These were proudly carried back to the Smolny Institute where, as Obolensky-Osinsky recalled, "We solemnly emptied [them] from a special chamois bag on the table before Lenin." Alas, Lenin, unsatisfied, "demanded from us *money* and not the keys."[19]

To break the resistance of the State Bank employees, Lenin ordered his commissars to take more hostages from the Petrograd banking community, including Directors Epstein of the Azov-Don, Wavelberg of the Commercial Bank, Sologub of the Volga-Kama Bank, Sandberg of the Siberian Bank (the one implicated in Sumenson's money laundering), and Kritilichevsky of the Bank for

Foreign Trade. Lenin demanded a billion rubles for each hostage, before settling, on November 15, for 1 million rubles per "head." Even then, the bank directors required him to produce the proper paperwork for a withdrawal of 5 million rubles on behalf of Sovnarkom, and the employees took their sweet time processing the request in the bank vault. As Obolensky-Osinsky recalled, "The time seemed to drag on terribly." Only when he saw bank employees wheeling a steel pushcart out of the vault could he relax. The entire ransom of 5 million rubles, he proudly reported in *Pravda*, was then driven over to Smolny.[20]

Far from ending the crisis, the hostages-for-cash deal of November 15 turned out to be a one-off. The bank strike persisted, soon encompassing more than six thousand employees in Petrograd alone. In the absence of help from the staff, the Bolsheviks stationed "commissars" at banks in Petrograd and Moscow, charged with overseeing salary disbursements to workers, but, as they had no access to the vaults, they soon ran out of ready cash. Most of these Bolshevik commissars were former bank employees fired for incompetence or malfeasance. It did not take them long, as the frustrated manager of the Russian & English Bank told the British ambassador, to reduce the account books to "a hopeless condition from which it will take years to recover."[21]

The stakes in the bank strike were colossal. It was largely to break the strike that the soon-dreaded "All-Russian Extraordinary Commission to Combat Counterrevolution, Speculation, and Sabotage" (Cheka) was formed. As Lenin instructed the man chosen to run it, Felix Dzerzhinsky, a Polish noble-turned-Bolshevik, on December 7:

> The bourgeoisie are still persistently committing the most abominable crimes. . . . The accomplices of the bourgeoisie, notably *high-ranking functionaries and bank cadres*, are also involved in *sabotage and organizing strikes* to undermine the measures the government is taking with a view to the socialist transformation of society. . . . Exceptional measures will have to be taken to combat these saboteurs and counter-revolutionaries.[22]

Dzerzhinsky's Cheka was also tasked with containing the political fallout from the recent national parliamentary elections (conducted on November 12, it had taken until the end of the month for all the ballots to be counted). Considering the circumstances, the elections of November 1917 were conducted with remarkable integrity, with a turnout of 41 million, half of eligible voters. As expected, the SRs won a plurality, scoring just above 40 percent, with the Bolsheviks coming in second at 24 percent (though Lenin's party won nearly 50 percent of the army, including 70 percent of serving men in Moscow and Petrograd). Impressive though this was in comparison to where the Bolsheviks had stood just months earlier, it was hardly reassuring to a ruling party of usurpers that more than three quarters of the Russian electorate had voted against them, leaving them with only 175 seats out of 707. As one observer noted, the democratic verdict sat with the Bolsheviks like a "bone in the throat." And so Sovnarkom, refusing to ratify the results as legitimate, postponed the convocation of Russia's long-awaited Constituent Assembly, originally scheduled for November 28, until "electoral abuses" could be investigated, and it instructed the Cheka to close off Taurida Palace to prevent opposition forces from gathering there.[23]

Meanwhile, Lenin's war with the banks stepped into high gear. On December 14, the Soviet Finance Ministry abolished private banks in Russia while granting broad powers to a new managing director of the "Commissariat of Formerly Private Banks," Grigory Sokolnikov. There was an element of fantasy here, in that Sokolnikov, a young party activist with no experience in the banking industry, did not even know where many banks were (his first order to subordinates was literally to prepare a list of their addresses and phone numbers). The Bolsheviks having failed, owing to the employee strike, to obtain access to the vaults where state reserves (including gold) were stored, Sokolnikov instead laid claim to private bank *deposits*, with the exception of savings accounts held by proletarians not belonging to the "rich classes," with the cut-off at 5,000 rubles or a monthly income of 500. In this way, private property in Russia would be "annihilated."[24]

The first reports from the banks Sokolnikov surveyed bristled with talk of "sums of incredible size" on deposit. By confiscating the private savings of rich Russians, the Bolsheviks aimed to acquire 2 to 3 billion rubles—$1 billion to $1.5 billion at the time, the equivalent of $100 billion to $150 billion today. And so it came about that on December 21, 1917, notices appeared all over Petrograd announcing that, "to combat bank speculation and the regime of capitalistic exploitation . . . the late private banks have been occupied by armed forces." Next day more notices appeared, explaining that on December 23 "will take place the revision of the safes at the following banks: International, Siberian, Russian Commercial and Industrial, Moscow Merchants', and Moscow Industrial (late Junker's)." Explaining what "revision" meant, the notice stipulated that "owners of safes from Nos. 1 to 100 at the said banks are to appear with their keys at 10 a.m. Safes belonging to those not presenting themselves within 3 days will be opened by the Revision Committee at each bank with a view to the confiscation of the contents." Bolshevik commissars were instructed to record "the quantities of: foreign *valiuta* [currency], gold and silver coin and ingots and bars of gold, silver, and platinum, all of which are confiscated and handed over to the State Treasury." Just in time for Christmas, Lenin's government had launched the novel policy of mass armed robbery of the citizenry, with the newly formed Cheka providing the muscle.[25]

In their first two months in power, the Bolsheviks had not so much won over the Russian people as harassed and bludgeoned them into submission. The November elections had returned a negative verdict, and Lenin could only postpone the convocation of the Constituent Assembly for so long before the entire country rose up against him.

Lenin, however, had an ace in the hole. In a war-weary nation, the man who could bring peace might carry all before him. It was time to play the German card.

$$=== \ 15 \ ===$$

CEASEFIRE

I n view of the historic events taking place in Petrograd and Moscow, it is easy to forget that Russia was in the middle of a world war when the Bolsheviks seized power. Judging from the lack of attention paid to military developments in most histories of the October Revolution, one could be forgiven for concluding that Russia's war effectively ended with the Kerensky Offensive of June–July 1917.[1]

Such a view is erroneous. The Galician front remained active all through summer and fall 1917, with artillery fire exchanged almost daily. Russian Special Army, near Vorobin, saw regular action well into October. On October 14, Russian troops actually took enemy prisoners. As late as October 18, the men of Special Army were given instructions from Stavka to "hold the line" to relieve pressure on Russia's Italian allies: the decisive Twelfth Battle of the Isonzo ("Caporetto") was then heating up. On the night of October 24–25, even as Red Guards were fanning out across Petrograd, Russian infantry beat off a furious German offensive near Rovno. On October 26, while the Second Congress of Soviets was rubber-stamping Lenin's coup, the commander of Special Army, General Rudsky, reported from Vorobin that "the enemy opened strong rifle and artillery fire, and enemy pilots tried to surveille our trenches, only be beaten off by our fire." Russian guns, he continued, "began raining down fire on the enemy trenches, and we scored hits on an infantry column advancing from the second to first trench line," cutting the Austro-German offensive to pieces. Clearly there was still fight in the Russian army.[2]

This fight did not survive Lenin's seizure of power. Although the "decree on peace" passed by Sovnarkom on October 26 was more aspirational than binding, it was wired to Stavka and the area commands, where it became the subject of vigorous discussion. On the active Galician front, the initial reaction was hostile. Special Army polled the men and found that few supported Lenin. A soldiers' committee resolution flatly denounced the "seizure of power by the Bolsheviks in Petrograd," which they feared would "lead to fratricidal war." On the other hand, the soldiers endorsed "emergency measures to bring about a speedy peace." In neighboring Eleventh Army, instances of fraternization across the lines were reported as soon as October 28.[3]

Other fronts saw a similarly discordant pattern, with the Bolshevik seizure of power greeted coolly, although Lenin's "decree on peace" was welcomed. For every resolution denouncing the illegal Bolshevik coup, there was another condemning the Provisional Government for continuing the war. On the relatively inactive Romanian front, the divide was particularly pronounced. In Sixth and Ninth Armies, the Bolsheviks would poll only 15 and 11 percent, respectively, in the November elections—and yet soldiers' committees in these same armies passed resolutions denouncing the "half measures and vacillating policy" of the Provisional Government and advocating "immediate peace and the transfer of power to the Soviets." By refusing to fight and demanding a ceasefire, Russia's frontline soldiers were endorsing Bolshevism in practice, even if most of them condemned it in principle.[4]

Until the situation in Moscow and Petrograd settled down—and the parliamentary elections were held—the fate of Lenin's peace proposal remained unclear, as no one was sure his government would last. Even Lenin himself, in his remarks to the Second Congress of Soviets on October 26, had predicted that his peace policy would "meet with resistance on the part of the imperialist governments [e.g., the Allies]—we don't fool ourselves on that score." Over the next two weeks, Sovnarkom issued no further orders to the military commands, creating uncertainty at the front. Only at four a.m. on November 8 did Lenin send a radiogram to Stavka, cosigned by Trotsky and the commissar of war, Ensign N. V. Krylenko, instructing

Russia's commander in chief, General Dukhonin, to "address your-self to the military authorities of the enemy armies with a proposal of the immediate cessation of hostilities." Dukhonin chose not to reply on the grounds that the directive was sent without "number or date"—that is, without the proper paperwork of the Russian War Ministry, as employees there were on strike.[5]

On the same day, Trotsky handed a "formal proposal for an imme-diate armistice on all fronts" to the Entente ambassadors in Petrograd. With Sir George Buchanan protesting that Lenin's was only a "pre-tended government established by force and not recognized by the Russian people," the Allies rejected the proposal on November 9. On November 12, the Bolshevik peace decree was transmitted, en clair, to German military headquarters at Brest-Litovsk—the Germans having no diplomats in Petrograd to hand it to—where, interpreted as a unilateral ceasefire request, it met a much friendlier reception. In this way Lenin circumvented Russia's wartime allies, the Russian Constituent Assembly being elected *that very day*, and his own mili-tary commanders, to ask the Germans personally for an unconditional armistice. So stunning was Lenin's démarche that German diplomats across Europe were specially instructed, in a circular wired from Berlin on November 13, to "conceal their glee" at public receptions.[6]

Back at Stavka, the roof was falling in on Dukhonin. At two a.m. on November 9, the commander in chief was awakened with the ominous news that Lenin, Krylenko, and Stalin were on the Hughes apparatus, waiting to speak with him. Asked to explain why he had not contacted the Germans yet, Dukhonin stalled for time, stating that he had no authorization from Russia's co-belligerents to begin armistice negotiations. When Lenin insisted he reply, Dukhonin objected that "only a government . . . supported by the army and the country can have sufficient weight to impress the enemy." This was the insubordinate answer Lenin needed, and he informed Dukhonin that, "by the authority conferred upon us by [Sovnarkom] we dismiss you from your post for refusing to carry out the orders of the gov-ernment." In a final insult, Dukhonin was told that his replacement would be *Ensign* Krylenko—almost certainly the lowest-ranking offi-cer ever to command the armies of a great power.[7]

Lenin was not finished with Dukhonin. On November 9, he broadcast a proclamation "to all soldiers of the revolutionary army and sailors of the revolutionary navy," informing them that Dukhonin had been dismissed for "disobeying the orders of the government and for acting in the manner that was bound to lead to great calamities for the toiling masses of all countries." With a hint of menace, Lenin demanded that Russian soldiers "not permit counter-revolutionary generals to frustrate the great cause of peace." Mischievously, he suggested that troops might "surround" such recalcitrant generals "with guards, so as to prevent lynchings." Lenin also requested that "regiments at the front immediately elect representatives to open formal truce negotiations with the enemy," in effect authorizing them to fraternize with the Germans.[8]

Dukhonin was not ready to give in just yet. Although dismissed from his command over the wires, he had not yet been arrested, nor had he lost control of Stavka's communications equipment. True, the Allied ambassadors in Petrograd were under Lenin's thumb, but Allied military attachés in Mogilev were not, and they assured Dukhonin that Lenin's regime was still not recognized in Paris, London, or Washington, DC—an assurance that he broadcast to the troops, accompanied by the editorial remark that the "chief object" of "Lenin and Trotsky" was to "spread a fratricidal civil war."[9]

The diplomatic stakes were huge. According to the "London Convention" signed on August 23/September 5, 1914, none of the Entente powers were permitted to open separate armistice negotiations with the Central Powers. For the Bolsheviks to do so would invalidate the still-secret wartime treaties, including the Sazonov-Sykes-Picot Agreement by which Russia had been promised Constantinople, the Ottoman Straits, Armenia, and Kurdistan. In these territorial promises, the Allied ambassadors thought they had a trump card—but they had not reckoned on Trotsky's ability to retaliate. On November 2, a sympathizer in the Foreign Ministry handed Trotsky "the keys to the filing cabinet holding the secret treaties," and he used them. On November 10, Trotsky published a broadside against the "secret diplomacy" of the "imperialist powers" and announced that *Izvestiya* and *Pravda* would begin publishing the secret treaties, including not only Sazonov-Sykes-Picot but also the territorial bribes offered to goad Italy, Romania, and Greece into the war. In response, the Allied military missions warned that if Russia entered into a "separate armistice or suspension of hostilities" in violation of the London Convention, it would "entail the gravest consequences"—reputed to include a Japanese invasion of Siberia. In a wire broadcast to frontline armies, Trotsky denounced the Allied statement as "a flagrant interference in the domestic affairs of our country with the object of bringing about civil war." The Russian people, he declared, "did not overthrow the governments of the tsar and Kerensky just to become cannon fodder for the Allied imperialists."[10]

Dukhonin was in an impossible position. Having lined himself up with Russia's wartime allies, he was now held responsible for their every move, including those made in the secret treaties Trotsky was publishing. For many Russians, the last straw came when *Izvestiya* published, on November 12, news that the US government had suspended all Russia-bound shipments of military supplies and provisions. This was teed up perfectly for the Bolsheviks, who responded, "it would seem that the North American plutocrats are ready to trade locomotives for the heads of Russian soldiers." Dukhonin now appeared, to many Russian soldiers, like the man who wanted to continue the war for the benefit of (in the words of *Izvestiya*) "the New York kings of war industry."[11]

Meanwhile Ensign Krylenko was en route for Mogilev on a special military train, flanked by fifty-nine Red Guards. They reached Dvinsk on November 11. On November 12, Dukhonin dispatched the First Finnish Rifle Division to Orsha, 50 miles north of Mogilev on the main rail line, with instructions to allow Krylenko "either to return to Petrograd or to proceed to Mogilev alone," but authorizing the "use of force to prevent Krylenko's armed guard from proceeding to Mogilev." XVII Corps guarded the rail line between Orsha and Mogilev, ostensibly on behalf of Vikzhel, the railwaymen's union. Blocked, for the moment, from reaching Stavka, Krylenko set up operations in Dvinsk. In his first order to the troops as commander in chief, Krylenko asked his men to "stand firm" and "hold the front," but also instructed them to "treat with contempt the lies and the false appeals of General Dukhonin's gang." On November 15, Krylenko went further, issuing an order for "firing to cease immediately and fraternization to begin on all fronts." Preparing for a showdown, he ordered up reinforcements from Petrograd, assembling a strike force of three thousand sailors and garrison troops, who took up positions just north of Orsha.[12]

In the face of the Lenin-Trotsky-Krylenko propaganda barrage, Dukhonin's last support among nearby troops now crumbled. The Finnish Rifles declared neutrality and let Krylenko enter Orsha. Vikzhel and XVII Corps pledged to block the tracks to Mogilev, but reneged when delegates saw the size of Krylenko's force. Receiving word that Krylenko's path to Mogilev was clear, Dukhonin began loading up trucks with Stavka's technical equipment and wired to Kiev to ask the Rada for a safe-conduct permit through Ukraine (the answer was no). At dawn on November 20, Krylenko's train arrived, and his battalion took over the town. Informed by the local Soviet that Dukhonin had helped General Kornilov and his supporters escape from Bykhov prison, Krylenko's men began baying for Dukhonin's blood. Krylenko, to his credit, offered Dukhonin protection in his own railcar, but he could not stay the mob, which pushed Krylenko himself aside (though leaving him unharmed) and swarmed over the train. Krylenko's men bashed in the windows with their rifles and then stormed into the train car of the unfortunate Dukhonin, who was beaten and run through with bayonets. His body, according to witnesses, was then "stripped and exposed to repeated profanations."[13]

In this way the Bolsheviks seized control of Stavka, and the command of the Russian army was transferred from General Dukhonin to Ensign Krylenko. What was left of it, anyway, for the Russian Imperial Army was melting away as soldiers simply packed up and left. What muzhik wanted to be the last to man his post while the great parceling out of the land began back home? This was especially true for minority peoples, such as Ukrainians, who saw the opportunity of attaining independence. By the end of November 1917, Ukrainian soldiers had virtually disappeared from the eastern front. It would not be long, a German spy reported from Kiev, before Ukraine would move "to separate itself from Russia." On the northern front, where there were dreams of Estonian, Latvian, and Lithuanian independence, the situation was no better. By the end of

December, all of three junior Russian officers remained at Dvinsk, holding the entire Baltic front line against the Germans.[14]

Many high-ranking officers were fleeing the sinking ship of the Imperial Army to form the nucleus of a new one. General Kaledin was the first to organize serious armed resistance, declaring Don Cossack independence as soon the Bolshevik seizure of power was wired to the country on October 26. General Alekseev set off south on November 12. Kornilov, sprung from prison by Dukhonin on November 19, set off for the Don region on horseback. Also freed were Generals Lukomsky and Denikin, who adopted disguises and traveled by train. By early December 1917, this burgeoning anti-Bolshevik coalition had gathered in Rostov-on-Don, captured by Kaledin's Don Cossacks on November 30. There was even talk of joining up with an English expeditionary force in northern Persia, although the British high command warned Kaledin and Kornilov to stand down and wait for the Constituent Assembly to convene before doing anything.[15]

Far from resisting the disintegration of the Imperial Army, the Bolsheviks embraced it as a necessary step on the road to world revolution. In early December 1917, Krylenko began formally demobilizing the army, in part for material reasons. A report received at Stavka on November 28 revealed a "catastrophic situation" in army logistics, with shortages of food, fodder, and rolling stock so severe that the army needed to shed "3 to 4 million soldiers" immediately. Since the Bolshevik takeover in Petrograd and the lynching of Dukhonin, desertions had risen dramatically—but not dramatically enough. Krylenko's solution was blunt: entire annual classes would be released from service, beginning with draft year 1900, on December 9; further draft years would be released on a schedule determined by a "demobilization commission," with the corollary that the men would be allowed to leave with their weapons. Putting an ideological spin on the policy, Krylenko explained, in a directive dated December 8, 1917, that Sovnarkom had asked him to come up with a "plan to transform a standing army into an armed population," and here it was. Combined with a ceasefire request, the demobilization of "three to four million" heavily armed soldiers perfectly fulfilled Lenin's program of transforming an imperialist war into a civil war.[16]

The Germans were happy to oblige. From intelligence reports, the German high command knew that the Bolsheviks were in no position to continue the war, even if they wished to. An agent's report, filed in Stockholm on November 17, noted that it would cost Russia "50–60 million rubles a day" to continue prosecuting the war, which was clearly "impossible." The only real concern at Brest-Litovsk, after Trotsky's ceasefire request was received on November 13, was to ascertain who, exactly, this Trotsky fellow and the new Russian commander in chief (Ensign Krylenko) were, and whether they could be trusted. As the question was urgent, Major-General Max Hoffmann, the real brains at German eastern headquarters under the nominal command of Prince Leopold of Bavaria, phoned the high command in Belgium and requested to speak with General Ludendorff, the real commander in chief under the aegis of the elderly Field Marshal Paul von Hindenburg. "Is it possible to negotiate with these people?" he asked. Ludendorff, needing to free up troops for a spring offensive on the western front, answered yes.[17]

With both sides desperate to end the war in the east for different reasons, matters proceeded swiftly. As early as November 14, Krylenko sent three delegates across the lines near Dvinsk, and they were brought to German headquarters muffled and blindfolded. After the Germans contacted Berlin and Vienna for authorization, at midnight Krylenko was informed that the Germans would open armistice talks at Brest-Litovsk on November 19. On November 16, Trotsky informed the Allied ambassadors that a truce had been reached and invited them to participate at Brest-Litovsk. In view of the strategic consequences of the collapse of the entire east European front, Trotsky's proposal was discussed by the Allied Supreme War Council in Paris that day. Although the British and Americans expressed some sympathy, the French and Italians, with bitter defensive battles on their own soil under way, objected. The Allies, Trotsky was told on November 18, would not participate. The Bolsheviks would go to Brest-Litovsk on their own.[18]

The Germans would now experience the novel style of the regime they had helped create. Trotsky dispatched to Brest his Bolshevik brother-in-law, Lev Kamenev; a Jewish lawyer named Adolph Joffe whom Trotsky had known since their Menshevik days; the

Banks commissar, Grigory Sokolnikov; a Left SR delegate named S. Mstivlavsky; and, as a sop to feminist socialist ideals, the famous SR assassin Mme. Anastasia Bitsenko, just released from a Siberian prison (she had assassinated a governor-general in 1905). The delegation was rounded out by a trio of "authentic" worker, soldier, and sailor delegates. Everything seemed perfect until Joffe and Kamenev, motoring toward Warsaw Station, realized they did not have a "representative of the peasantry," and so plucked "an old man in a peasant's coat" named Roman Stashkov from a street corner. "Come to Brest-Litovsk," Stashkov was told, "and make peace with the Germans."[19]

There was something disarming about this motley crew that arrived at Brest-Litovsk on November 20/December 3, 1917, accompanied by nine tsarist officers brought along to deal with technical issues, and who were treated as hostages. As the Russians were the supplicants, it seemed that the Central Powers had all the leverage, but this was not to reckon on the propaganda side, where the Bolsheviks excelled. Foolishly, General Hoffmann consented to allow German soldiers to visit special "intercourse centers" behind Russian lines, and to permit the exchange of newspapers: the Bolsheviks were already printing two German-language dailies, *Die Fackel* (The Torch) and *Die Völkerfriede* (The People's Peace). Hoffmann also agreed to "the immediate exchange of civil prisoners and prisoners of war unfit for further military service," which would allow the Bolsheviks to propagandize enemy prisoners of war before sending them home. Joffe also insisted that peace talks be publicized to the world, and the Germans, amazingly, agreed. These concessions given, the Bolsheviks agreed to a twenty-eight-day armistice to begin on December 4.[20]

Trotsky's team was playing a different game. Just as the Entente ambassadors had not expected that Trotsky would embarrass them by leaking the secret treaties, the Germans never imagined that the Bolsheviks would cultivate world opinion by advertising their own military impotence against the Germans. But this is exactly what Trotsky and Lenin proceeded to do. On November 23, during a pause in the armistice talks, Trotsky admonished Russia's allies to "state clearly and definitely, before all humanity, for what causes the nations of Europe must continue shedding their blood during the fourth year of the war." Adding punch to this rhetorical browbeating was the threat, published in *Pravda* the same day, that the Bolsheviks might repudiate Russia's external debts—amounting to 60 billion rubles (the equivalent of some $3 trillion today), the bulk held by British, French, and American creditors. Trotsky then fired a shot across the German bow, announcing in a radio broadcast on December 4 that the ceasefire "was only on one front." With a hint of menace, Trotsky explained that "our real negotiations [at Brest-Litovsk] were with the German workers and peasants dressed in soldiers' uniforms."[21]

The only mercy Trotsky granted the Germans, as formal negotiations began at Brest-Litovsk on December 9, was not to show up in person. In his absence, the mood was oddly convivial, in part because of the holiday atmosphere (according to the Western calendar, the first round took place from December 22 to 28). Wine flowed freely. There was even surprising concord over Joffe's proposal that any peace treaty must not sanction "forcible annexation of territories seized during the war," although the Bulgarians and Turks balked at this. To massage the issue, the Germans and Austro-Hungarians, in a Christmas Day Declaration on December 12/25, made acceptance of the no-annexation principle conditional on Russia's western Allies agreeing to follow it, too.[22]

Joffe's real goal in the first round of talks was to stall for time, in the hope that, in Trotsky's words, the Bolsheviks could "arous[e] the workmen's parties of Germany and Austria-Hungary as well as those of the Entente countries" into staging their own revolutions. But two could play at the stalling game. The Germans knew how precarious Lenin's hold on power was. On December 8, the German consul in Stockholm spoke with Karl Radek, one of Lenin's closest confidantes. Radek openly confessed that the decrees of the "Smolny government" were not much followed outside of Petrograd, and that even in cities the Bolsheviks controlled, they were "nervous." The Bolshevik strategy in the countryside, Radek explained, was to demobilize propagandized soldiers with their arms and hope for the best. In Petrograd, a cholera outbreak was expected any day. Owing to the ongoing bank strike, the state was bankrupt and could not survive without "help from the German side for the reconstruction of the Russian [economy]." Most important, from the German perspective, was the collapse of the Russian army, which, according to the agent who spoke to Radek, "finds itself in a state of utter dissolution." The Bolsheviks' decision to let soldiers leave with arms in hand meant there was a thriving black market in weapons near the front: Russian machine guns were selling for as little as 60 marks. The Germans thus had good reason to believe, as this intelligence report concluded, that the Bolsheviks would accept "peace at any price."[23]

Ratcheting up the pressure on the Bolsheviks were burgeoning independence movements on the Russian periphery, which they had foolishly encouraged with a Sovnarkom declaration on "The Rights of the Peoples of Russia to Self-Determination," co-signed by Lenin and the nationalities commissar, Stalin, on November 2/15, 1917.* The first peoples to accept the invitation were the Georgians, Armenians, and Azerbaijanis, who formed a Menshevik-dominated congress in Tiflis called the Seim and proclaimed an independent "Transcaucasian Federated Republic." The Sublime Porte arranged independence plebiscites in formerly Ottoman Kars, Ardahan, and Batum. Finland declared independence on November 23. After liberal nationalists prevailed in the November elections, the Ukrainian Rada proclaimed independence, prompting Kiev's Bolsheviks to flee to Kharkov, where they set up their own "Ukrainian People's Republic," ostensibly independent, too, but with a pro-Lenin orientation. With Kaledin's Cossacks encamped at Rostov-on-Don, Ukraine stood on the brink of a three-sided civil war. Taking advantage of Bolshevik weakness, the Kiev Rada sent a delegation of three young representatives to Brest-Litovsk for the next round of negotiations.[24]

As peace talks resumed at Brest-Litovsk on December 27, there was little sign of the conviviality of the first session. Owing to their own intelligence—and the insult of the Rada's being allowed to send delegates from Kiev—the Bolsheviks now knew that the Germans had designs on Ukraine. The ideological stakes had also been raised

---

*In retrospect the decision seems bizarre, as the Bolsheviks would spend the next five years fighting to regain control of territories they had literally invited to secede. The usual explanation is ideology: self-determination was a refutation of capitalist "imperialism," to be encouraged everywhere, including Russia; the refusal of the Provisional Government to allow minorities to secede had been a Bolshevik talking point. Ideology clearly counted with Lenin, although a cynic might recall that it was Lenin's support for Ukrainian separatism that had first recommended him to his German sponsors.

by a speech given, on the day before talks resumed, by US president Woodrow Wilson. Trotsky's publication of the secret treaties, followed by the Bolshevik decree on minority self-determination and the Germans' apparent (albeit conditional) acceptance of it, had put the Allies in a bad light, stealing Wilson's thunder after he had proclaimed a war for democracy. On December 26, 1917/January 8, 1918, Wilson unveiled his "Fourteen Points," reupping the ante by denouncing "secret diplomacy" (point 1) and embracing minority self-determination (contrary to legend, this phrase appears nowhere in Wilson's address, although it is implied in talk of "autonomous development" for various "nationalities"). The stage was set for a rhetorical battle royale over Ukraine.[25]

With the stakes this high, Lenin asked Trotsky to attend in person, with the express mandate of "delaying" the Germans as long as possible. Trotsky gave the Germans a taste of what to expect as his train pulled into the station at Brest-Litovsk, when he and Lenin's confidant from wartime Switzerland, Karl Radek, ostentatiously tossed propaganda leaflets out of the windows at German soldiers along the platform. With Bolshevik propriety, Trotsky refused to bow to Prince Leopold of Bavaria, and insisted that the Russian delegation sleep and dine in separate quarters from their hosts. The holiday fun was over, along with the pretense of comity. Since the Allies had refused to accede to the Christmas Day Declaration on the no-annexation principle, the head of the German delegation, State Secretary Richard von Kühlmann, announced that it was null and void.

Now began a fascinating game of cat and mouse. Kühlmann and Trotsky wrestled back and forth for days over the real meaning of "self-determination," with their argument amplified as the proceedings were released to the press. Kühlmann browbeat Trotsky into accepting the Rada delegates as legitimate, but Trotsky, in turn, goaded the Germans into admitting they were not going to evacuate occupied territories. To speed things up, General Hoffmann at last presented Trotsky, on January 5/18, with a draft map of the proposed borders of postwar Russia, which detached territories already occupied by German troops, including Poland and most of the Baltic area, with the peoples living there granted "self-determination." As for the future of Ukraine, Hoffmann stated bluntly that this would be "discussed with the Rada delegates." Finally running out of steam, Trotsky requested a ten-day adjournment to consult with Lenin in Petrograd.[26]

The gloves were off. Although the Germans were paying lip service to self-determination, they had also baldly confessed their intention of dismembering Russia. The Bolshevik regime, for its part, unmasked its true nature when, on the same day Hoffmann confronted Trotsky with a fait accompli at Brest-Litovsk—January 5/18, 1918—Red Guards surrounded Taurida Palace and dispersed the Constituent Assembly by force after it finally convened, killing eight people in what the progressive novelist and veteran of 1905, Maxim Gorky, called another "Bloody Sunday." Three days later, in place of Russia's democratic parliament (whose deputies they denounced as "hirelings of bankers, capitalists, and landlords"), the Bolsheviks convened a "Third Congress of Soviets" composed exclusively of Bolsheviks and Left SRs, which recognized Sovnarkom as the only legitimate authority in Russia and formally inaugurated a new sovereign entity called the Russian Soviet Federative Socialist Republic (RSFSR).[27]

The dissolution of the Constituent Assembly liberated the Bolsheviks from accountability to public opinion. Inside the party, it weakened the hand of Lenin's populist critics, led by a Marxist theorist named Nikolai Bukharin, who were opposed to accommodation with the Germans and wished to unleash *partizanstvo* (partisan warfare) against the occupiers while stepping up revolutionary agitprop behind German lines. Lenin's own position was that the Bolsheviks must accept Germany's peace terms to win a *peredushka* (breathing spell) to consolidate power at home. Although he won over Kamenev, Zinoviev, and Stalin, Lenin's proposal was voted down 48 to 15 at a party congress on January 8/21, showing how little support his policy enjoyed in the party—let alone in the country. As in October, it was Trotsky who squared the circle with his inspired slogan of "No war, no peace." As he explained, he would simply "announce the termination of the war and demobilization without signing any peace." The Bolsheviks could thus turn Brest-Litovsk into a "pedagogical demonstration," refuting the rumor that they were "agents of the Hohenzollern crown" while showing the "working classes of the entire world" that an unjust treaty was being foisted upon Russia "by German bayonets." Trotsky's clever compromise passed the Central Committee, 9 to 7.[28]

Armed with this curious mandate, Trotsky put on one of his greatest performances in the third plenary session, which opened on January 28, 1918 (after January 14/27, 1918, the Bolsheviks switched Russia over to the Gregorian calendar). For the Central Powers, the great prize was Ukraine—its resources and above all its grain, desperately needed in Constantinople, Vienna, and Berlin. Trotsky knew that with the Russian Imperial Army having melted away from the front—he had seen as much every time he passed through Dvinsk en route to Brest-Litovsk—he had no real way of preventing the Germans from taking Ukraine if they wished to. Still, they had given him a megaphone for his "pedagogical demonstration," and he would use it. When the Germans let the Rada delegates speak for "independent Ukraine," Trotsky retorted that the Rada of "Ukraine" represented a territory no greater than the hotel rooms the Germans had rented for its delegation. Trotsky's remark amused even Hoffmann, who knew that the Rada was tottering in Kiev: the city would indeed fall to Red Guards, sent from Kharkov, on February 8. Next day the Germans played their trump, signing a separate peace treaty with the Ukrainian Rada and giving Trotsky 24 hours to sign, or face the resumption of hostilities. Now it was Trotsky's turn to play his own. On February 10, Trotsky informed the Germans that, although he could not "sign a peace of annexation, Russia declares, on its side, the state of war . . . as ended." Rather than sign a punitive peace treaty, the Bolsheviks would simply "giv[e] the order for a general demobilization of all our armies." The assembled delegates were stunned into silence by this bizarre proposal, until General Hoffmann exclaimed, "*Unerhört!*" (Unheard of!). It was likely with this exchange in mind that the American liaison at Brest-Litovsk, Colonel Raymond Robins, called Trotsky "a four-kind son of a bitch, but the greatest Jew since Jesus."[29]

The ceasefire had run its course. Trotsky, running in essence a giant bluff, had dared the Germans to resume hostilities even though there were no longer enemy troops opposing them. If they took the bait,

German imperialism would be nakedly exposed before the world, so nakedly that Germany's own socialists might even, the Bolsheviks hoped, launch their own revolution against a military clique intent on prosecuting a war against a country (Russia) without an army. But would Russia still exist in recognizable form by the time this happened?

=== 16 ===

RUSSIA AT LOW EBB

The once mighty Russian Empire now stood entirely at Germany's mercy. From the Baltic to the Black Sea, the Russian line had all but disappeared. The general demobilization Trotsky had announced was not only for rhetorical show. The Bolsheviks had no money to pay regular soldiers even in Petrograd, where the garrison still numbered 200,000 men on paper, although few of them were pretending to be active-duty soldiers. Lenin was struggling to pay Red Guards, too, for whom the going rate was 20 to 30 *kerenki* (Kerensky rubles) per day. And these were a finite resource, as trained personnel at the mint capable of printing them (or the more valuable tsarist-ruble notes) had all left, and the State Bank had disbursed only 5 million to Lenin. True, the Bolsheviks were now producing their own cheap-looking paper currency—printed without serial number or signature, with the back side blank, they were already contemptuously referred to as *sovznaki* (Soviet rubles)—but even these would not likely suffice. A crude budget report obtained by German intelligence in early February 1918 noted that government expenses for the year were pegged at 28 billion sovznaki, against 5 billion in expected "income." Simple math suggested that, whatever currency was used to pay its armed defenders, so long as the bank strike continued, the days of the Bolshevik regime were numbered.[1]

Its enemies were predictably multiplying in consequence. In the Don region, Generals Alekseev and Kornilov were assembling a "Volunteer Army" to fight for the cause of the deposed Constituent Assembly, under the protection of "Ataman" Kaledin's Don Cossacks, although Kaledin was unsure of their loyalties. After some friction over the chain of command, Alekseev agreed to give Kornilov command of the troops, while handling political, financial, and diplomatic matters himself. By February 1918, the Volunteers had four thousand men under arms, a force large enough to focus the Bolsheviks' attention. The few reliable troops the regime controlled, a force of some six to seven thousand men under the command of Vladimir Antonov-Ovseenko, were sent south to crush the Volunteers before it was too late. They reached Rostov on February 23, and Novocherkassk, the Cossack capital, on February 25. Abandoned by the Don Cossacks, who refused to fight, the outnumbered Volunteer Army fled south in a soon-legendary "Ice March." Kaledin, ashamed that his Cossacks had failed him, committed suicide. The Don Cossacks would elect a new ataman, General P. N. Krasnov, in May.[2]

It was a Pyrrhic victory for the Reds. By sending their best troops south against the Volunteers, the Bolsheviks had left Russia's northern and western flanks unguarded, while forfeiting any real chance of subduing rebellious Ukraine. In Finland, although a few Red Guards—mostly radical sailors from the Baltic Fleet—were holding out in Helsinki, an anti-Bolshevik army commanded by a former tsarist general, Carl Gustav Mannerheim, already controlled the rest of the country and was threatening Helsinki. In Ukraine, Kiev had already turned into a multinational battleground, with French, English, and tsarist Russian officers fighting on behalf of the Rada. The Bolsheviks, according to a German agent in Stockholm who had spoken to the senior Bolshevik Lev Kamenev, now "seriously reckoned on a war between Russia and Ukraine." In the Arctic port of Archangel, the British Royal Navy had a squadron offshore, with marines on board, ready to land to protect military stores sent to Russia before the October Revolution.[3]

In Siberia, the strategic picture for Moscow was still bleaker. Vladivostok, like Archangel, housed huge volumes of imported war matériel, which had been shipped across the Pacific from the United States. On January 18, 1918, two Japanese warships arrived in Vladivostok to prevent these stores from falling into hostile hands, whether Bolshevik or German. Quietly, the Japanese were already shipping weapons and ammunition to the head of the "Transbaikal

Cossack host," Grigory Semenov, who controlled much of northern Manchuria. After hearing an alarming report that French and British merchants in Irkutsk were being "exterminated" by armed Bolsheviks and "their property destroyed," the French government mooted a proposal for a multinational force (French, British, American, Japanese, and Chinese) to "proceed from Manchuria to cut the Trans-Siberian Railway." So far had Russia fallen that lowly China was now among her oppressors, in a neat reversal of the humiliating "Eight-Power Expedition" of 1900: China had already sent more than a thousand troops into Siberia.[4]

Would the Germans take the plunge, too? At a crown council on February 13, 1918, Ludendorff proposed a bold offensive into Russia, threatening to occupy Petrograd if the Bolsheviks refused to sign the draft treaty of Brest-Litovsk. Paradoxically, he argued that this was the only way to end things quickly enough in the East to make possible his great spring offensive on the western front. Speaking for the Foreign Office—which still retained a soft spot for the regime it had helped spawn—Kühlmann cautioned against being drawn into the "center of revolutionary contagion," and proposed that the Germans revert to their policy of 1917, standing down on the eastern front so as not to provoke a patriotic Russian counter-revolution against Lenin. Kühlmann had a good case, but Kaiser Wilhelm II, incensed that the Bolsheviks had incited his soldiers to mutiny, sided with Ludendorff.[5]

Wilhelm II had also been impressed by intelligence reports speaking of the "madness reigning in Petrograd," which had become a real concern for the German high command now that Hoffmann was contemplating occupying the city. German agents in Petrograd (in particular a reactionary naval officer, Walther von Kaiserlingk) were telling alarming tales of assaults on private property across the entire Baltic region. Estonia was of particular concern because of its huge population of prosperous Baltic Germans, many of whom were being targeted for "expropriations." It is notable that two reports warning of "accelerating terror" were filed by German agents on February 6—the very day on which Lenin, in a celebrated editorial in *Pravda* outlining the Marxist imperative of "expropriating the expropriators," encouraged Russian proletarians to rob their better-off neighbors. "The bourgeoisie," Lenin wrote, "is concealing its plunder in its coffers . . . The masses must seize these plunderers and force them to return the loot [i.e., capital accrued through exploiting proletarian labor]. You must carry this through in all locations. Do not allow [the bourgeoisie] to escape, or the whole thing will fail . . . When the Cossack asked if it was true that Bolsheviks were looters, the old man replied: 'Yes, we loot the looters.'"[6]

In the face of such frightening reports, Kaiser Wilhelm decided that he had endured enough prevarication. "The Bolsheviks are tigers," he remarked, "and must be exterminated in every way." Although the question of a German occupation of Petrograd was left unresolved for now, the kaiser made it clear that he wished to secure at least the "Germanic" Baltic region, to prevent further Bolshevik horrors there. Ludendorff, for his part, emphasized the need to seize Ukraine before it was destroyed by Bolshevism. Hoffmann was authorized to resume the offensive on the eastern front, an offensive unsubtly code-named *Faustschlag* (literally "fist-punch") on February 17. The news was celebrated across Germany, according to a correspondent of *Vossische Zeitung*, "with school holidays, street rejoicings, and in some towns with the ringing of bells."[7]

After a cursory aerial reconnaissance of all-but-nonexistent enemy formations, at dawn on February 18 the German armies marched forward and seized Dvinsk, which had recently housed Russian Fifth Army headquarters, and pushed northward into Estonia. In Galicia, the Germans seized Lutsk the first day and rapidly descended into southwestern Ukraine, en route for the Crimean Peninsula. A Russian-language proclamation gave a political rationale to the German occupation, denouncing the Bolshevik dictatorship that "has raised its bloody hand against your best people, as well as against the Poles, Latvians, and Estonians."[8]

There was little resistance. In the first five days, along a line from the Baltic to the Carpathians, the Germans advanced 150 miles. At one railway station, seven German soldiers received the surrender of six hundred Cossacks. Russia's commander in chief, the overmatched Ensign Krylenko, observed sadly, "we have no army. Our demoralized soldiers fly panic-stricken before the German bayonets, leaving behind them artillery, transport, and ammunition. The divisions of the Red Guard are swept away like flies." General Hoffmann wrote in his diary, with a healthy dose of *schadenfreude*: "It is the most comical war I have ever witnessed. We put a handful of infantry men with machine-guns and one gun on a train and push them off to the next station; they take it, make prisoners of the Bolsheviks, pick up a few more troops, and go on. This proceeding has, at any rate, the charm of novelty."[9]

Trotsky had outsmarted himself. To stage his "pedagogical demonstration," the Bolsheviks had invited Russia's enemies to destroy her. When Krylenko, in a wire to Brest-Litovsk, begged Hoffmann to stop, the German refused. "The old armistice," Hoffmann replied, "is dead and cannot be revived," although he allowed that the Russians were perfectly free to petition for a new one. In the meantime, "the war is to go on . . . for the protection of Finland, Estonia, Livonia, and the Ukraine." The Germans promptly captured Tartu (Dorpat), Reval (Tallinn), Narva, and Lake Peipus. Only after the Germans had secured Estonia did Hoffmann, on February 23, send revised (much harsher) peace terms and invite the Bolsheviks to return to Brest-Litovsk to sign them.[10]

Lenin summoned the Bolshevik Central Committee on the night of February 23–24 to discuss Hoffmann's terms—and his own proposal to accept them. Trotsky, losing heart, softened his opposition, but could not quite bring himself to vote for peace. Bukharin, holding firm to his policy of partizanstvo, voted no, along with three other "left Communist" dissenters. With Trotsky and three others abstaining, Lenin's proposal to accept German peace terms needed five votes to pass: he got seven. He then proceeded to Taurida Palace to put the matter before the Congress of Soviets, whose approbation on foreign treaties was required according to the RSFSR statutes written up in January. Against stout opposition, Lenin argued that Russia had no choice but to "sign this shameful peace in order to save the world Revolution." By majority vote (116 to 85, with 26 abstentions), his motion passed. At 4:30 a.m. on February 24, 1918, a wire was dispatched to Berlin explaining that Sovnarkom "finds itself forced to sign the treaty and to accept the conditions of the Four-Power Delegation at Brest-Litovsk." The only remaining problem was who would agree to go to Brest-Litovsk and sign the humiliating treaty. This dubious honor fell to Sokolnikov, the banks commissar.[11]

Still the Germans marched on, seizing Minsk and Pskov and rolling up White Russia. On March 1, German troops marched into Kiev, which enabled Hoffmann to draw up terms with the Rada, arranging for the transfer of desperately needed Ukrainian grain to Berlin, Vienna, and Constantinople. On March 2, German warplanes even dropped bombs on Petrograd. Getting the point, which was hard to miss, on March 3 Sokolnikov signed the diktat peace treaty of Brest-Litovsk.[12]

The terms were draconian. In addition to the "full demobilization of the Russian army," the Germans insisted that Lithuania, Latvia, Estonia, Finland, the Åland islands in the Baltic, and Ukraine "must immediately be cleared of Russian troops and Red Guards," along with, at Turkish insistence, "the districts of Ardahan, Kars, and Batum in the Caucasus." Stripped of sovereign control over these provinces, Russia lost 1.3 million square miles—one fourth of the territory of the old tsarist empire—on which lived 62 million people, or 44 percent of her population. Estimated economic losses amounted to a third of agricultural capacity, three quarters of Russian iron and coal production, 9,000 out of 16,000 "industrial undertakings," and 80 percent of sugar production. Although Article 9 stated that "no indemnities" would be levied, reparations were hinted at in Article 8, which spoke of "reimbursement" for the cost of interning prisoners of war (in that millions more Russians had been captured by Germany than vice versa). German nationals were granted extraterritorial status inside Russia, exemption from property nationalizations, and sweeping economic concessions. In a special insult, the Bolsheviks were required to recognize the Kiev Rada. Russia's Black Sea Fleet was ordered to return to its Ukrainian ports and "be interned there until the conclusion of a general peace or be disarmed."[13]

Although Sokolnikov had signed the humiliating treaty, in political terms Lenin owned it. When Lenin arrived in Taurida Palace on the night of February 23–24, Left SR delegates had greeted him with shouts of "Down with the traitor!" "Judas!" and "German spy!" Lenin, unperturbed, had asked his critics whether they believed that "the path of the proletarian revolution was strewn with roses." In the pages of *Pravda* on March 6, Lenin took a similarly condescending tone, admonishing Bukharin and the other "Left Communists" to study military history to learn the value of tactical truces, such as the "Tilsit Peace" signed by Tsar Alexander I with Napoleon in 1807, which had bought time for Russia's ultimate victory. "Let's cease the blowing of trumpets," Lenin concluded, "and get down to serious work."[14]

On March 7, as if to disprove allegations that he was a tool of Berlin, Lenin ordered the evacuation of the government from Petrograd to the Moscow Kremlin, out of range of German warplanes, where it has remained to this day. Significantly, Lenin asked the French military mission for help in arranging logistics. With the Germans bludgeoning Russia into submission, it made sense to leverage the Entente powers against Germany—while, that is, Russia still had any leverage. As a show of good faith, on March 1 Trotsky authorized the landing of Allied troops at Archangel and Murmansk: five days later, 130 British Royal Marines landed. On March 5, Trotsky handed a note to Colonel Raymond Robins, the US liaison officer to the Bolsheviks, asking whether the "Soviet government" could "rely on the support of the United States of North America . . . in its struggle against Germany." Trotsky also courted Bruce Lockhart, a young Scottish "Russia hand" sent to Russia as a private envoy by the British cabinet. Although Trotsky was unable to obtain any concrete promises of military aid (or an Allied pledge to restrain the Japanese in Siberia), by the time the Brest-Litovsk treaty was formally ratified on March 14, he had done a great deal to improve relations with London and Washington. Paris would be a tougher nut to crack because of Lenin's decision to announce the repudiation of all Russian state debts on February 10, 1918. In France, owing to massive prewar investments in the tsarist regime, there were more than a million infuriated Russian bond-holders. Nonetheless, their very desperation to recover these losses gave the Bolsheviks a certain back-handed leverage against France.[15]

With a wary eye on both the Entente and the Central Powers, Lenin and Trotsky were quietly rebuilding Russia's armed forces, jettisoning the socialist dream of partisan militias for a proper professional army. On January 28, Sovnarkom had created the Red Army of Workers and Peasants (RKKA, henceforth Red Army) to take the place of the now-demobilized Imperial Army, with an initial outlay of 20 million rubles. On March 13, Trotsky resigned the Foreign Ministry and took over as commissar of war. (His successor as foreign minister, the former Menshevik Georgy Chicherin, came from an old noble family of diplomats, in another sign of the regime's grudging shift toward professionalism.) Significantly, Lenin and Trotsky agreed, against stout opposition from Krylenko and the Central Committee, to hire ex-tsarist officers as *voenspetsy* (military specialists) to train recruits, a policy formally authorized by Sovnarkom on March 31. In the course of his negotiations with Lockhart and Robins in March 1918, Trotsky even requested that British and American officers help train the Red Army, a request London and Washington approved on April 3, on condition that the Bolsheviks consent to a Japanese landing in Vladivostok (this condition was enough to kill the proposal). A new Commissar Bureau was established on April 18, which instituted the practice, maintained throughout the entire Soviet era, of assigning political commissars to keep watch over military officers. On May 8, Lenin and Trotsky even brought back Stavka, now styled the "All-Russian Main Staff." In all but its name and the assignment of political commissars, Lenin and Trotsky had re-created the Russian Imperial Army.[16]

Far-sighted though these reforms were, they did little to meet the immediate threats the regime faced on the Russian periphery. By legally cordoning off Russia from her former provinces in Finland, Ukraine, and the Transcaucasus, Brest-Litovsk was less "breathing spell" than incitement to invasion. The Germans landed troops in southern Finland in early April. Teaming up with Mannerheim's force of "White Finns" advancing from the north, the Germans conquered Helsinki on April 13, eliminating the last Bolshevik stronghold in Finland. On the White Russian front, the Germans seized Mogilev, which had been Russian military headquarters. On the western borderland of Ukraine, the Romanian speakers of Bessarabia, who had already declared an independent Moldavian People's Republic, pledged loyalty to Romania in April 1918. Although this union would not become official until the postwar treaties were ratified, Bessarabia was lost to Russia. All the Bolsheviks could do in retaliation was to seize Romania's gold reserves, which had foolishly been shipped to Petrograd in 1916 for safekeeping.*

Ukraine was the great prize. By mid-March 1918, even the hapless Austro-Hungarians had gotten in on the game, seizing Berdichev in northern Ukraine and then wheeling south to take Odessa with German help. A southern German army group, led by the formidable General August von Mackensen (architect of the German breakthrough at Gorlice-Tarnow in 1915), conquered Nikolaev, home to Russia's Black Sea dockyards, and Kherson, before invading the Crimean Peninsula. Rubbing Lenin's nose in defeat, Mackensen marched into the great naval base of Sevastopol on May Day 1918. In eastern Ukraine, a German advance guard, under General Wilhelm Gröner, marched into Kharkov on April 8 and quickly overran the strategic Donets (Donbass) region, with its abundant coal mines and factories. By May 8, the Germans had troops as far east as Rostov-on-Don (where they initiated contact with the Don Cossacks and Volunteers) and Taganrog, with scouting teams sent east to Tsaritsyn (later Stalingrad), on the Volga. In ten weeks, the German armies had conquered Russian territory larger than Germany. Twisting in the knife, Hoffmann wrote in his diary that "Trotsky's theories could not resist facts."[17]

The Germans were not the only ones taking advantage of Russian weakness. In an astonishing turnabout, considering how close Russia had come to crushing her ancient Turkish enemy in 1916–1917, the Ottoman armies thrust forward, encountering little resistance as they reconquered Trabzon, Erzincan, and then fortress Erzurum by March 12, obliterating Russia's hard-won gains from her 1916 victories in a matter of days. By month's end, the 1914 borders were restored. On April 4, the Turks marched into Sarıkamış, erasing the memory of a memorable Ottoman defeat during the first winter of the war. After

---

* The Bolsheviks also inherited Romanian artifacts, jewels, and manuscripts. Although little known outside Romania, the saga of the "lost national treasure" is an obsession there. Lenin decreed that the reserves might be returned if the "Romanian proletariat" ever came to power. When Nicolae Ceaușescu, the Romanian Communist dictator, reminded Brezhnev of this fifty years later, Moscow duly returned several cracked Thracian gold plates, which are now pathetically on display in the National History Museum in Bucharest. The gold bullion was never returned.

rolling up Ardahan province, the Ottoman commander, Vehip Pasha, took the surrender of Batum on April 12. On April 25, the First Ottoman Caucasian Army marched unopposed into Kars. In two months, the Ottoman Empire had turned the clock back forty-one years in her eternal war with Russia, restoring the 1877 borders.[18]

Under cover of the German and Ottoman advances, meanwhile, the Volunteer Army began to regroup in the north Caucasus. Although, in a blow to the cause, General Kornilov was killed by a shell on April 13 while bending over a map in a farmhouse outside Ekaterinodar, the Volunteers found another fine commander in General Anton Denikin, another low-born career soldier in Kornilov's mold. In early May 1918, just as the Germans were entering the Don region, the Volunteers returned to Novocherkassk in triumph and promptly made contact with General Gröner. Bolshevik-controlled Russia was now pinched between the Ural mountains and the German armies north, west, and southwest of Moscow and Petrograd, and cut off by the Volunteers from the coal-producing and industrial areas of Ukraine and from Baku and the oil-producing Caspian basin.

To counter the invading Central Powers, the Bolsheviks were forced to swallow their pride and request help from Russia's "capitalist" wartime allies. Begging London and Washington to hold off the Japanese at Vladivostok, Trotsky and Lenin won an early trick: Red Guards duly seized control of the city on March 24. But the victory was short-lived. On April 4, armed bandits (who may not have had any connection to the Bolshevik Red Guards) held up a Japanese-owned shop in the city. Next day, in retaliation, 500 Japanese marines landed and promptly spread out across the city. The Japanese now had a foothold in Asiatic Russia, which they would not easily surrender.

Making the situation in Vladivostok more explosive, the Allied consuls there were eagerly awaiting the arrival of an improvised legion of nearly fifty thousand Czechoslovak soldiers, most of them former Habsburg subjects taken prisoner by the Russians on the eastern front. The idea was that the Czechs would embark at Vladivostok on a roundabout sea journey to France, where they would reinforce the Allies on the western front. In a gesture to show good faith with Paris, London, and Washington at a time when the Central Powers were hammering him hard, Lenin had signed the Czech laissez-passer on

March 15. In retaliation for the Japanese landing at Vladivostok on April 5, the Bolsheviks ordered the legion, then proceeding eastward from Penza across the Trans-Siberian, to halt. Under ferocious pressure from the Allies (especially the French, who had the most to gain if the Czechs made it to France), the Japanese agreed to withdraw their marines from Vladivostok on April 25. For a moment in early May 1918, it seemed that the Bolsheviks and the Entente might come to terms out of shared antipathy to the rapacious Central Powers: the Germans were just then carving up the Don region.[19]

Fate then intervened along the Trans-Siberian. On May 14, an episode occurred at once utterly accidental yet emblematic of the chaos engulfing Bolshevized Russia in 1918. Even while the Czechoslovak Legion, keen to fight for the Entente to make a claim for postwar independence, was heading east on the Trans-Siberian, a detachment of pro-German freed Hungarian prisoners of war were heading home in the other direction. At a railway siding in Cheliabinsk, the two trains carrying antagonistic former Habsburg subjects pulled alongside each other. A quarrel broke out, and a Hungarian hurled a huge piece of scrap iron (or possibly a crowbar) at a Czechoslovak soldier, hitting him on the head and killing him. The victim's Czech comrades lynched the Hungarian and used the incident as a pretext to take over the railway station—and then, after the local Soviet protested, the arsenal, and finally the entire town of Cheliabinsk.[20]

Lenin now had reason to regret his decision to allow the Czechoslovaks to leave Russia with their arms. He had inherited this problem, like so many others, from Kerensky, who had originally authorized the creation of the legion to buttress his Galician offensive of June–July 1917 (two divisions had actually seen action then). At the time Lenin made his decision in mid-March 1918, the interests of the Bolsheviks, Allies, and Czechoslovaks had aligned. The legion's troops had been stationed in western Ukraine, in the face of the Austro-German advance; in a few areas they actually fought the invaders in late February. In a painful illustration of the state to which Russia had been reduced, Lenin had agreed to let a heavily armed legion of fifty thousand foreigners cross Ukraine and south Russia en route for Penza, just a few steps ahead of the invading armies of the Central Powers. The Bolsheviks had added the condition, signed by nationalities commissar Stalin on March 26, that the legion be partially disarmed in Penza, being allowed to proceed onto the Trans-Siberian with only 168 rifles and a single machine gun on each train, traveling "not as fighting units but as a group of free citizens, taking with them a certain quantity of arms for self-defense." But this condition proved difficult to enforce, and the Czechoslovaks had predictably kept most of their weapons.[21]

It was the Bolsheviks' bad luck that, at the time of the Hungarian provocation in Cheliabinsk, the men of the Czechoslovak Legion were strung out along the Trans-Siberian railway from Penza to Vladivostok, constituting everywhere they stood the strongest armed force for miles around. On May 18, the legion convened a "Congress of the Czechoslovak Revolutionary Army" in Cheliabinsk. On May 21, Trotsky ordered the legion disarmed, and had the members of the Czechoslovak National Council in Moscow—a sort of political liaison to the legion—arrested. On May 23, the Cheliabinsk Congress, defying Trotsky, resolved not to disarm. On May 25, Trotsky issued a follow-up order that amounted to a virtual declaration of war: "All Soviets are hereby instructed to disarm the Czechoslovaks immediately. Every armed Czechoslovak found on the railway is to be shot on the spot; every troop train in which even one armed man is found shall be unloaded, and its soldiers shall be interned in a war prisoners' camp."

If war is what Trotsky wanted, war is what he got. But the order of battle did not favor him. By May 25, the legion, under the command of a self-styled "general" named Rudolf Gajda, had already seized control of the railway and telegraph stations at Mariinsk and Novonikolaevsk (Novosibirsk), severing Moscow's connections with eastern Siberia. On May 28, the Czechs took Penza. Tomsk fell on June 4, and Omsk on June 7. On June 8, eight thousand Czechoslovak soldiers captured the regional capital of Samara, as one of them later recalled, "in the same way that one grabs hay with a pitchfork." In early July, Ufa fell. On July 11, the Czechs wrenched control of Irkutsk from Austro-German prisoners of war who made up the local Red Guard. With an advance guard having already seized Vladivostok, the Trans-Siberian Railway—from Penza to the Pacific—was now in Czechoslovak hands.[22]

Under cover of the Czech advance, Russia's beleaguered liberals and non-Bolshevik socialists mounted a comeback. In Omsk, a committee proclaimed the "Government of Western Siberia" on June 1. In Samara, deputies who had fled Petrograd after the Bolsheviks dissolved parliament in January formed a "Committee of the Constituent Assembly" (Komuch) devoted to restoring its authority. To cultivate Entente support, Komuch abrogated the Brest-Litovsk treaty and promised to honor the Russian state debts Lenin had annulled. While its authority did not yet extend beyond Samara, Komuch had laid down an important marker, as the cause of the deposed Constituent Assembly was one that millions of Russians, including the men of Denikin's Volunteer Army, could rally around.[23]

By July 1918, Russia had been reduced to a shadow of its former self. Siberia's cities were ruled by Czechs and Slovaks, its hinterland by Siberian Cossacks. Semenov's Transbaikal Cossacks lorded it over Manchuria, while his Japanese sponsors eyed Vladivostok. Finland was lost for good. Formerly Russian Poland, the Baltic area, White Russia, and Ukraine were German satellites, patrolled by a million occupying troops: there were 600,000 German soldiers in Ukraine alone. The Don region was controlled by Don Cossacks, the north Caucasus by Kuban Cossacks and Volunteers, while the Transcaucasus was being carved up by Turks. A German expeditionary force was in Georgia. Far from escaping the world war, Lenin's peace policy had turned Russia into the playground of outside powers. The future of Bolshevism looked bleak.

=== 17 ===

REPRIEVE

If there was a silver lining in the collapse of Soviet power in Siberia, it lay in the realm of diplomacy. The Czechoslovak Legion's improbable conquest alarmed not only the Bolsheviks, but also the Germans. On May 20, just as the war of words between Trotsky and the Czech Legion was heating up, the German government informed Adolf Joffe, now Soviet ambassador in Berlin, that Hoffmann's offensive in the east was concluded, and that the Germans had no intention of occupying Moscow or Petrograd. Ludendorff had run into serious problems on the western front, where his offensive launched on March 21, though bringing large territorial gains, had failed to reach Paris or break enemy morale. In the east, meanwhile, the Germans were putting out fires from Finland to the Black Sea. On April 30, just as the first German field batteries sighted Sevastopol, Russia's last two Black Sea dreadnoughts, which the Germans had hoped to seize intact, were sunk by their own Bolshevized crews, along with twenty torpedo boats, destroyers, and transport ships. The Ukrainian Rada had proven utterly incapable of delivering the grain it had promised. In Kiev, where the Germans had naively assumed that "milk and honey" would flow freely, as General Gröner wrote Ludendorff, "we cannot even get bread." On April 28, Gröner ordered German troops to disperse the Rada and arrest its leaders (the interior minister escaped by jumping out the window). He appointed in its stead a tsarist army veteran, Pavlo Skoropadsky, descendant of the Zaporozhian Host of Cossacks who had run most of Ukraine between 1649 and 1764, to rule as its hetman (ataman).

In danger of losing the war on both fronts, and with Ukraine turning into a huge headache, Ludendorff was forced to soften his opposition to the Bolsheviks.[1]

He still wanted, however, to keep Lenin on a short leash. The German high command was enraged by the Bolsheviks' scuttling of the Black Sea Fleet, and by their refusal to cease propagandizing the German army (and repatriating German prisoners of war), as mandated by Article 2 of Brest-Litovsk. In late April, the Germans had opened an embassy in Moscow under ambassador Count Wilhelm von Mirbach. To prop up Lenin's government, the German Embassy was directly subsidizing the Red Army, in particular the Latvian Rifles commanded by General I. I. Vatsétis, the only Imperial Army unit to survive demobilization intact. Even so, Mirbach had endured a series of insults, from the refusal of Lenin to greet him on arrival, to an astonishing military parade of Bolshevized German prisoners of war in Red Square, who had carried a German-language banner reading, "German comrades, throw off your kaiser as the Russian comrades have thrown off their tsar." The idea of occupying Moscow and Petrograd and overthrowing Lenin's obnoxious regime was never far from Ludendorff's mind, and he proposed it once again on June 9, arguing that "we can expect nothing from this Soviet Government even though it lives at our mercy." With a front row view of the chaos in Russia, Mirbach and his deputy, Kurt Riezler, agreed with Ludendorff, on condition that the Foreign Office revise Brest-Litovsk to make it acceptable to a less radical Russian government, possibly including the right SRs and Kadets, with whom Riezler had opened negotiations. The Kadet leader Pavel Milyukov, who had fled to Ukraine, had opened a line of communication with the German authorities in Kiev, even as Denikin's Volunteers were in contact with the German armies in the Don region.[2]

Kaiser Wilhelm II now faced a momentous decision. In a reprise of the policy battle of February, State Secretary Richard Kühlmann, speaking for the Foreign Office, assailed Ludendorff's proposal in a long memorandum for the kaiser. Having failed to prevent the wasteful allocation of resources to a large-scale occupation of European Russia, Kühlmann now cautioned against reinforcing failure. "We have only one overriding interest," he argued: "to promote the forces of decomposition and to keep the country weak for a long time to come." Rather than intervening further "in this country's internal affairs," he proposed that the kaiser allow the Bolsheviks to "remain at the helm for the time being," as they were forced, by their very weakness, to "maintain toward us the appearance of loyalty and keep the peace." It was a persuasive argument. On June 28, the kaiser, more out of resignation than enthusiasm, sided with Kühlmann, stipulating that the Germans would "undertake no military operations in Russia." He ordered Mirbach and Riezler to break off negotiations with the Kadets and Right Socialist Revolutionaries (SRs), and to inform Lenin's beleaguered government "that it could safely withdraw troops from Petrograd and deploy them against the Czechs."[3]

The kaiser's decision gave a reprieve to the Bolsheviks at a critical time. On July 1, the long-awaited cholera outbreak crashed into Petrograd, with 456 cases recorded the first week alone and another 4,247 by July 14; nearly a quarter of its victims died. By abandoning Petrograd, the Bolsheviks had escaped the epidemic, but they had also consigned the city to oblivion. A census in June showed that the population of Petrograd had declined by nearly half since early 1917, from 2.3 million to less than 1.5 million, and this was *before* cholera began ravaging the city. Most of the decline owed to food shortages so severe that by summer 1918 the Bolsheviks had created special "food procurement brigades" to wrest grain by force from nearby peasant farmers. Behind the brick walls of the Moscow Kremlin, Lenin's beleaguered government was safe from cholera and guarded by thirty-five thousand crack Latvian Rifle troops, whose salaries were subsidized by the German Embassy.

Owing to the kaiser's timely intervention, Lenin was able to unleash the Latvians against the Czechoslovak Legion, which in mid-June 1918 had entered Perm province, threatening both Ekaterinburg, in the Ural Mountains to the southeast, and Kazan, to the southwest. Kazan was home not only to the Red Army's eastern command, but also to half of the imperial gold reserves, nearly 500 metric tons of bullion, worth $330 million then or $33 billion today. The Czechs were only 90 miles from Ekaterinburg, which city, owing to a recent decision to move the captive Romanov family there from Tobolsk, had become almost as strategically important as Kazan. The arrival of the Latvians in Perm province in early July came just in time to prevent the former tsar from being captured by the Czechs, who might have handed him over to the Allies.[4]

By releasing the bulk of his loyal Latvians, however, Lenin had left Moscow vulnerable to internal opponents. Since the showdown over Brest-Litovsk, the Left SRs, who had earlier tolerated the Bolshevik government, had seethed in opposition to what they called "the rule of the commissars." Because their political support came from peasants, Left SRs were incensed by the Bolsheviks' violent food requisitions, which had sparked massive protests. The feeling was mutual. Lenin had expelled the Left SRs from attending Sovnarkom sessions in early April, after the government had finally broken the bank strike. By allowing 4,000 of 6,000 strikers to return to their posts, the Bolsheviks gained access to the old regime's cash and gold reserves. Right SRs, Mensheviks, and Kadets, meanwhile, had never given their consent to Lenin's government, and they opposed Brest-Litovsk just as vehemently as the Left SRs.[5]

The renewal of the Bolshevik-German partnership at the end of June 1918 was the last straw for Russian patriots. The Left SRs had resolved, at a secret party congress held just days before, to put forward a resolution demanding the abrogation of Brest-Litovsk at the Fifth Congress of Soviets, which convened in the Bolshoi Theater in Moscow on July 4. Whereas in February they had denounced Lenin as a "traitor," this time Left SR taunts were aimed at the German ambassador, Count Mirbach—who made an easy target, sitting in the diplomatic loge. "Down with the Mirbach dictatorship!" they shouted, dismissing Lenin as irrelevant. As if to prove their point about Bolshevik cooperation with the Germans, Trotsky actually requested permission from the Congress to have opponents of German occupation forces who resisted arrest "shot on the spot." Although the Left SR resolution to repudiate Brest-Litovsk was voted down by the Bolshevik majority, the Left SRs worked themselves into a bloodlust against the "German butchers" oppressing Russia. Later that night, the charismatic Left SR party leader Maria Spiridonova, a legendary assassin of the 1905 revolution, hired an assassin to murder Mirbach, both as an act of symbolic protest and as a signal for a Left SR uprising.[6]

Even as the Left SR plot was unfolding in Moscow, a Right SR plot was being launched simultaneously on the Volga northeast of the capital. The latter was the work of Boris Savinkov, the former commissar who had been Kerensky's acting war minister during the Kornilov affair. After the October Revolution, Savinkov had traveled to the Don and made contact with Generals Alekseev and Kornilov. A more impatient soul than they, Savinkov formed his own "Union for the Defense of Fatherland and Freedom" and pitched plans for an anti-Bolshevik rebellion to the Allies. The French ambassador gave Savinkov 2.5 million rubles, which he used to recruit former officers, including a formidable war hero, Lieutenant Colonel A. P. Perkhurov. Savinkov's idea was to seize Yaroslavl, northeast of Moscow on the only direct rail line to Murmansk, and hold it until the Allies would reinforce him from the north. Subsidiary risings would be launched at nearby Rybinsk and at Murom, a station on the eastbound Moscow–Kazan railway. At around two a.m. on July 6, Savinkov's organization took up arms, seizing Yaroslavl (where the competent Lieutenant Colonel Perkhurov was in charge) with ease.[7]

Back in Moscow at two o'clock that afternoon, two killers recruited by Spiridonova, posing as Cheka agents, entered the German Embassy on Denezhnyi pereulok, in the Arbat district. What followed was a grotesque affair reminiscent of Rasputin's murder. The assassins unleashed a hail of bullets at Mirbach and Riezler that somehow all missed. One assassin threw a bomb—which also missed. Finally, the other chased down Mirbach and shot him in the back of the head. By 3:15 p.m., the ambassador was dead.[8]

So shocking was the crime, so potentially damaging to Soviet relations with Berlin, that Lenin himself went to the German Embassy at five p.m. to express condolences to Riezler (who had survived the assault) in person. It was an extraordinary scene, not least because Riezler was the very man who had overseen the Germans' Lenin policy in 1917 while stationed in Stockholm, only to turn against the Bolsheviks after he had seen Lenin's regime up close in May–June 1918. Unimpressed with Lenin's apology, on July 10 Riezler requested permission from the Wilhelmstrasse to "temporarily" break off relations until the Bolsheviks showed "proper atonement for the murder."[9]

Meanwhile, the Left SRs used the assassination as a springboard to a rebellion, of sorts. Cheka headquarters, in Lubyanka Square, were seized by Left SR sailors, who took the Cheka chief, Dzerzhinsky, hostage. After seizing the Telegraph Bureau, the Left SRs sent out a message over the national wires claiming credit for the murder of Mirbach and denouncing the Bolsheviks as "agents of German imperialism." At seven p.m., the Congress of Soviets reopened in the Bolshoi Theater with a passionate speech by Spiridonova. Were the Left SRs going to seize power? No one seemed quite sure. Toward midnight, Lenin summoned Vatsétis, commander of the Latvian Rifles, who, after reinforcing Perm and the Volga region, had only about 3,300 men left in the Moscow area, facing 2,000 or so armed sailors fighting for the Left SRs. At five a.m. on July 7, the Latvians stormed the city center, reconquered the Lubyanka, and surrounded the Bolshoi Theater. Although the Germans still wanted justice for Mirbach's murder, the rebellion was over.[10]

The crisis of authority Lenin's government faced in July 1918 unleashed the inner savagery of Bolshevism. Food requisitions in the countryside were stepped up. In Moscow, Petrograd, and nearby towns, 650 Left SR party members were arrested. In Moscow, the Bolsheviks had 13 ringleaders executed, although they showed clemency to Spiridonova, who retained a certain mystique as a hero of 1905. The crackdown in Yaroslavl was more serious, owing to the brutal nature of the fighting there. Only on July 21 was Yaroslavl retaken by the Red Army, after days of shelling that "gutted" the ancient city center. This time, no mercy was shown. Although Perkhurov himself escaped, another 428 of Savinkov's followers were shot, in the first mass execution carried out by the Bolshevik regime. It would not be the last.[11]

The next victims of the burgeoning Bolshevik terror were the Romanovs. It had been a year of trials for the former tsar, his wife, Alexandra, their children, and the few family servants (such as Nicholas's doctor, Evgeny Botkin, and the tsarina's ladies-in-waiting) who had stayed loyal to them. During the months of house arrest in Tsarskoe Selo after the February Revolution of 1917, there had been some hope of salvation owing to an invitation from the tsar's English cousin, King George V. But the Petrograd Soviet had objected, causing the

British Labour Party (and a wide swathe of English public opinion) to pressure the king into rescinding his invitation. Tsarskoe Selo was close enough to Baltic ports that a rescue plot was launched by sympathetic military officers, though it had not come off. After the July Days of 1917, Kerensky had shipped the Romanovs, in dead of night under heavy guard, to Tobolsk, where they were safe from the Bolsheviks—but thousands of miles from any port. There had been a whisper of hope of escape in the chaos after the October Revolution, until Red Guards seized Tobolsk in March 1918.[12]

The Bolsheviks' original plan, after securing the Romanovs, was to bring them back to Moscow and force "Bloody Nicholas" to stand trial. But in the chaos of 1918, especially after the Czechoslovak uprising in Siberia, there was a serious risk the family could be captured en route. And so the Romanovs were transferred west to Ekaterinburg, only for the Czechs to threaten this regional capital, too. In early July, the head of the local Cheka, Yakov Yurovsky, took personal control of the house where the captives were being held, commandeered from an engineer named Ipatiev. Yurovsky's orders from Moscow were simple. He was to take a careful inventory of all the Romanovs' property prior to "expropriating it." Then he was to execute them. On the night of July 16–17, Yurovsky ordered Nicholas II, Tsarina Alexandra, her ladies-in-waiting, their five children, and Doctor Botkin down into the basement. After reading out a perfunctory verdict of guilt against the tsar (for "continued aggression against Soviet Russia"), Yurovsky's execution squad opened fire. Only Nicholas, the main target, was killed immediately (the gun that fired the fatal shot was later put on display in the Museum of the Revolution in Moscow). The other victims were finished off one by one at close range, execution-style. What transpired next was gruesome. In the words of Yurovsky's own, rather clinical recollection,

> it was discovered that Tatiana, Olga, and Anastasia were dressed in some kind of special corsets . . . the detachment began to undress and burn the corpses. A. F. was wearing a whole pearl belt. . . . Around each girl's neck was a portrait of Rasputin with the text of his prayer sewn into the amulets. The diamonds were instantly removed. They amounted to about eighteen pounds. . . . After we

put everything valuable into bags, the rest of what was found on the corpses was burnt and the corpses themselves were lowered into the mine . . . [13]

The "Four Brothers mine" where the bodies were initially dumped, alas, turned out to be too shallow to afford much camouflage if the Czechs, or another hostile anti-Bolshevik force, came through. And so the corpses were lifted up again and put back in a truck. Because of heavy rain, the roads were soon impassable. After some debate, the Bolshevik disposal team simply stopped along the Ekaterinburg–Moscow road, dumped the bodies, and poured sulfuric acid all over them. Yurovsky then covered the bodies with brushwood and ran over them repeatedly with a truck to mangle the corpses beyond recognition in case they were discovered. Buried in a shallow grave, the remains lay undisturbed until 1989. For good measure, on the next day, July 18, the tsar's blood relatives held at nearby Alapaevsk—including two Romanov grand dukes, a grand duchess, and their children—were strip searched, robbed of valuables, shot, and dumped in a mineshaft while at least several of the victims may still have been alive.[14]

Although the Romanov murders represented a political victory of sorts for Lenin, it was a fleeting one. Ekaterinburg fell to the Czechs on July 25, along with the nearby Four Brothers mine where the Romanovs had been initially buried, in which investigators, sent by Komuch (the Committee of the Constituent Assembly) in Samara, discovered a 10-carat platinum gold brilliant, a jeweled cross with emeralds and diamonds, porcelain miniatures, silver portrait frames, imperial belt buckles, coins, thirteen intact pearls, and various damaged jewelry (emeralds, earrings, almandines, adamants, topazes), scattered amid body parts (including a human finger), ripped corsets, and "the corpse of a female dog."[15]*

---

* The investigators did not discover the Romanov remains, nor the 18 pounds of diamonds stripped from the bodies of the tsar's daughters, which Yurovsky had buried prior to the Czech advance; these would be shipped to Moscow only after the Reds secured the area for good in 1919. Rumors of "buried treasure" percolated around Ekaterinburg for years. Well into the 1930s, Cheka agents regularly frisked locals, searching for saleable valuables.

Damaging as the fall of Ekaterinburg was for the Bolsheviks, in material terms it paled in significance next to the Czech capture of Kazan—and its banks—on August 7. The Czechoslovak Legion hereby acquired nearly 500 tons of gold, 100 million tsarist paper rubles (worth, at official par, $50 million then, or $5 billion today), platinum stocks, and a huge quantity of other valuables. The impotence of the Red Army was also nakedly exposed. The fall of Kazan to the Czechs prompted an acid response from Trotsky, who proclaimed the restoration of the death penalty for desertion in the Red Army on August 14 with his customary flourish, warning officers that "if any part of the army retreats of its own . . . the first to be shot will be the commissar and the second, the commander. Cowards and traitors will not escape the bullets."[16]

Bolshevik fortunes had now sunk so low that Lenin was forced to cough up still more concessions to the Germans, in effect paying them protection money. In a Supplementary Agreement to Brest-Litovsk signed on August 27, 1918, the Bolsheviks agreed to pay 6 billion marks of reparations, about $1.4 billion at the time, equivalent to $140 billion today. The Bolsheviks also agreed to recognize Georgia (that is, as a German satellite), and to ship to Germany 25 percent of the future oil production of Baku. In exchange, the Germans promised to evacuate White Russia, Rostov and part of the Don basin; not to encourage separatist movements on Russian territory; and to help the Red Army expel the Allied troops from Murmansk and Archangel. With the Bolsheviks duly shipping to Berlin the first two of five planned reparations installments in September, including 100 tons of gold, it appeared that the German investment in Lenin had paid off handsomely. With the German armies retreating on the western front, and 250,000 fresh American "doughboys" arriving in France every month, Berlin and Moscow were now locked in a desperate embrace to ward off catastrophe.[17]

If a shrewd observer were to wager on which partner would buckle first, it would not have been the Germans. Americans or no Americans, the Germans were fighting fiercely and the Allies had still not breached the Siegfried or "Hindenburg" line on the western front, believed to constitute "five miles of the most formidable defensive position in the history of warfare." From official memoranda,

264 — THE RUSSIAN REVOLUTION

we know that British and French commanders believed, well into September 1918, that the war would continue into summer 1919 at least. Even if the Allies broke through the last major fortified trench line, the Germans could easily retreat beyond the Rhine and blow the bridgeheads. With an eastern empire conquered with German blood, guarded by a million occupying troops, the Germans had every reason to fight on, and all indications suggested that they would do so.[18]

The Bolsheviks, meanwhile, were hanging on for dear life. Western intervention in Russia, spurred along by the success of the Czechoslovak Legion, was getting serious. On August 3, Komuch issued a formal invitation for the Allies to intervene militarily in Russia's civil war. The United States and Japan promptly signed an agreement on proposed troop deployments to Siberia. By month's end, Britain had forty thousand troops on the ground in Russia, mostly at Archangel and Murmansk. Although France had few troops to spare, Paris declared unequivocal support for intervention on August 7. In a clear declaration of intent, Britain's envoy to Lenin's regime, Bruce Lockhart, funneled 10 million rubles to General Alekseev and the Volunteer Army, still in the Don region. In retaliation for these interventionist moves, the Cheka arrested two hundred British and French nationals in Moscow. "A veritable panic has overtaken Moscow," Karl Helfferich, Mirbach's successor as German ambassador, reported to Berlin. "The craziest rumors imaginable are rife, about so-called 'traitors' who are supposed to be in hiding around the city."[19]

These rumors were not without foundation. Just past nine p.m. on August 30, three bullets were fired at Lenin, allegedly by a woman named Fanny Kaplan, as he emerged from the "Hammer and Sickle" (formerly Mikhelson) factory. The first missed him entirely, but the second lodged in his shoulder, and the third punctured his lung, forcing Lenin to slump to the ground before bodyguards carried him back to the Kremlin. Kaplan belonged to an underground SR cell affiliated with Savinkov's Union for the Defense of Fatherland and Freedom, believed to be plotting another coup. Lending credence to the theory, earlier that same day in Petrograd the head of the city Cheka, Moisei Uritsky, was assassinated outside Cheka headquarters. Suspecting British involvement, the Bolsheviks arrested Bruce Lockhart and interrogated him in the Lubyanka. Although Lockhart survived (he was later allowed to leave Russia in a "prisoner exchange" for Maxim Litvinov, his counterpart as Soviet plenipotentiary in London), the British envoy was made the scapegoat of a so-called Lockhart plot to create a military dictatorship in Moscow.* Fanny Kaplan was not so lucky. At four p.m. on September 3, she was executed with a bullet to the head.[20]

Whatever the truth about Lockhart's involvement, the political consequences of the Lenin assassination plot and the Uritsky murder on August 30 were immediate and terrible. Blaming the two crimes on "Socialist-Revolutionaries of the Right, hirelings of the British and French," on August 31, the chairman of the Bolshevik Central Executive Committee, Yakov Sverdlov, summoned "all Soviets of Workers,' Peasants,' and Red Army Deputies" to launch "merciless mass terror against the enemies of the revolution." Later that day, the head of the Cheka, Dzerzhinsky, and his assistant, Jan Peters, ordered that "anyone caught in illegal possession of a firearm will be immediately executed," while "anyone who dares to spread the slightest rumor against the Soviet regime will be arrested immediately and sent to a concentration camp." By September 3, *Izvestiya* announced that more than five hundred hostages had been shot by the Cheka. On September 5, twenty-nine more "counterrevolutionists" were executed in Moscow, including tsarist officials such as the ex–interior minister, A. N. Khvostov, and former Okhrana chief S. P. Beletsky. In an eerie echo of the French Revolution prison massacres of 1792, tribunals were set up in Moscow's jails, which summarily executed hundreds of suspected spies. This was not fast enough for G. I. Petrovsky, the people's commissar of internal affairs, who sent these extraordinary instructions to all provincial Soviets on September 4:

> The time has come to put a stop to all this weakness and sentimentality. All the right Socialist Revolutionaries must be arrested immediately. A great number of hostages must be taken among the officers and the bourgeoisie. The slightest resistance must be

---

*Cheka records confirm that Lockhart confessed under interrogation, although, of course, it may have been coerced. In a telegram only recently discovered, Lockhart spoke of "Savinkov's proposals for counter-revolution. . . . Bolshevik barons will be murdered and military dictatorship formed."

greeted with widespread executions . . . The CHEKAs and the other organized militia must seek out and arrest suspects and immediately execute all those found to be involved with counterrevolutionary practices . . . No weakness or indecision can be tolerated during this period of mass terror.[21]

Red Terror now spread across the country, its only mercy lying in the fact that Bolshevik rule did not extend beyond the Volga, and was bounded north, west, and south by German occupying troops in the Baltics, White Russia, and Ukraine. A Sovnarkom decree on September 5 legalized summary executions and *kontsentratsionnye lageri* (concentration camps), which were soon erected near all military fronts. Trotsky applied terror to the Red Army, announcing on August 31 that "twenty deserters were shot yesterday. The first to go were the commissars and commanders who left their posts; next came the cowardly liars who played sick; and finally the Red Army soldiers who deserted. Death to the coward! Death to the traitor-deserter!" The Terror reached Penza on September 10, where a local count, two tsarist army officers, and an old regime gendarme were shot; then Astrakhan, where "nine Socialist-Revolutionaries of the Right were shot"; Perm (36 shot); Viatka Guberniia (70 arrested); Orel (23 shot); then Vitebsk (8 shot), Voronezh (4), Petrozavodsk (4), Grodno (1), and finally Penza yet again, where, in retaliation for the death of a "Petrograd worker," the local Bolshevik committee executed 152 people on September 25, and promised that "severer measures will be taken . . . in the future."[22]

Given that Lenin was in a Kremlin hospital while all this transpired, he cannot be held personally responsible for the onset of Red Terror. Documents uncovered after the fall of Communism, however, suggest that he was thinking along similar lines before he was shot, owing to the increasingly sharp resistance of Russian peasants to Bolshevik requisitions. On August 8, Lenin ordered that "in all grain-producing areas, twenty-five designated hostages drawn from the best-off of the local inhabitants will answer with their lives for any failure of the requisitioning plan." On August 9, he instructed the Nizhny Novgorod Soviet to "introduce mass terror," to execute anyone "caught in possession of a firearm," and to begin "massive deportations of Mensheviks and other suspect elements." That same day, he ordered the Penza Soviet to intern "kulaks, priests, White Guards, and other doubtful elements in a concentration camp." On August 10, Lenin wired Penza that

> the kulak uprising in your five districts must be crushed without pity . . . You must make an example of these people. (1) Hang (I mean hang publicly, so that people see it) at least 100 kulaks, rich bastards, and known bloodsuckers. (2) Publish their names. (3) Seize all their grain. (4) Single out the hostages per my instructions in yesterday's telegram. Do all this so that for miles around people see it all, understand it, tremble.

Lenin certainly raised no objections to the wave of terror launched on his behalf, which claimed nearly fifteen thousand lives in the first two months alone—more than twice the total number of prisoners of all kinds executed in the last *century* of tsarist rule (6,321).[23]

Red Terror was a bridge too far for the Germans. By agreeing to help the Bolsheviks expel the Allies from Russia, the German government was now complicit in their crimes, to Ludendorff's disgust. To hedge the Wilhelmstrasse's bet on Lenin, the German high command had negotiated its own deals with the anti-Bolshevik Kuban and Don Cossacks, seeding them with 15 million rubles, more than Britain spent on the Volunteer Army. Unbeknownst to the German Foreign Office, which had requested that he contribute "six or seven divisions" for anti-Allied operations in north Russia, Ludendorff inserted the operational option (code-named "Schlußstein") that they would proceed to Murmansk and Archangel by way of Petrograd—where they would forcibly depose the Bolsheviks. The Germans also had operational plans to occupy Baku and secure the Caspian oil fields. (The Turks beat the Germans to Baku, arriving on September 15. Even so, Ludendorff issued an order to "plant the German flag on the Caspian" as late as September 29.) After learning of the assassination attempt on Lenin, Ludendorff ordered a division of German warplanes north from Kiev to the Baltics. On September 4, Ludendorff ordered preparations for Operation Schlußstein "to begin as soon as possible."[24]

Had Operation Schlußstein been carried out, it is difficult to see how Lenin's regime could have survived. A German occupation of Petrograd would have left Moscow isolated, an island of Bolshevik rule in a raging sea of foreign armies. Instead, the Bolsheviks were granted another improbable reprieve, on a hitherto obscure front in the world war: the Macedonian. Owing to diplomatic fallout from Brest-Litovsk, which had seen Bulgaria's co-belligerents deny her hoped-for spoils from the carving up of Russia, morale in the Bulgarian army holding the line in Macedonia against an Allied expeditionary army based at Salonica since 1915 had begun to crack. On September 15, the Allied commander at Salonica, Louis-Félix-François Franchet d'Espèrey, ordered a general attack that quickly blew a hole 20 miles wide in the Bulgarian line, opening up a clear path for the Allied armies to Belgrade—and Vienna. At the high command, Ludendorff threw up his arms, telling aides that "the war was lost." On September 27, he called off Operation Schlußstein for good, granting Lenin—who had just left Moscow to convalesce at Nizhny Novgorod (Gorky)—a stay of execution. On September 29, the Allies breached the Siegfried line, prompting the Germans to sue for peace.[25]

The impact of the German collapse in the west was felt immediately in the east. In a flash, the prestige of the conquerors was erased. Brest-Litovsk, a German diplomat reported from Moscow on October 10, "is a dead letter. Our influence with the Bolsheviks is completely exhausted. They do with us now what they wish." Soviet officials confiscated the diplomatic bags used by the German Embassy in Moscow. After the western armistice was finalized on November 11, the Bolsheviks looted the German consulate in Petrograd, where they found 250 million tsarist rubles stuffed into thirty diplomatic mailbags. Accounts of German nationals in Russian banks, which had been exempted from confiscation at Brest-Litovsk, were turned over to the "German Revolutionary Worker and Soldier Council of Moscow," assembled out of pro-Bolshevik German prisoners of war.[26]

No one felt greater relief than Lenin at the German collapse. Since his return to Russia under German military escort in April 1917, he had been pilloried as a tool of German imperialism. With Germany on her knees and her diktat peace a dead letter, Lenin was vindicated, just as his survival from near fatal wounds inflicted by an assassin was being talked up by party propagandists as a "miracle" befitting a savior. Truly sovereign at last, the Bolsheviks could realize the promise of Lenin's revolution.

PART IV

THE BOLSHEVIKS IN POWER

The working class hoped to achieve its liberation. The outcome has been even greater enslavement of human beings.

—"What We Are Fighting For," Declaration of the
KRONSTADT REVOLUTIONARY COMMITTEE,
March 8, 1921

= 18 =

War Communism

While the world war still raged, there was a kind of aster-isk placed on the economic policies of Lenin's govern-ment. Until Ludendorff's collapse on the western front, German-owned businesses in Russia had remained exempt from nationalization decrees. Even some British and English firms had been accorded protection for diplomatic reasons, until the Allies tipped over into outright intervention in August 1918.

Even so, enormous damage had been done to the Russian econ-omy. In the early flush of revolutionary enthusiasm, Sovnarkom had passed decrees outlawing "all payments of interest on investments and dividends on shares" (January 11, 1918), nationalizing iron and steel production and the insurance industry (February 5 and 10, 1918), and forbidding the private "purchase, sale, or leasing" of commercial and industrial enterprises (April 1918). Because most of these enterprises had been owned by "capitalist" banks that had been "abolished" in December 1917, all that was really accomplished by these sundry nationalization decrees was the choking off of cash from industry, as the great Russian bank-industrial conglomerates were sacked of whatever moveable assets could be secured without the cooperation of striking bank employees. The upshot of this crude industrial asset stripping, compounded by fuel shortages, was a mass shuttering of factories. By May 1918, unemployment in Petrograd's factories had reached nearly 90 percent on paper. Urban employment figures were soon meaningless, as so many jobless workers fled to the countryside to get closer to the food supply.[1]

The nationalization of foreign trade, decreed by Sovnarkom on April 22, 1918, represented, both literally and figuratively, the logical culmination of the maximalist socialist program. Having gutted the industrial economy by starving private enterprise of the capital (and subsequently the labor) it needed to function, the Bolsheviks were forced to import the manufactured goods Russia was no longer producing. But what could a country producing almost nothing of value "trade" for imports? All that was available for export via the Gulf of Finland were a few leftover stocks of flax, hemp, and linseed oil sitting in warehouses in Petrograd since 1917; and these were enough to barter for only about $3.5 million worth of (mostly Swedish) manufactures. As there remained no way of shipping tsarist gold ingots safely and securely across the Baltic, the Bolsheviks instead smuggled tsarist and "Kerensky" rubles into Stockholm, which they had acquired from looting private bank accounts. By the end of 1918, Bolshevik couriers had deposited "not less than 200 million rubles" in Swedish banks, to securitize imports.[2]

Even these deals had been held up, meanwhile, owing to the German naval screen imposed after Brest-Litovsk, which blocked military imports. The western armistice of November 11 was thus not only strategically but economically significant. In November 1918, the Bolsheviks placed orders for hundreds of millions of rubles' worth of Swedish military imports, including gun barrels, locomotives, aero-engines, and black leather "bomber" jackets favored by Cheka agents.[3]

It was not to be. Even as Sweden's factories cranked up war production for Lenin, the British fleet took position in the Baltic Sea, imposing a blockade that made the earlier German screen look amateurish. Over the next ten months, only five Swedish ships, carrying exclusively civilian goods, got through, delivering agricultural items, such as grindstones, seeds, scythes, and saws, that were of little immediate use, as most of Russia's peasant farmers were being conscripted into the Red Army.[4]

Cut off from the world in 1919, the Bolsheviks would have to improvise a new kind of war economy entirely on their own. In a sense, the autarky imposed by the Allied blockade was ideologically appropriate, giving the regime a tabula rasa to build Communism without capitalist "infection" from abroad. In the Brest-Litovsk era, Lenin had been assailed by Bukharin's "Left Communists" for encouraging foreign concessions in the Russian economy and thus reintroducing the "germs of capitalism." Lenin was vindicated for signing the peace, but his critics won the economic argument. There would be no more compromises with foreign businessmen. Instead what remained of Russian industry would be exclusively state-owned and state-controlled, under the auspices of the Supreme Council of the National Economy (VSNKh). Created on paper in December 1917, VSNKh became truly operational in August 1918 when Sovnarkom delineated its powers and gave it a budget. This bureaucratic leviathan, comprising delegates from the Commissariats of Food, Transport, Labor, Agriculture, and Finance, was authorized "to regulate and organize all production and distribution and to manage every enterprise of the Republic."[5]

The creation of VSNKh was a seminal moment in the revolution. Later renamed (from 1921) the State Planning Commission (Gosplan), VSNKh was the "brains" of Communism. With private property abolished, the state now controlled, in theory at least, all economic activity in Russia. Entire sectors of the economy were assigned to planning agencies based on the commodities being produced (Glavsol for salt, Glavlak for paint, Glavbum for paper, and so on). As one industry after another was subordinated to VSNKh, the leviathan grew, reaching twenty-five thousand full-time employees by the end of 1919, who beavered away in a huge building in central Moscow on Myasnitskaya ulitsa.[6]

In material terms, the results of all this VSNKh paper-shuffling were meager, if not downright counterproductive. Economic indices declined even more precipitously than before. In the revolutionary chaos of 1917, industrial production had declined to some 77 percent of the last prewar year, 1913. In 1919, it fell to 26 percent of the 1913 total; in 1920, to 18 percent. This was true even of energy and raw materials output, with output of oil falling to 42 percent of prewar levels; coal falling to 27 percent; cotton yarn, to 5 percent; and iron ore, to a woeful 2.4 percent. Agricultural production in central Russia declined less in relative terms, about 38 percent from 1913 (78 million tons) to 1920 (48 million), although, owing to transportation problems, the impact on Russia's northern cities was especially severe.[7]

The only Soviet bureaucracy that rivaled VSNKh in its growth was the Mint. By 1919, demand for the printing of *sovznaki* (Soviet rubles) was almost insatiable, to enable the government to pay the metastasizing number of its own bureaucrats, along with millions of ordinary Russians thrown onto the payrolls of nationalized enterprises that produced little revenue on their own. There was an ideological component as well, in that many of the party's Marxist theorists, such as Nikolai Bukharin, wanted to destroy the ruble, pursuant to introducing a moneyless economy. The abolition of money was formally adopted in the Bolshevik Party program in March 1919. On May 15, 1919, the State Bank (now renamed the "People's Bank") was authorized to emit as much currency as it desired. By the end of 1919, the Mint employed more than 13,000 workers and was churning out currency by the truckload. That year, the number of rubles in circulation quadrupled to 255 billion. In 1920, the quantity would pass 1 trillion. By the end of 1921, more than 13 trillion rubles were being printed each month.[8]

The economic wages of "War Communism," as this period was retroactively labeled after the more extreme measures of state control were abandoned after 1921, were devastating. By 1920 Moscow and Petrograd, once the crown jewels of a fabulously wealthy empire, had become ghost towns. The pre-1917 population of Petrograd (about 2.5 million) had been reduced to 750,000. Emaciated city residents stumbled around in a perpetual half-stupor, with barely the energy to stand on line at government rationing centers for bread (which sold on the black market for thousands, then millions, of rubles). Both Petrograd and Moscow had nearly run out of fuel, with entire buildings being torn down for wood. Water pipes had cracked in the cold, leaving residents without running water. With streetlamps having ceased to function, the streets were dark and menacing at night. Trams and trolleys had stopped running. Colonel Edward Ryan, an American Red Cross commissioner, crossed Bolshevik lines from Estonia without official authorization in early 1920 to investigate the humanitarian situation. He left behind a vivid description of the horror that had overtaken Russia's once-great capital cities: "Both

Moscow and Petrograd are indescribably filthy in outward appearance . . . [I] was told the streets had not been cleaned for more than three years . . . The dirt and rubbish is in all places at least ankle deep and in most places it is up to one's knees, and there are many places where it is as high as one's head."[9]

The government's own employees, with access to the highest level of ration cards, ate better than did ordinary people, but this was little consolation to those who fell ill. With garbage piling up in the streets and shortages of everything from soap to running water to medicine, epidemic disease was rampant. Cholera hit Petrograd in summer 1918, soon followed by typhus and dysentery. There was little solace for sick patients in the hospitals, because the doctors and nurses were dying, too. Colonel Ryan, on an impromptu visit to a hospital in central Moscow favored by regime elites, learned that "during the preceding three months seventy-five percent of the personnel of this hospital had died." This comparatively well-off facility had sheets and mattresses, at least, but surgeries were still rarely performed because there were "very few surgical instruments and few anesthetics." Ryan was not allowed to visit hospitals in poorer districts, which, presumably, were even worse off. In the frigid swamps of Petrograd, matters were even worse, with so many people dying by 1919 that the morgues and cemeteries could not keep up: corpses lay around for months waiting to be buried.[10]

The atrocious situation in Russia's capital cities could be blamed, at least in part, on the collapse of transport. There was a snowball effect as fuel shortages—significantly, the Bolsheviks were cut off from Baku and its oilfields until April 1920—grounded rail engines, which, in turn, prevented supplies from reaching the cities. Even had enough fuel been available, rolling stock was disappearing, too. The production of locomotives, like everything else, plummeted in 1919 to only forty for the entire year, as against a thousand annually prior to 1917. Trying to find a catchall explanation for the dire state of the economy, Lenin's roving trade commissar, Leonid Krasin, wrote to his wife (herself settled in Stockholm) in 1919, "Distribution is very difficult with the railways in such a state of disorder . . . Any number of factories are idle; the Volga fleet is paralysed for lack of fuel." Or as one of Krasin's purchasing agents, Georgii Solomon, put it, by

1919, functioning train cars in Russia "had become an archaeological curiosity."[11]

Krasin's explanation for the economic catastrophe overtaking Russia, although inadequate, was not without some merit. If Russia's railways ever came back online, conditions would surely improve in the cities. In March 1919, Krasin, a trained engineer who was a rare Bolshevik with genuine business experience, was appointed Soviet commissar of ways of communication, with a sweeping mandate to restore and, hopefully, modernize Russia's rail network by placing major import orders abroad, and was authorized to spend as much as 800 million rubles on locomotives and spare parts. Shuttling between Petrograd, Stockholm, Copenhagen, and Berlin, Krasin put together a blockbuster deal, to be financed by Soviet gold shipments to Stockholm.[12]

So long as the British were blockading the Baltic, however, Krasin's rail deal remained stuck at the drawing board. The Entente powers had imposed a ban on Russian gold exports, viewing the old tsarist reserves acquired by Lenin's government as "looted property," to be held against the debts the Bolsheviks had repudiated. Gold bullion was heavy, difficult to move, and easy to trace. Imperial Russian ingots were clearly marked with a tsarist stamp, familiar to bankers all over the world.

Unable to ship gold across the Baltic in 1919, the Bolsheviks tried smuggling cash instead. But the western Allies were on high alert, and they pressured Finland and Sweden to crack down on illicit ruble transactions, circulated lists of suspected Bolshevik agents in Stockholm and monitored wire traffic. These efforts paid off handsomely. In January 1919, Sweden's government forbade the buying and selling of paper rubles on Swedish territory. In April 1919, Lenin's old Zurich associate, Fritz Platten, was arrested at the Finnish border, en route for Stockholm, carrying no less than 100 million rubles in his personal luggage.[13]

Cut off from major European suppliers by the Allied blockade, for most of 1919 the Bolsheviks were reduced to haggling with small-time smugglers and con men. The greatest of these was an ambitious operator named Franz Rauch, who hailed from the German-speaking communes of the lower Volga region. Captured by the Czechoslovak

Legion at Orenburg in spring 1918, and then freed when they withdrew from the area in October, he offered his services to the Bolsheviks and was sent to Berlin to negotiate. Rauch proposed to smuggle German manufactures (chemicals and dyes for paper factories, equipment for textile spinning mills, glass and kitchen wares, optical equipment, and pharmaceuticals) into Russia illicitly, avoiding Allied checkpoints. The scheme looked promising until Rauch explained to the German government that the Bolsheviks would pay for these imported wares with the 250 million tsarist rubles they had stolen from the German Consulate in Petrograd. This was the last anyone in Moscow heard from Franz Rauch.[14]

A particular import priority, outlined by the Soviet Trade Commissariat in March 1919, was paper, along with the chemicals needed to treat it, both for the Mint and for propaganda—the mother's milk of Communism. A Serbian trader was given a 150,000 ruble commission in May 1919 to import typewriters and ink cartridges. A trained engineer was sent to Finland with 20,000 British pounds sterling, acquired in the looting of bank safes, to cover the purchase of "technical material and accessories" for Russia's languishing paper mills (he was rebuffed and placed the order in Stockholm instead). But very few of these materials, owing to the Baltic blockade, reached Russia in 1919.[15]

Drawing blanks in the Baltic region, the Bolsheviks tried the southern smuggling routes. In early July 1919, the Foreign Trade Commission placed an order for 63 million rubles of Persian tobacco, dried fruit, oranges, and opium, although as fighting continued in the Caucasus, it would take almost a year for these goods to reach Russia. Another Persian trader did arrive in Moscow earlier in 1919 with several tons of opium. With Red Army doctors deprived of European medicines and painkillers, the Bolsheviks jumped at the chance to isolate some morphine. The People's Bank dipped into its dwindling supplies of tsarist rubles and paid the Persians 500 per kilogram of opium.[16]

This was about it for 1919, a year in which Russia's foreign trade fell no less precipitously than the domestic production that imports were intended to replace. The prewar volume of Russian exports had often surpassed 50 million tons annually, which ensured a positive

trade balance in most years against smaller volumes of imported manufactures. Exports had already dropped severely during the war and
revolution, dwindling to 60,000 tons in 1918, against 300,000 tons of
imports, most from Germany and Sweden. In 1919, Russian imports
plummeted to a positively anemic 16,000 tons; Soviet exports that
year measured a mere *1,500 tons* of leftover flax and hemp. It was as
if an entire continent, once central to the functioning of the world
economy, had dropped off the map.[17]

The decline in trade volume, at least, could plausibly be blamed
on the Allies. In addition to the British fleet patrolling the Baltic,
the lands of the former tsarist empire were now occupied by foreign
troops—Czechoslovak, British, French, American, Japanese—who
offered the regime a scapegoat for the privations ordinary Russians
were enduring. In political terms, it is not always a bad thing for a
government when its people suffer hardship in wartime, when shared
sacrifices can bring people together against a common enemy.

Emblematic of the social logic of War Communism was the introduction, on October 31, 1918, of "universal labor duty," which was
soon expanded to include *subbotniks* (compulsory weekend work battalions). Private labor unions were then abolished, which effectively
eliminated the right to strike. As Trotsky, turning Marx's idea about
the "emancipation of labor" on its head, explained the imperatives of
War Communism, "As a general rule, man strives to avoid work . . .
the only way to attract the labor power necessary for economic tasks
is to introduce *compulsory labor service*."[18]

Surrounded by domestic and foreign enemies, with her put-upon
workers and peasants conscripted into either the Red Army or universal labor duty, Lenin's Russia was mobilized for war in every possible sense of the word.

═ 19 ═

RED ON WHITE

Civil war occupied an important place in Bolshevik thinking. Far from an unplanned or unwelcome occurrence, it was the culmination of cataclysmic proletarian revolution. As we have seen, Lenin's imperative was to transform the "imperialist war" into a civil war. The idea was that Russia's peasants and urban workers, armed by the tsar to fight against Germans, Austrians, Hungarians, and Turks, would turn their weapons against "class enemies." Lenin's program had been literally implemented after the October Revolution when Ensign Krylenko "democratized" and "demobilized" the army, releasing entire draft classes of men from service while retaining their weapons. But for most of 1918, the class war had been complicated by the presence of so many foreign armies on Russian soil. By the terms of Brest-Litovsk (Article 5), the Germans had expressly *forbidden* Russia from fielding an army ("Russia will, without delay, carry out the full demobilization of her army *inclusive of those units recently organized by the present government.*") Still, the Germans had chosen to look the other way as Trotsky assembled the Red Army, seeing it as a useful bulwark against the Allied incursions in Siberia and at Murmansk. So long as the German army, 1 million strong, remained in the East, the Bolsheviks had not really been masters of their own house.[1]

The first and most critical result of the German collapse on the western front was therefore simple: the Red Army could be expanded without German interference. As early as October 1, 1918, after he learned of the Allied breakthrough at the Siegfried line, Lenin ordered general conscription to begin, with the aim of building an army of 3 million men by spring 1919. It was an ambitious goal, not only logistically but also politically, as an army of that size could only be recruited among the peasant population, which remained mostly hostile to Lenin. An army of millions would also need officers to train and command it, who could only be found among veterans of the Imperial Army. Trotsky had already begun enlisting tsarist officers in the Red Army in spring 1918, but only about eight thousand had signed up so far; Lenin's proposed army would require ten times that many. Moreover, many of Trotsky's early officer recruits had enlisted in the hope of fighting the Germans (then carving up Ukraine, White Russia, the Baltics, and Finland)—only to discover, by fall 1918, that their most likely opponents would be either Russia's former allies, or worse, their fellow tsarist officers in the Volunteer Army.[2]

Even so, the German collapse made Trotsky's task, in political terms, a bit easier. In spring and summer 1918, the Allied landings at Murmansk, Vladivostok, and Archangel had been small-scale and, in theory at least, friendly. Only after the Czechoslovak rebellion and Boris Savinkov's uprising at Yaroslavl in July had relations between the Entente powers and Moscow tipped over toward outright hostility, and even then it stopped short of armed combat. The November 1918 armistice, ending the world war, tore off the mask of friendliness. Any continued Allied military presence in Russia would be ipso facto hostile, which the Bolsheviks could plausibly describe to peasant recruits, or to ex-tsarist officers, as a foreign invasion. True, officers irredeemably opposed to Bolshevism could still join the Volunteer Army, and more than fifty thousand did. But for some patriotic officers, it now appeared that the Bolsheviks, for all their strange economic policies, were fighting for Russia, while their enemies were collaborating with foreigners. Small wonder that thousands of veteran officers joined the Red Army that winter, with as many as 75,000 serving by summer 1919, including 775 generals.[3]

The strategic picture facing Moscow in November 1918 was menacing, but far from hopeless. Finland and the Baltic states were lost, along with the Transcaucasus; but the embryonic states in these areas were mostly wrapped up in their own affairs, having no aggressive designs on Russian territory.

In Ukraine, the situation was fluid. The Germans were withdrawing very slowly (concerned about Bolshevik penetration, the Allied Supreme Command had stipulated in the November 1918 armistice that German troops should leave only "as soon as the Allies shall think the moment suitable, having regard to the internal situation"). The western Allies, pursuant to the Mudros armistice they signed with Turkey on October 30, now controlled the Black Sea, which enabled a British-French landing at Novorossiisk, in the Kuban area in the rear of the Volunteer Army, on November 23. The Volunteer Army itself was entrenched in the north Caucasus, under protection of the Kuban Cossacks, but General Denikin's cool relations with the Don Cossack ataman, General Krasnov, complicated any advance farther north. While still under German patronage, Krasnov's Don Cossacks had attacked Tsaritsyn, on the lower Volga, repeatedly in fall 1918, only to be beaten off in a brutal series of battles best remembered for the quarrel between Stalin, who had unleashed a reign of terror against ex-tsarist officers, and a furious Trotsky, who recalled Stalin to Moscow. Britain and France did control Russia's Arctic ports of Murmansk and Archangel, with more troops (including 5,000 Americans) landing there all the time. Still, Archangel was 770 miles from Moscow along a jerry-built railway very easy to sabotage, and Murmansk another 500 miles farther still. In Siberia, there were 70,000 Japanese and 7,000 American troops on the ground. But most of them were stationed in the Far East between Vladivostok and Harbin, 5,000 miles from Moscow.[4]

The most serious threat to the Bolsheviks came from Samara, 650 miles southeast of Moscow, where Komuch, the organization that claimed the mantle of the deposed Constituent Assembly, was issuing its own decrees under the protection of the Czechoslovak Legion. This would-be Russian government controlled, at its peak in late August 1918, Samara and Ufa provinces, in which lived about 12 million people, mostly Socialist Revolutionary (SR)–voting Russian peasants. Owing to the existence of a rival "Siberian Provisional Government" at Omsk, its authority did not extend farther east, but the territory Komuch controlled was more strategic, straddling the Volga River basin from Nizhny Novgorod to the Caspian. Komuch had even articulated a serious agricultural policy, turning over the land to peasant communes and freeing up grain prices. Komuch had begun recruiting its own "People's Army," although this numbered fewer than thirty thousand by the end of summer 1918, a force still overshadowed by the Czechoslovaks. Even so, Trotsky had sent his best troops, the Latvian Rifles under Vatsétis, to deal with Komuch, and arrived himself in August 1918 to take personal charge of a new "Eastern Army Group." On August 27, Trotsky narrowly escaped capture at Sviazhsk, in a close-run battle that turned out to be the high-water mark for the Czechs. Kazan fell to the Reds on September 10; Simbirsk, on September 12; and then Samara, on October 7. The Czechoslovak troops, unsure what or whom they were fighting for, were demoralized by these defeats. By the time the armistice was signed in November ending the world war on the western front, the Czech-Komuch alliance was in disarray. What remained of Komuch and the Siberian Army retreated east to Ufa and Omsk.[5]

Like the departure of the Germans from Ukraine, however, the disintegration of the Czech Legion removed a buffer between Moscow and the Allies. The shift from Samara to Omsk also changed the political complexion of the resistance in Siberia, weakening the hand of the radical Left SRs who, after breaking with the Bolsheviks in the botched uprising of July 1918, had fled east and come to dominate Komuch. Russia's Kadets, the liberal party of Milyukov, now returned from the political wilderness, forming a five-man "Directory" with moderate SRs. On October 24, Viktor Chernov, the Left SR ex–agriculture minister, issued a "manifesto" denouncing the Kadet-dominated Directory as "counter-revolutionary." This alarmed the Kadets and military officers in Omsk, who rallied around the former Black Sea Fleet commander Admiral A. V. Kolchak as a possible political savior. After dramatically resigning his command in June 1917 by throwing his sword overboard, Kolchak had escaped Russia, visited the Admiralty in England, and then traveled to the United States, where he gave lectures at the Naval War College in Newport, Rhode Island. A fervent Anglophile, Kolchak was liked and trusted by the British, especially Major-General Alfred W. F. Knox, the head of the British military mission in Siberia. In an eerie replay of the odd diplomacy of the Rasputin affair, a conspiracy was hatched in Omsk by a combination of ex-tsarist officers and Siberian Cossacks, which, on the night of November 17–18, 1918, brought Admiral Kolchak to power as "Supreme Ruler" of a new "All-Russian Provisional Government," with "warm approval" expressed by (and possibly the covert support of) Major-General Knox and the British military authorities in Siberia.[6]

The Kolchak coup in Omsk, coming hard on the heels of the western armistice, clarified the political stakes in the Russian Civil War. Previously a confusing, multiparty conflict, the war now appeared to be a bilateral affair pitting pro-Bolshevik "Reds" against right-leaning "Whites," who were backed by the western "imperialist" powers.* After General Alekseev, the titular head of the Volunteer Army, died of natural causes in October 1918, Kolchak was unrivaled as the political leader of the Whites. While posing as a simple patriot who disavowed *partiinost'* (party politics), Kolchak summed up his war aims as an uncompromising "struggle against Bolshevism."[7]

If the emergence of Kolchak as supreme ruler brought clarity to the political goals of the White armies, it did little to clear up the military chain of command. The area between Omsk and the Volunteers in the north Caucasus was Red-controlled, which meant that communications between Kolchak and Denikin needed to be routed by way of Vladivostok—and the Allied Supreme Command in Paris. Nor were the Allies agreed on which front to prioritize. The British were all in with Kolchak, but the French wanted to focus on Ukraine. The Americans were cool on Kolchak, too, owing to Woodrow Wilson's reservations about the antidemocratic coup in Omsk (the president also believed, erroneously, that the Whites planned to restore the Romanov monarchy).

Nor was it clear where the Whites, cut off from Russia's industrial centers, would obtain arms. The most logical supplier was the United States, which meant shipping weapons all the way across the Pacific Ocean to Vladivostok, and then thousands of miles along the Trans-Siberian. But Kolchak's government had little money of its own, and

---

*"Whites" was a Red insult, as this color of the French Bourbons implied a reactionary attachment to monarchy. None of the "White" leaders, who all pledged to restore the authority of the Constituent Assembly (not the tsar), ever accepted the term. Still, with apologies to the Whites, it is a useful shorthand.

the Czechoslovaks refused to hand over the Kazan gold reserves he might have used as security. In the end, the only weapons Kolchak could afford were British army surplus—600,000 rifles, 6,831 machine guns, 192 field guns, and 500 million rounds.[8]

The Bolsheviks enjoyed a more unified command and more favorable geography. Moscow was ideally located in strategic terms, at the center of a ramshackle but still functioning hub-and-spoke railway network from which troop trains could be dispatched northwest to Petrograd, northeast to Archangel, south toward the Don region, or east to the Urals and western Siberia. Ruling over central European Russia, the Bolsheviks could also recruit soldiers from a homogeneous population of "Great Russians," even as their White opponents, operating on the periphery of the old tsarist empire, had to rely on Cossacks, Ukrainians, Estonians, Finns, and other minorities of uncertain loyalties. The Red Army also inherited the bulk of the old tsarist Army arsenal, including 2.2 million rifles, 18,036 machine guns and 3 billion clips, 430,000 midrange or light guns, 500 Vickers heavy guns, 1.56 million hand grenades, and 167,000 officers' pistols and revolvers. The Bolsheviks also controlled the arms factories of Tula. Although production capacity was now severely limited, these factories were still critical assets.[9]

Despite laboring under material disadvantages, both Denikin and Kolchak put together real armies during the winter lull in fighting between November 1918 and March 1919. The departure of the Germans from the Don basin helped, by costing the Don Cossacks their patron and forcing their ataman Krasnov into an alliance of convenience with Denikin. On January 8, 1919, Krasnov accepted Denikin's command, instantly enlarging the Volunteer Army by 38,000 men. By mid-February 1919, Denikin's "Southern Army Group" counted 117,000 men, 460 guns, and 2,040 machine guns. The departure of the Germans from Ukraine and the collapse of their puppet Hetmanate in Kiev (replaced by a short-lived "Ukrainian People's Republic") opened up a new front for operations for Denikin, who could now outflank the Reds to the west and maybe even link up with the Polish army forming, led by Marshal Jozef Pilsudski, under Allied auspices. While this was bad news for the 30 million people of Ukraine, whose second dawn of independence would last less than two months, it was good news for the Whites.[10]

On paper, Kolchak's Army was even stronger than the Volunteers. By February 1919, Kolchak had 143,000 men under his command, enough to outnumber the Red Eastern Army Group, which counted only 117,600 (although the Reds had another 150,000 or so in reserve east of Moscow, in case of a White breakthrough). The Red Eastern Army Group was superior in both artillery (372 guns to 256) and machine guns (1,471 to 1,235), but owing to British aid, the Whites had enough stocks to sustain an offensive, if not indefinitely. The critical factor in western Siberia, where the armies (unlike in south Russia) were already poised in striking range of one another, was timing. After Lenin's October 1918 call for three million soldiers, it was only a matter of time before the Reds could overwhelm the Whites by force of numbers. To have any chance of a decisive victory threatening Moscow, Kolchak would have to strike quickly.[11]

Kolchak, a navy man, entrusted army operations planning to D. A. Lebedev, a former Stavka staff officer. But Lebedev had little material to work with, as there were fewer experienced officers in western Siberia than in the Don region—or in central Russia, where the Reds had an almost infinite supply of ex-tsarist officers to draw from. Only one of the veterans in Omsk, M. V. Khanzhin, had ranked as high as general. There was the self-declared "General Gajda" of the Czech Legion, but he was a Habsburg war prisoner with no command experience other than in the railway skirmishes of 1918.[12]

Despite these myriad deficiencies, the Siberian People's Army acquitted itself well in Kolchak's offensive, which began in mid-March when the Siberian winter began to ease (though crucially, before the ground had thawed out). In the first month, the Siberian Army, advancing along a 700-mile-wide front between Perm and Orenburg, pushed the Reds back nearly 400 miles, nearly to the Volga River. The Whites captured Ufa with ease, even while a southern army pushed southwest into the steppe above the Caspian, targeting Astrakhan. By the end of April, Kolchak's armies were threatening to retake Samara and Kazan. Meanwhile, a cascading series of anti-Bolshevik peasant uprisings in the rear of the Reds seemed to herald a major strategic breakthrough. In Omsk, the atmosphere was euphoric, with bold talk of linking up with the Allies at Archangel or Murmansk. The Japanese liaison officer to Kolchak, General Kasat-kin, even offered to send Japanese troops to reinforce his armies (for a price, of course, which included territorial concessions in the Far East). In panic, Trotsky ordered all available reinforcements to the eastern front.[13]

Trotsky's panic was short-lived. By May, Kolchak's eastern offensive had run into the same problem that bedeviled armies invading Russia from the West: the rains came, and the roads turned to mud. Mean-while Trotsky reorganized the command structure of Eastern Army Group, making two inspired appointments. M. N. Tukhachevsky, a high-born tsarist officer famous for escaping from a German fortress-prison, was made commander on the central front, while M. V. Frunze, a low-born Communist fanatic who had directed operations in Turkestan in 1918, was put in charge of the southern army group on the lower Volga. On April 28, Frunze struck at a vulnerable hinge point between the White central and southern armies at Sterlitamak, on the Belaya River, capturing prisoners and, significantly, a White operational directive from Omsk. Learning that his right flank was safe, Frunze pushed forward. By mid-May, he had punched a substan-tial gap in between the two White Siberian armies.[14]

Frunze's coup came at a critical moment in the Russian Civil War. In the burst of optimism that had followed Kolchak's early victories, the western Allies had begun drawing up conditions for continu-ing to supply his armies, not realizing how precarious his strategic position actually was. Despite energetic lobbying at the Paris Peace Conference by such old-regime diplomats as Izvolsky and Sazonov, the Whites simply had no diplomatic leverage, as they discovered when their request for a role in the postwar Ottoman Straits regime, pursuant to the old Sazonov-Sykes-Picot Agreement, was summarily dismissed. As the Bolshevik regime, despite having defaulted on all treaty and financial obligations to the Allies, was making no such demands regarding the Ottoman settlement, the Allies had even allowed President Wilson, against the fervent objections of Sazonov and Izvolsky, to send a mission to Moscow in March 1919, led by William Bullitt. (Bullitt's subsequent recommendation, that Allied diplomats meet Bolshevik representatives for formal peace talks on Prinkipo Island in the Sea of Marmara south of Constantinople, was vetoed by the French.)

To remind Kolchak who had the leverage, the Allied Supreme Council in Paris informed him, on May 26, that the Allies would continue to supply his armies only if he immediately convened a new Constituent Assembly and joined the nascent League of Nations (in both cases to appease Woodrow Wilson); if he agreed to honor all debts contracted by tsarist Russia (to satisfy the French); if he recognized the independence of Poland and Finland, and accepted mediation on the status of the new states in the Baltic region (to please the British). Kolchak, barely holding on against the Red tide, was forced to agree to these onerous terms, although he summoned enough patriotic stubbornness to insist that Finnish independence could be recognized only by the Russian Constituent Assembly, if it ever reconvened. To reassure Woodrow Wilson in particular, Kolchak declared, on June 4, that "there cannot be a return to the régime which existed in Russia before February 1917."[15]

While the Allies were putting the squeeze on Kolchak, the White position in western Siberia was falling apart. The Reds stormed into Ufa on June 9, pushing the Whites back to the Ural Mountains. Serious dissension was now brewing in the White command, with "General" Gajda, in charge of the northern front between Ufa and Perm, complaining that Lebedev had starved him of resources. Owing to the leverage still enjoyed by the Czechs—although they were no longer fighting at the front, they still held most of the Kazan gold reserves—Lebedev was forced to sack Khanzhin, the Whites' only experienced corps-level commander from the world war, and put Gajda in charge of the entire central and northern sectors. It was a poor decision. By the end of June, the Whites had fallen back to Ekaterinburg. In mid-July, Tukhachevsky's Fifth Army captured Zlatoust and, on July 24–25, Cheliabinsk, driving a deep gap in the White center. Farther south, Frunze was pushing east along what is now the border between Russia and Kazakhstan, threatening to outflank the entire White army on the right.[16]

If there was a silver lining in Kolchak's reverses, Trotsky's heightened focus on the eastern front did open up room for Denikin in the south. In mid-June 1919, just as the Siberian Army was falling back to the Urals, the Volunteers advanced into the Donbass region. Kharkov fell on June 21, opening up the path through central Ukraine to Kiev. On Denikin's right flank, a Caucasian Army, commanded by Baron P. N. Wrangel, a highly decorated cavalry officer of Baltic German stock, crossed the Kalmyk steppe and closed on Tsaritsyn, where the Reds had spent all winter digging trenches and erecting barbed wire. Deploying two British tanks, Wrangel's army breached these defenses and crashed into Tsaritsyn on June 30, capturing some forty thousand Red prisoners. Wrangel's was a signature victory in the Civil War.[17]

Timing did not favor the Whites, however. Far from coordinating his advance with Kolchak—a virtual impossibility, owing to the lack of a direct telegraph connection—Denikin's Volunteers had reached the Volga at Tsaritsyn at a time when Kolchak's forces were retreating all across the line, their own high water mark, less than 50 miles from the Volga east of Saratov, having been reached nearly two months earlier. It was a similar story in Ukraine, where France's own limited intervention had petered out long before Denikin finally went on the offensive in June. Because France had sustained such terrible losses on the western front, the sixty-five-thousand-odd "French" expeditionary force, which was commanded by Franchet d'Espèrey, and had landed at Odessa and on the Crimean Peninsula in December 1918, consisted mostly of Greek, Romanian, and French colonial troops from Senegal, none of whom had shown much enthusiasm for fighting in Russia's Civil War. In the first week of April 1919, a disgusted Franchet d'Espèrey simply evacuated the lot of them, along with forty thousand "White" civilians, including Grand Duke Nicholas— the first of many waves of Russian émigrés to leave via the Black Sea and Constantinople (where there was soon a large Russian colony, the glamorous women of whom titillated Muslim men not accustomed to seeing unveiled women in public).[18]

The French withdrawal from Crimea was hardly an encouraging omen for the Volunteer Army as it poured into Ukraine. The Allied Supreme Command in Paris had some hope that Pilsudski's new Polish army might put pressure on the Red Army from the West. The Poles indeed fought a series of small border engagements with the

Red Army in spring and summer 1919 in Lithuania and White Russia. But for Polish nationalists to cooperate with Denikin's Volunteer Army of Russian patriots and Cossacks would require something of a political miracle. True, Kolchak had promised to recognize an independent Poland; but he had clearly done so under duress, and Denikin, fighting under the well-publicized slogan "Russia, one and indivisible," had made no such promises regarding Poland. Pilsudski therefore remained distinctly cool to Allied requests that he coordinate his operations with the Volunteer Army.[19]

The diplomacy of the war was still more complicated in the Baltic theater. Here, just as in Ukraine, the Germans had withdrawn their troops slowly after the armistice, owing to Allied concerns about Bolshevik encroachment. The Germans also had troops in southern Finland, operating under the aegis of Carl Gustav Mannerheim's Finnish Army, which caused the Allies to view Mannerheim's "White Finns" skeptically and even, at one point in April 1919, demand that Mannerheim call off an offensive in Karelia just as he neared Petrograd. In Lithuania and White Russia, the Reds moved into Vilnius and Minsk after the German withdrawal in early 1919, only to lose these cities to Pilsudski's Polish army in April and August 1919, respectively. In Riga, veterans of the Latvian Rifles, after doing such great service to Lenin in 1918 by seeing off the Czech threat in Perm province and crushing the Left SR uprising in Moscow, returned home in triumph in January 1919, helping to establish a "Soviet" (that is, pro-Moscow) Latvian government.

The situation in Estonia was the most bewildering of all. After the armistice, the Red Seventh Army invaded from Petrograd, galvanizing resistance from a motley assortment of Estonian patriots, German soldiers who had never withdrawn, Baltic German locals, freed German prisoners of war, "White" refugees fleeing Petrograd, and tsarist officers returning east from German captivity. For a time, this anti-Bolshevik "Northern Corps" was commanded by a German general, Count Rüdiger von der Goltz. Nikolai Yudenich, the conqueror of Erzurum and (despite his notorious and now overweening corpulence) one of tsarist Russia's greatest war heroes, then arrived in late April and fashioned Northern Corps into a "Northwestern (NW) Army" of 16,000, augmented by 20,000 ostensibly allied

Estonian troops, who were commanded independently by General Johan Laidoner. On May 13, Yudenich's NW army crossed into Soviet Russian territory and swiftly captured Pskov.[20]

By summer 1919, despite Kolchak's reverses in western Siberia and the French withdrawal from Ukraine, the Bolshevik regime appeared to be in serious danger. The threat from the east had receded, but there were at least four active military fronts, two threatening Petrograd, and two Moscow. Mannerheim's White Finns threatened Petrograd from the northeast, while Yudenich's NW Army was encamped at Pskov, less than 200 miles from the city's southwestern perimeter. There were no armies this close to Moscow, but Pilsudski's Poles were at Minsk, just a simple rail connection away, and Denikin's Volunteers were advancing north of Kharkov on a broad front less than 300 miles south of Moscow, approaching Kursk and Voronezh. If these four armies achieved even a modest level of cooperation, Lenin's regime would not likely last out the year.

Once again, the Bolsheviks were fortunate in their enemies. In May 1919, Yudenich and Mannerheim came to an agreement, in principle, to coordinate a joint attack on Petrograd. But these plans ran aground owing to diplomatic complications. Some of the difficulty was rooted in Kolchak's stubbornness over Finnish independence, although Yudenich himself agreed to this condition on June 19. Four days later, Kolchak sent a telegraph to Mannerheim, requesting that his Finns attack Petrograd and even consenting to a Finnish occupation of the city, so long as Russian troops were present. But the British refused to cooperate with Mannerheim's Finns, whom they viewed as pro-German. The British Foreign Office took a blinkered view of Yudenich, too, owing to the "German" origin of his NW Army. In the British cabinet, only the minister of war and munitions, Winston Churchill, favored greater cooperation with Mannerheim and Yudenich, and he was overruled. With his Russian interventionist policy discredited owing to British hostility, Mannerheim was forced to stand for election in Finland in July 1919, and he lost. Having dodged a bullet in Finland, on August 31 the Bolsheviks offered peace—and diplomatic recognition—to Estonia. General Laidoner then chose to stand down his Estonian army, refusing to fight alongside Yudenich.[21]

Pilsudski, for his part, was content to observe the unfolding conflict from Warsaw, holding Vilnius and Minsk as bargaining chips. The longer the Russian Civil War continued, the better for Poland, as whichever side emerged triumphant would be all the more exhausted in case Pilsudski chose to fight to adjust Poland's borders eastward (the "Curzon line" drawn up by Britain's foreign secretary, Lord George Curzon, had drawn Poland's eastern frontier along the Bug River from East Prussia to Galicia). Although willing to parley with both Lenin and Denikin, Pilsudski had concluded, by September 1919, that it was "a lesser evil to help Soviet Russia defeat Denikin," and so he decided not to engage the Reds during Denikin's fall offensives. Pilsudski secretly informed Moscow of his decision in early October, which allowed Trotsky to transfer forty-three thousand troops south to face Denikin.[22]

In the absence of diversionary help from the French, Poles, Estonians, or Finns, and with Kolchak's Siberian army reeling, Denikin's Volunteers would have to fight on their own as they slogged their way north. On July 3, Denikin issued Secret Order No. 08878, stating his goal as "the occupation of the heart of Russia, Moscow." This "Moscow directive" envisioned an advance along three fronts, with Wrangel's Caucasian Army targeting Saratov, Penza, Nizhny Novgorod, and ultimately Moscow from the east, while V. I. Sidorin's "Don army" would march on Voronezh and Ryazan. The main thrust, led by the original Volunteer Army, would target the war factories of Tula by way of Kursk and Orel, even while dispatching rearguard troops to secure the Crimean ports abandoned by the French and, possibly, Kiev.[23]

As Denikin's armies marched into the heart of Ukraine, the Russian Civil War approached its sinister climax. The Volunteers quickly captured Red-held territory. But Denikin's supply lines were soon stretched to the breaking point, and they were thinly guarded. Ukrainian peasants were no more well disposed to the Whites than they had been to the German occupiers or the Reds, who had set grain requisition quotas even higher than the Germans had. The posture of most Ukrainian peasants was "a pox on all your houses," with farmers hiding their produce underground to deny them to marauding armies. By the time the Whites moved in, there were a half-dozen partisan armies operating in Ukraine, ranging from right-populists led by the Cossack hetman Semen Petliura to the far-left anarchists led by Nestor Makhno, a kind of T. E. Lawrence of the Russian Revolution, who blew up troop trains and robbed the survivors. Given an army commission by Trotsky in December 1918, Makhno had turned against the Reds. On August 1, 1919, Makhno issued his own Order No. 1, which called for the extermination of the White Russian "bourgeoisie" *and* of Red commissars.[24]

The one thing Ukrainian partisans had in common was xenophobia, encompassed in slogans like "Ukraine for Ukrainians" and "Ukraine without Moscovites or Jews." Long before the Whites had moved in, pogroms had erupted in the old Pale of Settlement on both sides of the shifting military lines. The Terek Cossacks, notorious Jew-haters, reached western Ukraine in October 1919 and crashed into Kiev, Poltava, and Chernigov. In a single pogrom in Fastov, outside of Kiev, 1,500 Jews were slaughtered, including 100 who were reportedly burned alive. Denikin, concerned about the erosion of discipline, condemned such atrocities and even tried, on several occasions, to convene courts-martial. Still, the evidence is abundantly clear that thousands of his troops, including regulars, officers, and Cossacks, indulged in terrible pogroms.[25]

As ugly as the situation was in Denikin's rear, the vistas opening up in front of him seemed endless. On August 10, a flying brigade of eight thousand Cossack cavalrymen, led by General K. K. Mamontov, captured Tambov and Voronezh, inducing panic in Moscow. On September 12, Denikin ordered all his armies, "from the Volga to the Romanian border," on the offensive, with Moscow the objective. Kursk fell on September 20, and there were signs of collapsing Red morale, with some units deserting en masse to the Whites. On October 13–14, the Volunteer Army conquered Orel, only 250 miles from Moscow, and less than half that distance from Tula and its munitions factories.

Meanwhile in Pskov, Yudenich had launched his own assault on Petrograd on October 12, not so much in coordination with the Volunteers as in defiance of the British, who had demanded, on October 6, that he transfer his forces to Denikin's front. The British did contribute six tanks, along with their British crews, to NW Army, along with naval support. Other than this, Yudenich's NW Army, now seventeen thousand strong, was on its own: Laidoner's Estonians refused to fight. The British tanks were rendered useless after the Reds blew up the bridge over the Luga River. Nonetheless Yudenich reached Gatchina, only 30 miles from Petrograd, on October 16. In the next five days, NW Army rolled into Pavlovsk, Tsarskoe Selo, and finally Pulkovo, just 15 miles from the capital. Covered by the British fleet, a detachment of Yudenich's marines also landed at Krasnaya Gorka, opposite Kronstadt, northeast of Petrograd. In Paris, Sazonov made one last desperate plea for Finnish intervention to help Yudenich, proposing to Allied diplomats that they could use the "Brest-Litovsk" gold the Bolsheviks had shipped to Germany (now in Allied hands) to pay for it. In this aim he was supported by Mannerheim himself, who, after being ejected from power in July, had gone to Paris to lobby with everyone else. Would the Allies back Yudenich when it counted?[26]

It was a moment of truth for the Bolshevik regime. Lenin, more worried about Moscow, wanted to abandon Petrograd and reinforce the southern front against Denikin. Zinoviev, the Bolshevik Party boss in Petrograd, suffered a "nervous collapse" when he heard of Yudenich's approach. And so it was left to Trotsky to save the city. Arriving in Petrograd on October 17, the commissar of war ordered that the "capital of the revolution" be defended "to the last drop of blood." Demonstrating real physical courage, Trotsky went to Pulkovo, abandoned the armored train car he usually traveled on, and rallied Red troops on horseback. With reinforcements pouring in from Petrograd, Trotsky pushed NW Army back to Gatchina on November 3, and then into Estonia. The only mercy for Yudenich was that Lenin, following the advice of Foreign Minister Georgy Chicherin, ordered Trotsky not to pursue Yudenich beyond the border, so as to drive a wedge between accomodationists and "interventionists" in London (Chicherin mentioned Churchill by name, displaying a keen grasp of British cabinet politics).[27]

Almost simultaneously with Yudenich's comeuppance, the Reds turned the tide against Denikin. Reinforcements had been pouring in all through September and early October to plug the gap north of Orel. The most important units dispatched south were the Second and Third Latvian Brigades. On October 18–19, just as the Volunteers were approaching Tula, the Latvians smashed into Denikin's left flank, in brutal action that saw the Latvians lose nearly 50 percent of their men, including 40 percent of their officers. That same day, a Red Cavalry Corps, commanded by Semen Budennyi, surprised Mamontov's increasingly disorderly Cossacks—weighed down by war booty—above Voronezh, threatening to encircle the Volunteers from the southeast. Denikin was forced to retreat to Kursk and then, in early December, to Kharkov. Red Moscow was safe.[28]

Such was the conclusion of British prime minister Lloyd George, who now abandoned Britain's commitment to the Whites so swiftly that he shocked even Chicherin and Lenin, who had expected a proper cabinet row over the matter. Without giving prior notice to his colleagues of a change in policy, Lloyd George simply announced, at the lord mayor's banquet at London's Guildhall on November 9, that Britain was giving up. "Russia is a quicksand," he intoned darkly: it was time for Britain to escape before she was sucked in further. The coming winter months, he suggested, would give all sides time to "reflect and reconsider." When the text of this historic speech was published and transmitted to Russia, the effect on White morale, a British journalist accompanying Denikin's army later wrote, "was electrical." Within days, "the whole atmosphere in South Russia was changed . . . Mr George's opinion that the Volunteer cause was doomed helped to make that doom almost certain."[29]

It was not over quite yet for the Whites. Fighting fiercely to the end, the Volunteers held on in Kiev until December 16. On Denikin's right flank, Tsaritsyn was abandoned only on January 3, 1920. Novocherkassk and Rostov fell on January 7, and the Whites prepared to evacuate beyond the Don. By now the Don Cossacks had ceased fighting, leaving Denikin with no option other than to reenact a less inspiring version of the Ice March of 1918, pulling back toward the Kuban River. Denikin's retreat turned into a general evacuation of "White Russia," with civilian émigrés from the northern cities, joined by local Kalmyk, Tatar, Cossack and Circassian notables who had collaborated with Denikin, fleeing on foot with whatever they could carry. "The exodus of the Russian people," as one White officer called it, "reminded me of Biblical times." In March 1920, Entente journalists recorded tearful scenes at Novorossiisk, as crowds of refugees tried to evacuate on the last British and French ships before the vengeful Reds closed in. Crimea, protected from the mainland by the easily defended Perekop Isthmus, was safe for now, guarded by a small rump army of Whites led by General Slashchev (who would soon surrender his command to Wrangel). But it could not be long before this last beachhead, too, was breached by the advancing Red armies.[30]

In Omsk, meanwhile, Kolchak and what remained of the Siberian Army had been hanging on for dear life after the fall of Cheliabinsk in late July 1919. Instead of pursuing immediately, Tukhachevsky and Frunze had paused to wait on reinforcements, knowing that time was on their side. As the thinning White armies retreated toward Omsk, the front contracted to about 200 miles from north to south. By October, the Reds enjoyed a two to one advantage in manpower (about 100,000 to 50,000) at the front, with massive Red reserves in the rear. On October 14, just as the decisive battles were being joined on the northwestern and southern fronts, Frunze, who had taken over the overall command of Red Eastern Army Group, ordered Third and Fifth Armies to attack. The Whites fell back behind the Ishim River at Petropavlovsk, and then evacuated farther east when the Reds crossed the river, the last natural barrier before Omsk, on October 31.[31]

Refugees now streamed into Omsk in terror of the advancing Reds, swelling the population of this provincial capital from 120,000 to over half a million. As one English officer recalled the scene: "Peasants had deserted their fields, students their books, doctors their hospitals, scientists their laboratories, workmen their workshops . . . we were being swept away in the wreckage of a demoralized army." On November 14, the Reds conquered Omsk without a fight, and the White exodus continued east into the vastness of the Siberian winter. The Trans-Siberian was clogged with bedraggled refugees, with thousands succumbing to typhus in the cramped, unsanitary railcars. The Czechoslovak Legion, hopeful of avoiding the epidemic, began halting the eastward movement of trains from Omsk, stranding even "Supreme Commander" Kolchak, who had planned to set up a new government in Irkutsk. For most of November and December 1919, Kolchak was held ransom by Czechoslovak guards at Nizhneudinsk, prior to being handed over to a Bolshevik Military-Revolutionary Committee in Irkutsk on January 21, 1920. The details of the negotiations remain murky, but the upshot is that the Czechoslovaks turned over Kolchak and 285 tons of the Kazan gold reserves to the Bolsheviks in exchange for their freedom.* On the night of February 6–7, 1920, Kolchak was shot following a "trial" reminiscent of the one given the tsar in Ekaterinburg, and his body was pushed under the ice of the Ushakovka River. So ended the White movement in Siberia.[32]

In the Baltics, the Bolsheviks played a more subtle game. By not pursuing Yudenich into Estonia, Trotsky had levered Lloyd George into a policy of accommodation, just as Chicherin had promised Lenin. Toward the end of October 1919, the British fleet began easing up on the Baltic blockade of Soviet Russia, stopping only ships with actual weapons aboard while letting dual-use items through. On November 20, Lloyd George informed the House of Commons that the blockade would be lifted in even this form as soon as the winter snows melted. Wired to the world, this declaration was music to Bolshevik ears—and to interested parties in Stockholm, where lucrative Soviet orders for everything from field and machine guns to locomotives, armored cars, and aero-engines were on hold.[33]

To capitalize on Lloyd George's stunning announcement, in December 1919 Lenin sent his roving trade commissar, Leonid Krasin, to Estonia, to negotiate peace terms. Because Petrograd's ports on the Gulf of Finland were ice-bound for much of the winter—they had also been severely damaged during the revolution—access to the great Baltic port of Reval (Tallinn) was critical. Krasin did not disappoint. By the terms of the Tartu (Dorpat) Treaty, ratified on February 2, 1920, Estonia granted official recognition to Soviet Russia, the first country to do so since Germany in the now-defunct Brest-Litovsk Treaty, while guaranteeing unlimited Soviet Russian use of her rail network for commercial freight. The treaty even created "special

---

*Nearly 100 tons of the original Kazan reserves had been lost. A few tons were shipped to San Francisco as security against White arms imports. The rest appears to have been spirited away by the Czechs—unless, as one rumor had it, it was dumped into Lake Baikal in the hope of future recovery, only to sink without trace into the fathomless depths of the world's largest freshwater lake.

zones" in Estonian ports, use of which would be set aside exclusively for the Bolsheviks.[34]

With their enemies in disarray and a window to the world opened on the Baltic, Lenin's government could begin to breathe freely at last. After two and a half years of isolation, international Communism was open for business.

= 20 =

The Communist International

B y 1920, all the familiar elements of Soviet Communism were in place, including single-party rule,* grain requisitions, a centrally planned economy with state ownership of the means of production, official atheism, the Cheka, Red Terror, and concentration camps housing "class enemies," of which camps there were now eighty-four. Some of these measures, such as the abolition of private property and state control of agriculture and industry, derived unambiguously from Marxist theory. Others had emerged from a blend of doctrine and necessity. The Cheka had been created to suppress a state-employee strike, only to evolve into a heavily armed, black-leather-jacket-clad army of ideological enforcers employing, by the end of 1920, some 280,000 people. Red Terror, launched in retaliation for assassination attempts on Lenin and Uritsky, had metastasized into a permanent class war against ever-growing categories of "enemies of the people" targeted in Cheka decrees: hoarders, "kulaks" (i.e., peasants accused of hoarding or hiding grain from requisitioners), "the rich," White officers, "Menshevik counterrevolutionaries," "bandits," those guilty of "parasitism, prostitution, or procuring," "ancien régime functionaries," "hostages from the haute bourgeoisie," "doubtful elements," and so on.[1]

Terrible as these Bolshevik policies were for class enemies, concentration camp inmates, and ordinary Russians reduced to abject

---

*In 1918 the party had been formally renamed the "All-Russian Communist Party (Bolsheviks)."

poverty, it was undeniable that, in military terms, at least, they worked. The Red Army was not the most efficient fighting force. Soviet sources suggest that Trotsky lost 1.76 million deserters in 1919 alone, out of 3.6 million peasant recruits (even if many of these later returned to their units). Despite public executions of deserters (about 600 in the second half of 1919), desertions continued into 1920 even after the Reds had defeated Denikin and Yudenich, suggesting that the loyalty of peasant recruits to Lenin's regime was weak to non-existent. Still, the salient fact was that, in a war against a world of enemies—from White armies supported by the Entente powers, to Finns, Poles, Cossacks, and partisans—the Reds had won.[2]

It was in recognition of this military verdict that Lloyd George had lifted the Baltic blockade, that Estonia had recognized the Bolshevik government, and that "capitalist" weapons suppliers were now lining up in Sweden and Germany to sell Lenin the proverbial "rope" he (allegedly) prophesied the Communists would use to hang them. Maxim Litvinov, the former Soviet plenipotentiary to London, current deputy foreign secretary and a future foreign minister, was appointed Soviet ambassador to Estonia. Together with Lenin's roving trade commissar, Leonid Krasin, Litvinov spread word throughout the Baltic region that the Bolshevik regime had cash to burn; its gold reserves, augmented by the Czech hoard acquired in Irkutsk, now surpassed 500 tons (worth $350 million).[3]

The regime was coming into other wealth, too. On the day after the Tartu Treaty was signed between Soviet Russia and Estonia (February 3, 1920), Lenin signed a Sovnarkom decree creating a clearinghouse on Strastnaia (Pushkin) Square in Moscow, mandated to store the vast quantities of confiscated platinum, diamonds, gold, silver, and jewelry now pouring in from reconquered provinces and from bank safe deposit boxes in Moscow and Petrograd, many only now being opened by a special branch of the Finance Ministry devoted to safe-cracking, the Safes Commission. This new "State Treasury for the Storage of Valuables" (Gokhran), directed by Nikolai Krestinsky, collected and appraised, in its first eight months alone, $245 million worth of confiscated valuables (equivalent to $24.5 billion today), including 51,479 carats of diamonds, 39,840 carats of pearls, 35,000 items of gold jewelry, and one hundred tons of silver.

The one exception to its collection mandate was in Petrograd, where Krasin instructed the Commissariat of Foreign Trade on February 16 to take "immediate measures" to register and appraise "all reserves of materials, wares, goods, and valuable antiques in the vicinity of the northern district," preparatory to their export via Estonia.[4]

With 500 tons of gold bullion and a jewelry hoard nearly as valuable on hand, the Bolsheviks were liquid buyers. Krasin's credit line, confirmed by a Politburo decree, was $150 million, the equivalent of $15 billion today. His first major deal, a locomotive order with the Nydquist & Holm consortium signed in Stockholm on May 15, 1920, was worth 100 million Swedish crowns (about $23.5 million then, or $2.35 billion now). In a critical test of the British posture on the Baltic, Nydquist & Holm required the Bolsheviks to ship 8,000 kilograms (8.82 tons) of gold to Stockholm as security—gold clearly marked with the old tsarist insignia, still banned from Entente capital markets. With Britain's fleet standing down, the gold arrived without incident on June 1. A range of Swedish, Danish, and German firms now signed deals with Krasin, too. By mid-June, more than 33 tons of gold had already been shipped from Reval to Stockholm, where the Swedish Royal Mint melted down looted tsarist ingots, put a Swedish stamp on them, and then sold these, at huge profit, to London and Wall Street buyers. In exchange for this laundered gold, arms dealers, inking deals in Reval, shipped to Russia supplies desperately needed by the Red Army, from locomotives and rolling stock (69 factories in Sweden alone were working on this order for Lenin), to precut "greatcoat" wool for Red army uniforms, leather boots and boot soles, Roche pharmaceuticals from Switzerland, and Mauser rifles and machine guns, sold in steeply discounted German marks.[5]

The arms import surge began just in time. In 1919, the Red Army had expended 70 to 90 million rounds per month, four times faster than clips were being produced in Tula, nearly exhausting the stock inherited from the tsarist arsenal. Scarcely had the White fronts quieted down than another foreign invasion came in spring 1920, from Poland. After observing the destruction of Denikin and Yudenich with satisfaction, Pilsudski had made methodical preparations all winter, assembling an army of 320,000. Taking a page from the German playbook, Pilsudski signed a treaty, on April 21, 1920, with a three-man "Directory of the Independent Ukrainian People's Republic," headed by the Cossack hetman Semen Petliura, who came to Warsaw to sign. Petliura conceded eastern Galicia to Poland in exchange for recognition of his authority in Kiev. Like the Germans, the Poles invaded Ukraine by formal invitation, which helps explain why it took them only two weeks to reach Red-held Kiev, which fell to a combined Polish-Ukrainian force on May 7, 1920, the Poles losing only 150 dead and 300 wounded. Wits in the Ukrainian capital noted that it was the fifteenth change of regime in three years.[6]

The Polish invasion-by-invitation of Ukraine, dangerous as it was, was also tailor-made for Red propaganda. Pilsudski and Petliura were over-the-top reactionaries, the former an avowed Polish imperialist and the latter a Cossack strongman harking back to the seventeenth century. The agitprop nearly wrote itself: indeed in Britain, linchpin of the wavering western Alliance, the Bolsheviks barely even had to try. By jettisoning the Baltic blockade, Lloyd George had already gone halfway toward accommodating the Bolsheviks. Under mounting pressure from the Labour Party, he would now go the other half. In fall 1919, he had agreed to send arms to Pilsudski's Poles. After the fall of Kiev on May 7, stevedores at the East India Docks went on strike, refusing to load a consignment of field guns and ammunition destined for Danzig. With the Labour Party in an uproar and believing (correctly) that the British public was weary of the failed intervention in Russia, Lloyd George's cabinet spokesman informed the House of Commons on May 17, 1920, that "no assistance has been or is being given to the Polish Government." Although none of the Entente powers had recognized Lenin's government, the reversal in British policy was nearly complete.[7]

Behind Red lines, the Polish invasion rallied many Russians to the Soviet regime out of simple patriotism. On May 30, 1920, *Izvestiya* published an appeal from the former commander in chief, General Brusilov, urging tsarist officers to enroll in the Red Army to see off the foreign invaders. Enough did to make a difference. In early June, Budennyi's First Cavalry Army pierced Polish lines outside Kiev. On June 12, Pilsudski sounded the retreat, allowing the Reds to take Kiev—in the sixteenth regime change of the revolution. By early July, the Polish retreat had turned into a rout, with a southwestern Red

Army Group under Colonel A. I. Egorov advancing on Lvov, and a Western Army Group, commanded by Tukhachevsky, advancing into White Russia and Lithuania. By early July, the Poles had been chased back to the Vistula, with Tukhachevsky's armies seizing Minsk (July 11), Vilnius (July 14), Grodno (July 19), and Brest-Litovsk on August 1. "Over the corpse of White Poland," Tukhachevsky exhorted his men, "lies the path to world conflagration . . . On to . . . Warsaw! Forward!"[8]

Whether or not Warsaw would fall to the Reds, the Soviet counteroffensive provided a perfect backdrop for the Second Congress of the Communist International, which opened in Petrograd on July 19, 1920, just as the Red armies were entering Poland. The First Congress, held in Moscow in March 1919, had been something of a dud, in that only 5 out of 54 delegates, owing to logistical difficulties, actually arrived in Russia from abroad, the remainder being composed of Russians and released prisoners of war, mostly Germans and Hungarians. Although the western front against Poland was active in summer 1920, the Baltic was now open, enabling Europe's socialist leaders to make their first pilgrimage into Red Russia.[9]

The Second Congress was a coming-out party for international Communism. In the nomenclature of socialism, the new Communist International (Comintern), was the "Third," the idea being that the Second International (1889–1914) had perished when socialist parties in belligerent countries' parliaments voted for war credits on August 4, 1914, abandoning the socialist cause for patriotism (or "chauvinism," as antiwar Marxists called it). Attendance was much higher than in 1919, with over two hundred legitimate foreign delegates making the trip, including Marcel Cachin, a rising French star; Giacinto Menotti Serrati, Benito Mussolini's successor as editor of the socialist paper *Avanti!*; and from Germany, not only members of the German Communist Party (KPD) formed out of the radical socialist faction known as the Spartacist League in winter 1918–1919, but four delegates from the Independent German Socialist Democratic Party (USPD) and also Klara Zetkin, creator of International Women's Day.

Not all European Marxists accepted the supremacy of Lenin's party, but Russian prestige was soaring and few could resist the lure of coming to Russia to see the great Communist experiment for themselves.

Upon arriving in their hotel rooms in Petrograd, delegates received a copy of Lenin's latest effusion, a condescending pamphlet called *"Left Wing" Communism, An Infantile Disorder*, which counseled foreign comrades to show greater patience and discipline, ruling out premature putsches (such as the botched German Spartacist Uprising of January 1919) until they were as strong as the Bolsheviks. The delegates were then shown the revolutionary sights, including the palaces of Tsarskoe Selo, which, after being occupied by grubby soldiers during the long civil war (when the town had been known colloquially as Soldatskoe Selo), had been transformed into "proletarian children's" homes for orphans of the revolution (it was now called Detskoe Selo). Back in Petrograd, the delegates were shown around the Smolny Institute, Bolshevik headquarters during the October Revolution. On Nevsky Prospekt, they were treated to a reenactment of "The Storming of the Winter Palace," staged under Maxim Gorky's direction on the steps of the now-silenced Petrograd Stock Exchange. Red flags blustered in the wind atop the Winter Palace as warships on the Neva lit up the hammer and sickle with searchlights. As one of the starry-eyed socialist delegates recalled, "it was like a dream."[10]

After a few ceremonial days in Petrograd, everyone took the train to Moscow, where the real business began on July 23. Although Grigory Zinoviev, now party boss in Petrograd, was the official chair, it was Lenin who stole the show as he mounted the rostrum in the Kremlin throne room to deliver the gala address. The timing was ideal, as the Red Army was then approaching Warsaw—en route, possibly, for Berlin, Prague, Budapest, or the other capitals of Europe. As Lenin cabled to Stalin, in Kharkov, earlier that very morning: "The situation in the Comintern is superb. Zinoviev, Bukharin and I, too, think that the revolution should be immediately executed in Italy. My own view is that to this end one should Sovietize Hungary and perhaps also Czechoslovakia and Romania."[11]

Over the next two weeks, the symbolism of the Kremlin throne room became reality. Before the Congress convened, Lenin and Zinoviev had crafted twenty-one conditions of membership to be imposed on foreign Communist parties, including the expulsion of "reformists and centrists," the imposition of "strict party discipline," the infiltration of labor unions, and the creation of a "parallel illegal organization" inside every party, ready to assume control come the revolution. Lenin's model of international Communism was a military chain of command, with an Executive Committee of the Communist International (ECCI) in Moscow issuing binding orders to national "sections," which must obey on pain of being ejected from the Comintern. Knowing that not all European socialists would swallow this, ECCI instructed delegates to return home and call snap votes in national party congresses, "splitting" them into "Communist parties" loyal to Moscow, and rump socialist groups that would be denied patronage.[12]

The lever used to pry open the proud socialist parties of Europe was simple: money. The Bolsheviks now possessed a gold reserve that had, in 1914, been the largest in Europe, even if it had since been reduced by the German reparations sent west in September 1918, the nearly 100 tons spirited away by the Czech Legion, and the bullion shipped to Stockholm to be melted down. More relevant for the Comintern was the world's largest jewelry hoard piling up in the Moscow Gokhran—jewels that could easily be smuggled into Europe. In 1919, Bolshevik couriers, according to one historian of the Comintern, had financed the embryonic Communist parties of Germany, Britain, France, and Italy with diamonds, sapphires, pearls, rings, bracelets, brooches, earrings and "other tsarist treasures" worth "hundreds of thousands of [tsarist] rubles." After the Second Comintern Congress, delegates were given diamonds to bring home, stitched into jacket cuffs or hidden in double-bottomed suitcases. Others carried cash, especially US dollars, which soon became the official currency of the Comintern, in which all accounts were kept (the official language, owing to the enduring prestige of Marx, was German).[13]

Armed with Moscow funds, delegates from the Second Congress would have imposing leverage when they returned home to carve Communist sections out of their parent socialist parties. But, owing to a somewhat reckless tour the Bolsheviks arranged in Ukraine to showcase their victory, forty foreign delegates were nearly stranded behind when their train was ambushed, three times, by Nestor Makhno's partisans. The Comintern VIP train made an inviting target in a land ravaged by three years of civil war; it was so lavishly outfitted that the curtains were drawn when it passed through populated areas, lest hungry locals storm the train. Somehow, Makhno kept missing his target—blowing up one railway bridge a few moments too late; then tearing up the tracks too early, allowing the conductor to brake and pull up short; then blanketing a small station with his partisans just minutes after the train had pulled through. In this way, a near disaster for Moscow, which might have seen Bolshevik prestige ruined had Makhno blown up their famous foreign guests, turned into a kind of beatification. As a Ukrainian peasant told one of the German Communist VIPs, "If even the Popes from abroad are in favor, then the Bolsheviks, these scoundrels, must be in the right and will win."[14]

It was in a similarly expansive spirit that the Bolsheviks convened a "Congress of the Peoples of the East" in Baku on September 1, 1920. After rolling down the Caspian through Daghestan, the Reds had entered Baku unopposed on April 28 and secured the oilheads. Although Armenia and Georgia, unlike Azerbaijan, remained independent, they were now pinched in between the Reds and the Turkish armies to the west. Georgia, abandoned by her German patrons in 1919 and distrusted by the Entente powers, was in little position to bargain. The fervently pro-Entente Armenian Republic, meanwhile, had thrown in with the Whites in 1919, and was now reaping the ill wind of their defeat.[15]

Whereas the Second Comintern Congress was aimed at European socialist elites, the Congress of the Peoples of the East targeted those of Asia, the Middle East, and Africa, broadcasting the message that Soviet Russia stood with the world's colonized and oppressed against European imperialism. In propaganda terms it was a brilliant idea, although owing to geographic limitations the Congress was predictably dominated by Russians, along with a few Tatars from Russian Central Asia and northern Iran, and Turks from Ankara, with tiny contingents from China and India. Because Christian Armenia and Georgia boycotted the conference (although a few Armenians and Georgians went anyway), it took on the air of a Muslim-Communist alliance against the West, or as Zinoviev put it in his opening address, of a "holy war" against "British imperialism." His abandonment of the "imperialist" Whites and Poles notwithstanding, Lloyd George was burned in effigy (as was, even more bizarrely, a by-now invalid

President Woodrow Wilson). The presence of Ottoman wartime generalissimo Enver Pasha added frisson. He was sent to Baku by the Soviet Foreign Ministry, which entertained hopes that he would return to Turkey to supplant Mustafa Kemal (the future Atatürk), First Speaker of the newly formed Grand National Assembly in Ankara, at the head of the Turkish nationalist movement—only for Enver to be denounced by Turkish Communist delegates as an "imperialist" war criminal.[16]

In retrospect, the Baku Congress was a political watershed, a first stab at the "anti-imperialist" message that would serve Communists so well during the twentieth century. At the time, though, its impact was muted by the darkening strategic picture for Moscow. When the Second Comintern Congress had convened, the Red Army had been triumphant. Pilsudski, falling back for a last-ditch defense of Warsaw, was outnumbered nearly two to one, with nearly 220,000 Red troops in Poland against his 120,000. On August 14, just after the Second Congress closed, Trotsky issued orders for the final offensive against Warsaw to begin. Somehow, despite tall odds, Pilsudski struck back with a blistering counterattack against Tukhachevsky's flank on August 16, capturing ninety-five thousand prisoners and forcing three Red armies to pull back in what Poles christened the "Miracle on the Vistula." By September 1920, the Reds were retreating all along the line, falling back all the way into Ukraine, where Wrangel's rump White Army was still encamped in Crimea. Capitalizing on the reverse in Red fortunes, in late September, Mustafa Kemal ordered Kâzim Karabekir's Turkish Fifteenth Corps to advance into then-Armenian Ardahan and Kars. The coronations in Moscow and Baku had been premature.[17]

Realizing this, Lenin and Trotsky sued Warsaw for peace. On October 12, 1920, Soviet diplomats signed a preliminary peace treaty at Riga, conceding huge swathes of western Ukraine in which lived nearly 3 million people (mostly Belorussians and Ukrainians), marking the final Polish boundary 120 miles east of the Curzon line drawn at Versailles. Eight days later, after transferring troops east to achieve a crushing superiority over the Whites (133,600 to 37,220), the Red Army attacked the Perekop Isthmus. It was all the over-matched Wrangel could do to screen an evacuation from Sevastopol, aboard French and Russian ships bound for Constantinople. (There were no British vessels, as Lloyd George had stipulated in the cabinet on November 11, to Churchill's horror, that Britain must not give Wrangel assistance even in evacuating women and children, much less fighting forces.) On November 14, the last White troops, along with civilians lucky enough to talk their way aboard—in all 83,000 people—left the Crimea; most would never see their homeland again. Some 300,000 unfortunate collaborators were left behind to face Bolshevik firing squads or be interned in concentration camps. In retaliation for helping Denikin and Wrangel, the Don Cossacks were expelled en masse from their homesteads. The Whites were finished.[18]

The departure of the Whites and the Poles also removed, however, the most plausible scapegoat the Bolsheviks could blame for the privations of War Communism. Foreign intervention had offered a common enemy shared by urban Reds and pox-on-all-your-houses peasants. This enemy gone, the real civil war, long simmering in the background, could now begin, pitting Russia's Communist rulers against her own people.

21

THE IDES OF MARCH

A s long as foreign or foreign-supplied armies fought on Russian soil, Lenin's single-party government had an excuse for draconian policies, such as forced "grain tribute" from the peasants (the notorious *prodrazvërstka*). Foreign intervention, along with the British blockade, had won the Bolsheviks a certain grudging sympathy from their rural subjects, as both fought the same enemies and suffered, to at least some extent, the same material deprivations. The Red Army was itself a marriage of convenience between the Communist regime and Russia's peasant masses, who supplied the manpower that allowed the Reds to defeat their foreign enemies largely by sheer weight of numbers.

In November 1920, the political dynamic was turned upside down. With the blockade lifted, the Bolsheviks were free to import as much military equipment as their tsarist gold bullion and Gokhran jewelry could buy—while facing, after the departure of the Whites and the Poles, only internal opposition from peasant partisans resisting grain requisitions, which now ratcheted up sharply.

Historians are still reconstructing the outlines of Russia's peasant wars. Cheka files opened after 1991 have revealed the astonishing scope of peasant bunts that erupted behind (or sometimes across) military lines during the Russian Revolution and Civil War. More than four thousand "peasant disturbances" were recorded in 1917 alone, from old-style manor burnings in the last days of the tsarist regime to anti-Bolshevik agitation after the October Revolution, with protests against the Provisional Government in between. The end of the world war in October–November 1918 saw a new spike, with forty-four separate armed uprisings. There was another surge after the defeat of Denikin and Wrangel in February–March 1920, when the so-called Pitchfork Rebellion, encompassing an irregular peasant army of fifty thousand stretched out between the Volga and the Urals, forced Red commanders to deploy cannons and heavy machine guns. Pilsudski's invasion in April had, in strategic terms, piggybacked on the Pitchfork Rebellion, which so distracted Trotsky that he had temporarily left Ukraine and White Russia undefended. The peasant wars may, in the end, have been a greater test of strength for the Bolshevik regime than the more publicized conflicts with the Whites, Entente expeditionary forces, Finns, and Poles. As Lenin himself pointed out, Russia's peasants were "far more dangerous than all the Denikins, Yudeniches, and Kolchaks put together, since we are dealing with a country where the proletariat represents a minority."[1]

The brief pause at the end of the Polish war allowed the Red Army high command to prepare its first serious inventory of stocks depleted during the Civil War. The news was not good. Nearly 1.8 million rifles of the 2.2 million inherited from the tsarist arsenal had been either lost, captured, or stopped working since 1918, leaving only 437,377 functioning rifles. Russia's factories could produce, in an ideal year, only one third of the 2 million rifles the Red Army needed. Of 18,036 machine guns the Bolsheviks inherited in 1917, only 5,000 were still operational, and Tula could manufacture, even at full annual capacity, less than half the 13,000 machine guns needed to replace the ones lost, and a quarter of the 3 billion clips these would require. Officer pistols and revolvers had been nearly wiped out; only 15,012 of 167,264 acquired from tsarist stores remained in the Red arsenal. Hand grenades were nearly gone, with only 91,000 left of the 1.56 million inherited in 1918. Only 200 Vickers guns remained of the old tsarist stores of 500. Many other crucial items—binoculars, gun sights, flares and signaling equipment, incendiary rounds, and explosive cartridges—were not manufactured in Russia at all. All these things would need to be imported.[2]

Even these inadequate figures assumed, meanwhile, that war production could be cranked up to pre-1917 levels in Tula, Moscow, and Petrograd. But Russia's war factories needed massive imports of ferrous metals simply to keep operating at all. Enormous orders for lead, tin, zinc, steel, and pure tungsten were placed all through 1920, although it was not until September that the metals began arriving in Reval, and then only the lead. The tin, zinc, and steel did not start arriving in bulk until December 1920, and the tungsten (owing to the critical attention of Allied spies) would be shipped still later.[3]

In the meantime, the regime was forced to pay top dollar for finished, high-end military equipment. Trotsky oversaw some critical deals himself, including an order for Russian-style Mosin-Nagant "3-line" repeating rifles manufactured in the American Westinghouse foundry, in accordance with a tsarist commission from 1915. A Swedish firm called Tjernberg & Leth Aktiebol had 1.2 million of these, although it drove a hard bargain with Trotsky, agreeing to sell him 300,000 Nagants and 5 million rounds for $9 million in gold bullion. After this firm fulfilled the rifle order to Trotsky's satisfaction, the Red Army's special foreign procurement agency (Spotekzak), signed a more ambitious deal with Tjernberg & Leth Aktiebol on January 11, 1921, worth 40 million Swedish crowns' worth (another $9 million) of gold bullion, to supply Moscow with "150,000 sets complete Outfittings," each consisting of a 3-Line Nagant Rifle with 1,800 cartridges, a "cleaned and disinfected" English khaki uniform, a pair of black leather top boots, and a woolen blanket, at a price of 269 Swedish crowns per set. [4]

The Bolsheviks could now fight the peasant wars in style, with state-of-the-art foreign weapons and uniforms. This was all to the good, for Cheka reports on partisan unrest submitted to Lenin had, by fall 1920, become almost numbing in their repetitive quality. "Yaroslavl. Banditry is widely spread in the entire province." "Ryazan. Rebellions are going on connected to food supply." "Tula: Gangs of bandits are present." "Vitebsk: The bandits are well organized . . . they number 3,000." "Pskov: Opochka region. A band of 300 is active." "Petrograd: Yamburg [district]. Green bandits [that is, partisans or anarchists, supporting neither Reds nor Whites] are active." "Vyatka . . . the attitude of peasants towards Soviet power is sharply hostile." "Perm: The disposition of the population is counterrevolutionary." "Kuban: The mood . . . is counterrevolutionary." "Tomsk . . . rebellions broke out often which embraced this entire province." "The Urals: The attitude of the population toward Soviet power is unfriendly due to the pumping out of grain." "Samara: Discontent is on the rise . . . Shows itself in peasant unrest." "Voronezh: The attitude of population towards Soviet power is hostile. . . . a band of greens is operating numbering 400."[5]

The motivation of partisan rebels varied from region to region, district to district, but certain themes were obvious. The forced grain requisitions of War Communism were universally detested. The prodrazvërstka, in force from 1919 to 1921, saw requisition levels set by planning officials in Moscow, without regard for the size of any local food surpluses (where they even existed). Meeting resistance everywhere they went, Bolshevik requisitioners armed themselves, creating *prodarmii* (food armies) and *voenprodotriady* (military foot brigades) to bludgeon recalcitrant peasant hoarders into submission. To the peasants working the land, it was like a second serfdom, particularly the new "labor and cart obligations" imposed by Communist officials, whom they now referred to contemptuously as *pomeshchiki* (landlords). As peasants at one village assembly in Tambov province complained, the regime must "put an end to the serfdom of horses and men from this day onward."[6]

In October–November 1920, as if in lockstep with the departure of the last foreign armies from Russian soil,* the most ferocious peasant rebellions yet erupted against the Bolshevik dictatorship in the eastern Ukraine (led by Nestor Makhno's partisans, who now numbered about 15,000), western Siberia, the northern Caucasus, Central Asia, the Volga region, and in Tambov province, only a few hundred miles from Moscow. The partisans in the North Caucasus had about 30,000 under arms, in western Siberia as many as 60,000. In Tambov, a rebel chieftain named Alexander Antonov, drawing on no less than 110,000 Red Army deserters hiding out in the surrounding countryside, put together a partisan army of 50,000 men, divided up into eighteen or twenty military "regiments."[7]

This new class war pitted heavily armed Red Army troops or Cheka enforcers against peasant farmers, many of whom fought with

---

*With the exception of the Japanese, who occupied Vladivostok until June 1922, and northern Sakhalin Island even after this. For peasants west of the Urals, however, this Far Eastern intervention might as well have been on the other side of the moon.

pitchforks. In a typical Cheka directive in the north Caucasus, on October 23, 1920, Sergo Ordzhonikidze ordered that inhabitants of Ermolovskaya, Romanovskaya, Samashinskaya, and Mikhailovskaya "be driven out of their homes, and the houses and land redistributed among the poor peasants." The Cheka agents obliged, reporting to Ordzhonikidze three weeks later: "Kalinovskaya: town razed and the whole population (4,220) deported or expelled. Ermolovskaya: emptied of all inhabitants (3,218)." In all, some 10,000 peasants had been expelled, with another 5,500 shortly to suffer the same fate.[8]

There was a self-reinforcing quality to the peasant wars. Each clash between the Cheka or "food armies" and partisan rebels fueled a vicious cycle, as peasants hid their grain or deliberately stopped growing crops, leading frustrated Communist requisitioners to denounce the "kulak grain hoarders" and demand yet more brutality in dealing with them. By winter 1920–1921, huge swathes of rural Russia were approaching famine conditions. In Tambov province, where Antonov's peasant rebellion was so huge that the Red Army was called in, the commander in charge of suppressing the partisans, Vladimir Antonov-Ovseenko, openly admitted that, by January 1921, "half the peasantry was starving." In the Volga basin, conditions were even worse. In Samara province, the commander of the Volga military district reported that "crowds of thousands of starving peasants are besieging the barns where the food detachments have stored the grain . . . the army has been forced to open fire repeatedly on the enraged crowd." In Saratov, heavily armed partisans, after obtaining rifles from Red Army deserters, had recaptured the grain stocks requisitioned by the food armies. Ominously, the local Soviet reported to Moscow that "whole units of the Red Army have simply vanished." Between January and March 1921, Soviet sources indicate, the regime lost control of whole areas of the middle Volga and western Siberia, including the provinces of Tyumen, Omsk, Cheliabinsk, Ekaterinburg, and Tobolsk—and of the Trans-Siberian railway itself.[9]

The food wars now crashed into Moscow and Petrograd. On January 22, 1921, the bread ration in both cities was reduced by one third, to 1,000 calories a day, for even the privileged laborers of heavy industry, costing Lenin's government the support of even its diehard backers; only 2 percent of factory workers now belonged to the party. Strikes and protests rocked Petrograd. On February 22, a new "Plenipotentiary Workers' Assembly" was formed, which, according to Cheka reports, was "strongly Menshevik and Socialist Revolutionary in character." The Assembly's inaugural decree demanded an end to Bolshevik dictatorship, freedom of speech and assembly, and a release of political prisoners, and called a general strike to achieve these aims. The Cheka responded with force, firing into a group of workers on February 24 and killing twelve, before arresting another thousand protestors. On February 26, Zinoviev, the party boss in Petrograd, warned Lenin that if he did not receive reinforcements, "we are going to be overrun."[10]

Just when it seemed things could not possibly get worse for the regime, the rebellion reached Kronstadt, which had provided Lenin his most reliable support in 1917 during the July Days and October Revolution. More than four thousand Kronstadt Communists had already torn up their party cards. On February 28, Zinoviev reported to Lenin that a sailors' mutiny had broken out in the harbor, and that all the factories were on strike. On March 1, a massive protest was held, involving fifteen thousand people—fully a quarter of the population. Four days later, Trotsky arrived in Petrograd to take charge of the counterattack. Although he denounced the protestors as "White Guards," the tenor of the Kronstadt rebellion was, as Trotsky surely knew, anarchist-socialist. On March 8, the local *Izvestiya* hit the Bolsheviks where it hurt. "In carrying out the October Revolution," the paper announced, "the working class hoped to achieve its liberation. The outcome has been even greater enslavement of human beings." Instead of freedom, Russia's urban workers now faced "the daily dread of ending up in the torture chambers of the Cheka," while her peasant masses were being "drenched with blood." A "third revolution" was at hand, in which "the long suffering of the toilers has drawn to an end."[11]

Trotsky had other ideas, and the order of battle favored him. By March 1921, the Red Army had gorged itself on five months' worth of imported war matériel. The rebels, meanwhile, were isolated, especially after the Bolsheviks, learning that foodstuffs were being smuggled to the Kronstadt rebels from Sweden, laid down the law on March 16, ordering the Swedish foreign minister to cut them off (anxious to preserve the profitable Bolshevik gold-laundering business in Stockholm, he did as he was told).[12]

With tens of thousands of Red Army regulars, well clothed and well armed, supplied with enough artillery shell to bombard the rebels from the mainland without interruption for ten days, the outcome was never really in doubt. On the night of March 16, fifty thousand Red troops, under cover of darkness, set out over the ice from Oranienbaum and Peterhof, reaching Kronstadt harbor before they were marked by armed defenders, who were outnumbered four to one. The rebels fought fiercely, inflicting ten thousand casualties on the Reds before succumbing on the morning of March 18. Trotsky had vowed the rebels would be "shot like partridges," and he was good to his word. Of rebel survivors, 2,103 ringleaders were executed and another 6,459 sent to prisons or concentration camps, mostly forced-labor facilities in the Arctic far north, where nearly three quarters would die within a year. Battle deaths were so heavy that the Finnish government requested the removal of corpses from the ice, "lest they should be washed up on the Finnish coast and create a health hazard following the thaw." Those Kronstadters fortunate enough to escape across the ice to Finland received a cold welcome, being interned by border authorities. Promised an amnesty, some five thousand of these returned to Russia in 1922 and were promptly sent to concentration camps.[13]

Trotsky's assault on Kronstadt in March 1921 marked a point of no return. There was no longer even a whiff of pretense that the Communist government had the support of the people over whom it ruled. The Red Terror had been aimed at "class enemies"; the Civil War was a struggle against "imperialists and White Guards." Even the peasant wars had pitted, in theory at least, proletarians against "capitalist farmers." But now the world's first "proletarian" government had begun slaughtering urban proletarians, too. It is no wonder that "Kronstadt" became, in addition to a black mark on Trotsky's record, a byword of Bolshevik betrayal for European socialists who refused to bow to Moscow.

Harder to explain is why it was in this very week in March 1921 that Lenin's Communist dictatorship was beatified by Britain, after months of diplomatic courtship. Lloyd George affixed his signature to the historic Anglo-Soviet Accord on March 16, the very day the Bolsheviks blackmailed Sweden into cutting off the Kronstadt rebels and on which Trotsky launched his final bloody assault. Although on paper a mere "trade agreement," the accord granted Soviet and British trade officials rights equivalent to those of consular personnel, from the use of ciphers and sealed diplomatic bags, to the recognition of valid passports. By agreeing to Soviet demands that the British government vow never to "take possession of any gold, funds, securities or commodities . . . which may be exported from Russia in payment for imports," the accord formally ended the gold blockade, forfeiting any leverage Entente governments still had to force Moscow to pay old debts. Lloyd George's protestations aside, his government had granted de facto recognition to Lenin's, giving up the right to "express an opinion upon the legality or otherwise of its acts," as the British Court of Appeals ruled as early as May 1921, and as British courts have ruled ever since.[14]

For a hitherto isolated Moscow, the Anglo-Soviet Accord opened the diplomatic floodgates. By the end of 1921, Lenin's government had signed formal trade agreements with Sweden, Norway, Finland, Latvia, Lithuania, Poland, Germany, Czechoslovakia, Austria, and Italy, and sent trade missions to Kemal's Turkey (which had also come to diplomatic terms with Moscow, giving up Azerbaijan and Batum in exchange for Ardahan and Kars), Persia, and China. The only holdouts of note were France, Japan, and the United States, whose leaders refused to give in like the British had. In view of the opening of the London capital market, this was a small concern. Absolutely anything could be imported by the Bolsheviks now, from millions of yards of prime English wool worth $11 million ordered in 1921, to $8,200 worth of spare parts for Lenin's 1915 model Rolls-Royce (requisitioned from Michael Romanov), to dozens of state-of-the-art English warplanes mounting Rolls-Royce engines, such as the wonderfully named Kangaroo Bombing Aeroplane, designed by the Blackburn Aeroplane & Motor Co. of Leeds.[15]

The influx of arms helped the regime crush Alexander Antonov's partisan army in Tambov province. On April 27, 1921, the Civil War hero General Tukhachevsky was given command of a special army "for the Internal Defense of the Republic," numbering more than 100,000, backed by Cheka execution squads. Tukhachevsky's army enjoyed greater mobility compared to those he had commanded against the Whites: his cavalry rode on imported horse saddles, his lorries were well supplied with tires, spark plugs, and spare parts, and he could deploy foreign warplanes for surveillance and area bombing. Imported incendiary rounds enabled his men to torch villages suspected of "assisting or collaborating" with Antonov. Tukhachevsky also had chemical weapons, which Zinoviev had purchased in Halle while attending the German Communist "Splitting" Congress in October 1920. On June 11, 1921, Tukhachevsky issued Order No. 171: "The forests where the bandits are hiding are to be cleared out by the poison gas. This must be carefully calculated, so that the layer of gas penetrates the forest and *kills everyone hiding* there." Houses of "bandit families" were "to be burned or demolished," with their property redistributed "among peasants who are loyal to the Soviet regime." By July 15,000 peasants had been shot or gassed to death, with another 50,000 partisans sent off to forced-labor camps. The rebellion was broken. Tambov was the last major battle of the peasant wars, which had cost the Red Army alone 237,908 casualties—against opponents who, lacking firearms, fought mostly with farm implements.[16]

The only mercy for Russia's peasants in this *annus horribilis* was that Lenin's government began dismantling the policy that lay behind all the trouble. On March 23, 1921, even as the last Kronstadt rebels were being rounded up, Lenin announced the end of the hated prodrazvërstka, replacing grain tribute quotas with a lower "tax in kind" on agricultural produce, the *prodnalog*. It would take months to work out the details of this "New Economic Policy" (NEP), but the key principles were established: local soviets—in effect the old rural communes, and not Moscow—would determine the obligations of each peasant household, and some kind of market in grain would be tolerated.[17]

In political terms, Lenin's *smychka* (truce) with the peasantry was a masterstroke, robbing partisan leaders of their principal argument. But it came a year too late for millions of peasants who, by spring 1921, faced starvation on an unprecedented scale. In the end, Russia's peasant wars were not so much won by the Communists as lost by their opponents, who were too weakened by hunger to fight.

— 22 —

"TURN GOLD INTO BREAD": FAMINE AND THE WAR ON THE CHURCH

After an all-too-brief snowmelt, a terrible drought descended on European Russia in May and June 1921. The Volga flowed at its lowest level in years. The water table plunged, and wells ran dry. Amid scorching heat, wheat literally burned as it came up from the ground. Grain reserves, already at dangerously low levels owing to a poor fall harvest, disappeared within days. With no feed for livestock, cows and pigs succumbed, or were slaughtered before they were too scrawny to eat. Desperate peasants consumed burnt wheat, grass, weeds, bark, and rodents to survive, until these ran out, too. Before long millions of hungry peasants were wandering the countryside in a daze. In such conditions, epidemic diseases—typhus, cholera, typhoid fever, and smallpox—spread rapidly. By mid-June, nearly a quarter of the landmass of European Russia, bounded by Viatka in the north, Astrakhan to the south, Penza to the west, and Ufa at the foot of the Ural Mountains in the east, had become virtually uninhabitable. Outside of the black earth belt of Ukraine, itself undergoing a severe drought, these were ordinarily among the most fertile lands in Russia, so there was no surplus elsewhere to be had. After hiding the truth for weeks, on June 21, *Pravda* admitted that about 25 million people were on the brink of starvation, including 7 million children. Even this figure was underplayed, as the Cheka was reporting that another 7.5 million faced imminent starvation in Ukraine, making a total of more than 33 million people.[1]

A famine on this scale was a long time in the making. Even in tsarist times, the short growing season in the central and northern grain belt had left Russia vulnerable to shortages in bad harvest years. More than 400,000 peasants had died in the Volga famine of 1891–1892, although the subsequent improvement in yields, especially after the Stolypin reforms, had cushioned the blow in the last major drought years of 1906 and 1911. In 1913, Russia had exported 20 million tons of surplus grain, which suggested that the days of famine were behind her. Then came the war, which pulled millions of peasants from the land. Even so, the problem of urban bread prices in 1917, in view of the fact that Russia had stopped exporting grain, was more a matter of poor distribution than of shortages. Yields had remained robust during the war, despite the decline in the rural population owing to the draft. It was only after 1918, with the onset of civil war and the draconian requisitions of War Communism, that grain production levels truly plummeted. The first danger signs in the Volga region were picked up by Cheka reports as early as 1919. The dry summer of 1920 tipped the scale toward famine: the peasant wars raging that fall were fought in large part over control of a dwindling food supply. Any peasant caught hoarding produce was "tortured and whipped to the blood." Angry farmers fought back with whatever tools they had on hand, bludgeoning to death, according to the regime's figures, eight thousand Bolshevik food requisitioners in 1920 alone. The peasant masses of the Volga region, one Cheka agent reported to Moscow, now genuinely believed that the "Soviet regime is trying to starve all the peasants who dare resist it."[2]

The regime's abandonment of the *prodrazvërstka* in March 1921 was a step in the right direction, but Lenin's truce with the peasants was belied by his reaction to the famine. The regime did spend some money on food imports in May and June, but these were for the cities, and they mostly consisted not of grain and seed, but perishable luxuries such as Persian fruits, Swedish herring (40,000 tons), Finnish salted fish (250 tons), German bacon (7,000 tons), French pig fat, and chocolate. As one of Lenin's own purchasing agents later recalled with a shudder, Communist elites in Moscow and Petrograd were consuming "truffles, pineapples, mandarin oranges, bananas, dried fruits, sardines and lord knows what else" while everywhere else in Russia "the people were dying of hunger." Far from easing up on the starving peasants of the Volga basin, on July 30, 1921, Lenin instructed all regional and provincial Party committees to "bolster the mechanisms for food collection" and to "provide the food agencies with the necessary party authority and the total power of the state apparatus of coercion."[3]

Fortunately for the starving, there were other Russians with a conscience in Moscow and Petrograd who shamed the government into action. The *Pravda* article of June 21 was inspired by the research of a team of agronomists from the Moscow Agricultural Society. Earlier in June, this group had formed a "Social Committee for the Fight Against Famine," recruiting, among others, journalist Ekaterina Kuskova, the wife of a good friend of renowned novelist Maxim Gorky. Gorky had known Lenin for over two decades, and had raised money for the Bolsheviks before the war. Although he had criticized many of the regime's repressive policies, his international fame furnished him protection during the Red Terror. Once Gorky learned of the scale of the famine, he agreed to issue an appeal "To All Honorable People" on July 13, 1921, soliciting aid from the international community. He also lent his name to the new "All-Russian Public Committee to Aid the Hungry" (Pomgol), an ostensibly private (actually regime-controlled) charity organization founded on July 21, which enabled Lenin's Communist government to solicit foreign aid without appearing to beg for bread from "capitalists."[4]

It worked. On July 23, US secretary of commerce Herbert Hoover, whose American Relief Administration (ARA) had disbursed American food aid in stricken postwar Belgium and Hungary, responded to Gorky's appeal. Negotiations were then carried out in Riga, in which the lack of trust was obvious. Hoover insisted on independence from Soviet government interference, along with the release of US nationals held in Communist prisons and concentration camps. Lenin was so infuriated by these demands that, while agreeing to sign, he ordered the Cheka to infiltrate the ARA with "the maximum number of Communists who know English." Lenin also issued a public appeal "to the workers of the world" on August 2, in which he alleged that "the capitalists of all countries . . . seek to revenge themselves on the Soviet Republic. They are preparing new plans for intervention and counter-revolutionary conspiracies." Before they went to work alleviating the Volga famine, Hoover's aid workers had already been placed under suspicion (and surveillance) as "counter-revolutionaries."[5]

Nonetheless, they performed heroically. Primed by an appropriation of over $60 million from the US Congress, the ARA established a first-class operation in Russia. By the end of 1921, the ARA, along with other "bourgeois" charity organizations, such as the American Red Cross, Quakers, and the Federated Council of the Churches of Christ, had shipped to Russia over two million tons of grain and foodstuffs, enough to adequately feed 11 million people, along with seed sufficient for the next two years' harvests. Although 5 million died in the Volga famine that summer and fall, by early 1922 reports of starvation had virtually ceased. So efficient was the ARA's work that the Soviet government expressly requested that the ARA curtail aid shipments into the ports of Reval, Riga, and Petrograd, "owing to their inability to handle such large quantities."[6]

The success of the "capitalist" Americans in feeding millions of Russians starving under Communist rule was politically embarrassing. In August 1921, Lenin created a "proletarian" aid front in Berlin, run by a trusted friend from his Zurich days, Willi Münzenberg, the chairman of the Communist Youth International. Although Münzenberg's committee raised little money in Europe, its New York branch, with the appealing name "Friends of Soviet Russia" (FSR), did better. "Give," the FSR instructed American readers of the *Nation* and the *New Republic*, "not only to feed the starving, but to save the Russian Workers Revolution. Give without *imposing reactionary conditions as do Hoover and others*." Judging by the amount of money collected by the FSR—$125,000 by October 1921 (although $73,000 of this was wasted on agitprop and overhead)—these appeals were effective, not least in smearing Hoover, whom the *Nation* accused of "us[ing] his food to overturn the Soviet government."[7]

The Volga famine also brought to a boil long-simmering tensions between the Communists and the Russian Orthodox Church. Patriarch Tikhon, elected by church elders shortly after the Revolution (the first patriarch since Peter the Great had abolished this office in the eighteenth century), had been a thorn in Lenin's side ever since he responded to a Bolshevik assault on the Alexander Nevsky Monastery in Petrograd in February 1918 with an encyclical calling down anathema on "the monsters of the human race . . . who are striving to destroy Christ's cause by sowing everywhere, in place of Christian love, the seeds of malice, hatred, and fratricidal strife." The Cheka had even charged Tikhon in the August 1918 murder attempt against Lenin, although, owing to Lenin's fear of turning him into a martyr for Russia's pious peasants—whose support he needed in the Civil War—the patriarch was not executed, but placed under house arrest.[8]

The Church had not escaped the depredations of the revolution, but as long as the Bolsheviks had needed to keep the peasantry reasonably quiet, there had been limits. Although church property was nationalized in January 1918, very little had actually been taken, owing to Lenin's fear of arousing popular resistance. For most of the Civil War, the Bolshevik assault on the clergy remained on low boil—a dozen-odd priests or bishops "chopped to pieces with axes" by Red Guards here, a church or monastery defiled and looted there. The Orthodox community certainly did not escape the Red Terror. Still, Soviet records suggest 1,500 deaths out of 140,000 clergymen: significant but not quite genocide, either. Lenin had even provided an exception, in the Gokhran's nationwide mandate over saleable jewels, artwork, and antiquities, for items set aside for use by "religious communities, like objects of worship." As late as April 1921, Lenin warned his Politburo colleagues that they must give "absolutely no offense to religion."[9]

In view of what was shortly to ensue, these words seem astonishing. But they reflected, like most of Lenin's utterances, an ice-cold grasp of power relationships. With the war against Antonov's army just then entering its climactic stages, Lenin had reason to worry about pushing Russia's angry peasants too far. The onset of an almost nationwide famine in June 1921, compounded by the snuffing out of the Tambov rebellion, altered the equation. Peasant resistance was now crumbling, overriding Lenin's reservations about targeting the Church. Meanwhile, Patriarch Tikhon had embarrassed Lenin no less badly than had Hoover with his own response to the famine. By the end of June 1921—more than a month before Lenin had issued his own appeal to global "proletarians"—Tikhon had printed up 200,000 copies of a moving appeal to Russia's Christians to "take the suffering into your arms with all haste . . . with hearts full of love and the desire to save your starving brothers." The patriarch then established his own famine relief committee, which collected 9 million rubles. On August 22, 1921, Tikhon wrote to Lenin, asking permission for the Church to be allowed to buy food supplies directly and organize relief kitchens in famine areas. Enraged by the patriarch's impudence, Lenin ordered Tikhon's famine relief committee dissolved, arrested its leaders, and exiled them to Russia's far north. Tikhon, still under house arrest, continued receiving donations, but he was forced to turn these over to the government.[10]

By sticking his neck out for the starving peasants of his flock in summer 1921, Tikhon had provided Lenin a pretext to end his truce with the Orthodox Church. The war might have started right then and there, except that Lenin's health was beginning to slip. Suffering from chronic headaches and sleeplessness, Lenin cut back his work schedule in fall 1921, decamping to his country dacha south of Moscow. In his absence, Trotsky took over the "famine" brief for the Politburo, by which was meant not food aid—Hoover's ARA was taking care of this—but the *politics* of famine.

In November 1921, Trotsky was appointed to head a new commission overseeing the sale of Gokhran treasures abroad, ostensibly for famine relief. The idea was to seek out such treasures in the Church. Trotsky dropped hints in the press that the Church was not "doing enough" for relief. Why were clergymen not, one article demanded, using their "gold and silver valuables" to buy "grain [which] could save several million of the hungry from starvation"? "Citizen letters" were then published in *Izvestiya* and *Pravda*, supporting confiscations of Church valuables. Many of these came from "progressive" clergymen of middle rank—regime collaborators known as renovationists—who hinted darkly (and absurdly) that Patriarch Tikhon was threatening famine donors in the Church with excommunication.[11]

Tikhon fell for the bait. After the All-Russian Central Executive Committee (VTsIK) ordered the expropriation of Orthodox Church valuables for famine relief on February 23, 1922, Tikhon declared this Bolshevik decree a "sacrilege" and threatened to excommunicate anyone who removed "sacred vessels" from the Orthodox Church, "even if for voluntary donation." Tikhon did allow, on February 28, that parishioners might donate saleable Church valuables to help feed the hungry, so long as they "had not been consecrated for use in religious ceremonies." Such vessels could be surrendered to the government, Tikhon and the Orthodox Metropolitan of Petrograd, Veniamin, declared, only if the Bolsheviks could provide assurance that resources were exhausted, that "proceeds would truly benefit the hungry," and that Orthodox clergymen would be allowed to "bless the sacrifice." For thus calling the Bolsheviks' bluff, Veniamin and Tikhon were labeled "enemies of the people." The government now had its bogeyman for the looting campaign: reactionary ("Black Hundred") clergymen. Trotsky's inspired agitprop slogan "Turn gold into bread!" invited popular mobs to sack churches in good conscience.[12]

The assault on the Church was motivated, in part, by the official atheism of the Communist regime. The government had gone to great lengths, in the early months of the revolution, to mock Orthodox "superstitions" about saints, opening tombs revered by pilgrims to expose sacred relics as mere bones, rags, and straw. Lenin even ordered one monastery near Moscow popular with pilgrims, the Troitsky-Sergievskaia Monastery in Sergiyev Posad (Zagorsk), converted into a "museum of atheism." Predictably, such insults led most peasants to double down on their Orthodox faith.[13]

There was more to the Church looting campaign launched on February 23, 1922, however, than ideology. The dire financial straits cited in Trotsky's agitprop were real, although Trotsky was lying about the reason the government suddenly needed the money so badly. Hoover's ARA was providing famine relief to Russia essentially free of charge, and it was this very month that the Soviet government, satisfied with Hoover's performance to date, requested that the ARA *slow down* shipments of food aid, as Hoover personally informed US President Warren Harding on February 9. Earlier that same week, in a development unrelated to either the ARA or to famine relief, the last shipment of tsarist gold bullion (44 tons) left Reval on February 6, destined for Stockholm. On February 7,

Trotsky revoked authorization for Soviet purchasing agents abroad. In terms of gold bullion—which they needed not for famine relief, but to pay for weapons and other strategic imports—the Bolsheviks were, by February 1922, effectively broke.[14]

Trotsky knew that the regime was approaching bankruptcy beforehand, of course. The church looting campaign was settled on long before its announcement on February 23, 1922, and the Patriarch's pitch-perfect protest lodged in response. It had been meticulously planned out in advance the previous December at a series of closed-door sessions of Sovnarkom, the Politburo, and the party's Central Committee, culminating in a top-secret VTsIK resolution "on the liquidation of Church property" passed on January 2, 1922, which explicitly stated that valuables obtained from the Church would go not to famine victims, but to the State Treasury of Valuables (Gokhran). All trains on which looted Church vessels were transported would be guarded by Red Army officers, who were required to inform the Gokhran, by telegram, of "the number of the train, the number of the wagon, and the time of departure." All communications from looting teams in the field were to be conducted only with senior Gokhran officials. Small wonder an operation ostensibly devoted to famine relief was entrusted to the Red Army and the Cheka, now renamed the State Political Directorate (GPU), and directed by Trotsky, the commissar of war.[15]

By mid-April 1922, 1,414 "bloody excesses" had already taken place in confrontations between the GPU and Church defenders, according to *Izvestiya*. Resistance was predictably fierce in the countryside, but there were also violent incidents in Rostov-on-Don, Smolensk, Novgorod, Moscow, and Petrograd. The most notorious episode occurred in Shuia, a textile factory town northeast of Moscow. There, the government's looting team entered the local church on the Sabbath—Sunday, March 12. The crowd of worshippers was strong enough to repel them, which was the idea. On Wednesday, the GPU returned and deployed troops equipped with machine guns, opening fire on the parishioners. Four or five people were killed, and ten or eleven injured. Incensed, Trotsky convened a Politburo meeting to discuss the Shuia incident, which was then reported to Lenin, still convalescing. On March 19, Lenin issued a top-secret dictation from his dacha. "Concerning the events at Shuia," he stated,

> I believe that the enemy here commits a major strategic blunder . . . the present moment . . . offers us a 99% chance of overwhelming success in shattering the enemy and assuring our position for decades. It is now and only now, when in the famine regions there is cannibalism, and the roads are littered with hundreds if not thousands of corpses, that we can (and therefore must) carry through the confiscation of Church valuables with the most rabid and merciless energy . . . so as to secure for ourselves a fund of several hundred million gold rubles . . . Without such capital no government work is possible, no economic reconstruction, and especially no defense of our position at [the upcoming inter-Allied debt settlement conference in] Genoa. We absolutely must take into our hands this capital of several hundred million (or perhaps several billion) rubles . . . no other moment except that of desperate hunger will give us such a mood among the broad peasant masses such as will assure us [their] neutrality, that victory in the battle to remove the [Church] valuables will remain unconditionally and completely on our side.[16]

In Lenin's mind, the Volga famine had conjured up not sympathy but opportunity.

After Shuia, the gloves were truly off. An *Izvestiya* editorialist, writing on March 28, 1922, briefly remembered to ask, "What should the workers and peasants do, if they do not wish the deaths of millions of dying peasants?" He then answered his own question, showing it had been merely rhetorical: "Give a rebuff to this band of rabid 'dignified' priests. Burn out the 'most holy counterrevolution' with a hot iron. Take the gold out of the churches. Exchange the gold for bread."[17]

In April 1922, the hot iron of repression descended on Moscow, home to "forty times forty churches," each one housing the priceless treasures of a thousand years of Russian history: illuminated bibles and rare manuscripts mounted on silver bindings, icons embroidered with pearls, gold vessels, chalices encrusted with precious gems. Targeting these saleable assets were Bolshevik looting commissions assigned to each of the seven main districts in Moscow, staffed by around twenty-five men, of whom ten were heavily armed enforcers from the security organs (either the GPU or the Red Army). By April 5, these armed enforcers had removed 6.5 tons of treasures from forty-three Orthodox cathedrals and monasteries in Moscow. High profile targets included the Church of the Epiphany in the Khamovnichesky district, a cathedral constructed in 1625 that frequently hosted Orthodox religious councils. Over three thousand parishioners gathered to defend the church on April 5, but they were overwhelmed by the heavily armed GPU men; looters carted off 500 pounds of Orthodox treasures. The Bolsheviks also sacked the Church of Christ the Savior on the Moscow River. Constructed to commemorate the victory over Napoleon, this stunning cathedral contained five towering gold domes, one of which reached as high as a seventeen-story building. Fourteen silver church bells had been lifted into the belfries, which together weighed 65 tons. The walls were adorned with 177 marble panels, each depicting heroic battles against Napoleon. The very size of these endowments, however, made their removal a logistical nightmare—looters were able to cart off "only" 1,250 pounds of church vessels. (Dynamited on Stalin's orders in 1931, the Church of Christ the Savior was rebuilt, at colossal expense, after the fall of the Soviet Union, and consecrated on Transfiguration Day 2000.)[18]

Things went more smoothly for the GPU in Moscow's less illustrious churches, which had fewer defenders. Between April 5 and 8, fully 106 different Moscow churches were raided, yielding nearly 13 tons of valuables. After a brief pause to digest this huge haul, Bolshevik looting squads pulled off an even more stupendous feat between April 24 and 26, attacking 130 churches and three chapels from which they carted off another 13 tons of silver, and about 50 pounds of gold, plus untold quantities of sacred Church vessels. The GPU also looted several Armenian and Greek Orthodox facilities in Moscow in April, one Protestant-Evangelical church, and several Jewish synagogues. The most lucrative acquisition was Armenia's national Church treasure, which—like the Romanian patrimony—had ironically been brought to Moscow for safekeeping back in 1915.[19]

Petrograd, a more modern city, had fewer churches than Moscow, and they were newer, housing less in the way of ancient church vessels and icons. What they lacked in liturgical history, however, they made up for in wealth, especially in diamonds. By the end of April 1922, Petrograd looting committees had collected 30 tons of silver from local churches, about 145 pounds of gold, 3,690 diamonds, and 367 precious stones. Most of the gold and silver was forwarded to the Moscow Gokhran, but about two thirds of the diamonds (2,672) remained in the vaults of the Petrograd looting commission, to lessen the risks of losses to sabotage or theft en route.[20]

In the provinces, Orthodox churches and monasteries were less well endowed, but there were so many of them that mere volume sufficed to produce a cornucopia of riches. Viatka and Kaluzhskaia provinces yielded 20 tons of church loot. Nizhny Novgorod yielded just under a ton of silver and 3 pounds of gold. The story was similar in Astrakhan, Kazan, Cheliabinsk, Penza, and Ukraine. By June 1922, provincial teams had looted a quarter-ton of gold, 167 tons of silver, 12,124 diamonds and brilliants (1,145 carats), 48 pounds of pearls, and 26,708 precious stones, weighing 14 pounds.[21]

The armed robbery of Russia's churches met with considerable popular resistance, just as Trotsky had hoped. On April 13, thirty-two clergymen were arrested in Moscow, and another twenty-two the following week. Trotsky ran the press campaign, smearing defendants as "black hundreds" and "counterrevolutionaries." On April 26, the first great show trial opened in the Moscow Polytechnic Museum. Eleven priests were sentenced to death, the first of hundreds to follow, as the show trials moved on to Petrograd (86 defendants, 4 executed), Shuia (3 death sentences), and other cities. Lenin, from his dacha, asked to be informed "on a daily basis" how many priests had been shot. According to the government's figures, at least 28 bishops and 1,215 priests were killed in 1922, although not all by gunfire: two bishops, in Perm and Tobolsk, were drowned to death instead. As many as 20,000 or so ordinary parishioners also perished, many of them elderly Old Believers, who still practiced Russian Orthodox rites dating to before a seventeenth-century Church reform, and who defended their churches with pitchforks.[22]

These figures, terrible as they are, paled in comparison to those of the Red Terror of 1918 or the atrocities committed by both sides in the Civil War. In a sense, the looting of the Church had been expected: revolutionaries had always targeted ecclesiastic wealth, from Henry VIII's going after England's Catholic monasteries to the French Revolutionaries nationalizing Church property in 1790. But the Bolsheviks were breaking new ground in sacrilege. In May, a looting team invaded the Petropavlovsk Cathedral in Petrograd, where tsars were traditionally buried. They removed the silver coffin of one tsarina, and a pearl necklace from the corpse of Catherine the Great. When the team reached the tomb of Peter the Great, however, even these ruthless Bolsheviks were given a "violent shock" by the sight of his body, which had been so "carefully embalmed" that it looked "as if he had just been placed there." Unable to rob what appeared to be a living emperor, the looters, it was said, "insisted that the coffin should be closed immediately, and would not allow anything to be taken off his body."[23]

The church robberies shocked European and American opinion. As the *New York Times* reported in April: "[Russians] have seen their churches invaded by bands of armed men who seem quite as eager to destroy as to remove the sacred ornaments . . . in many places parties of men, women and children, unarmed but determined, have formed a circle round their church and dared the Soviet troops to do their worst." Amsterdam's *De Telegraaf* ran sensational headlines all spring: "Desecration of Minsk churches"; "Orthodox priests sentenced to death for resistance"; "Bloody clashes in Kiev."[24]

Undeterred by negative foreign press coverage, Lenin and Trotsky plowed on. The pace of confiscations remained brisk through the summer and fall of 1922, although not everything made its way to the Moscow Gokhran. Despite its impractical bulk, silver (except in the case of dinnerware) was the material that regional looting committees most easily parted with, because it offered the least temptation for pilfering. All but about 90 of the 434 tons of silver collected in the provinces by November 1922 was shipped to Moscow. By early 1923, so much Church silver had accumulated at Gokhran, on Strastnaia (Pushkin) Square, that a nearby building was emptied to house it. By contrast, only half of the 1,200 pounds of gold confiscated in the provinces was forwarded to Moscow, a seventh of the 35,000 diamonds, and one tenth of the 505 pounds of pearls.[25]

Icons were also confiscated in enormous quantities, although no accurate count was kept. Many of these unique Russian artistic treasures ended up in street bazaars, where they were snapped up by foreign collectors, such as Olof Aschberg, the Swedish financier whose Nya Banken had helped finance Lenin in 1917. Aschberg bought 277 Orthodox icons, most of them now on display in Stockholm museums. We can be grateful for collectors like Aschberg, for few of the icons looted in 1922 that stayed in Russia survived intact. Those sent to the Gokhran had their bindings dismantled for scrap silver. Antiquarian manuscripts and religious service books, too, were ripped from their bindings. Vestments and chasubles, crosier and miter, crosses and cups—everything that contained Church silver—was melted down and sold by volume.[26]

Destroying the sacred objects of the Orthodox Church, the last pillar of traditional Russian civilization still standing, must have been richly satisfying for Lenin, Trotsky, and other fanatical Communists. In material terms, however, it did them little good (to say nothing of Russian famine victims, who were not even considered). By year's end, the intake of saleable metals from the Church amounted to 939 pounds of gold and 550 tons of silver. At prevailing prices, this hoard could have netted the Bolsheviks only $10 million, enough to pay for a month of strategic imports. Gokhran files actually show a *decline* in income in 1922 from the furious pace of 1920–1921, with only 40 million gold rubles ($20 million) of valuables sorted and appraised from January to October. Most of this hoard, meanwhile, remained basically illiquid, as any significant foreign sales of diamonds or pearls threatened to collapse the price.[27]

The sad truth was that a looting campaign launched in February 1922 to secure, in Lenin's words, a "fund of several hundred million gold rubles" yielded forty or fifty times less. So desperate was the Soviet government for revenue that Grigory Sokolnikov, the former banks commissar, began soliciting appraisals of the "Romanov jewels," which the Bolsheviks, in March 1922, had finally discovered in the Kremlin armory where Kerensky had hidden them after the July Days. Sokolnikov did receive one promising appraisal of 900 million gold rubles ($450 million, equivalent to $45 billion today). And yet who would spend this kind of money on the world's most famous stolen treasure, on which self-declared Romanov heirs and Entente creditors were already staking legal claims? The collection could be sold off piecemeal, but then the point of its august provenance would be lost, along with its inflated valuation.[28]

At best, the "Romanov treasure" (or the Gokhran jewelry hoard) might serve as collateral for loans. But this would require a deft touch. After the Bolshevik repudiation of Russian state debts of February 1918—the largest default in recorded financial history—bankers were understandably reluctant to lend money to Lenin's outlaw government, especially those in the Entente countries that had lost the most. The Anglo-Soviet Accord of March 1921 had allowed the Bolsheviks to sell tsarist gold bullion without fear of sequestration, but this had simply brought them closer to bankruptcy once this finite resource had run out. Viewing Paris, London, and New York as dead ends, the Politburo resolved to focus its loan drive on "capitalists from neutral countries" instead. Having blown through the inherited capital of tsarist Russia, the Communists had no other choice. It was time to reactivate the German-Swedish connection that had brought Lenin to power in the first place.[29]

23

RAPALLO

Lenin's instructions that the Bolsheviks exploit starvation-induced peasant weakness to "confiscate church valuables with the most rabid and merciless energy," callous as they were, reflected a solid grasp of the regime's financial position in March 1922. What he had in mind was the upcoming international economic conference at Genoa in April, when critical questions pertaining to postwar reconstruction, inter-Allied debt and a return to the prewar gold standard, German reparations, and the Bolshevik default of 1918, would be discussed. The last thing Lenin wanted was to give in to Allied demands over repayment of Russian debts in exchange for fronting the new loans his government needed so badly. But after the final hoard of tsarist gold bullion was exported across the Baltic in February, the last capital reserves of the Communist government were gone, and revenues from the church looting campaign were so far nugatory. Would the Bolsheviks have to come to terms with the despised Western "capitalist" powers at Genoa after all?

Signs of economic desperation in Soviet Russia were hard to miss. The Volga famine was an international embarrassment. Hyperinflation was raging. In September 1921, monthly currency emissions had passed the trillion ruble mark. Nearly 2 trillion rubles were printed in October, and 3.35 trillion in November. In December, emissions doubled again, to over 7 trillion. Tax collection remained anemic. By early 1922, fully 97 percent of the domestic operating expenses of the Soviet government (then running at 13.5 trillion paper rubles per month) was being met with the printing press.[1]

The final plunge into thirteen-digit hyperinflation in Russia followed, as if by clockwork, the disappearance of the last remaining gold coins from circulation. The first danger sign had come in July 1921, when the Politburo resolved to begin covering major expenses, such as food purchases in Persia and Red Army officer salaries, with silver. Silver rubles would now be cast for the Bolsheviks in Finland, where the Helsinki Mint took a contract to coin 500 million. In November 1921, the Politburo created a gold commission to account for vanishing reserves; it was a sub-branch of this commission, led by Trotsky, which directed the Gokhran-Church confiscations of 1922.[2]

Parallel to these measures to shore up precious metal reserves, the Politburo sent trade delegations to Berlin and Stockholm. The key foreign intermediary was Olof Aschberg, the Swedish banker whose Nya Banken had been the conduit for German funds sent to Lenin in Russia in 1917. Aschberg's bank had been put on an Entente blacklist, its American and British assets frozen. Undeterred, Aschberg sold his shares, formed a new Stockholm bank out of his personal capital called "The Swedish Finance Company, Limited" (SEA) and continued doing business with the Bolsheviks. After the Anglo-Soviet Accord was ratified on March 16, 1921, Aschberg, misreading Lloyd George's deal as a softening of Entente hostility to the Bolsheviks, visited the French Embassy in Berlin and tried to negotiate a similarly generous, open-ended trade deal. Aschberg proposed that Paris forgive Russian debts in exchange for Soviet oil and mining concessions. As a sweetener, he would allow French banks to buy $50 million in tsarist gold bullion to pay for Soviet imports from France. Aschberg's SEA would handle all transactions. Predictably, Aschberg was shown the door by the French ambassador, which hardened his resolve to cut a deal with the Germans instead.[3]

In August 1921, Aschberg met with Lenin in Moscow. In a kind of last financial will shortly before he left for his country dacha, Lenin granted Aschberg's SEA the "exclusive right to direct financial operations for the Soviet government in Scandinavia and Germany," along with titles to Russia's raw materials and petroleum reserves, to be sold abroad as Aschberg saw fit. Lenin's banker was also given title to 55 tons of gold, 100 million tsarist and Kerensky rubles, and 25 million Romanian lei. The rubles were to be spent in areas of Prussia,

White Russia, and Poland where they were still accepted, and the lei to finance imports from Romania. The gold—the last hoard of imperial bullion left in Russia—was intended as bait for the German government.[4]

In a revealing declaration of intent, Aschberg was accompanied to Berlin by Nikolai Krestinsky, the director of the Gokhran. In a time of straitened finances, every asset counted, and the Gokhran's hoard of jewelry and artwork might prove critical. Parallel to the church looting campaign, Krestinsky had created a new Financial Inspectorate to keep track of the intake of church loot, which answered to an accounting bureaucracy called the "Workers' and Peasants' Inspectorate" (Rabkrin). Rabkrin, originally created alongside the Gokhran in February 1920 to root out the inevitable corruption involved in a nationwide looting operation, was run by Stalin, who used it to amass dirt on rivals—whom he could then, in his capacity as chairman of the party's Organization Bureau (Orgburo), promote, blackmail, or fire as he saw fit. With Lenin bowing out of the government's day-to-day operations, and Trotsky's Red Army fading in importance after the end of the Civil War proper, the Stalin-Krestinsky connection was critical, linking the ever-growing Soviet bureaucracy to the Gokhran hoard expected to finance everyone's salaries.[5]

The problem Krestinsky and Aschberg needed to solve for Stalin was complex, although not insuperable. Since what the Bolsheviks themselves had called their "annihilation" of tsarist Russian debts in February 1918, the Soviet government had been unable to secure a single new loan. Tsarist assets abroad, including bank accounts and real estate, had been frozen in retaliation for the default. The laundering of gold and platinum in Scandinavia—and then direct sales in England after the Anglo-Soviet Accord of March 1921—had allowed Lenin's government to muddle through the Civil War, buying weapons with cash and gold. But no government can survive for long without credit, especially one that has destroyed its own economy and tax base. Instead of a reliable stream of tax revenue to offer lenders as collateral, the Soviet government had a massive collection of looted precious metals, jewelry, and artwork—goods that its deposed creditors viewed as stolen property, anyway. How, in view of the Allies' insistence that any saleable Bolshevik assets be used to pay off old

Russian debts, could the Gokhran hoard be used to collateralize new foreign loans for Moscow?

The answer was found in Berlin. Germany, like Soviet Russia, was a pariah state in 1922, under surveillance by an Allied Control Commission that monitored financial transactions to prevent her from rearming. The precarious "Weimar" government, viewed by many patriotic Germans as the illegitimate bastard child of the Versailles Treaty, had nearly been toppled by the Spartacist Uprising of January 1919, by a right-wing "Kapp putsch" of March 1920, and by Communists in the botched "March Action" of 1921. In the German Foreign Office and General Staff, a group known as "easterners," wished to spurn the western Allies and resuscitate the old connection to Russia forged at Brest-Litovsk in 1918. Their arresting slogan was that "the Bolsheviks must save us from Bolshevism." By fall 1921, a secret team of German arms experts ("Sondergruppe R," for "Russia") was in Moscow, scoping out production facilities including an airplane factory at Fili, and an airfield at Lipetsk, south of Moscow, to test warplanes.[6]

Cognizant of the easterners' views, Aschberg and Krestinsky lured the Germans in. On August 24, 1921, shortly after Lenin had given Aschberg title to his government's remaining gold reserves, one of his top SEA deputies, Boris Stomoniakov, informed the German Reichsbank that the SEA was willing to send 38 metric tons of Russian bullion to Berlin as security against German imports. The Reichsbank would extend Moscow dollar-denominated import credits against this gold, calculated at $664.60 per kilogram. In exchange, the Germans expected the Bolsheviks to place orders with German industry worth at least 2 billion reichsmarks—about $50 million at the current rate of exchange. The Germans even offered rent-free facilities in Berlin for the Soviet trade team. It was a fantastic deal; but Aschberg told Stomoniakov to hold out for still more. His instinct was sound. In a follow-up meeting held at the Wilhelmstrasse, the Foreign Office instructed the Reichsbank to promise Aschberg that Berlin would "take pains to fulfill the wishes of the Russian government . . . to the furthest extent possible."[7]

All winter, the Bolsheviks worked over the Germans, crafting terms ever more favorable to Moscow. In January 1922, Lenin's old friend, Karl Radek, threatened Germany's foreign minister, Walter Rathenau, that Moscow would sign a deal with France unless the Germans coughed up import credits. Rathenau, shaken, offered a blanket credit of 50 to 60 million gold marks (about $15 million), only for Radek to reject this as inadequate. While Radek went after Rathenau, Krestinsky lobbied the German chancellor, Joseph Wirth, proposing to sell Gokhran treasures via German auction houses. Wirth, anxious to recoup the 150 million marks his administration had already spent on "Sondergruppe R," responded favorably, putting Krestinsky in touch with Rudolf Lepke, who ran an auction house on Berlin's Potsdamerstrasse. Krestinsky also courted German generals who hoped to pursue secret rearmament in Russia, meeting with commander in chief Hans von Seeckt in the Berlin apartment of General Kurt von Schleicher on December 8, 1921. Here, in the home of a future chancellor, the chief of the German General Staff shook hands with the looter in chief of Bolshevik Russia.[8]

The Germans' lust for a deal was obvious, which enabled the Russians to write up almost any terms they wished. Radek insisted that Berlin write off all prior Russian debts owed to German banks or firms (including those incurred since the war for Soviet arms imports), and the Germans agreed, in exchange for a nonbinding promise that the Soviets would place most of their future arms orders in Germany. To pay for these imports, the Russians were encouraged to auction off Gokhran treasures at Lepke's. Krestinsky insisted on immunity against lawsuits filed by Russian émigrés who might recognize their property in auction catalogs, and he got it. In exchange for having their debts forgiven and being given an open-ended credit line for importing German weapons—despite sending no gold to Berlin—all the Bolsheviks had to do was permit German firms, including Albatross Werke, Blohm & Voss, Junkers, and Krupp, to manufacture and test new weapons on Soviet territory—where Soviet engineers could inspect (and possibly copy) German designs. The draft treaty was written up in advance by Russian experts in conjunction with Seeckt and Sondergruppe R. On April 16, 1922, after slipping out of Genoa to meet in a hotel room in nearby Rapallo, Radek and Rathenau signed the draft (according to legend, in their pajamas) without altering a word.[9]

Although Seeckt and the German generals got what they needed at Rapallo, Rathenau did not read the fine print very carefully. Only two days later would the Germans discover that Bolshevik gold exports had been cut off by Trotsky. On April 20, 1922, the Soviet delegation in Berlin confessed to Reichsbank officials that the Germans would not be able to purchase Soviet gold as they had been expecting. In a sudden panic, the German trade team at Genoa sent an urgent telegram to Berlin on May 3, demanding copies of all SEA contracts dating to the previous fall. It was too late: Aschberg had sold the last tsarist bullion in Stockholm to a *French* banking house, as the Germans would learn from the Swedish newspapers. The Reichsbank would get no gold at all out of Rapallo. Small wonder the notorious treaty turned into a money pit for the Germans, with one of the main firms investing in Russia, Junkers, going bankrupt in 1925.[10]

The reaction to Rapallo in the Entente capitals, though predictably hostile, was tinged with a certain schadenfreude, at least in Paris. The French actually wheedled more gold out of Moscow than the Germans did. Officials at the Quai d'Orsay, having read through Aschberg's terms the previous year more closely than Rathenau had done at Rapallo, better understood what Aschberg and Lenin were up to. The French knew that, in the words of an official Quai d'Orsay memorandum on Rapallo written on May 20, without new "foreign credits," the Bolsheviks "will not be able to finance their propaganda, or to pay for their import orders in Sweden, England, and Germany," which they needed to "equip their army with the materials it needed [to fight]." Had Germany's diplomats not been so blinded by rage and her generals by greed, they would have realized that the strategic question at Genoa had been whether the Bolsheviks, whose "last gold reserves were exhausted," would be forced "to pay Russia's debts" to obtain new credits. The answer at Rapallo was emphatic: no, they would not.[11]

Rather than meet Western governments, and the millions of expropriated creditors they spoke for, halfway, the Bolsheviks would not meet them at all. True, this meant that Soviet Russia remained a pariah state, unrecognized by the Western powers and cut off from their capital markets. But a lifeline had been opened to Germany, Russia's fellow pariah, which would allow Moscow to import almost everything the regime required, from Mausers to motor cars, from pencils to pharmaceuticals. By refusing to ship bullion to Germany, Krestinsky and Radek had enabled Moscow to hold onto just enough gold to provide 25 percent backing to a new ruble, worth ten tsarist rubles ($5), called the *chervonetz*. Lenin, embarrassed by the return to sound "bourgeois" money, vowed that once Communism swept the world, gold would be used only to build toilets.[12]

In November 1922, Aschberg opened a bank in Moscow to handle the Communist regime's foreign transactions. As part of the New Economic Policy, which had seen the relegalization of the grain trade and small private retail, the Communist government now allowed private banks to be chartered, though under strict supervision. Aschberg's "Russian Bank of Commerce" (Ruskombank), given a prime location near the Kremlin at the corner of Petrovka and Kuznetsky Most, was the flagship, designed to attract both Russian savings deposits (relegalized in April 1922) and foreign capital via the sale of bonds in Stockholm and Berlin, along with a flood of remittances from Russians abroad, mostly small sums ($5 or $10) wired from the United States. Ruskombank was also given title to "gold, platinum, precious stones, diamonds and pearls" from the Gokhran, to be sold to collectors both in Russia and abroad. Lepke's auction house in Berlin was the main conduit for foreign sales, but not the only one. Aschberg himself sold $50 million worth of Gokhran treasures between 1921 and 1924, mostly in Stockholm, raising the foreign exchange equivalent of some $5 billion today for the Soviet government.[13]

Aschberg handled the German side of the Rapallo trade, too. In November 1922, he chartered the "Garantie- und Kreditbank für den Osten" in Berlin to handle business with Moscow. The bank raised funds to finance Bolshevik arms purchases through stock issue on the Berlin bourse, through sales of Gokhran treasures at Lepke's via another new Aschberg firm (Russische Edelmetallvertrieb AG), and by floating "worker bonds" for Moscow with Germany's powerful unions. Incredibly, the flow of gold even reversed under Aschberg's system, with German gold sent to *Russia* in 1926 in exchange for a particularly lucrative sale of Gokhran jewels. Symbolic of the Rapallo partnership between Berlin and Moscow was the appointment of

Nikolai Krestinsky, founder of the Gokhran, as Soviet ambassador to Germany, an office he would hold until 1930.[14]

Rapallo marked the coming of age of international Communism. What had begun as an alliance of convenience between the German Foreign Office and a band of Bolshevik conspirators in 1917 had come full circle, with the conspirators now recognized as equals—and curiously treated with great deference, as if they were superiors—by their German benefactors. On the international chessboard, it was a masterstroke. After a half-decade of bitter trials, Communism had proved it was here to stay. Secure in Russia, it could be exported to the world.

== Epilogue ==

THE SPECTER OF COMMUNISM

After five years of revolutionary turmoil and civil war, something resembling peace came to Russia at last after the Bolsheviks had snuffed out the last popular resistance to the Church robberies. Thanks to the tireless efforts of Hoover's ARA and its brave Russian employees, the Volga region enjoyed a bumper harvest in summer 1922. Over the preceding year, the Soviet government had quietly relegalized many private economic activities, from the retail sale of agricultural and manufactured goods (July 19, 1921) to real estate transactions (August 1921), publishing (December 1921) and small-scale manufacturing (June 1922). The critical month was April 1922, when the Bolsheviks, by restoring the right to own hard currency and precious metals without fear of confiscation, effectively re-legalized money. By the time the gold ruble was in circulation and Ruskombank was chartered in November 1922, the wages of this "New Economic Policy" (NEP) were clear, if unexpected. With the exception of heavy industry, banking, and foreign trade, which Lenin famously called the "commanding heights" of the economy, Russia's Communist rulers had brought back—capitalism.[1]

A put-upon Russian peasant farmer finally allowed to sell his surplus grain in the market again could be forgiven for wondering what the point had been. The convulsions of the Russian Revolution, the Red Terror, the Civil War, the peasant wars, and the Volga famine had cost the lives of some 25 million people across the territories of the former tsarist empire—a figure eighteen times higher than Russia's losses in the world war from 1914 to 1917 (1.3 to 1.4 million). Bolshevik Party propagandists had spent years denouncing tsarist police repression, only to erect a secret-police apparatus geometrically larger and more murderous in its place. Even the most obvious political transformation, the end of single-man monarchical rule wrought by the revolution and made official by the murder of the Romanovs in July 1918, was undermined when Stalin exploited Lenin's January 1924 funeral to erect a quasi-religious personality cult, embalming the body of the Bolshevik Party leader and then erecting a mausoleum in Red Square to house it as a site of pilgrimage. In terms of the relationship between government and governed, ruler and ruled, it seemed that one Russian autocracy had simply been substituted for another.[2]

Nonetheless, the Russian Revolution had fundamentally transformed the political landscape, although not in the direction intended by the men who began it. Russia's liberals had dreamed of a constitutional monarchy in which the tsar ruled through cabinets answerable to the Duma and public opinion, allowing them to revamp Russia's supposedly floundering war effort and her allegedly moribund economy (even though the liberals themselves admitted there was no real bread shortage in the capital in February 1917). Instead, their dangerous palace plots and inept stab at riding the Petrograd garrison mutiny to power unleashed political chaos and gravely undermined Russia's war effort. True, it was not the Provisional Government that issued the discipline-destroying Order No. 1, which sundered the fighting morale of the Russian Imperial Army just as it was poised to turn the table on the Germans in 1917 after achieving overwhelming superiority in manpower and war matériel—and as Russia stood on the cusp of a historic victory over her ancient Ottoman enemy to the south. Still, the inability of the liberal ministers of the Provisional Government—Lvov, Guchkov, and Milyukov—to corral the irresponsible socialists of the Petrograd Soviet who did issue Order No. 1 spoke ill of their capacity for statesmanship. Ruling the vast, multiethnic Russian Empire turned out to be far more difficult than these men had expected, and the liberals certainly performed no better than the tsar and his appointed ministers did. Indeed, if we are to judge by the army's declining battlefield performance in spring and summer and the utter collapse of the Russian economy by fall 1917, they did far, far worse.

After Bolshevik-inspired mutinies reached the frontline armies—and Petrograd—in July 1917, Kerensky tried to square the circle between revolutionary socialism and military discipline, only to fail even more spectacularly than the liberals had done. Rarely has a man been as fortunate in his enemies as Lenin. Just as Kerensky's Justice Department unearthed the first smoking guns proving Lenin's treasonous contacts with the Germans, Kerensky, to pursue his vendetta against Russia's most popular general, decided to rehabilitate the party that had tried to topple him by force—and in Trotsky's case, had publicly called for his assassination. The Kornilov affair completed the process that had seen a revolution launched by liberal pan-Slavists, such as Milyukov, to rededicate Russia to the war against Germany bring to power a man literally on the German payroll, whose first major act in power was to ask the enemy for an unconditional ceasefire.

The crazy twists and turns of the Russian Revolution should give us pause in drawing pat historical lessons from it. Far from an eschatological "class struggle" borne along irresistibly by the Marxist dialectic, the events of 1917 were filled with might-have-beens and missed chances. The most critical mistake of the tsarist government was the decision to go to war in 1914, a decision warmly applauded by Russian liberals and pan-Slavists but lamented by conservative monarchists. For this reason, it is hard to fault Nicholas II for refusing to take liberal advice during the war, to surrender power to ambitious politicians who had already shown poor judgment. Strange as it may seem to modern sensibilities that the tsar preferred the counsel of the peasant faith healer Rasputin to that of elected Duma leaders such as Rodzianko, the fact is that, had he listened to Rasputin instead of Rodzianko in 1914, he might have died peacefully on his throne instead of being butchered by the Bolsheviks in July 1918.

Still, even after the critical mistake to go to war was made, the tsar's fate was not sealed. Absent the break in the weather on International Women's Day in February 1917, a popular disturbance in Petrograd would surely still have occurred at some point, although it might not have produced the chain reaction that led to a garrison mutiny. Even after the mutiny erupted, decisive measures could easily have turned the tide. The tsar abdicated his throne and called off the punitive military expedition from the front that might have saved it because he foolishly listened to General Alekseev, who in turn made the cardinal mistake of trusting in Rodzianko's ability to master the situation in Petrograd. Even after the abdication, the tsar might later have made a comeback as a constitutional monarch had the liberals not blown their chance so badly, or had Kerensky not chosen to immolate himself in the Kornilov affair. The only lesson we can safely draw from these events is that statesmen bear grave responsibility, especially in wartime, and that a country pressed to the limits of its endurance must pray that its leaders display better judgment than the tsar, Rodzianko, and Kerensky did in 1917.

For all the contingency involved in Lenin's improbable path to power, for all the times in which fortune alternatively frowned or smiled upon him as if to mock any notion of Marxist determinism, it was not simply a matter of dumb luck. From his dramatic arrival at the Finland station in April until October 1917, Lenin remained steadfast in his pursuit of his goals. In some ways Trotsky displayed better tactical instincts, as in his suggestion to wait for the Second Congress of Soviets to convene and rubber-stamp the Bolshevik power seizure. But it was Lenin's ferocious will to power that truly set him apart from rival politicians like the nervous Rodzianko, the gun-shy Guchkov, and the volatile Kerensky. Above all, Lenin had a clear, unambiguous political program. His promise to end the war was the Bolsheviks' winning argument in Russia in 1917, just as the insistence of first the liberals, and then Kerensky, on continuing it, was a losing one.

It is well to remember this, for there was a kind of bait and switch in the October Revolution that bedevils understanding of Communism to this day. The Bolsheviks, who lost the November 1917 elections and forcibly suppressed the Russian Constituent Assembly in January 1918, never received a formal democratic mandate to rule. Nonetheless there was a *kind* of mandate for Lenin's peace program, which was overwhelmingly supported by soldier committees and ratified on the ground when millions of frontline troops voted with their feet, leaving the front and walking home. Controversial though it was with the Socialist Revolutionaries (SRs) and liberals, even Lenin's decision to ratify the Brest-Litovsk Treaty in March 1918 had an implied popular legitimacy, in view of the mass desertions and abandonment of frontier posts that had preceded it. It was on the peace plank, and it alone, that the Bolsheviks gained a solid foothold with the Russian public—certainly not on the peasant-appeasing "decree on land" that Lenin shamelessly ripped off from the SRs, in which he promised something not in his power to give.

What the Russian masses did not know was that peace in the world war was, for Lenin, only a means to a very different end. After spending 1917 denouncing the death penalty in the Imperial Army and encouraging men to mutiny against officers, once in power the Bolsheviks invited those same officers back to command their new Red Army and reinstated the death penalty in August 1918. Peace in the "imperialist" war, it turned out, was mere prelude to a far bloodier civil war between the Bolsheviks and all manner of real and imagined domestic and foreign "class enemies" opposed to Communist rule.

Lenin's civil war was from the outset an international conflict. The entire point of the war was to spread Communism or "really existing socialism"—from the abolition of private property and a centrally planned, state-owned economy, to the vast apparatus of surveillance and coercion necessary to achieve this dubious goal—as far as the Red Armies would go. Sold a program of peace at any price, Russia's long-suffering muzhiks were instead conscripted into an armed ideological crusade very few of them could possibly have understood. The reward Trotsky's peasant conscripts were given for their help in expelling the Whites and foreign armies from Russian soil was to suffer the wrath of the victorious Bolsheviks when the latter turned their guns on the peasants' villages and farms in 1920–1921.

Victory in the Russian Civil War won the Communist regime respect from its subjects, however grudging, and from foreign powers, even if formal recognition came only later. But far from vindicating the efficiency of maximalist socialism (or "War Communism," as the period 1918–1921 was labeled in retrospect after the introduction of the "New Economic Policy," or NEP), in fact the Red Army won the Civil War with the inherited capital of the old, "capitalist" regime. Most of its officers had been trained by the tsarist army. Its weapons were tsarist army surplus. When these stores were exhausted in 1920, the Reds bought weapons manufactured by foreign (mostly German and American) capitalists, with tsarist gold bullion laundered in

Sweden. When this gold ran out in February 1922, all Lenin and Trotsky could think of was to rob Russia's churches, until the German General Staff rescued the Bolsheviks from impending bankruptcy at Rapallo. Only years later, in Stalin's time, was the Communist economy able to mass-produce weapons domestically—and even then much of the capital invested in Stalin's steel mills and tank factories (most of which were themselves designed by American and German "capitalist" engineers) came from foreign auctions of looted Russian art and antiquities.[3]

For all the crude, reductive violence of their policies, the Bolsheviks were masters of propaganda, and they succeeded, with the aid of sympathetic chroniclers, such as John Reed, in electrifying millions around the world with the drama of their story. Reed's best-selling *Ten Days That Shook the World* (1919), a blend of reporting and propaganda beatified by Lenin himself (who wrote the introduction), painted flattering portraits of Lenin and Trotsky (less so of Stalin, who did not like the book) that influenced generations of readers, along with those who watched movies based on it, from Sergei Eisenstein's *October* (1929) to Warren Beatty's *Reds* (1981). That Reed was paid 1 million rubles by the Soviet government for writing this book, that he later recanted his earlier views after witnessing the misery of the Volga region on a boat tour, does not undermine his political importance. Like the "fellow travelers" who sang Stalin's praises after being taken on conducted tours of Soviet Russia in the 1930s, Reed saw what he wanted to see in the October Revolution, and he tapped into a huge market. Millions of foreign sympathizers, too, wanted to see their dreams of a better world realized in Communist Russia, even if very few wanted to go there in person to experience it for themselves.[4]

For those less sympathetically inclined, the Russian Revolution produced a catalog of horrors that hardened the political resolve to resist the Communist International (1919–1943) and its agents. Hostility to the Bolshevik regime in France, among all but members of the French Communist Party (PCF), was baked into the cake by the Bolshevik default of February 1918 and the cynical Soviet-German alliance signed at Rapallo, and would remain potent for decades. In Britain, despite the policy reversal of Lloyd George, a political weathervane who sensed the emerging power of the Labour Party, most Liberals and Tories viewed Communism with horror. As early as the Bolsheviks' bank nationalization campaign of 1917–1918, reports pouring into London described maximalist socialism as a "lunatic asylum." As Churchill put it colorfully during the debate over the Anglo-Soviet Accord, "One might as well legalize sodomy as recognize the Bolsheviks." In the United States, despite the popularity of Reed's book and the fund-raising success of "Friends of Soviet Russia," respectable opinion remained resolutely opposed to reconciliation with Lenin's outlaw regime. Only in 1933 did the United States recognize Russia's Communist government—and even then the controversial decision by FDR's administration to do so roiled domestic politics well into the 1950s.[5]

The Russian Revolution polarized world politics as never before. In the struggle for world opinion, Lenin and Trotsky won an early trick by publishing the "secret treaties" in November 1917, nakedly exposing the imperialism of the Entente powers and forcing even the idealist of the western alliance, Woodrow Wilson, on the defensive, as he strained to offer alternative explanations, in his Fourteen Points, of how the slaughter in the trenches might lead to a better world. To the men fighting, bleeding, and dying in the world war, the Communist critique of a war waged for "imperialist" gain made good sense: it was easier for many to grasp than the abstract arguments of Wilson and the Allies about "civilization," "self-determination," and "democracy." The Bolsheviks' request for a ceasefire in November 1917 won them goodwill not only with the Russian peasants they baited-and-switched, but also with millions of disillusioned Europeans.

This promising beginning, however, was squandered by the horrendous body count of the Red Terror and Civil War, and especially (for socialists) by Trotsky's brutal crackdown at Kronstadt in March 1921. Each successive stage of Communism—from Brest-Litovsk to Rapallo, from War Communism through the partial "retreat" into capitalism of NEP, to Stalin's abandonment of NEP and resuming of the socialist offensive in 1928—became a matter of intense ideological argument both inside and outside Russia. By the time of Stalin's ascendancy, doctrinal shifts in the Comintern shaped domestic politics across Europe, from the "class against class" era of 1928–1934 that pitted socialists and Communists against one another and helped enable Hitler's rise to power in Germany, to the Popular Front era of 1934–1939, when the leftist parties belatedly teamed up against fascism—only to pull another abrupt about-face in August 1939 when Stalin signed his pact with Hitler and Communists began defending the Nazis. Hitler then ended the pro-Nazi era of Communism by invading Russia in June 1941. After the Red Army crashed into Berlin in May 1945, conjuring up the danger of a Stalinist wave overwhelming Europe, the specter of Communism literally divided the world into two hostile military blocs, each of which would soon possess a nuclear arsenal capable of eradicating civilized life on earth.

Lenin would surely have been pleased. Pilloried as an extremist during his years of Swiss exile, then as a German agent in the early months after his return to Russia, Lenin had always been certain in his own mind that he was serving the cause of world revolution. What distinguished Lenin from more doctrinaire socialists was not a lack of principle, but a willingness to make compromises in pursuit of the final goal—from accepting German aid in 1917, to signing the diktat peace of Brest-Litovsk in 1918, to inviting ex-tsarist officers to train the Red Army, to the adoption of a pseudo-capitalist New Economic Policy in 1921–1922 that appeared, to many socialists, like a betrayal of Communism. Lenin himself conceded at the Tenth Party Congress in May 1921 that NEP entailed "the restoration of capitalism to some extent," although he predicted at the next Party Congress in spring 1922 that "the last and decisive battle with Russian capitalism" would occur "in the near future, though it is impossible to determine the date precisely." Building a state-planned economy would evidently take longer than Lenin first thought—but he consistently insisted that the Communist utopia was still worth the candle.[6]

Since Lenin died in 1924, four years before Stalin abandoned NEP and resumed the Communist offensive with the First Five-Year Plan, it is impossible to know for certain what he would have thought of the forced collectivization of agriculture of the early 1930s, which Ukrainians now refer to as the Holodomor (hunger-extermination), or of Stalin's crash industrialization drive and the gulag network of murderous forced-labor camps that followed in its wake, or of the Great Terror that began in 1936, targeting not only "enemies of the people" as in Lenin's time, but also (indeed especially) high-ranking Communist functionaries. Nor can we do more than guess what Lenin might have made of the Communist regimes in China; in Stalin's East European satellites; or in North Korea, Cuba, Cambodia, Vietnam, and Ethiopia, which followed Russia's example in everything from property nationalization and economic collapse, to ubiquitous secret-police surveillance and concentration camps for regime enemies, to industrial-agricultural "collectivization" and the subsequent state-induced famines that, in the Chinese case, killed tens of millions.

One suspects, nonetheless, that Lenin would have viewed these developments favorably, as the historical dialectic churned ever onward toward the final triumph of Communism. In each of these cases, just as in Russia in 1917, the advent of Communist rule came in the wake of pitiless armed conflict. This should not have been surprising. The program of maximalist socialism, outlined by Marx in the *Communist Manifesto*, required "despotic inroads on the rights of property," which obviously required armed force. Lenin's genius lay in recognizing the opportunity presented to socialist maximalizers by armies mobilized in wartime. Once modern states had armed huge masses of men to fight their foreign opponents, it was a simple task to propagandize them into unleashing their most atavistic impulses against their social betters at home instead, combining jealousy with bloodlust in mass looting campaigns. In retrospect the shocking thing is not that this happened in wartime Russia in 1917, but that Lenin's insight about turning "imperialist war" into civil war had never occurred to anyone before.

Like the nuclear weapons born of the ideological age inaugurated in 1917, the sad fact about Leninism is that, once invented, it cannot be uninvented. Social inequality will always be with us, along with the well-intentioned impulse of socialists to eradicate it. Fortunately, most social reformers accept limitations on the power of government to direct economic life and tell people what they are permitted to do and say. But the Leninist inclination is always lurking among the ambitious and ruthless, especially in desperate times of depression or war that seem to call for more radical solutions. When a nation is suffering as badly as Russia was in 1917, Yugoslavia in 1945, China in 1949, Cuba in 1959, or Cambodia in 1975, it is easy to be lured in by the siren song of Communism, or to reduce one's guard when enforcers come pounding on the door.

If the last hundred years teaches us anything, it is that we should stiffen our defenses and resist armed prophets promising social perfection. The Russians who followed Lenin in 1917 had good grounds for resenting the tsarist government that had plunged them into a terrible war for which they were unprepared, and they had little reason to expect that the regime they were creating would unleash far greater terrors. They could not have known, then, what Communism truly meant.

A century of well-catalogued disasters later, no one should have the excuse of ignorance. Even so, history can play tricks on us. The popularity of Marxist-style maximalist socialism is on the rise again in the United States and other Western "capitalist" countries, even as its appeal is all but dead in those countries where it was actually tried, from still nominally Communist-ruled China and Vietnam, to the liberated countries of the former Soviet Union and eastern Europe, where the hangover from Communism has shifted politics far to the right. Today's Western socialists, dreaming of a world where private property and inequality are outlawed, where rational economic development is planned by far-seeing intellectuals, should be careful what they wish for. They may just get it.

Acknowledgments

The Russian Revolution is a huge subject, and I could not have tackled it without a lot of help over the years. My scholarly interest in Russia was first piqued at UC Berkeley by Yuri Slezkine, the late Reggie Zelnik, and especially the late Martin Malia, who, already retired when I met him, had ample time to indulge my curiosity. It was during my Berkeley years that I began visiting Moscow, helped along by a number of grants from ACTR, FLAS, and IREX, all supported, directly or indirectly, by the US government, in days of happier Russian-American relations when this was a badge of honor, not grounds for suspicion. My last research trip to Russia was funded by a Franklin Grant from the American Philosophical Society, which Linda Musemeci was generous enough to approve, despite a few mishaps with the application paperwork.

Some of the research on which I draw in this book was carried out during my years teaching in Turkey, which enabled frequent travel to nearby Russia. For this opportunity I owe debts to Ali Doğramaci of Bilkent University, who gave me my first real job in academe, and Norman Stone, who provided the introduction and founded Bilkent's Turco-Russian Centre where I worked for many years. Norman's seminal work *The Eastern Front* (1975) was a landmark and inspiration for my own work on the First World War, and his encouragement over the years has been very important to me.

More recently, I have been graced with institutional support from Bard College in Annandale-on-Hudson, New York, for which I owe thanks to President Leon Botstein, former dean Michèle Dominy, current dean Rebecca Thomas, and also Vice President Jonathan Becker, a fellow Russianist whose connections in St. Petersburg, where Bard runs a campus at Smolny, proved invaluable. In Petersburg, Olga

Voronina, Oleg Minin, and Maria Sonevytsky were immensely helpful, and it has been a privilege to join Bard's Russian and Eurasian Studies program. Cecile Kuznitz and Jonathan Brent helped arrange a fruitful visit to the Bund archives at the Yivo Institute in Manhattan, hosted by Leo Greenbaum. Despite its famously unimposing endowment, Bard is a wonderfully rich place to teach and work, and I have been made to feel at home in both history and politics by such colleagues as Richard Aldous, Mark Lytle, Greg Moynahan, Omar Encarnacion, Michelle Murray, Roger Berkowitz, Walter Russell Mead, Simon Gilhooley, Rob Culp, Omar Cheta, Miles Rodriguez, Tabetha Ewing, Christian Crouch, Carolyn Dewald, Myra Armstead, Alice Stroup, Drew Thomson, and Wendy Urban-Mead.

Over the past few years, I have also benefited enormously from the wisdom of fellow scholars at World War I centennial conferences. Dennis Showalter, one of America's most prolific and accomplished military historians, has been an invaluable resource. Eric Lohr invited me onto two fine panels on Russia's war, where I was able to learn a great deal from him, Ronald Bobroff, Joshua Sanborn, and David Stone. Bruce Menning suggested fruitful avenues of research on Russian army morale. We may never agree about Russia and the July crisis, but I have tremendous respect for Bruce's pathbreaking work on the Russian army.

It was in the Russian archives that this project truly came to life, where I was able to lean on the expertise of many fine archivists. At RGAVMF (the tsarist naval archives) in St. Petersburg, Elena Viktorovna helped me evade touchy regulations about what materials one is allowed to photocopy when working on an explosive topic like the mutinies of 1917. At RGVIA (the Imperial Army Archives) in Moscow, Tatiana Yurevna Burmistrova (in the reading room) and Director Irina Olegovna Garkusha have approved my sometimes overwhelming photocopying requests. Sergei Mironenko helped open doors at GARF (the State Archive of the Russian Federation), including those leading to the special collections of RGAE (the Russian State Economics Archive). Sasha Alekseevich Nazarov, the photocopy workhorse of both GARF and RGAE, put up with many imposing photocopying requests on short notice, and he came through brilliantly.

My real archival home in Russia, however, has always been the Communist Party Archives (as I call them) on Bolshaya Dimitrovka, known officially as RGASPI (the Russian Archive of Social-Political History). I was privileged to dine with Director Andrei Sorokin several years ago in Budapest, and he has done wonders with the place. In the reading room on the fifth floor, Vera Stepanova (in the old days) took great care of me, and more recently Irina Petrovna has been a godsend. But above all, I salute Misha, the notorious muse of the document registers, whose sometimes erratic mood swings have scared off a few researchers. I have learned, over the years, simply to trust Misha's impassioned counsel, as no one knows this archive better. In 2015, Misha introduced me to a new Lenin fond, along with the witness depositions taken by Kerensky's Justice Department after the July Days of 1917. I will remain forever in his debt. Samuel Hirst and Daniel Repko also went out of their way to process my complex document scan orders from the Moscow archives, which always take more time to process than one has. In St. Petersburg, Katya Gavroeva was generous enough to share her own digital files, which included a hard-to-find document collection. Sergei Podbolotov was also a great help.

I also draw on material from European and American archives in this book, although many of these run so efficiently that little extra help is required. Still, I must give a shout out to Mareike Fossenburger of the German Foreign Office archives in Berlin, who performed wonders for me. In Paris, Dominique Liechtenhan introduced me to the Quai d'Orsay archives. At the Hoover Archives, Linda Bernard, Carol Leadenham, and Elena Danielson have been advisers and friends ever since my undergraduate days at Stanford, and it was a great pleasure to connect with them once again this past winter.

My agent, Andrew Lownie, did a great deal to turn this ambitious project into reality. Lara Heimert, of Basic Books, is the best editor one can hope for. Roger Labrie once again cleaned up my prose. I must also salute the hospitality of my wife's generous parents, Süheyla and Yüksel Ersoy, in whose splendid home on the Sea of Marmara I have gotten so much writing done over the years, and in which I sit now. Turkey is perhaps not as welcoming as it was when I first arrived in 2002, but her traditions of hospitality live on in the Ersoy household, where I, my wife, Nesrin, and our lovely children, Ayla and Errol, have spent so many happy days. As I write, Turkey is being roiled by its own political drama, which gives a painful reminder of just how fragile civilization is. Fascinating as the Russian Revolution is to me, I hope and pray that my children will not have to live through times quite so interesting themselves.

Abbreviations

AAB   Arbetarrölsens Arkiv och Bibliotek. Stockholm, Sweden.

AN   Archives Nationales. Paris, France.

AVPRI   Arkhiv vneshnei politiki Rossiiskoi Imperii (Archive of the Foreign Policy of the Russian Empire). Moscow, Russia.

BA/MA   Bundesarchiv Militärabteilung (German Military Archives). Freiburg, Germany.

BB   Bundesarchiv Bern. Bern, Switzerland.

DBB   Deutsches Bundesarchiv Berlin. Lichterfelde, Berlin, Germany.

GARF   Gosudarstvennyi Arkhiv Rossiiskoi Federatsii (Government Archive of the Russian Federation). Moscow, Russia.

HS   "Hoover Stavka." Collection "Russia Shtab Verkhovnogo Glavno Komanduiushchego" (e.g., Stavka, or Russian Military Headquarters), Hoover Institution Archives, Stanford, California, USA.

IBZI   *Internationale Beziehungen im Zeitalter des Imperialismus.* Ed. M. N. Pokrovskii. 8+ vols. Berlin: R. Hobbing, 1931–.

KA   *Krasnyi Arkhiv* (The Red Archive). Secret Documents from the Tsarist Archives, especially the running "diary" of the Imperial Russian Ministry of Foreign Affairs. 106 vols.

NAA   National Archives Annex. College Park, Maryland, USA.

PAAA   Politisches Archiv des Auswärtigen Amtes (Political Archive of the Imperial German Foreign Ministry). Berlin, Germany.

PBM   Peter Bark Memoirs. Columbia University Rare Book & Manuscript Library. Columbia University, New York, USA.

PRO   National Archives of the United Kingdom. Kew Gardens, London, UK.*

QO   Archives of the Quai d'Orsay. Paris, France.

RAT   *Razdel Aziatskoi Turtsii. Po sekretnyim dokumentam b. Ministerstva inostrannyikh del* (The Partition of Asiatic Turkey, According to Secret Documents from the Former Ministry of Foreign Affairs).

RGAE   Rossiiskii Gosudarstvennyi Arkhiv Ekonomiki (Russian Government Archive of Economics). Moscow, Russia.

RGASPI   Rossiiskii Gosudarstvennyi Arkhiv Sotsial-Politicheskii Istorii. (Russian Government Archive of Social-Political History). Moscow, Russia.

RGAVMF   Rossiiskii Gosudarstvennyi Arkhiv Voenno-Morskogo Flota (Russian Government Archive of the Imperial Navy). St. Petersburg, Russia.

RGIA   Rossiiskii Gosudarstvennyi Istoricheskii Arkhiv (Russian Government Historical Archive). St. Petersburg, Russia.

RGVA   Rossiiskii Gosudarstvennyi Voennyi Arkhiv (Russian Government Military Archive). Moscow, Russia.

RGVIA   Rossiiskii Gosudarstvennyi Voenno-Istoricheskii Arkhiv (Russian Government Military-Historical Archive). Moscow, Russia.

RSU   Riksarkivet Stockholm Utrikesdepartement. Stockholm, Sweden.

TRMV   *Tsarskaia Rossiia v mirovoi voine* (Tsarist Russia in the World War).

TsGIASPb   Tsentral'nyi Gosudarstvennyi Istoricheskii Arkhiv Sankt-Peterburga (Central Government Historical Archive of St. Petersburg). St. Petersburg, Russia.

VSHD   Vincennes. Service Historique de la Défense (French military archives). Vincennes, Paris, France.

---

*Although it has been years now since the Public Record Office was renamed the National Archives, for the sake of tradition, and to preserve common currency, I continue to reference it in this book as the PRO.

NOTES

Introduction: The First Century of the Russian Revolution

1. Sheila Fitzpatrick, *The Russian Revolution*, 51. For an example of a non-Marxist historian who engages strongly with Marxist arguments about the revolution, see Norman Stone's celebrated final chapter in *The Eastern Front 1914–1917* (1975).

2. Pipes, *The Russian Revolution* (1990), xxiv and passim. This is not to slight Leonard Shapiro's excellent *Russian Revolutions of 1917* (1986). Shapiro's book, however, is more of an analytical study, not really a work of historical scholarship.

3. Timothy Shenk, "Thomas Piketty and Millennial Marxists on the Scourge of Inequality," *Nation*, April 14, 2014.

4. As by, for example, the hundreds of scholars involved in the multivolume, multidisciplinary study of *Russia's Great War and Revolution, 1914–1922*. For an overview, see http://russiasgreatwar.org/index.php.

Prologue: The Blood of a Peasant

1. Cited in Pipes, *Russian Revolution*, 255.

2. Citations in Radzinsky, *Rasputin File*, 434.

3. Rodzianko was not, at first, taken in by Yusupov's hysterical gossip. But eventually Felix had his way. After the revolution, Rodzianko, falling in with the crowd, penned a gossipy memoir-apologia titled *The Reign of Rasputin: An Empire's Collapse*. On the importance of Princess Zinaida in spreading rumors of "dark forces" surrounding Rasputin, see George Katkov, *Russia 1917*, 196–201. Yusupovs richer than the Romanovs: see N. V. Kukuruzova, *Wealthier Than the Romanovs?* (2006).

4. Cited in Fuhrmann, *Rasputin. The Untold Story*, 174. The leading proponent of the theory that Grand Duke Dmitri Pavlovich fired the fatal bullet is Edvard Radzinsky, in *The Rasputin File* (2001).

5. Cited in Cook, *To Kill Rasputin*, 252.

6. Cited in ibid., 158.

7. This the assessment of Joseph Fuhrmann, the leading Western scholarly expert, in *Rasputin. The Untold Story*, 147.

8. Cited in Pipes, *Russian Revolution*, 262. "Would liquidate Rasputin": cited in Cook, *To Kill Rasputin*, 74. The theory of Rayner's involvement has recently inspired new studies of the Rasputin murder based on British files. Cook, in *To Kill Rasputin* (2006), even claimed that Rayner fired the fatal shot, causing a minor scandal in British-Russian relations (this was the year when Alexander Litvinenko was fatally poisoned in London with polonium-210, allegedly by Russian agents, in an intriguing mirror-imaging of what Cook claims Rayner did in 1916).

9. Cook, *To Kill Rasputin*, 173–175. Fuhrmann, in *Rasputin. The Untold Story* (205), claims that the conspirators hoped that "strong tides would carry [Rasputin's body] to the Gulf of Finland," where it would "simply disappear." But this seems inconsistent with the effort put into purchasing weights and chains to ensure the corpse would sink.

10. Cook, *To Kill Rasputin*, 149–150 and passim.

11. Citation in ibid., 197.

12. Fuhrmann, *Rasputin. The Untold Story*, 207–213.

13. Cited in Pipes, *Russian Revolution*, 267.

1. The Old Regime, and Its Enemies

1. Moynahan, *Russian Century*, 7. The Pobedonostsev quote in the part epigraph is cited in Geoffrey Hosking, *Russia and the Russians*, 318.

2. McMeekin, *History's Greatest Heist*, xvi–xvii; and *Russian Origins*, 6–7.

3. The phrase is Robert Massie's, in *Nicholas and Alexandra*, 8.

4. Norman Stone, *Europe Transformed*, 150.

5. Nechaev, *Catechism of a Revolutionary* (1869), available in English translation at https://www.marxists.org/subject/anarchism/nechayev/catechism.htm.

6. Sebag-Montefiore, *Young Stalin*, 86.

7. Figes, *People's Tragedy*, 46.

8. Sebag Montefiore, *Young Stalin*, 111–114.

9. Okhrana file on Vladimir Ulyanov (Lenin), in RGASPI, fond 4, opis' 3, del' 68, 29, 29 ob, 30.

10. Pipes, *Russian Revolution*, 5–10.

11. Fuller, *Civil-Military Conflict in Imperial Russia 1881–1914*, 88–91.

12. H. Shukman, "The Relations Between the Jewish Bund and the RSDRP, 1897–1903," unpublished D. Phil Thesis, Oxford University, 37. On comparative membership numbers: Figes, *People's Tragedy*, 141n.

13. Shukman, 237.

14. F. Roger Devlin, "Solzhenitsyn on the Jews and Tsarist Russia," *Occidental Quarterly* 8, no. 3 (Fall 2008): 75–76.

15. Cited in Fuller, *Civil-Military Conflict*, 79.

16. Fuller, *Strategy and Power*, 373.

17. On Ayastefanos: Dilek Kaya Mutlu, "The Russian Monument at *Ayaste-fanos* (San Stefano): Between Defeat and Revenge, Remembering and Forgetting," *Middle Eastern Studies* 43, no. 1 (January 2007): 75–86; and "Ghost Buildings of Istanbul" at http://www.hayal-et.org/i.php/site/building/ayaste fanos_ant.

18. David R. Stone, *Russian Army*, 35–36.

19. Ibid.

20. Tolstoy, *The Cossacks* (1863).

21. Stone, *Russian Army*, 36–37.

22. Norman Stone, *Eastern Front*, 20–22.

2. 1905: Shock to the System

1. For a sympathetic rendering of the episode, see Massie, *Nicholas and Alexandra*, 49–56.

2. See McMeekin, *Ottoman Endgame*, chaps. 1–2.

3. Cited in McDonald, *United Government*, 13.

4. Citations in ibid., 70–72.

5. Cited in Fuller, *Strategy and Power*, 397.

6. Ibid., 397–401.

7. Cited by Orlando Figes, in *People's Tragedy*, 172.

8. Pipes, *Russian Revolution*, 24–26.

9. Sebag-Montefiore, *Young Stalin*, 128–129.

10. Fuller, *Civil-Military Conflict*, 134–135.

11. Cited in Fuller, *Strategy and Power*, 405.

12. H. P. Willmott, *The Last Century of Sea Power: From Port Arthur to Chanak, 1894–1922*, 115–121.

13. Citation and figure in Sebag Montefiore, *Young Stalin*, 135.

14. Citations in Bascomb, *Red Mutiny*, 129–132.

15. Ibid., 138–141 and (for the journey to Constanza) 231–242.

16. For the statutes of the "Bulygin Duma": see US Ambassador Meyer to Secretary of State, July 13, 1905, available at http://novaonline.nvcc.edu/eli/evans/his242/documents/frus/bulyginduma.html. For the university reform, see Pipes, *Russian Revolution*, 35–36.

17. Miliukov, *Political Memoirs*, trans. Carl Goldberg, 41–42; and Pipes, *Russian Revolution*, 28.

18. Bolshevik pamphlets and newssheets put out by the Military Organization in 1905–1906 are preserved in the Bund archives of the Yivo Institute in New York City, ME1-88 and ME1-103.

19. Scharlau and Zeman, *Merchant of Revolution*, 76–81.

20. Cited in Pipes, *Russian Revolution*, 38 (Pipes's translation).

21. Cited in Massie, *Nicholas and Alexandra*, 107.

362 — Notes

22. "Manifesto of 17 October 1905."

23. Citations in Fuller, *Civil-Military Conflict*, 138.

24. Pipes, *Russian Revolution*, 49–50; and (for details on Trotsky and Parvus) Scharlau and Zeman, *Merchant of Revolution*, 88–92.

25. Sebag Montefiore, *Young Stalin*, 147–150.

26. Fuller, *Civil-Military Conflict*, 139–141.

27. Pipes, *Russian Revolution*, 157–159.

3. The Fragile Giant: Tsarist Russia on the Precipice of War

1. Figures in ibid., 169.

2. Alexander Zenkovsky, *Stolypin: Russia's Last Great Reformer*, trans. Margaret Patoski, 2 and passim.

3. Pipes, *Russian Revolution*, 170.

4. Cited in Zenkovsky, *Stolypin: Russia's Last Great Reformer*, 11. "Thank God for the Tsar": cited in Stone, *Europe Transformed*, 226. "I cannot tell you": cited in Massie, *Nicholas and Alexandra*, 216. The Okhrana file on Vladimir Ulyanov (Lenin) compiled in 1909 does not even mention the 1905 revolution. In RGASPI, fond 4, opis' 3, del' 68, 29, 29 ob, 30.

5. Cited in Pipes, *Russian Revolution*, 178.

6. McMeekin, *History's Greatest Heist*, 1 and passim.

7. Stone, *Europe Transformed*, 228.

8. Cited in the protocol of the meeting of the Council of Ministers held on January 21/February 3, 1908, reproduced (in German translation) in M. N. Pokrovskii, ed., *Drei Konferenzen*, 25, 30.

9. Citations in D. C. B. Lieven, *The End of Tsarist Russia*, 214, and McDonald, *United Government*, 143. *Russkoe Slovo* (January 28, 1909): clipped and reproduced by the Foreign Ministry of Austria-Hungary, in HHSA, Russland Berichte 1909 I-IX, Karton 134. On the Austrian side, see Manfried Rauchensteiner, *Der Tod des Doppeladlers*, 18. On the Ottoman side, see McMeekin, *Ottoman Endgame*, chap. 2.

10. Cited in Lieven, *End of Tsarist Russia*, 224.

11. Cited in Ascher, *P. A. Stolypyin*, 293–294. On Sazonov's appointment and the Kaiser-Tsar summit, see Baron Szilassy from Petersburg to Aehrenthal, June 9, 19, and 26, 1909, in HHSA, Russland Berichte 1909 I-IX, Karton 134. Although Sazonov would not officially take the reins until fall 1910, his appointment was announced to the diplomatic community of St. Petersburg in June 1909.

12. See British Embassy aide-mémoire dated November 30, 1910, and Quai d'Orsay memorandum labeled "Russie-Angleterre. Juillet 1914," both in QO Russia Politique Etrangère, File 50. For analysis, see also Lieven, *End of Tsarist Russia*, 236–237.

13. Pipes, *Russian Revolution*, 189.

14. Cited in McDonald, *United Government*, 159.

15. McMeekin, *Ottoman Endgame*, chap. 3.

16. On the French view of Krivoshein, see the Quai d'Orsay backgrounder on "Principaux Personnages Politiques Russes," prepared for President Raymond Poincaré's visit to St. Petersburg in July 1914, in QO, Russia. Politique Intérieure, vol. 4.

17. Cited in Lieven, *End of Tsarist Russia*, 263.

18. Cited in McDonald, *United Government*, 191.

19. See McMeekin, *Russian Origins*, chap. 1.

20. Sazonov to Tsar Nicholas II, January 6, 1914, reproduced in the *Krasnyi Arkhiv*, vol. 6, 41 and passim; and conference protocol for January 13, 1914, reproduced in Pokrovskii, *Drei Konferenzen*, 40–42.

21. Resolutions 1 through 6 of the original February 8/21, 1914, conference transcript, in AVPRI, fond 138, opis' 467, del' 462, list' 23 (and back). Regarding Kokovtsov's resignation, there was also gossip that he had incurred the displeasure of Rasputin. And yet the timing seems off, as the two men met only once, in February 1912.

22. Durnovo Memorandum to Tsar Nicholas II, February 14, 1914, widely available in English translation, as here: http://www2.stetson.edu/~psteeves/classes/durnovo.html.

23. A copy of Durnovo Memorandum was found among the tsar's valued personal papers when he was arrested in 1917, which suggests that Nicholas II had come, over time, to realize the wisdom of Durnovo's warning. But Durnovo's message was unheeded in 1914, when it might have made a difference.

24. Bark memoirs in Bark collection at Columbia University, box 1, 15–21 and passim.

25. Citations in Fuhrmann, *Rasputin*, 114–115.

26. Cited in ibid., 119.

27. Entry for July 17/30, 1914, in Schilling, 64.

28. Cited in Fuhrmann, *Rasputin*, 129.

4. Russia's War, 1914–1916

1. Stone, *Russian Army in the Great War*, 56. On draft riots in 1914, see Joshua Sanborn, "The Mobilization of 1914 and the Question of the Russian Nation: A Reexamination," *Slavic Review* 59, no. 2 (2000): 267–289.

2. Geoff Wawro, *Mad Catastrophe*, 179, 188–193.

3. Citations in Stone, *Russian Army in the Great War*, 69.

4. The scene is movingly recreated in Solzhenitsyn's *August 1914*, 467–469. Loose radio communication has long been a popular explanation of the Russian disaster at Tannenberg, although its importance has often been exaggerated. As David Stone notes in *Russian Army in the Great War* (69), *any* army advancing into enemy territory in 1914 faced this problem, including

the Germans invading France, who likewise broadcast numerous messages en clair.

5. Fuller, *Foe Within*, 129, 161, and Norman Stone, *Eastern Front*, 68–69.

6. As noted by Norman Stone in *Eastern Front*, 53n.

7. Norman Stone, in *Eastern Front* (chapter 7) disputed the importance of shell shortage to Russia's battlefield performance, calling it, at bottom, "a hard luck story." David Stone, in his new *Russian Army in the Great War* (228 and passim) disagrees.

8. Stone, *Russian Army in the Great War*, 134; Fuller, *Foe Within*, 132.

9. Fuller, *Foe Within*, 1–2.

10. Citations in ibid., 163–164.

11. "A very difficult struggle with Judentum lies in store for us": Yanushkevitch to Goremykin, September 19/October 2, 1914, document 349 in IBZI, vol. 6, 270–272. On Yanushkevitch's anti-Semitic spy mania at Stavka, see Fuller, *Foe Within*, 177. On the wartime deportations of Jews and Germans, see Eric Lohr, "Russian Army and the Jews," and *Nationalizing the Russian Empire*.

12. Stone, *Russian Army in the Great War*, 146–161.

13. David Stone, *Russian Army in the Great War*, 161–175, and Norman Stone, *Eastern Front*, chap. 8.

14. Yakhontov minutes for August 24/September 6, 1915, in *Soviet Ministrov Rossiiskoi Imperii v gody pervoi mirovoi voiny. Bumagi A. N. Yakhontova* (St. Petersburg, 1999), 239; and citations in Katkov, *Russia 1917*, 143.

15. Yakhontov minutes for August 21/September 3, 1915, in *Soviet Ministrov Rossiiskoi Imperii v gody pervoi mirovoi voiny*, 236.

16. Stone, *Russian Army in the Great War*, 229.

17. Police report on the meeting at Chelnokov's house on September 6/19, 1915, reproduced in Grave, *Burzhuaziia nakanune fevralskoi revoliutsii*, 46–49.

18. Katkov, *Russia 1917*, 163 and passim. For more on freemasonry, see Semion Lyandres, *The Fall of Tsarism*, biographical notes on Nekrasov (142 and passim) and Tereshchenko (245 and passim). German intelligence: see Herr Steinwachs to Minister Bergen, January 18, 1916, passing on "A. Stein" from Stockholm, January 9, 1916, reproduced in English translation by Z. A. B. Zeman, ed., *Germany and the Revolution in Russia, 1915–1918* (henceforth "Zeman"), 11–13.

19. Norman Stone, *Eastern Front*, 208–211.

20. David Stone, *Russian Army in the Great War*, 222, 228–229.

21. "Svodka Svedenii o sostoyanii i nastroenii nashei deistvuiushchei armii . . . s' 15 dekabrya 1916 g. po 1 yanvarya 1917 goda" (henceforth "Northwestern Army December 1916 Morale Report") in RGVIA, fond 2031, Opis' 1, Del' 1181, list' 20–22 (and backs), 23.

22. Citations in Aleksandr Astashov, *Russkii front v 1914–nachale 1917 goda: voennyi opyt i sovremennost'*, 622–626.

23. See McMeekin, *Russian Origins*, chap. 8, and *Ottoman Endgame*, chap. 12.

24. The fullest account of the battle in English is Timothy Dowling, *The Brusilov Offensive*. On the Austro-Hungarian side, see Graydon Tunstall, "Austria-Hungary and the Brusilov Offensive of 1916," *Historian* 70, no. 1 (Spring 2008): 30–53. The best recent estimates on casualties are in David Stone, *Russian Army in the Great War*, 248–249. On the Russian side, see also Fuller, *Foe Within*, 207.

25. Alekseev to Stürmer, September 1/14, 1916, in RGIA, fond 1276, opis' 15, del' 45. For more, see McMeekin, *Ottoman Endgame*, chap. 14.

26. Rodzianko, *Reign of Rasputin*, 174–177. Confusingly, Protopopov was a trusted protégé of Rodzianko, who had even recommended him to the tsar as a possible minister in a "government of public confidence." But Protopopov did not bother to inform his patron about his appointment until after the fact, which enraged Rodzianko.

27. A. I. Guchkov to Mikhail Vasil'evich' Alekseev, August 15/28, 1916, original copy in RGIA, Fond 1276, opis' 15, del' 51, list' 1–4. For analysis, see A. S. Senin, *Aleksandr Ivanovich Guchkov*, 96–97.

28. See Katkov, *Russia 1917*, 185–187. On the blaming of Guchkov, see Senin, *Aleksandr Ivanovich Guchkov*, 97.

29. Ruzsky to Stürmer, September 17/30, 1916, in RGIA, Fond 1276, opis' 15, del' 48; and police report, ca. October 1916, cited in Pipes, *Russian Revolution*, 243.

30. February 1916: cited in Katkov, *Russia 1917*, 189.

31. Milyukov's speech is reproduced in English translation by Emanuel Aronsberg, in Frank Golder, ed., *Documents of Russian History 1914–1917*, 154–166.

32. See prologue above.

5. Full of Fight

1. Citations in Fuhrmann, *Rasputin: The Untold Story*, 1, and Douglas Smith, "Grigory Rasputin and the Outbreak of the First World War," in *Historically Inevitable?*, 65.

2. Frank Golder diary, entry for Thursday, April 13/26, 1917, in Frank Golder collection, Hoover Institution Archives, box 2, folder 2 (henceforth "Golder diary"). On Rasputin and Sukhomlinov, see Fuller, *Foe Within*, 209–211, 228–231.

3. Cited in Pipes, *Russian Revolution*, 268.

4. Guchkov deposition by the Muraviev Commission, in *Padenie tsarkogo rezhima*, vol. 6, 278–280. On Guchkov's anti-Rasputin war chest: Senin, *Aleksandr Ivanovich Guchkov*, 97. On his importuning of Denikin: "Zapis' besedyi A. I. Guchkova s N. A. Bazili," in *Aleksandr Ivanovich Guchkov rasskazyivaet* (henceforth "Basily-Guchkov interview"), 10–11.

5. Cited in Katkov, *Russia 1917*, 176.

6. Senin, *Aleksandr Ivanovich Guchkov*, 99. On the "troika" and the timing and logistics of the planned "palace coup": Basily-Guchkov interview, 17–23. For details on Kossikovsky, see Lyandres, *Fall of Tsarism*, 272 and passim.

7. Citations in Katkov, *Russia 1917*, 161–162, 218; Pipes, *Russian Revolution*, 269. See also Gurko, *Features and Figures of the Past*, 582, and Grave, *Burzhuaziia nakanune fevralskoi revoliutsii* 59, and passim.

8. Rodzianko interview conducted by M. A. Polievktov, May 16/29, 1917, transcript cited in Lyandres, *Fall of Tsarism*, 106. Katkov, *Russia 1917*, 43.

9. Cited in Katkov, *Russia 1917*, 211 and 211n.

10. Rodzianko, *Reign of Rasputin*, 244–245.

11. Rodzianko interview conducted by M. A. Polievktov on May 16/29, 1917, cited in *Lyandres, Fall of Tsarism*, 106.

12. Kolchak directive dated February 8/21, 1917, in RGAVMF, Fond 716, Opis' 1, del' 267. For more details, see McMeekin, *Russian Origins*, chap. 9, and *Ottoman Endgame*, chapter 14, and Norman Stone, *Eastern Front 1914–1917*, 282.

13. "Doklady o nastroenii voisk 5-i armii po pis'mam . . . 31 December 1916," in RGVIA, Fond 2031, opis' 1, del' 1181. There were differences inside other Russian armies: units in heavily forested areas ate less well than those billeted near farmland.

14. Ibid.

15. "Doklad' o nastroenii voisk' 5-i armii po pis'mam za fevral' mesyats' 1917 g," in RGVIA, fond 2031, opis' 1, del' 1181; and "Northwestern Army December 1916 Morale Report."

16. "Doklad' voenno-tsenzurnago otdeleniya Shtaba III-i armii po 514/ts Fevralya 19 dnya 1917 goda"; and, for First Army, "Doklad' o nastroenii voisk' i naseleniya po dannyim ochetov voennyikh' tsensurov raiona 1-i armii za Ianvar' mesyats' 1917 goda, both in RGVIA, fond 2031, opis' 1, del' 1181. On Galician protests: David Stone, *Russian Army in the Great War*, 278; and F. Akimov, "Bolsheviki v bor'be za soldatskie massy Iugo-Zapadnogo fronta (1914–fevral' 1917 g.)," *Voenno-istoricheskii zhurnal*, no. 2 (1977): 87–88.

17. Norman Saul, *Sailors in Revolt*, 52–53.

18. Oleg Airapetov, "Sud'ba Bosforskoi ekspeditsii," 236. See also Halpern, *Naval History of World War I*, 237.

19. Evan Mawdsley, *Russian Revolution and the Baltic Fleet*, 2–5.

20. For statistics on the food situation in Petrograd in February 1917, see graphic reproduced in Golder, *Documents of Russian History*, 186–187. On the German Foreign Office and the strike movement of January 1916, see Minister in Copenhagen to the Chancellor, January 23, 1916, reproduced in Zeman, 14–16; and also Scharlau and Zeman, *Merchant of Revolution*, 185–188.

21. Protest in the name of the "Predstavleniya Tsentral'nogo voenno-promyishlenogo komiteta," addressed to Chairman of the Council of Min-

isters Golitsyn, February 3/16, 1917, in RGIA, fond 1276, opis' 13, del' 33. For details see also Katkov, *Russia 1917*, 233–235; and Pipes, *Russian Revolution*, 270–271.

6. A Break in the Weather

1. International Women's Day, like May Day, was a creation of the Marxist "Second International" (1889–1914), designed to teach working women that their true "sisters" were laborers in other countries, not fellow countrywomen of different classes.

2. Telegram from Protopopov to Count N. D. Golitsyn, February 25/ March 10, 1917, in RGIA, fond 1276, opis' 13, del' 36; Golder diary, entry for Thursday, March 8, 1917 (February 23); and Okhrana report cited in Pipes, *Russian Revolution*, 275.

3. V. Zenzinov, "Fevral'skie Dni," entry for February 24, 1917, excerpted in Kerensky and Browder, eds., *Russian Provisional Government*, 27–28.

4. *Rech'* editorial on the food situation, February 25/March 10, 1917, reproduced in Kerensky and Browder, eds., *The Russian Provisional Government 1917*, 30. Rodzianko: May 16/29 interview, cited in Lyandres, *Fall of Tsarism*, 107. Golder diary, entry for March 9, 1917 (February 24); and Khabalov directive published in *Novoe Vremia* on February 24, 1917, excerpted in Kerensky and Browder, ed., *Russian Provisional Government*, 27–28.

5. The incident is discussed in Zenzinov's entry for February 25, 1917, and in an Okhrana reported dated February 26, 1917, excerpted in ibid., 32, 37. For the regime's estimates on the number of protestors on each of the first three days: Protopopov to Golitsyn, February 25, 1917.

6. Zenzinov on February 25, 1917. Milyukov to Kerensky: cited in Katkov, *Russia 1917*, 257. "German woman": cited in Pipes, *Russian Revolution*, 275.

7. Tsar's orders to Khabalov, February 25, 1917, Khabalov deposition by the Muraviev Commission, and police decree of February 26, 1917, cited in Katkov, *Russia 1917*, 267–269; and Golder, diary entry for Sunday March 11, 1917 (February 26). For more on the day's critical events, see Leonard Shapiro, *Russian Revolutions of 1917*, 41; and Pipes, *Russian Revolution*, 277.

8. Katkov, *Russia 1917*, 271–273.

9. On Balkashin's last stand, see Hasegawa, *February Revolution*, 360–361.

10. Golder diary, Monday night March 12 (February 27) to Tuesday morning, March 13 (February 28).

11. Orlando Figes, *A People's Tragedy*, 320–221. On the sacking of Okhrana headquarters: Pipes, *Russian Revolution*, 280–281.

12. Rodzianko to Tsar Nicholas II, February 26, 1917, reproduced in (among many other places) Golder, *Documents of Russian History*, 278. For Council of Ministers: Katkov, *Russia 1917*, 287–289.

13. Rodzianko to Tsar Nicholas II, February 27, 1917, reproduced in Golder, ed., *Documents of Russian History*, 278.

14. The first list of members is reproduced in Golder, ed., *Documents of Russian History*, 281. For more details, see especially Katkov, *Russia 1917*, 296–297.

15. Alekseev diary, entries for February 27–28 (March 12–13), 1917, in Alekseev collection, Hoover Institution Archives, folder 1-20 (henceforth "Alekseev diary"). For more on the timeline see Pipes, *Russian Revolution*, 284–286.

16. Katkov, *Russia 1917*, 289.

17. Alekseev diary, entry for February 28 (March 13), 1917, and Katkov, *Russia 1917*, 282–284.

18. Engelhardt interview conducted on May 4, 1917, and Kerensky interview conducted on May 31, 1917, in Lyandres, *Fall of Tsarism*, 59, and 223–224; and Katkov, *Russia 1917*, 359–365. The Sokolov quote is cited in Allan Wildman, *End of the Russian Imperial Army*, 172.

19. Documents reproduced in Golder, ed., *Documents of Russian History*, 280–282.

20. Cited in Melgunov, *Martovskie Dni*, 160–161. Emphasis added.

21. Rodzianko to "Moskva Gorodskomu Golove Chelnokovu," February 28/March 13, 1917, and Rodzianko "Komanduyushchemu Voiskami Generalu Mrozovskomu," February 28, 1917, both in RGIA, fond 1278, Opis' 10, del' 3. For details on Bublikov and the Transportation Ministry: Nekrasov interview conducted on May 25, 1917, cited in Lyandres, *Fall of Tsarism*, 151; and Katkov, *Russia 1917*, 311.

22. See Katkov, *Russia 1917*, 316–317.

7. Army in the Balance: March

1. Mawdsley, *Russian Revolution and the Baltic Fleet*, 12–14.

2. Rusin from Helsingfors, March 1, 1917; Kapnist' from Admiralty Petrograd; and Nepenin from Helsingfors, March 1, 1917 (10:00 a.m. and again 2:30 p.m.), all in RGAVMF, fond 716, opis' 1, del' 277.

3. "Doklad' o nastroenii vois' 5-i armii po pis'mam za mart' mesyats 1917 g.," in RGVIA, fond 2031, opis' 1, del' 1181.

4. "Doklad' o nastroenii voisk' i naseleniya po dannyim' otchetov voennyikh' tsenzurov' raiona 1-i armii za Mart' mesyats 1917 g."

5. Alekseev passed on by Lutsk command, March 1, 1917 (4:25 a.m.); and Gerua operation reports from Lutsk, March 2, 1917 (10:40 a.m.) and March 3, 1917 (10:30 p,m,), and March 7, 1917 (10:00 p.m.), all in RGVIA, fond 2067, opis' 1, del' 394.

6. See McMeekin, *Ottoman Endgame*, chap. 14 ("Russia's Moment").

7. Cited in Katkov, *Russia 1917*, 303.

8. Rodzianko to Alekseev, March 2/15, 1917, in RGIA, fond 1278, opis' 10, del. 5; and Rodzianko conversation with Ruzsky on the "Hughes apparatus," 2:00 a.m. to 7:00 a.m. on March 2, 1917, cited in Katkov, *Russia 1917*, 304n.

9. Cited in Katkov, *Russia 1917*, 390.

10. Bonch-Bruevich, *Na boevyikh postakh fevral'skoi i oktyabr'skoi revoliutsii*, 12–13; Lyandres, *Fall of Tsarism*, 67n31 and 207n17; Wildman, *End of the Russian Imperial Army*, 182–188; and Katkov, *Russia 1917*, 370–373.

11. The "final" version is reproduced in English translation by Wildman in *End of the Russian Imperial Army*, 187–188. For the subtleties of the drafting and changes in published versions, see Katkov, *Russia 1917*, 370–373.

12. Cited in Pipes, *Russian Revolution*, 305.

13. Hasegawa, *February Revolution*, 361–367. On early defections in the army, see Wildman, *End of the Russian Imperial Army*, 173–174 and 207–211.

14. The draft manifesto is reproduced, in English translation with accompanying commentary and annotation, by its author in Nicholas de Basily, *The Abdication of Emperor Nicholas II of Russia*, 125.

15. Citations in Wildman, *End of the Russian Imperial Army*, 208.

16. Cited in Katkov, *Russia 1917*, 322.

17. Cited in ibid., 329–330.

18. Cited in ibid., 331.

19. Melgunov, *Martovskie Dni*, 291.

20. Wildman, *End of the Russian Imperial Army*, 190.

21. The abdication scene is rendered in great detail, including a long transcript of the proceedings, in Melgunov, *Martovskie Dni*, 291–304. For analysis of possible discrepancies in the different accounts, see Katkov, *Russia 1917*, 340–345. As Katkov notes, it is hard to credit Guchkov's argument that the tsar's action was legally reviewable by Rodzianko's Duma committee, itself created without precedent.

22. Transcript of Rodzianko conversation with Ruzsky, 5:00 a.m., on March 3/16, 1917, reproduced in Kerensky and Browder, eds., *Russian Provisional Government*, 109–110.

23. Alekseev to all front commanders, 7:00 a.m. on March 3/16, 1917, reproduced in Kerensky and Browder, eds., *Russian Provisional Government*, 112–113. Alekseev to Lukomsky: cited in Katkov, *Russia 1917*, 346–347.

24. Milyukov's version of the event is excerpted in Kerensky and Browder, eds., *Russian Provisional Government*, 115–116.

25. "The Refusal of the Grand Duke Mikhail Aleksandrovich to Assume the Supreme Power," reproduced in ibid., 116. Nicholas II to Michael, March 3, 1917: cited in Donald Crawford, "The Last Tsar," in Brenton, *Historically Inevitable?*, 85.

26. Reproduced in the Alekseev collection, Hoover Institution Archives, box 1-20. Members of the Romanov dynasty arrested: cited in Pipes, *Russian Revolution*, 324.

27. Details in Leonard Shapiro, *Russian Revolutions of 1917*, 57; and in Wildman, *End of the Russian Imperial Army*, 202.

28. Guchkov order as "Naval Minister" to the fleet (with copy to army), March 4/17, 1917, in RGAVMF, 716-1-277, list' 54–55.

29. "War Minister Guchkov" to the army and fleet, March 5/18, 1917, in RGVIA, fond 2031, opis' 1, del' 1537, list' 46.

30. Rodzianko to the army and fleet, March 6/19, 1917, passed on (in this case) by Ruzsky at northern army command, in RGVIA, fond 2031, opis' 1, del' 1537, list' 22.

31. Alekseev and Danilov, ms. signed order no. 1998, ms. dated March 6, 1917, in RGVIA, fond 2031, opis' 1, del' 1537, list' 26 (and back); and "Prisyaga," dated March 7, 1917, signed Prince Lvov, in RGVIA, fond 2031, opis' 1, del' 1537, list' 55.

32. "Telegrafnoe vozzvanie k' armii ot' Vremennago Pravitel'stva," cosigned by Chairman Lvov and War and Naval Minister Guchkov, March 7/20, 1917, in RGVIA, fond 2031, opis' 1, del' 1537, list' 72 (back) and 73.

33. "Prisyaga," March 13/26, 1917, in RGVIA, fond 2031, opis' 1, del' 1534, list' 9.

34. Alekseev to Guchkov, March 26, 1917, and Guchkov reply, passed on to front commanders the next day, in RGVIA, fond 2031, opis' 1, del' 1534, list' 57 and back.

35. Alekseev to Northern Front Command at Pskov (Ruzsky), March 26, 1917, in RGVIA, fond 2031, opis' 1, del' 1537, list' 331 and back. Order No. 2 is reproduced in Golder, ed., *Documents of Russian History*, 388–390. See also Wildman, *End of the Russian Imperial Army*, 230–233.

36. Nepenin to Admiralty, 1:30 a.m. on March 4/17, 1917, in RGAVMF, fond 716, opis' 1, del' 278, list' 7–8. For a lurid account of Nepenin's murder: see letter from B. Dudorov to Kolchak, March 10, 1917, in the Kolchak fond at RGAVMF, fond 11, opis' 1, del' 57. For casualties in the navy, Wildman, *End of the Russian Imperial Army*, 234n.

37. Golder diary, entry for March 15/28, 1917. On the origins and nature of Kerensky's dual mandate, see Shapiro, *Russian Revolutions of 1917*, 55 and passim.

38. In the operation reports of the southwestern command at Lutsk, for March and Arpil 1917, the first mention of desertions (all of two soldiers) occurs at 5:45 p.m. on April 18/31, in RGVIA, fond 2067, opis' 1, del' 394, list' 352. For a summary of figures for March 1917, see Wildman, *End of the Russian Imperial Army*, 235.

39. See Pipes, *Russian Revolution*, 303–304 and 304n.

8. The German Gambit

1. *Westminster Gazette*, March 7/20, 1917; and *Le Matin*, March 12/25, 1917, clipped in RGIA, fond 1358, opis' 1, del' 1945.

2. Barbara Tuchman, *Zimmermann Telegram*.

3. Wilson declaration to Congress, April 2, 1917, widely available online, as here: http://www.firstworldwar.com/source/usawardeclaration.htm.

4. *Le Temps* March 9/22, 1917; and *Le Matin* March 13/26, 1917 ("Les événements de Russie"), clipped in RGIA, fond 1358, opis' 1, del' 1945.

5. *Berliner Lokal-Anzeiger*, March 7/20 and 11/24, 1917, and *Berliner Tageblatt* March 7/20, 1917, clipped in RGIA, fond 1358, opis' 1, del' 1945.

6. Report of "K.k. Ministerium des Innern. Staatspolizeiliches Bureau," August 16, 1914, in RGASPI, fond 4, opis' 3, del' 48, list' 1 and following documents.

7. Wangenheim via Zimmermann, January 9, 1915, reproduced in Zeman, 1–2.

8. Kesküla collection, Hoover Institution Archives, box 1, folder 1-5 ("1960"). For German sources on Kesküla's connection with Romberg and Lenin: Romberg to Bethmann Hollweg from Bern, September 30, 1915, and Steinwachs to Bergen (with information on sums disbursed), May 8, 1916, reproduced in Zeman, 6–8, 16–18.

9. As translated by R. Craig Nation, in *War on War*, 1.

10. For a full statement of Lenin's views on the war, see his *Socialism and War* (1915). On Zimmermann's intervention, see Katkov, *Russia 1917*, 76–77.

11. Lenin, *Collected Works, Volume 23 (August 1916–March 1917)*, 253.

12. The final terms, confirmed by Romberg on April 5, 1917, are reproduced in Zeman, 38–39. For more on the negotiations and the appropriation of funds, see Scharlau and Zeman, *Merchant of Revolution*, 208 and passim; and Pipes, *Russian Revolution*, 391–392. The best single account of the voyage, based on German sources, is Werner Hahlweg, *Lenins Rückkehr nach Russland*.

13. Memorandum by Ow-Wachendorf, Berlin, April 11, 1917, reproduced in Zeman, 44–45. Ow-Wachendorf insisted, less than credibly, that the German hotel rooms in Sassnitz in which Lenin and the Russians had stayed were "locked." On Jansson joining the Russians: Bussche to Bern, April 5 and 7, 1917, reproduced in Zeman, 37–38 and 40. On the two German officers: citations in Michael Pearson, *Sealed Train*, 81–82.

14. One witness, Subaltern D. S. Ermolenko, became briefly famous when he testified that Lenin was working for Berlin, famous enough for his credibility to be attacked by generations of Soviet historians, and more recently by Semion Lyandres, in *The Bolsheviks' "German Gold" Revisited* (1995), 1–3 and passim. Lyandres (1) calls Ermolenko's testimony "shaky." Lyandres is not wrong to be skeptical about Ermolenko's more fanciful claims, such as that he was called in by the German General Staff for a debriefing. But Ermolenko's more important claim that Lenin's journey across Germany, and his views on Ukraine, were known to Russian prisoners of war there is corroborated by multiple witnesses deposed by the Provisional Government.

15. Cited in Scharlau and Zeman, *Merchant of Revolution*, 208. See also telegram from Stockholm, May 14, 1917, noting that "257 Russian emigrants expected tomorrow morning," intercepted by Russian intelligence, in RGASPI, fond 4, opis' 3, del' 39, list' 31. "Much more raving mad": cited in Pipes, *Russian Revolution*, 390.

16. Grünau passing on Steinwachs from Stockholm, April 17, 1917, received at Spa April 21, 1917, reproduced in Zeman, 51. On Lenin's arrival, see Sukhanov, *Russian Revolution 1917*, 272–273, and also Pipes, *Russian Revolution*, 393. The April Theses are reproduced in Lenin, *Collected Works* (trans. Bernard Isaacs), vol. 24, 21–26. Golder: Golder diary, entry for Wednesday, April 5/18, 1917.

17. Kamenev: cited in Bunyan and Fisher, eds., *Bolshevik Revolution 1917–1918*, 7. Stalin: Cited in Leonard Shapiro, *The Russian Revolutions of 1917*, 59.

18. Krasnyi testimony, in "Materialyi predvaritel'nogo sledstviya o vooruzhennom vyistuplenii v Petrograde 3(16) – 5(18) iyulya 1917 goda," RGASPI, fond 4, opis' 3, del' 41, list' 153 and passim.

19. On the print runs, see Pipes, *Russian Revolution*, 410.

20. Ibid., relying on Nikitin, *Rokovye gody*, 109–110. On the now well-documented role of Olof Aschberg's Nya Banken in Stockholm as principal conduit for German funds to Lenin, see McMeekin, *History's Greatest Heist*, esp. chap. 5.

21. Nikitin, *Rokovy gody*. Such was the conclusion of Semion Lyandres, in *The Bolsheviks' "German Gold" Revisited* (1995). Sumenson withdrawal: Kerensky, *Crucifixion of Liberty*, 326.

22. Natal'ya Ferdinandovna Gerling, Al'fred Mavrikievich Rudno, Mariya Mikhailovna Rudenko, Aleksei Alekseevich Konde, Bronislaw Andreevich Veselovskii, Mikhail Nikolaevich Lebedev, Nikolai Martyinovich Medvedev, and Romana Vladimirovna Fyurstenberg depositions in "Materialyi predvaritel'nogo sledstviya o vooruzhennom vyistuplenii v Petrograde 3(16)–5(18) iyulya 1917 goda," RGASPI, fond 4, opis' 3, del' 41, list' 101–102, 139–140, 161–164, 202–203, 251, 325–326, 336, and passim.

23. Intercepted telegram no. 34 from Kozlovskii in Petrograd to Fuerstenberg in Stockholm (Saltsjöbaden), June 5/18, 1917, and follow-up no. 90 (July 2/15, 1917), confirming the transfer into Russo-Asiatic Bank, in RGASPI, fond 4, opis' 3, del' 39, list' 124. For the best estimates of German expenditure, see Baumgart, *Deutsche Ostpolitik 1918*, 213–214, n19.

24. Summary of depositions of Malinovskii, Vissarianov, and Beletskii, in "Materialyi predvaritel'nogo sledstviya o vooruzhennom vyistuplenii v Petrograde 3(16)–5(18) iyulya 1917 goda," RGASPI, fond 4, opis' 3, del' 41, list' 87–88. For more on Kshesinskaya's, see Sukhanov, *Russian Revolution 1917. A Personal Record*, 211.

25. Evgeniya Ivanovna Shelyakhovskaya deposition, in "Materialyi predvaritel'nogo sledstviya o vooruzhennom vyistuplenii v Petrograde 3(16)–5(18)

iyulya 1917 goda," in RGASPI, fond 4, opis' 3, del' 41, list' 112–113 (and back of 112).

26. Ibid.; Kondrat'evich deposition, in RGASPI, fond 4, opis' 3, del' 41, list' 98.

27. Nikitin, *Fatal Years*, 114.

9. Twilight of the Liberals

1. "First Declaration of the Provisional Government," March 7/20, 1917, reproduced in Golder, *Documents of Russian History*, 311–313. On Guchkov's sacking of generals: Stone, *Russian Army in the Great War*, 280–281.

2. In Kerensky and Browder, *Russian Provisional Government*, 196–215.

3. "Milyukov's Note," March 5/18, 1917, "Call by the Petrograd Soviet to the Peoples of the World," 14/March 14/27, 1917, and "Secret Diplomacy," March 18/31, 1917, reproduced in Golder, *Documents of Russian History*, 323–327.

4. Citations in Chernov, in *The Great Russian Revolution*, 193, 200. Trepov: Pipes, *Russian Revolution*, 257–258.

5. Guchkov telegram to Stavka, March 19, 1917, in Basily collection, Hoover Institution Archives, box 11; Bazili to Pokrovskii from Stavka, February 26/March 11, 1917, in AVPRI, fond 138, opis' 467, del' 493/515, list' 1 (and back). French pledge: cited in C. Jay Smith, Jr., *Russian Struggle for Power, 1914–1917*, 465. Milyukov: cited by Richard Stites in "Milyukov and the Russian Revolution," foreword to Milyukov, *The Russian Revolution*, xii.

6. As published in *Rech'* the next day (March 23/April 5, 1917), reproduced in Kerensky and Browder, *Russian Provisional Government*, vol. 2, 1044–1045.

7. Bazili to Milyukov, March 23/April 5, 1917, in AVPRI, fond 138, opis' 467, del' 493/515, list' 4–6 (and backs). On the surveillance probe: Usedom to Kaiser Wilhelm II, April 16, 1917, in BA/MA, RM 40-4. Seven seaplanes: René Greger, *Russische Flotte im Ersten Weltkrieg*, 61.

8. "Russia's Control of the Straits," *Manchester Guardian*, April 26, 1917, reproduced in M. Philips Price, *Dispatches from the Revolution*. "Obligations assumed towards her allies": cited in Smith, *Russian Struggle for Power*, 472. The statement of March 27 is reproduced in Golder, *Documents of Russian History*, 329–331.

9. Lenin, "The War and the Provisional Government," first published in *Pravda* on April 13/26, 1917, in *Collected Works (April–June 1917)*, vol. 24, 114.

10. As recalled by Chernov in *The Great Russian Revolution*, 194.

11. Details in Pipes, *Russian Revolution*, 400; Chernov, *Great Russian Revolution*, 200; and Kerensky, *The Catastrophe*, 135. Kerensky elides the argument about his intentions, emphasizing the "unanimity" of the government behind the "note of April 18."

12. Pipes, *Russian Revolution*, 400–401.

13. Shelyakhovskaya deposition, and Golder diary, April 21/May 4, 1917.

14. Shelyakhovskaya deposition, and Pipes, *Russian Revolution*, 402–404.

15. Ibid.

16. Ibid., and Lenin, "Draft Resolution on the War . . . written between 15 April and 22 April 1917," in *Collected Works*, vol. 24, 161–166.

17. Citations in Sukhanov, *Russian Revolution*, 319–320, and Pipes, *Russian Revolution*, 402–403.

18. Protocol of the Provisional Government, sittings no. 69 (May 5/18, 1917) and 71 (May 6/19, 1917), in RGIA, fond 1276, opis' 14, del' 2. For the ghost parliament: "Materialyi chastnogo soveshchaniya chlenov Gosudarstvennoi Dumyi . . . ," May 4/17, 1917, in RGIA, fond 1278, opis' 10, del' 22.

19. "Rukovodiashchiia ukazaniia General'Komissaru oblastei Turtsii, zanyatyikh' po pravu voiny," May 15/28, 1917, in AVPRI, fond 151, opis' 482, del' 3481, list' 81–82.

10. Kerensky's Moment

1. Alekseev to Lvov, March 14/27, 1917, reproduced in Kerensky and Browder, *Russian Provisional Government*, vol. 2, 862–863.

2. "Doklad' a nastroenii vois' i naseleniya po dannyim' otchetov voennyikh' tsenzurov' raiona I-i armii za Mart' mesyats 1917 g.," in RGVIA, fond 2031, opis' 1, del' 1181, list' 225–226 and backs.

3. "Instructions to the Military Committee," March 19/April 2, 1917, reproduced in Kerensky and Browder, *Russian Provisional Government*, vol. 2, 865. Alekseev's request: cited in Feldman, "Russian General Staff and the June 1917 Offensive," 528. See also Wildman, *End of the Russian Imperial Army*, 253–258.

4. "Order No. 8," May 8/21, 1917, reproduced in Kerensky and Browder, *Russian Provisional Government*, 880–881.

5. Stone, *Russian Army in the Great War*, 281.

6. Russian military censors' report on "bratanie" (fraternization), April 23/May 6, 1917, in RGVIA, fond 2031, opis' 1, del' 1181, 262–263 and backs.

7. Military censors' report on fraternization in the northern army, May 12/25, 1917, in RGVIA, fond 2031, opis' 1, del' 1181, 287–288 and backs.

8. "General Nivelle's Replies to Alekseev's Messages," March 15, 1917, reproduced in Kerensky and Browder, *Russian Provisional Government*, vol. 2, 928.

9. Alekseev to Brusilov, May 18/31, 1917, reproduced in ibid., 931. "Russia is perishing": cited in Feldman, "Russian General Staff and the June 1917 Offensive," 534.

10. Brusilov to Kerensky, May 20/June 2, 1917, reproduced in ibid., 932.

11. G. W. Le Page to Captain H. G. Grenfell from aboard the *Almaz* at Sevastopol, April 29 and May 23, 1917, in PRO, ADM 137/940. On Kerensky's

visit with Kolchak: Rusin to Sevastopol, May 15/28, 1917, in RGAVMF, fond 716, opis' 1, del' 277. On Tiflis: Kazemzadeh, *Struggle for Transcaucasia*, 61; and Wildman, *End of the Russian Imperial Army*, vol. 2, 141.

12. Golder diary, entry for May 1/14, 1917; and Wildman, *End of the Russian Imperial Army*, vol. 2, 23–24.

13. Citations in ibid., 26–27; and in Pipes, *Russian Revolution*, 413.

14. Wildman, *End of the Russian Imperial Army*, vol. 2, 23–24.

15. Baluev from Vorobin, May 18/31, 1917, 1:40 p.m., and, for the desertions, Sollogub from Vorobin, May 18/31, 1917 (5:40 p.m.) and May 19/June 1, 1917 (6:00 p.m.), in RGVIA, fond 2067, opis' 1, del. 395, list' 138–139, 140, 145.

16. Gerua from Vorobin, April 20/May 3, 1917 (10:15 p.m.), and April 23/May 6, 1917 (10:45 p.m.), in RGVIA, fond 2067, opis' 1, del. 394, list' 371 and 395.

17. Cited in Scharlau and Zeman, *Merchant of Revolution*, 207–208. For desertions, see Baluev from Vorobin, May 18/31, 1917; Sollogub from Vorobin, June 3/16 and 7/20, 1917, in RGVIA, fond 2067, opis' 1, del. 394, list' 326 and 355.

18. Protocols from the First All-Russian Congress of Soviets, June 6 and 12, 1917, in Kerensky and Browder, *Russian Provisional Government*, vol. 2, 939. The resolution stated, "until the war is brought to an end by the efforts of revolutionary democracy, the Russian revolutionary democracy is obliged to keep its army in condition to take either the offensive or defensive," with this question decided "from the purely military and strategic point of view."

19. Feldman, "Russian General Staff and the June 1917 Offensive," 536.

20. Lieutenant General Il'kevich to Brusilov, June 15, 1917, in RGVIA, fond 2067, opis' 1, del' 395, 416 and back. Stamped "received" at Stavka, June 15, 1917.

21. Citations in Wildman, *End of the Russian Imperial Army*, vol. 2, 28, 52–53.

22. Ibid.

11. Lenin Shows His Hand

1. Feldman, "Russian General Staff and the June 1917 Offensive," 539; Wildman, *End of the Russian Imperial Army*, vol. 2, 89–91.

2. Cited in Wildman, *End of the Russian Imperial Army*, vol. 2, 92.

3. Kerensky's Order to the Army and the Fleet, reproduced in Golder, *Documents of Russian History*, 426–427.

4. Cited in Feldman, "Russian General Staff and the June 1917 Offensive," 539.

5. Wildman, *End of the Russian Imperial Army*, vol. 2, 95–96.

6. Baluev to Brusilov from Vorobin, June 23/July 8, 1917, in RGVIA, fond 2067, opis' 1, del' 396, list' 13 and back.

7. Wildman, *End of the Russian Imperial Army*, vol. 2, 98, and Feldman, "Russian General Staff and June 1917 Offensive," 539.

8. Citations in Wildman, *End of the Russian Imperial Army*, vol. 2, 98–99.

9. Citations in ibid., 93–94; and, for Special Army, see Baluev operations reports from Vorobin, June 22 and 26, 1917, and from Gen. Valter, July 6, 1917, all in RGVIA, fond 2067, opis' 1, del' 396, list' 56, 67, 130.

10. Kollontai's April 1917 speeches to the First Machine Gun Regiment were recalled by nearly all witnesses deposed after the July Days, such as Aleksandr Stepanovich Emel'yanov, Fedor Dmitrievich Ryazantsev, Anatolii Vasil'evich Sokolov, and Fedor Ivanovich Loshakov, in "Materialyi predvaritel'nogo sledstviya o vooruzhennom vyistuplenii v Petrograde 3(16)–5(18) iyulya 1917 goda," RGASPI, fond 4, opis' 3, del' 41, list' 36, 38, 41–43.

11. A. V. Sokolov deposition, July 15/28, 1917, in RGASPI, fond 4, opis' 3, del' 41, list' 21 and back. On the Moscow Guard Reserves: "Postanovlenie," on the July 3–4 uprising, taken by "Prokuror. Petrogradskago Sudebnyoi Palatyi," ca. late July 1917, in TsGIASPb, fond 1695, opis' 2, del' 1, list' 17–19. For Semashko's contacts with the Bolshevik Military Organization at Kshesinskaya's, see "Report of the Public Prosecutor on the Investigation of the Charges Against the Bolsheviks," reproduced from *Rech'* in Kerensky and Browder, *Russian Provisional Government*, vol. 3, 1371.

12. Cited in Wildman, *End of the Russian Imperial Army*, vol. 2, 125; and Golder letter to "K." (probably Harvard historian Robert J. Kerner), June 5/18, 1917, cited in Emmons and Patenaude, ed., *Passages of Frank Golder*, 74–75.

13. Nikitin, *Fatal Years*, 133. See also Pipes, *Russian Revolution*, 421.

14. Nikitin, *Fatal Years*, 124–132.

15. Afanasii Efimovich Zamykin and I. P. Slesarenok depositions, July 15/28, 1917, in RGASPI, fond 4, opis' 3, del' 41, list' 34, 42.

16. "The *Izvestiia*'s Account of the Uprising," July 4/17, 1917, reproduced in Golder, *Documents of Russian History*, 445; Golder diary, entry for July 3/16; and (for other infantry regiments), Pipes, *Russian Revolution*, 423.

17. Mawdsley, *Russian Revolution and the Baltic Fleet*, 55; Shapiro, *Russian Revolutions of 1917*, 83; and, for the estimate of six thousand armed sailors from Kronstadt, "Postanovlenie" dated July 21/August 3, 1917, in "Materialyi predvaritel'nogo sledstviya o vooruzhennom vyistuplenii v Petrograde 3(16)–5(18) iyulya 1917 goda," in RGASPI, fond 4, opis' 3, del' 41, list' 81.

18. Lev Nikolaevich Ginnerman deposition, in RGASPI, fond 4, opis' 3, del' 41, list' 24.

19. Cited in Pipes, *Russian Revolution*, 427–428.

20. Shelyakhovskaya deposition. For estimates on crowd size, see Pipes, *Russian Revolution*, 428 and footnotes.

21. "The *Izvestiia*'s Account of the Uprising," *Izveztiia* no. 108, July 4/17, 1917, reproduced in Golder, *Documents of Russian History*, 445–447.

22. Colonel Nikitin later mused that the Bolsheviks had been assaulted by "an imaginary force of Cossacks." But they were not imaginary. Frank Golder recorded in his diary that "the bolsheviki soldiers fired and killed a number of

Cossacks and their horses, which I saw lying on the Liteinyi." Nikitin, *Fatal Years*, 140. Golder: diary entry for July 4/17, 1917. *Izvestiia* reported: no. 108.

23. Pipes, *Russian Revolution*, 426–427.

24. Zamyikin deposition.

25. Ibid., 429; Sukhanov, *Russian Revolution 1917*, 445–447; and Nikitin, *Fatal Years*, 149–150.

26. Zamyikin deposition.

27. Nikitin, *Fatal Years*, 154.

28. Ibid., 160; and Pipes, *Russian Revolution*, 431–432. The exposé was first published in *Zhivoe Slovo* on July 5/18, 1917, reproduced in Kerensky and Browder, *Russian Provisional Government*, 1364–1365.

29. Nikitin, *Fatal Years*, 166; Pipes, *Russian Revolution*, 434. On Stalin negotiating the surrender: Mawdsley, *Russian Revolution and the Baltic Fleet*, 56.

30. Nikitin, *Fatal Years*, 172 and passim.

31. "The Bolshevik Denial of the Charges That Lenin Received German Money," from *Listok Pravdy*, July 6/19, 1917, reproduced in Kerensky and Browder, *Russian Provisional Government*, 1366; "Trotsky's Letter to the Provisional Government," July 10/23, 1917, reproduced in Golder, *Documents of Russian History*, 460–461.

12. Army on the Brink

1. S. V. Gagarin, B. V. Lobachevskii, V. V. Kurochkin, and I. P. Vasil'ev depositions, July 11–14/July 24–27, 1917, in RGASPI, fond 4, opis' 3, del' 41, list' 17–20, 31.

2. "Statement from [Ispolkom]," *Izvestiia*, no. 110, July 6/19, 1917, and "Report of the Public Prosecutor on the Investigation of the Charges Against the Bolsheviks," *Rech'*, July 22/August 4, 1917, both reproduced in Kerensky and Browder, *Russian Provisional Government*, vol. 3, 1367, 1370–1377. Emphasis added.

3. Sukhanov, *The Russian Revolution 1917*, 471.

4. "Pereverzev's Comments on the Charges," *Novoe Vremia*, July 7/20, 1917, reproduced in Kerensky and Browder, *Russian Provisional Government*, 1367; and Bonch-Bruevich, *Na boevyikh postakh*, 89–90. For Nikitin's view: *Fatal Years*, 169.

5. "Views of Tereshchenko, Nekrasov, and Kerensky on the Charges Against the Bolsheviks and on the Restoration of Pereverzev," *Novoe Vremia* July 8/21, 1917, reproduced in Kerensky and Browder, *Russian Provisional Government*, 1367. "Essential to accelerate the publication of the evidence": cited in Abraham, *Kerensky*, 221.

6. "Resignation of Members of the Kadet Party from the Ministry," July 3/16, 1917, reproduced in Golder, *Documents of Russian History*, 440–441; and "The Acceptance of the Resignation of the Kadet Ministers and the Submittal

of the Resignation of Prince Lvov," *Zhurnal* no. 125, July 7/20, 1917, reproduced in Kerensky and Browder, *Russian Provisional Government*, 1385.

7. Citations in Wildman, *End of the Russian Imperial Army*, vol. 2, 125–126.

8. "Prince Lvov on Kerensky as His Successor as Minister-President," *Russkoe Slovo*, July 12, 1917, reproduced in Kerensky and Browder, *Russian Provisional Government*, 1389.

9. Lucius von Stoedten from Stockholm, July 20, 1917, in PAAA, R 10080. Kerensky into Winter Palace: Abraham, *Kerensky*, 244 and passim.

10. Citations in Wildman, *End of the Russian Imperial Army*, 124–127.

11. David Stone, *Russian Army in the Great War*, 290–291; and Stel'nitskii to Brusilov, July 12/25, 1917, in RGVIA, fond 2067, opis' 1, del' 396, list' 207.

12. Excerpt from soldier's letter in Fifth Army, July 17/30, 1917, in RGVIA, fond 2031, opis' 1, del' 1181, list' 360. For commander of Forty-Second Division: cited in Wildman, *End of the Russian Imperial Army*, vol. 2, 129.

13. Cited in Stone, *Russian Army in the Great War*, 292. One hundred prisoners: soldier's letter from northern army, ca. late July 1917, in RGVIA, fond 2031, opis' 1, del' 1181, list' 362.

14. Pipes, *Russian Revolution*, 442.

15. "Kerensky's Speech Before the Executive Committees," *Izvestiia*, July 13/26, 1917, reproduced in Golder, *Documents of Russian History*, 482.

16. "Account of the Moscow State Conference," *Rech'*, August 13/26, 1917, reproduced in Golder, *Documents of Russian History*, 491.

17. "Kerensky's Opening Address," reproduced in Kerensky and Browder, *Russian Provisional Government*, vol. 3, 1457–1462.

18. "Second Day," *Izvestiia*, August 15/28, 1917, reproduced in Golder, *Documents of Russian History*, 493–495.

19. Ibid., and for more on the impact of Kaledin's speech, Wildman, *End of the Russian Imperial Army*, vol. 2, 186.

20. Cited in Pipes, *Russian Revolution*, 447–448.

21. David Stone, *Russian Army in the Great War*, 292–297.

22. Mawdsley, *Russian Revolution and the Baltic Fleet*, 67–69.

23. "General Lukomskii's account," reproduced from his memoirs in Kerensky and Browder, *Russian Provisional Government*, vol. 3, 1549–1550.

24. Ibid., 1550–1551.

25. "Statement of Savinkov," given to a journalist from *Birzhevyia Vedomosti*, September 12, 1917, reproduced in Kerensky and Browder, *Russian Provisional Government*, vol. 3, 1554–1555.

26. "General Lukomskii's Account"; and, "From the Memoirs of V. N. Lvov," reproduced in Kerensky and Browder, *Russian Provisional Government*, vol. 3, 1563. The main difference in the two accounts is that Lukomskii claims the meeting took place on the morning of August 25, not 10:00 p.m. on August 24.

27. "Kerensky's Account of His Second Meeting with Lvov and His Conversation Over the Hughes Apparatus with Kornilov," reproduced in Kerensky and Browder, *Russian Provisional Government*, vol. 3, 1568–1569.

28. An original copy of Kerensky's radio-telegram of August 27, 1917, received in Pskov at northern army headquarters, is preserved in RGVIA, fond 2031, opis' 1, del' 1558, list' 7–9. For more details, see Pipes, *Russian Revolution*, 456–457.

29. An original copy of Kornilov's reply (received at northern army headquarters at Pskov) is preserved in RGVIA, fond 2031, opis' 1, del' 1558, list' 36, 38, 39, 40. On Savinkov's attempted intervention, see "Statement of Savinkov."

30. Pipes, *Russian Revolution*, 461–462.

31. Lukomskii to Kerensky, copied to all front commanders, 1:00 p.m. on August 27, 1917, in RGVIA, fond 2031, opis' 1, del' 1558, list' 31–33; transcript of conversation between Alekseev and Kornilov, conducted on August 30 between 1:00 p.m. and 3:00 p.m., in RGVIA, fond 2031, opis' 1, del' 1558, list' 81–82 (and backs).

32. "The Arming of the Workers," *Izvestiia*, August 29, 1917, and "Negotiations for the Release of Certain Individuals Arrested in Connection with the July Days," *Izvestiia*, August 31, 1917, reproduced in Kerensky and Browder, *Russian Provisional Government*, vol. 3, 1590–1591.

13. Red October

1. Men'chukov from Vorobin, August 12/25, 1917, in RGVIA, fond 2067, opis' 1, del' 397, list' 136; and Svechin from Dvinsk, July 28, 1917, in RGVIA, fond 2031, opis' 1, del' 1555, list' 163–165.

2. Lukomskii to Kerensky, August 27, 1917; Baluev from western army headquarters, and Shcherbachev from Romanian front headquarters, August 28, 1917, in RGVIA, fond 2031, opis' 1, del' 1558, list' 26–27, 29. Denikin: cited in Wildman, *End of the Russian Imperial Army*, vol. 2, 197.

3. "Excerpts" from soldiers' letters "on the Kornilov affair," September 1/14 to 15/28, 1917, in RGVIA, fond 2031, opis' 1, del' 1181, list' 378–385 (and backs).

4. Men'chukov from Vorobin, September 6/19, 11/24, 16/29, and September 21/October 4, 1917, in RGVIA, fond 2067, opis' 1, del. 397, list' 344, 375, 407, 453.

5. Wildman, *End of the Russian Imperial Army*, vol. 2, 201.

6. Svechin from Dvinsk, September 1/14, 1917, in RGVIA, fond 2031, opis' 1, del. 1555, list' 240 and back.

7. Parskii report on morale in Twelfth Army, September 28, 1917, in RGVIA, fond 2031, opis' 1, del' 1543, list' 14–18.

8. "Condition of the troops at the front," Army Intelligence Report for October 2–13, 1917, reproduced in Bunyan and Fisher, *Bolshevik Revolution 1917–1918*, 24.

9. Cited in Mawdsley, *Russian Revolution and the Baltic Fleet*, 96. German spies: agent report filed from Stockholm on September 16/29, 1917, in BA/MA, RM 5/2596. On Operation Albion, see Stone, *Russian Army in the Great War*, 299–304.

10. Pipes, *Russian Revolution*, 466–467.

11. Chernov deposition, in RGASPI, fond 4, opis' 3, del' 41, 308–309.

12. Lebedev deposition, in RGASPI, fond 4, opis' 3, del' 41, 325.

13. Cited in Melgunov, *Kak bol'sheviki zakhvatili vlast'*, 13.

14. Kerensky's speech to the Petrograd Democratic Congress, September 14/27, 1917, reproduced in Kerensky and Browder, *Russian Provisional Government*, vol. 3, 1674–1675; and, for the explosive second half (which Kerensky's own edition cuts out), Golder, *Documents of Russian History*, 544–545. Kamenev's "Bolshevik resolution": reproduced in Golder, *Documents of Russian History*, 551–553.

15. "The Resignation of Alekseev," September 9, 1917, reproduced in Kerensky and Browder, *Russian Provisional Government*, vol. 3, 1621.

16. For election figures in Moscow, see Matthew Rendle, "The Problem of the 'Local' in Revolutionary Russia: Moscow Province, 1914–22," in Badcock et al., eds., *Russia's Home Front in War and Revolution*.

17. See the files preserved in folder labeled "Telegramma nachal'nika Petrogradskoi militsii vsem komissaram o poluchenii ordera . . . na arrest V. I. Ul'yanova (Lenina) . . . obvinyaemogo po delu o vooruzhennom vosstanii 3(16)–5(18) iyulya 1917 g. v Petrograde," in RGASPI, fond 4, opis' 3, del' 45.

18. See Wildman, *End of the Russian Imperial Army*, 270–277.

19. Lenin, "The Crisis Has Matured," September 29/October 12, 1917, in *V. I. Lenin. Selected Works*, vol. 6, 231–232.

20. *Izvestiia* transcripts of Soviet meetings held on September 21 and 23, 1917, reproduced in *Petrogradskii Sovet rabochikh i soldatskikh deputatov*, eds. B. D. Galperina and V. I. Startsev, vol. 4, 382–385.

21. "Otchet 'Petrogradskoi gazetyi' ob obshchem sobranii," October 3, 1917, reproduced in ibid., 446–448.

22. The transcript of the critical October 10 meeting of the Bolshevik Central Committee is reproduced in Kerensky and Browder, *Russian Provisional Government*, vol. 3, 1762–1763; also Bunyan and Fisher, *Bolshevik Revolution 1917–1918*, 56–58. Kamenev's objection: cited in Figes, "The 'Harmless Drunk,'" in *Historically Inevitable?*, 132.

23. Sukhanov, *Russian Revolution 1917*, 562; and, for October 18, citation in Pipes, *Russian Revolution*, 480.

24. Kerensky to London: cited in Abraham, *Kerensky*, 313. To Buchanan (ca. October 3–4/16–17, 1917): cited in German agent report from Stockholm,

October 17/30, 1917, passing on report dated October 5/18, 1917, in BA/MA, RM 5/2596.

25. Ibid. On Kerensky's new warrant: German agent report from St. Petersburg, filed in Stockholm on October 26/November 8, 1917, in BA/MA, RM 5/2596. Kerensky tells Buchanan: citation in Pipes, *Russian Revolution*, 477–478.

26. Citations in Wildman, *End of the Russian Imperial Army*, vol. 2, 291–292.

27. Ibid., 293; and Abraham, *Kerensky*, 315.

28. "Order of the Commander of the Petrograd Military District," October 24/November 6, 1917, and "Petrograd Proclaimed in a State of Insurrection," Kerensky's speech to the Pre-Parliament, also October 24/November 6, 1917, both reproduced in Bunyan and Fisher, *Bolshevik Revolution 1917–1918*, 85–91.

29. "Declaration of the Military Revolutionary Committee," October 24/November 6, 1917, and "Lenin Urges the Immediate Seizure of Power," letter of same day reproduced in Bunyan and Fisher, *Bolshevik Revolution 1917–1918*, 95–96. Lenin escapes the picket: Figes, "The 'Harmless Drunk,'" in *Historically Inevitable?*, 123.

30. The best account of the events of Tuesday night, based on a judicious reading of available sources, is Pipes's, in *Russian Revolution*, 490–491. On Kerensky, see also Abraham, *Kerensky*, 316 and passim.

31. Polkovnikov to Stavka by direct wire, 10:15 a.m. on October 25/November 7, 1917, reproduced in Bunyan and Fisher, *Bolshevik Revolution 1917–1918*, 98–99.

32. "Progress of the Insurrection," Levitsky to Dukhonin by direct wire, morning of October 25/November 7, 1917, reproduced in ibid., 98–99.

33. Ibid., and Mel'gunov, *Kak bol'sheviki zakhvatili vlast'*, 106–107.

34. Citations (including the report of rapes) in Pipes, *Russian Revolution*, 494–496. For more details on the action, see also "The Action of the Cruiser 'Aurora'" and "The Taking of the Winter Palace," reproduced in Bunyan and Fisher, *Bolshevik Revolution 1917–1918*, 107, 116–117.

35. "Petrograd on November 7," *Delo Naroda*, November 8, 1917, in Bunyan and Fisher, *Bolshevik Revolution 1917–1918*, 105; and Pipes, *Russian Revolution*, 495.

36. German agent report from Petrograd, November 2/15, 1917; German intelligence summary of Russian press reports, compiled in Stockholm on October 18/November 1 and October 31/November 12, 1917; and from Haparanda, October 4/17, 1917; and from Stockholm, September 16/29, 1917, all in BA/MA, RM 5/2596.

37. Pipes, *Russian Revolution*, 502. Pipes insists that the Bolshevik organization in Moscow was called the "Moscow Revolutionary Committee" instead of Milrevkom, because its mandate was rejected in the Moscow Soviet. But its files (located at GARF) show that the body still called itself the "Military Revolution Committee" (Milrevkom).

38. Moscow Milrevkom order "vsem' revolyutionnyim' voiskam' Moskov-skago Garnizona," November 1, 1917; "Prikaz' 1-oi zapasnoi artileriiskoi brigad'," "Prikaz' 2-oi artilleriiskog kolon'," and "Prikaz' v' polkovoi Komitet 193 pekhotnago zapasnago polka"; and Milrevkom situation report ("Vyisyilayutsya sleduyushchie otryadyi"), October 31, 1917, all in GARF, Fond P1, opis' 1, del' 3, list' 63, 66, 69, 75, 94. See also Edward Dune, *Notes of a Red Guard*, trans. Diane Koenker and S. A. Smith, 58–73.

39. "Prikaz' vsem' voiskam' Voenno-Revolyutsionnago Komiteta," November 2, 1917, November 3 and 5, 1917, in GARF, Fond P1, opis' 1, del' 3, list' 117, 135, 161.

14. General Strike

1. Citations in Figes, "The 'Harmless Drunk,'" in *Historically Inevitable?*, 138.

2. "Abolition of Capital Punishment," "Transfer of Authority in the Provinces to the Soviets," and "Proclamation on Peace," October 26/November 8, 1917, both reproduced in Bunyan and Fisher, *Bolshevik Revolution 1917–1918*, 124–128.

3. As noted by Pipes in *Russian Revolution*, 499. The full text of the "Decree on Land," issued on October 26/November 8, 1917, is reproduced in Bunyan and Fisher, *Bolshevik Revolution 1917–1918*, 128–132.

4. "The Soviet of People's Commissars," reproduced in ibid., 133–138.

5. Lukirskii to Dukhonin, October 26/November 7, 1917; Kerensky to Cheremisov, and Cheremisov to commanders of First, Fifth, and Twelfth Armies, October 27/November 8, 1917, reproduced in Bunyan and Fisher, *Bolshevik Revolution 1917–1918*, 143–145.

6. Krasnov, "The Advance on Tsarskoe Selo," reproduced in ibid., 150.

7. "Order of the Committee to Save the Country and the Revolution," and "Bulletin" of same, October 29/November 11, 1917, reproduced in ibid., 151.

8. "Krasnov's Peace Proposals," October 31, 1917, and accompanying Kerensky telegram, reproduced in ibid., 165.

9. Cited in Wildman, *End of the Russian Imperial Army*, vol. 2, 336.

10. "The October Revolution in Saratov," reproduced from the memoirs of Mikhail Vasiliev-Iuzhin, in Daly and Trofimov, *Russia in War and Revolution*, 117–120.

11. "On Establishing Bolshevik Rule in Viatka Province, December 1917," and "A Bolshevik Agitator in Perm Province, December 1917," in ibid., 120–124. For "drunken pogroms" in Perm province: see intelligence report passed on to Stavka, November 9/22, 1917, in RGVIA, fond 2031, opis' 1, del' 6, list' 150.

12. Vasiliev-Iuzhin memoirs. On Kornilov's flight, see Mawdsley, *Russian Civil War*, 27.

13. "Strike of the State Employees of Petrograd," resolution published in *Volia Naroda*, October 28/November 10, 1917, reproduced in Bunyan and Fisher, *Bolshevik Revolution 1917–1918*, 225.

14. "Vikzhel's Ultimatum to End the Civil War," October 29/November 11, 1917, reproduced in Bunyan and Fisher, *Bolshevik Revolution 1917–1918*, 155. For more on Vikzhel and the railway strike, see Shapiro, *Russian Revolutions of 1917*, 141–145.

15. "The Spread of the Strike of State Employees," *Delo Naroda*, October 28/November 10, 1917, and "Reasons for the Strike," *Delo Naroda*, November 8/21, 1917, both reproduced in ibid., 226–227; and McMeekin, *History's Greatest Heist*, 15.

16. Cited in ibid., 11.

17. Pipes, *Russian Revolution*, 528.

18. F. O. Lindley, "Report on Recent Events in Russia," November 12/25, 1917, in PRO, FO 371 3000/3743.

19. V. Obolensky-Osinsky, "How We Got Control of the State Bank," reproduced in Bunyan and Fisher, *Bolshevik Revolution 1917–1918*, 319.

20. Ibid. "1,000,000 rubles per head, but cash down only": Lindley, "Report on Recent Events in Russia." The 5 million ruble deal is also confirmed in a German intelligence report, dated November 17/30, 1917, in BA/MA, RM 5/2596.

21. Letter from the Manager of the Russian & English Bank, Petrograd, sent from Petrograd January 24, 1918, to the bank's London office, forwarded to the British Foreign Office, in PRO, FO 371/3701; and "The bank position," enclosure in Sir George Buchanan's dispatch No. 6 Commercial of January 6, 1918, in PRO, FO 371/3294.

22. Cited by Nicolas Werth, "The Iron Fist of the Dictatorship of the Proletariat," in *The Black Book of Communism*, 103. Emphasis added.

23. Tony Brenton, "The Short Life and Early Death of Russian Democracy," in *Historically Inevitable?*, 155–156.

24. "Proekt dekreta o provedenii v zhizn' nationalizatsii bankov i o neobkhodimykh v sviazi s etim' merakh'," December 14/27, 1917, in RGASPI, 670-1-35, 19–21; "Naimenovanie Bankov. Adres'. NoNo Telefonov . . . ," and Undated Doklad, ca. late December 1917, "Upravliaiushchemu Komissariatom byvsh. chastnykh bankov tov. Sokolnikovu," all in RGASPI, 670-1-35, 5–8 (and backs), 54.

25. "The bank position," enclosure in Sir George Buchanan's dispatch No. 6 Commercial of January 6, 1918, in PRO, FO 371/3294; "Opening of safes at banks," Enclosure in Sir G. Buchanan's desp. No./Commercial of January 5, 1918, in PRO, FO 371/3294; and Report from the British Consulate General, Moscow, forwarded to London via F.O. Lindley in Petrograd, January 28, 1918, in PRO, FO 368/1965.

15. Ceasefire

1. Pipes's classic *Russian Revolution* (1990) is typical. After his account of the botched Kerensky offensive, Pipes writes (418) that "since the old Russian army engaged in no significant operations after July 1917, this may be an appropriate place to tally the human casualties Russia suffered in World War I." More recent accounts by military historians, such as David Stone's *Russian Army in the Great War*, do a much better job keeping track of battlefield developments in 1917.

2. Field reports from Special Army (Vorobin), September 11/24 and 16/29, 1917; September 21/October 4, 1917, in RGVIA, fond 2067, opis' 1, del' 397, list' 375, 407, 453, 503; and for October 14, 18, 25, and 26, in RGVIA, fond 2067, opis' 1, del' 398, list' 99, 162, 241, 255.

3. Citations in Wildman, *End of the Russian Imperial Army*, vol. 2, 314–315.

4. Citations in ibid., 316–317.

5. "Order to Dukhonin to Open Armistice Negotiations," radiogram from Lenin, Trotsky, and Krylenko to Stavka, November 8/21, 1917, and "Dukhonin Declines," conversation by direct wire, 2:00 a.m. on November 9/22, both reproduced in Bunyan and Fisher, *Bolshevik Revolution 1917–1918*, 233–234. For Dukhonin's conditions: see Wildman, *End of the Russian Imperial Army*, vol. 2, 380.

6. Kurt Riezler from Stockholm, November 13/26, 1917, forwarded to German consulates and embassies abroad, in PAAA, R 2000. Lenin to the Second Congress of Soviets on October 26, Trotsky and the Allied Ambassadors: citations in Wheeler-Bennett, *Forgotten Peace*, 69–71.

7. "Dukhonin Declines."

8. "Lenin Urges the Soldiers to Negotiate with the Enemy," *Izvestiia*, November 9/22, 1917, in Bunyan and Fisher, *Bolshevik Revolution 1917–1918*, 236.

9. "Appeal of the All-Army Committee to the Soldiers," radiogram, November 8/21, 1917, reproduced in Bunyan and Fisher, *Bolshevik Revolution 1917–1918*, 240. On Dukhonin and Allied military attachés, see Wheeler-Bennett, *Forgotten Peace*, 72–73.

10. "Protest of the Allied Military Missions," November 10/23, 1917, and "Trotsky's Reply," November 11/24, 1917, reproduced in Bunyan and Fisher, *Bolshevik Revolution 1917–1918*, 245–246. For details on Trotsky burgling the filing cabinets: German intelligence report from Petersburg, November 16/29, 1917, BA/MA, RM 5/2596.

11. "Izvestiia's Comment on the French and American Notes," November 14/27, 1917, reproduced in Bunyan and Fisher, *Bolshevik Revolution 1917–1918*, 250–251.

12. "Krylenko's Order No. 2," November 13/26, 1917, reproduced in Bunyan and Fisher, *Bolshevik Revolution 1917–1918*, 256. Krylenko's fraternization order of November 15/28 is cited in Wheeler-Bennett, *Forgotten Peace*, 75.

13. Wildman, *End of the Russian Imperial Army*, 401. Wildman is citing eye-witness accounts of Krylenko's *supporters*, as there were no surviving witnesses from Dukhonin's side to tell the tale.

14. German intelligence reports, November 27/December 10, 1917, and December 4/17, 1917; in BA/MA, RM 5/2596. Dvinsk: German agent report from Brest-Litovsk, December 29/January 11, 1918, in BA/MA, RM 5/4065.

15. German intelligence report dated November 27/December 10, 1917.

16. Krylenko directive no. 19018, December 8/21, 1917; Novitskii tele-gram no. 6544, November 27/December 10, 1917, and Lukirskii telegram no. 6033, November 28/December 11, 1917, and accompanying documentation, in GARF, fond P375, opis' 1, del. 8, list' 1, 3, 8 (and back), 9 (and back).

17. Cited in Wheeler-Bennett, *Forgotten Peace*, 79. For German intelli-gence, see report labeled "Russland–Inneres," November 17/30, 1917, in BA/MA, RM 5/2596.

18. For a detailed summary of these negotiations, see Bunyan and Fisher, *Bolshevik Revolution 1917–1918*, 259–261.

19. Citation in Wheeler-Bennett, *Forgotten Peace*, 86–87.

20. The technical provisions of the agreement are preserved in the German Military Archives in Freiburg, BA/MA, RM 5/2596. On fraternization and propaganda, see Wheeler-Bennett, *Forgotten Peace*, 92–94.

21. Trotsky's December 4/17 radio address is reproduced, in German trans-lation, in BA/MA, RM 5/2596. His November 23 invitation to the Allies and December 8/21 address are reproduced in Bunyan and Fisher, *Bolshevik Rev-olution 1917–1918*, 270–271.

22. Joffe's conditions (stated on December 9/22) and the Austro-German reply penned by Count Ottokar Czernin are reproduced in Bunyan and Fisher, *Bolshevik Revolution 1917–1918*, 477–480. Stashkov: Wheeler-Bennett, *Forgotten Peace*, 114.

23. "Top Secret" transcript of von Lucius conversation with Radek in Stock-holm, December 8/21, 1917, German agent reports from Petrograd, Decem-ber 9/22 and December 10/23, 1917, in BA/MA, RM 5/2596. For dissolution of Russian army: German agent report from Brest-Litovsk, December 29/January 11, 1918. German "military intelligence summary" dated Decem-ber 21/January 3, 1918, in BA/MA, RM 5/4065. Trotsky: cited in Wheeler-Bennett, *The Forgotten Peace*, 115.

24. German agent's report from Petrograd, December 14/27, 1917, in BA/MA, RM 5/2596. On Transcaucasia, see Reynolds, *Shattering Empires*, 175–176.

25. The Fourteen Points are today widely available online, as here: http://avalon.law.yale.edu/20th_century/wilson14.asp.

26. Citations in Wheeler-Bennett, *Forgotten Peace*, 173–175; and Pipes, *Rus-sian Revolution*, 581. A Bolshevik pamphlet obtained by the military author-ities at Brest-Litovsk, dated December 25/January 7, 1918, can be found in BA/MA, RM 5/4065.

27. Pipes, *Russian Revolution*, 552–555. The Germans were well-informed about the dissolution of the Constituent Assembly. See agent reports dated January 5/18 and 6/19, 1918, in BA/MA, RM 5/4065.

28. Lenin's points on "peace" are reproduced in Bunyan and Fisher, *Bolshevik Revolution 1917–1918*, 500–502. Other citations in Wheeler-Bennett, *Forgotten Peace*, 185–186; and Winfried Baumgart, *Deutsche Ostpolitik*, 21.

29. Citations in Wheeler-Bennett, *Forgotten Peace*, 152, 226–228; and Pipes, *Russian Revolution*, 584. For German intelligence on the struggle in Kiev: see agent reports filed on February 2, February 12, and February 13, all in BA/MA, RM 5/4065.

16. Russia at Low Ebb

1. German military intelligence report filed in Berlin, January 9/22, 1918, in BA/MA, RM 5/4065; and Lindley report to Arthur Balfour, sent from Petrograd, February 8, 1918, in PRO, FO 371/3294.

2. Pipes, *Russia Under the Bolshevik Regime*, 15–23.

3. German military intelligence reports filed in Berlin, January 22, February 2, and February 12, 1918, in BA/MA, RM 5/4065. Kamenev: German agent's report from Stockholm, February 18, 1918, in BA/MA, RM 5/4065.

4. Ullman, *Anglo-Soviet Accord*, vol. 1, 89–92.

5. Citations in Baumgart, *Deutsche Ostpolitik*, 23–25.

6. V. I. Lenin, *Sochineniia*, vol. 22, 231. German intelligence reports: agent report from Petrograd, February 1, 1918, and two from February 6, 1918, in BA/MA, RM 5/4065.

7. Cited in Wheeler-Bennett, *Forgotten Peace*, 232. "Bolsheviks are tigers": cited in Pipes, *Russian Revolution*, 586.

8. Cited in Bunyan and Fisher, *Bolshevik Revolution 1917–1918*, 512.

9. Citations in Wheeler-Bennett, *Forgotten Peace*, 245, 258–259.

10. Cited in ibid., 246.

11. Ibid., 258–259; Bunyan and Fisher, *Bolshevik Revolution 1917–1918*, 519–520. Voting with Lenin were Stalin, Zinoviev, Sokolnikov, I. T. Smilga, Y. M. Sverdlov, and Elena Stasov, with Bukharin, A. S. Bubnov, A. Lomov, and Moisei Uritsky against. Abstaining were Trotsky, Joffe, Felix Dzerzhinsky and Nikolai Krestinsky. Kamenev was in Stockholm, en route for London on a diplomatic mission.

12. Baumgart, *Deutsche Ostpolitik*, 119–127.

13. The text of the treaty is reproduced, in English translation, in Wheeler-Bennett, *Forgotten Peace*, 403–408. For more on economic concessions, see McMeekin, *History's Greatest Heist*, chap. 5; and Pipes, *Russian Revolution*, 595.

14. Citations in Wheeler-Bennett, *Forgotten Peace*, 260, 279.

15. Citations in Ullman, *Anglo-Soviet Accord*, vol. 1, 124–125; and (for Robins) Pipes, *Russian Revolution*, 597–598. The decree on "Annulment of Russian

State Loans," February 10, 1918, is reproduced in Bunyan and Fisher, *Bolshevik Revolution 1917–1918*, 602.

16. The founding decree of the Red Army, and the appropriation of 20 million paper rubles, is preserved in RGVA, fond 1, opis 1 ("Kantselariya"). For other key dates, see Jacob W. Kipp, "Lenin and Clausewitz: The Militarization of Marxism, 1914–21," *Military Affairs* 49, no. 4 (October 1985): 188.

17. Baumgart, *Deutsche Ostpolitik*, 119–127. On Romania, see Mugur Isarescu, Cristian Paunescu, and Marian Stefan, *Tezaurul Bancii Nationale a Romaniei la Moscova—Documente*.

18. "Augenblicklichen Lage im Kaukasus," April 6, 1918, in BA/MA, RM 40/215; and Pomiankowski, *Zusammenbruch des Ottomanischen Reiches*, 335.

19. Ullman, *Anglo-Soviet Accord*, vol. 1, 146–151.

20. Serge P. Petroff, *Remembering a Forgotten War*, 1–2.

21. Stalin to Czechoslovak National Council, March 26, 1918; reproduced in Bunyan, *Intervention*, 81 and passim.

22. Pipes, *Russian Revolution*, 631–632; Petroff, *Remembering a Forgotten War*, 9.

23. On the formation of Komuch, see Pipes, *Russian Revolution*, 630–631.

17. Reprieve

1. Baumgart, *Deutsche Ostpolitik*, 124–129, 162, and Ullman, *Anglo-Soviet Accord*, vol. 1, 187. Jumped through the window: Wheeler-Bennett, *Forgotten Peace*, 322. On the Skoropadsky regime, see A. N. Artizov, *Getman P. P. Skoropadskii Ukraina na perelome 1918 god* (Rosspen, 2014).

2. Citations in Wheeler-Bennett, *Forgotten Peace*, 331, 335; and Baumgart, *Deutsche Ostpolitik*, 80.

3. Citations in Pipes, *Russian Revolution*, 633–634.

4. On the gold reserves at Kazan, see Charles Westcott, "Origin and Disposition of the Former Russian Imperial Gold Reserve," April 21, 1921, in NAA, M 316, roll 120. On the cholera outbreak and the population decline in Petrograd, see Alexander Rabinowitch, *The Bolsheviks in Power*, 256–259.

5. See McMeekin, *History's Greatest Heist*, chap. 5.

6. Citations in Wheeler-Bennett, *Forgotten Peace*, 338–339; and (for Trotsky), Rabinowitch, *Bolsheviks in Power*, 289.

7. Pipes, *Russian Revolution*, 646–649. For more on the Savinkov plot, see also Ullman, *Anglo-Soviet Accord*, 189–190, 230–231; Baumgart, *Deutsche Ostpolitik*, 228.

8. Pipes, *Russian Revolution*, 641–642. On Mirbach's assassination, see also Baumgart, *Deutsche Ostpolitik*, 224 and n50.

9. Riezler: cited in Baumgart, *Deutsche Ostpolitik*, 225.

10. Pipes, *Russian Revolution*, 640–643; Wheeler-Bennett, *Forgotten Peace*, 337–338.

11. "Executions at Moscow," from *Novaia Zhizn'*, July 14, 1918, and "Executions at Yaroslavl," *Pravda*, July 26, 1918, reproduced in Bunyan, *Intervention*, 227–228. The 428 figure is in Nicolas Werth, "The Red Terror," in *Black Book of Communism*, 73.

12. Edvard Radzinsky, "Rescuing the Tsar and His Family," in *Historically Inevitable?*, 163–177.

13. "Yakov Yurovsky's note on the execution of the imperial family," in Steinberg and Khrustalëv, *The Fall of the Romanovs*, 353–354.

14. Pipes, *Russian Revolution*, 779–780.

15. Sokolov, *Sokolov Investigation*, 91–107. Buried underground: "Yakov Yurovsky's note."

16. "Seizure of the Gold Reserve at Kazan," report of Lebedev to the Samara Government, reproduced in Bunyan, *Intervention*, 292. Trotsky: "Death for Deserters," August 14, 1918, reproduced in Bunyan, *Intervention*, 301.

17. The August 27, 1918, Supplementary Agreement, along with an accompanying "Note" from Hintze to Joffe and "Financial Agreement," are reproduced in Wheeler-Bennett, *Forgotten Peace*, 427–446. On the reparations shipments to Berlin, sent on September 10 and 30, 1918, see the April 7, 1919, German Foreign Office postmortem on the Brest-Litovsk supplementary treaty, titled "Aufzeichnung betreffend unsere handelspolitischen Beziehungen zu Russland," in DBB, R 901/81069, 339–345.

18. Citations in Nick Lloyd, *Hundred Days*, 139–140.

19. Cited in Nicolas Werth, "The Red Terror," 71; "Allied Plan for Armed Intervention," August 7, 1918, reproduced in Bunyan, *Intervention*, 111; and Baumgart, *Deutsche Ostpolitik*, 109–117.

20. See Martin Sixsmith, "Fanny Kaplan's Attempt to Kill Lenin. August 1918," in *Historically Inevitable?*, 178–199. The "Lockhart plot" has been taken seriously by Michael Kettle, among others, although Kettle credits British spy Sidney Reilly as the real mastermind. See Kettle, *Sidney Reilly. The True Story of the World's Greatest Spy*. Andrew Cook, in *Ace of Spies. The True Story of Sidney Reilly*, takes a more skeptical line on Reilly's activities.

21. Petrovsky and Dzerzhinsky/Peters: cited in Werth, "Red Terror," 75–76. Sverdlov: reproduced in Bunyan, *Intervention*, 237–238.

22. "Red Terror Legalized," Sovnarkom resolution of September 5, 1918, "Red Terror in the Provinces," compilation of press reports in *Izvestiia* from September 10 to 29, 1918, and "Trotsky's Announcement," reproduced in Bunyan, *Intervention*, 239, 242–243, 301.

23. All citations in Werth, "Red Terror," 72–73, 78.

24. Cited in Baumgart, *Deutsche Ostpolitik*, 116–117 and (for Caspian), 204–205.

25. Ibid., 116. Ludendorff: cited in David Stevenson, *Cataclysm*, 468.

26. A. Rosemeyer "Abschrift" sent from Moscow to Berlin, October 10, 1918, in DBB, R 901/86976, 84–87; report from gez. Leutnant Rey, head of the German military commission in Petrograd, sent to Petrograd on November 19, 1918, in PAAA, R 11207; and Franz Rauch's April 12, 1919, report to the German Foreign Office in Berlin after his return from Moscow, in DBB, R 901/82082, 22–25.

18. War Communism

1. For an account of the sacking of "industrial" banking conglomerates, see "Spravka o sostoianii svobodnogo kredita chastnykh bankov po spets. Tek. Schetov . . . ," January 22, 1918, in RGASPI, 670-1-15, 72.

On factory closings and layoffs, see Pipes, *Russian Revolution*, 558; and Sylvana Malle, *The Economic Organization of War Communism*, 50, 161.

2. "Svenskt motforslag. Avtal," October 28, 1918, with Russian translation, in RSU, box 4456, 153–158. On cash smuggling into Stockholm: "Stokgol'msky valiutny rynok v 1918 g.," in RGAE, 413-3-18, 11.

3. "Otchet torgovogo otdela pri Stokgol'mskoi missii RSFSR o deiatel'nosti za 1919 g.," in RGAE, 413-3-267, 65–68.

4. On Swedish shipments in 1918–1919, see German secret-agent report from Petrograd, January 1, 1919, labeled "Betrifft: Warenaustausch mit Russland," in DBB, R 901/81080, 316–317; and Soviet import table in RGAE, 413-3-242, 9.

5. "The Functions of the Supreme Council of the National Economy," Sovnarkom decree of August 8, 1918, reproduced in Bunyan, *Intervention*, 405–406.

6. On VSNKh employment figures: Pipes, *Russian Revolution*, 691.

7. Letter from Robert E. Olds, American Red Cross Commissioner to Europe, to Dr. Livingston Farrand, April 15, 1920, in RSU, HP 494. For industrial production indices: Pipes, *Russian Revolution*, 696.

8. Ibid., 686, and, for currency circulation figures, Sokolnikov report to Politburo, February 9, 1922, RGASPI, 670-1-25, 11–13.

9. Olds to Farrand, April 15, 1920.

10. Ibid., and, for Petrograd: Figes, *People's Tragedy*, 605.

11. Krasin: quoted by Lubov Krassin, in *Leonid Krassin: His Life and Work*, 105. Solomon: Solomon, *Unter den Roten Machthabern*, 131.

12. Krasin, *Voprosy vneshnei torgovli*, 245–249; and *O vneshnei torgovle i otnoshenii k nei russkoi kooperatsii*, 20–21. See also O'Connor, *The Engineer of Revolution*, 159, 235–236; and R. F. Karpova, *L. B. Krasin, sovetskii diplomat*, 51. For Allied intelligence, see *Echo de Paris* June 19, 1920, in QOURSS 481, 121.

13. See letter from Swiss intelligence to the Public Prosecutor, April 11, 1919, in BB, E 21, 11427, and French reports on Platten's arrest, in folder

labeled "Introduction en France de billets de banque altérés et d'origine dou-
teuse," in AN, F7/14769.

14. Rauch telegram from Moscow to Berlin, March 5, 1919, in DBB, R 901/81081, 199–201; and Rauch from Berlin, April 12, 1919, in DBB, R 901/81082, 22–25.

15. Narkomvneshtorg import plan for March 1919, RGAE, 413-3-245, 109, letter from Narkomtorgprom to the People's Commissariat of Foreign Affairs, May 20, 1919, and "Svidetel'stvo," June 8, 1919, in RGAE, 413-3-243, 65, 72, 175.

16. See funding request for 63,425,000 rubles, July 3, 1919, and accompanying documents, in RGAE, 413-3-243, 161–162, 179, 238.

17. On prewar trade, see Pasvolsky and Moulton, *Russian Debts and Russian Reconstruction*, 28–41. On figures for 1919, see "Der Außenhandel Sowjetrußlands," *Beilage des "Revaler Bote,"* December 7, 1921; and Georg Solomon, *Unter den Roten Machthabern*, 131–132.

18. Trotsky: cited in Pipes, *Russian Revolution*, 703. The key decrees ("The Unemployed Forbidden to Refuse Work," Decree of the Commissar of Labor, September 3, 1918, "Abolition of Workers' Control," October 18, 1918, "Relations Between Trade Unions and the Union of State Employees," October 18, 1918; and "Universal Labor Duty," Decree of Sovnarkom, October 31, 1918) are reproduced in Bunyan, *Intervention*, 407–408, 413, 417–419.

19. Red on White

1. "Treaty of Brest-Litovsk," signed on March 3, 1918, article 5, reproduced in Wheeler-Bennett, *Forgotten Peace*, 406.

2. Citation and figures in Pipes, *Russia Under the Bolshevik Regime*, 51–53.

3. Figures in Kotkin, *Stalin*, vol. 1, 297.

4. Ullman, *Anglo-Soviet Accord*, vol. 2, 6–7, 20–21, 233. Armistice terms: cited in Mawdsley, "Sea Change in the Civil War," in *Historically Inevitable?*, 200–201. On the Stalin-Trotsky feud, see Kotkin, *Stalin*, vol. 1, 300–307.

5. Mawdsley, *Russian Civil War*, 67–68; and Petroff, *Remembering a Forgotten War*, 80–81, 107–109.

6. Citations in Ullman, *Anglo-Soviet Accord*, vol. 2, 33–34 and 34n55. Conclusive evidence of British involvement has never emerged, although Knox was rebuked by the Foreign Office on December 1, 1918, for his "highly indiscreet . . . recent activity in political matters." For interpretations downplaying Knox's involvement, see Mawdsley, "Sea Change in the Civil War," and Pipes, *Russia Under the Bolshevik Regime*, 39–42. For a more critical account: Petroff, *Remembering a Forgotten War*, 113–225.

7. Cited in Ullman, *Anglo-Soviet Accord*, vol. 2, 30.

8. Figures in Mawdsley, *Russian Civil War*, 144, 167.

9. "Svodnaia Vedomost' raskhoda artilleriiskago imushchestva na grazhdanskuiu voinu/s 1/II–18–IV 20 g.," in RGAE, 413-6-5, 82; and "Vedomost' Predmetam Artilleriiskogo Imushchestva Podlezhaschikh Zakazu," October 7, 1920, in RGAE, 413-6-10, 155 and back, 156 and back.

10. Figures in Petroff, *Remembering a Forgotten War*, 155; and Mawdsley, *Russian Civil War*, 163–164.

11. Figures in Petroff, *Remembering a Forgotten War*, 171–173.

12. Mawdsley, *Russian Civil War*, 144–145.

13. Petroff, *Remembering a Forgotten War*, 173–179; and Pipes, *Russia Under the Bolshevik Regime*, 77–178.

14. Petroff, *Remembering a Forgotten War*, 198–1200.

15. Cited in Pipes, *Russia Under the Bolshevik Regime*, 79. For White negotiations in Paris: Uget' to Sazonov, March 24, 1919, in the Girs Collection, Hoover Institution Archives, box 1, folder labeled "Telegrams. From March 14, 1919, to April 22, 1919"; and, on Sazonov-Sykes-Picot, McMeekin, *Ottoman Endgame*, chap. 18.

16. Petroff, *Remembering a Forgotten War*, 202–204.

17. Pipes, *Russia Under the Bolshevik Regime*, 82–83.

18. Figures in ibid., 74–75. On the White émigré phenomenon in Constantinople, see Nur Bilge Criss, *Istanbul Under Allied Occupation 1918–1923*.

19. On these fractious negotiations, see Ullman, *Anglo-Soviet Accord*, vol. 3, 20–23; Pipes, *Russia Under the Bolshevik Regime*, 88–89; Mawdsley, *Russian Civil War*, 205.

20. Ibid., 116–119.

21. Ullman, *Anglo-Soviet Accord*, vol. 2, 258–265. On Laidoner breaking with Yudenich, see McMeekin, *History's Greatest Heist*, chap. 6.

22. Cited in Pipes, *Russia Under the Bolshevik Regime*, 90–91. On Pilsudski and the Polish border question, see Ullman, *Anglo-Soviet Accord*, vol. 3, 20–21.

23. Cited in Mawdsley, *Russian Civil War*, 172–173.

24. Vladimir Brovkin, *Behind the Front Lines of the Civil War*, 106–112.

25. Pipes, *Russia Under the Bolshevik Regime*, 106–108, and Werth, "Dirty War," 95–96; and Oleg Budnitskii, *Russian Jews Between Reds and Whites, 1917–1920*, trans. Timothy Portice, 257 and passim.

26. Ullman, *Anglo-Soviet Accord*, 283–285.

27. Ibid., 285.

28. Pipes, *Russia Under the Bolshevik Regime*, 127–129; and, on Mamontov's raid, M. Beller and A. Burovskii, *Grazhdanskaia Istoriia bezumnoi voiny*, 348 and passim. Oleg Budnitskii, in *Russian Jews Between Reds and Whites* (271) argues, plausibly, that Mamontov's force was weakened owing to his troops' penchant for pogroms and looting.

29. Citations in Ullman, *Anglo-Soviet Accord*, vol. 2, 306; and, for British journalist, Pipes, *Russia Under the Bolshevik Regime*, 129.

30. Mawsdley, *Russian Civil War*, 223–224.

31. Petroff, *Remembering a Forgotten War*, 223–231.

32. Ibid., 250–253; and Pipes, *Russia Under the Bolshevik Regime*, 117–119. On the Czechs and the gold: see Budnitskii, "Kolchakovskoe zoloto," in *Diaspora* IV (2002), 458, and *Den'gi russkoi emigratsii*. For contemporary accounts and rumors: "Tell of Kolchak's Gold," *New York Times*, September 30, 1919; "8 American Officers Reported Captured," *New York Times*, January 30, 1920 (which discusses Lake Baikal). On the estimated figure recovered by the Bolsheviks (285 tons), see "Russia's Gold Reserve," in State Department Reports on Russia, National Archives Annex (NAA), M 316, roll 119.

33. See report from Lucius von Stoedten, the German Minister in Stockholm, October 16, 1919, in PAAA, R 11207.

34. O'Connor, *Engineer of Revolution*, 231–232.

20. The Communist International

1. Werth, "The Red Terror," 68, 73–80.

2. Figures from Pipes, *Russia Under the Bolshevik Regime*, 59–60.

3. This is one of Lenin's most famous aphorisms, although no one seems quite certain when, or even if, he said it. It appears nowhere in his collected works.

4. On the foundation of the Gokhran, see "Postanovlenie soveta narodnykh komissarov ob uchrezhdenii gosudarstvennogo khranilishcha tsennostei," February 3, 1920, type-signed by V. Ulyanov (Lenin) for Sovnarkom, in RGAE, 7632-1-1, 1. For an inventory: "Spravka o nalichnosti tsennostei v kladovykh Gokhrana na 1-oe Dekabria 1920 g.," in RGAE, 7632-1-6, 17. Krasin: telegram to the Petrograd headquarters of NKVT, February 16, 1920, in RGAE, 413-3-242, 46 and back.

5. For Krasin's credit line: June 10, 1920, Politburo minutes, in RGASPI, 17-3-87. Sixty-nine Swedish factories: "Lokomotiven aus dem Ausland," *Revaler Bote*, September 8, 1921. Mausers: Kopp to Lezhav, and Lezhav's replies, in RGAE, 413-6-10, 43–44, 47, 53. Greatcoat wool: "Protokol no. 1 Zasedaniia pri Chusosnabarme ot 27-go Oktiabria 1920 g.," in RGAE, 413-6-2, 25; "Svedeniia o vypolnenii plana SPOTEKZAKA po 1 Noiabria 1920 goda," in RGAE, 413-6-3, 1–2. Boots: "Svedeniia o vypolnenii plana SPOTEKZAKA po 1 Noiabria 1920 goda," in RGAE, 413-6-3, 1 and back, 2 and back, 7 and back, 8 and back; and "Protokol no. 1 Zasedaniia pri Chusosnabarme ot 27-go Oktiabria 1920 g.," in RGAE, 413-6-2, 25. Roche pharmaceuticals: contract dated July 26, 1920, in RGAE, 413-6-8, 33–47.

6. Pipes, *Russia Under the Bolshevik Regime*, 179. On the Petliura-Pilsudski talks, see Ullman, *Anglo-Soviet Accord*, v. 3, 46–47 and 47n86.

7. Citations in ibid., 51, 54.

8. Cited in Pipes, *Russia Under the Bolshevik Regime*, 180. For military details, see Mawdsley, *Russian Civil War*, 250–253.

9. On the First Congress, see Julius Braunthal, *Geschichte der Internationale*, vol. 2, 181; and Angelica Balabanoff, *Impressions of Lenin*, 69–70.

10. McMeekin, *Red Millionaire*, 93–94.

11. Cited in Pipes, *Russia Under the Bolshevik Regime*, 177.

12. The Twenty-One Conditions are reproduced in Jane Degras, *The Communist International, 1919–1943: Documents*, vol. 1, 166–172. On the Second Congress, see Braunthal, *Geschichte der Internationale*, vol. 2, 189 and passim.

13. Citation in Jeremy Agnew and Kevin McDermott, *The Comintern. A History of International Communism from Lenin to Stalin*, 21. Delegates leaving the Second Congress with diamonds: Babette Gross, *Willi Münzenberg*, 99.

14. Max Barthel, *Kein Bedarf an Weltgeschichte*, 103–112. On the Makhno episode, see also Figes, *People's Tragedy*, 662.

15. Armenia sent diplomatic envoys to both Kolchak and Denikin in 1919. See Richard Hovannisian, "Bolshevik Movements in Transcaucasia," and "The May Uprising in Armenia," in *The Republic of Armenia*, vol. 3.

16. On the burning in effigy of Lloyd George and Wilson: Ullman, *Anglo-Soviet Accord*, vol. 3, 318. "Holy war": cited in Kotkin, *Stalin*, vol. 1, 369.

17. Ibid., and for details of the Polish-Soviet war, Mawdsley, *Russian Civil War*, 253–257, and Pipes, *Russia Under the Bolshevik Regime*, 187–192.

18. Ibid., 134–135. On the Polish settlement, and Lloyd George's decision not to help with evacuating the Crimea: Ullman, *Anglo-Soviet Accord*, vol. 3, 310–312 and 311n.

21. The Ides of March

1. Cited in Figes, in *Peasant Russia, Civil War*, 321. The most thorough study of the peasant wars in English is Figes, *Peasant Russia, Civil War* (1989). Vladimir Brovkin's *Behind the Front Lines of the Civil War* (1994) is not exclusively concerned with peasant partisans, but he had greater access to original Soviet sources. Mark Baker recently updated the bibliography in "War and Revolution in Ukraine: Kharkiv Province's Peasants' Experiences," in *Russia's Home Front in War and Revolution*. See also Alessandro Stanziani, "De la guerre contre les blancs a la guerre contre les paysans (1920–1922)," in *L'Economie en Révolution*, 281–304.

2. "Svodnaia Vedomost' raskhoda artilleriiskago imushchestva na grazhdanskuiu voinu/s 1/II–18–IV 20 g.," in RGAE, 413-6-5, 82; and "Vedomost' Predmetam Artilleriiskogo Imushchestva Podlezhaschikh Zakazu," October 7, 1920, in RGAE, 413-6-10, 155 and back, 156 and back.

3. "Izvlechenie iz Obshei Svodnoi Vedomosti otdela Metalla V.S.N.Kh. Predmety vypisyvaemye dlia voennoi nadobnosti," June 2, 1920, in RGAE, 413-6-2, 27; "Svedeniia o vypolnenii plana SPOTEKZAKA po 1 Noiabria 1920 goda," in RGAE, 413-6-3, 3 and back; and "Vedomost' gruzov, pribyvshikh iz zagranitsei," January 12, 1921, in RGAE, 413-6-3, 28.

4. The Tjernberg & Leth Aktiebol contract is in 413-6-10, 63; the rifles and ammunition only deal is outlined in Krasin's telegram to Chicherin, November 17, 1920, forwarded to Lenin and Trotsky, and their replies, in RGAE, 413-3-10, 52–53, 57–59. See also "Svedeniia o vypolnenii plana SPO-TEKZAKA po 1 Noiabria 1920 goda," RGAE, 413-6-3, 2 (back), 3; 8 and back, 9 and back.

5. These CHEKA reports filed personally for Lenin, from July to November 1920, are reproduced in Brovkin, *Behind the Front Lines*, 313, 320.

6. Citations in ibid., 313; and Figes, *Peasant Russia, Civil War*, 260–262.

7. Pipes, *Russia Under the Bolshevik Regime*, 377.

8. Citations in Werth, "The Dirty War," 101–102.

9. Citations in Werth, "From Tambov to the Great Famine," in *Black Book of Communism*, 111. Antonov-Ovseenko: cited in Figes, *People's Tragedy*, 754.

10. Citations in Werth, "From Tambov to the Great Famine," 112. Bread rations cut: Pipes, *Russia Under the Bolshevik Regime*, 379.

11. Cited in ibid., 383–384.

12. "I have no doubt," the head of the Bolshevik Trade Mission, Platon Kerzhentsev, wrote the Swedish Foreign Minister, Count Herman Wrangel, on March 16, 1921, "that the Swedish Government, which have commercial relations with the Russian Soviet Government, will neither help to such transportation for rebels against the Russian Soviet Government nor allow such transport to take place." In RSU, HP 495.

13. Werth, "From Tambov to the Great Famine," 113–114; and Pipes, *Russia Under the Bolshevik Regime*, 385–386.

14. Cited in Ullman, *Anglo-Soviet Accord*, vol. 3, 452–453.

15. For a French critique of the Anglo-Soviet trade accord, see the "Memoire sur l'accord commercial anglo-bolcheviste conclu a Londres le 16 mars 1921" prepared on behalf of the Quai d'Orsay, in AN, F7/13490. On Kemal's deal with Lenin, first agreed to by Ali Fuat Cebesoy in Moscow in March 1921 prior to official ratification at Kars on October 13, see Reynolds, *Shattering Empires*, 257–258.

English wool order: *Beilage des "Revaler Bote,"* December 28, 1921.

Lenin's Rolls-Royce: Russian Trade Delegation in London to Moscow in RGAE, 413-6-36, 89–90, 143.

Bomber: Prospectus labeled "Blackburn 'Kangaroo,'" sent to the Russian Trade Delegation in Stockholm, September 25, 1921, in RGAE, 413-6-13, 15–16, 35–38.

16. Citations in Werth, "From Tambov to the Great Famine," 116–117. For Red Army casualties, Pipes, *Russia Under the Bolshevik Regime*, 373. For Zinoviev's purchase of poison gas in Halle: "L'armeé rouge approvisionnée par la contrebande," *Echo de Paris*, November 20, 1920.

17. Pipes, *Russia Under the Bolshevik Regime*, 391–392.

22. "Turn Gold into Bread":
Famine and the War on the Church

1. H. H. Fisher, *The Famine in Soviet Russia 1919–1923*, 51.

2. Cited in Werth, "From Tambov to the Great Famine," 121. "Tortured and whipped to the blood": cited in Fisher, *Famine in Soviet Russia*, 500–501. Eight thousand food requisitioners murdered in 1920: Figes, *People's Tragedy*, 753.

3. Lenin and Molotov to all Provincial and Regional Party Committees, July 30, 1921, reproduced in Pipes, *Unknown Lenin*, trans. Catherine Fitzpatrick, 130–131. Purchasing agent: Solomon, *Unter den Roten Machthabern*, 198. Luxury perishables imported: "Aussenhandel," October 19, 1921, *Revaler Bote*; "Sowjetrusslands Import" and "Der Aussenhandel Sowjetrusslands," December 6 and 7, 1921, *Revaler Bote*. The chocolate order was placed in October 1920, although only fulfilled in 1921: contract with Aronstein & Co., Ltd., October 6, 1920, in RGAE, 413-6-27, 22.

4. Pipes, *Russia Under the Bolshevik Regime*, 416–417. On Gorky and the Arts Registration Commission: Waltraud Bayer, "Revolutionäre Beute," in *Verkaufte Kultur*, 23, and, for a typical looting of a Petrograd household, "Akt na osnovanii ordera Komendanta Petrogradskogo Ukreplennogo Raiona . . . ot 5-go Oktiabria 1919 g. . . . v d. no. 30, kv. 9 po naberezhnoi . . . ulitsa koresa," in RGAE, 7733-1-931, 4.

5. Cited in Willi Münzenberg, *Solidarität. Zehn Jahre Internationale Arbeiterhilfe*, 188. Infiltration of ARA: Lenin to Molotov, August 23, 1921, cited in Pipes, *Russia Under the Bolshevik Regime*, 417–418. Hoover's terms: McMeekin, *Red Millionaire*, 105.

6. Cited in Fisher, *Famine in Soviet Russia*, 545.

7. This is from a typical FSR letterhead, in RGASPI, Fond 538, opis' 2, del' 5, list' 1. Emphasis added. FSR advertised frequently in *Nation* and *New Republic*, which accused Hoover of "an implacable hostility to Bolshevism." Press citations in Fisher, *Famine in Soviet Russia*, 55–56.

8. Curtiss, *Russian Church and the Soviet State*, 67. Encyclical: cited in Pipes, *Russia Under the Bolshevik Regime*, 343.

9. Cited in Jonathan Daly, "'Storming the Last Citadel': The Bolshevik Assault on the Church, 1922" in Brovkin, ed., *The Bolsheviks in Russian Society*, 235. "Chopped to pieces with axes": "Bolshevik Atrocities," *Het Limburgsch Dagblad*, January 19, 1920. Gokhran exception: "Postanovlenie soveta narodnykh komissarov ob uchrezhdenii gosudarstvennogo khranilishcha tsennostei," February 3, 1920.

10. Citations in Natalya Krivova, *Vlast' i Tserkov' v 1922–1925 gg.*, 31; and in British intelligence dispatch from Mr. Hodgson, in Moscow, to Curzon, August 21, 1922, in PRO, FO 371/8212. See also Curtiss, *Russian Church and the Soviet State*, 107.

11. For Trotsky's famine/church looting commissions, see Politburo minutes of November 11, 1921, in RGASPI, 17-3-229; December 8, 1921, in RGASPI, 17-3-242; December 31, 1921, in RGASPI, 17-3-247; and March 20, 1922, in RGASPI, 17-3-283. Press citations in Daly, "Bolshevik Assault on the Church," 240–224.

12. Citations in Mitrofanov, *Istoriia russkoi pravoslavnoi tserkvi*, 210–213.

13. Volkogonov, *Lenin*, 374; and Pipes, *Russia Under the Bolshevik Regime*, 346.

14. Hoover to Harding, February 9, 1922. On the February 6, 1922, gold shipment from Reval, see report of Captain Kelley, assistant military observer at the U.S. Commission in Reval, March 20, 1922, in NAA 316, roll 121. On the revocation of purchasing authority: Chicherin telegram to Krasin/Solomon, which passes on Trotsky's order, February 7, 1922, in RGAE, 413-6-36, 96.

15. Citations in Krivova, *Vlast' i Tserkov' v 1922–1925 gg.*, 34–36.

16. The original of this notorious document can be found in RGASPI, 2-1-22947, 1–4. Long excerpts in the original Russian can also be found in Mitrofanov, *Istoriia russkoi pravoslavnoi tserkvi 1900–1927*, 217–218.

17. Cited by Curtiss, in *Russian Church and the Soviet State*, 115.

18. Krivova, *Vlast' i Tserkov' v 1922–1925 gg.*, 102–109.

19. Ibid., 106; and report of the British commercial attaché in Moscow to the Foreign Office, April 11, 1922, in PRO, FO 371/8212.

20. Krivova, *Vlast' i Tserkov' v 1922–1925 gg.*, 116.

21. Ibid., 117–118, and report of the British commercial attaché in Moscow to the Foreign Office, May 31, 1922, in PRO, FO 371/8212.

22. Figures from Pipes, *Russia Under the Bolshevik Regime*, 353–355; and Figes, *A People's Tragedy*, 748–749. On the show trials: Daly, "Bolshevik Assault on the Church," 252–253. Lenin asks how many priests shot: cited in Volkogonov, *Lenin*, 69.

23. "Report on the Removal of Valuables by the Soviet Authorities from Petropavlovsk Cathedral," forwarded from British intelligence in Petrograd to the Foreign Office, July 9, 1922, in PRO, FO 371/8212.

24. "Red Leaders Split on Robbing Churches," *New York Times*, April 7, 1922; and "Churches Resist Decree of Soviet," *New York Times*, April 14, 1922. "The Seizure of Russian Art Treasures," *De Telegraaf*, April 4, 1922; "Desecration of Minsk churches," *De Telegraaf*, May 12, 1922. "Bloody clashes in Kiev," *De Telegraaf*, June 1, 1922. "Confiscation of Russian church treasures," *De Telegraaf*, May 13, 1922. "Orthodox priests sentenced to death," *De Telegraaf*, May 14, 1922.

25. Krivova, *Vlast' i Tserkov' v 1922–1925 gg.*, 118.

26. Laserson, *In the Service of the Soviet*, 68–73.

27. "Otchet Gokhrana s 1 Ianvaria do 1 oktiabria 1922 g.," in RGAE, 7632-1-16, 2. On estimated revenues from the Church campaign: Krivova, *Vlast'*

i Tserkov' v 1922–1925 gg., 118–119. On the difficulties the Bolsheviks had selling diamonds and platinum abroad, see McMeekin, *Heist*, 71 and passim.

28. Sokolnikov memorandum addressed to M. K. Vladimirov, A. I. Rykov, and A. D. Tsiurupy, labeled *o perotsenke romanovskikh tsennostei*, May 27, 1922, and follow-up private letters to M. K. Vladimirov and Trotsky, in RGASPI, 670-1-36, 26–30.

29. Politburo minutes, October 17, 1921, RGASPI, 17-3-217, item 6.

23. Rapallo

1. Sokolnikov report to Politburo, February 9, 1922, RGASPI, 670-1-25, 11–13; and, for a postmortem on the hyperinflation, Sokolnikov's February 1, 1923, report, "Frantsusky assignat i sovetsky rubl'," in RGASPI, 670-1-36, 72–99.

2. Politburo minutes of July 7, 1921, meeting, item 32, in RGASPI, fond 17, opis' 3, del' 184; and July 9, 1921, meeting, item 1, authorizing 500,000 silver rubles to pay salaries in the Fifth Army, RGASPI, fond 17, opis' 3, del' 185. Silver minting contract: reported in the August 30, 1921, *Izvestiia*. Trotsky's commission: Politburo minutes of November 11, 1921, items 3z and 4, RGASPI, fond 17, opis' 3, del' 229.

3. Report of a conversation with Olof Aschberg by the Chargé d'Affaires of the French Embassy in Berlin, submitted to Paris on March 19, 1921, in QOURSS 482, 227 (and back), 228; and "Note Séjour à Paris du Financier Suèdois Aschberg" prepared by the Quai d'Orsay's "Service Financier," March 22, 1921, in QOURSS 482, 230.

4. Quai d'Orsay report labeled "Exportation des fonds d'Etat russes [*sic*]," August 25, 1921, in QOURSS 482, 252–253; and Delavaud report to the Quai d'Orsay from Stockholm, September 2, 1921, in QOURSS 482, 258 (and back).

5. "Pravila proizvodstva fakticheskoi revizii raboche-Krest'ianskoi Inspektsii bankovskikh vagonov," ca. early 1922, in RGAE, 7733-1-573, 68 (and back).

6. Gerald Freund, *Unholy Alliance*, 84–92. "Save us from Bolshevism": cited in Blücher, *Deutschlands Weg nach Rapallo*, 151.

7. "Entwurf eines Vertrages zwischen der Reichsbank und der Svenska Ekonomie Aktibolaget Stockholm," on the meeting in the Reichsbank on August 24, 1921; and minutes of meeting at the Wilhelmstrasse, September 6, 1921, both in PAAA, R 31956.

8. Hans-Ulrich Seidt, *Berlin, Kabul, Moskau*, 150. On Wirth and Krestinsky: Waltraud Bayer, "Erste Verkaufsoffensive: Exporte nach Deutschland und Österreich," in *Verkaufte Kultur*, 102. Radek and Rathenau: cited in Pipes, *Russia Under the Bolshevik Regime*, 427.

9. The original Russian-language terms are in *Sovetsko-Germanskie Otnosheniia ot peregovorov v Brest-Litovske do Podpisaniia Rapall'skogo Dogovora*,

479–481. As the signatory, Rathenau was blamed by German *völkisch* nationalists who viewed Rapallo as a treasonous accommodation with the "Jewish" regime in Moscow. Two months later, he was murdered by a German anti-Semite for being, in essence, a pro-Communist Jew.

10. Report from the German Minister in Moscow sent to Foreign Office Berlin, April 18, 1922; telegram from Reuter, in Genoa, to Berlin, May 3, 1922, and (for the Germans learning the French had scooped them), clipping from the *Svenska Dagbladet*, May 5, 1922, all in PAAA, R 31956. For Wittenberg and Aschberg: Letter from Wittenberg to Foreign Office, April 4, 1922, in PAAA, R 31956. Junkers bankrupt: see Freund, *Unholy Alliance*, 96, and Seidt, *Berlin, Kabul, Moskau*, 150–153.

11. Quai d'Orsay memorandum, intercepted by German intelligence, May 20, 1922, in DBB, R 43/I/132, 525. For Allied reactions to Rapallo, see "Germans Astound Genoa Conference by Announcing Compact with Russia, Granting All That Allies Reject," *New York Times*, April 18, 1922, and "Russia Must Respect Private Property, Powers Will Tell Her in Note Today," *New York Times*, April 29, 1922.

12. Cited in Pipes, *Russia Under the Bolshevik Regime*, 393–394.

13. Transcript of Aschberg interrogation at the Paris Préfecture de Police, 2; and Aschberg, "Wandering Jew," 56–63. On Ruskombank and its lubrication of German-Soviet trade, see Brockdorff-Rantzau from Moscow, November 17, 1922, in PAAA, R 94575.

14. On Aschberg's German concessions, see Foreign Office Memorandum "An die Bevollmächtigte Vertretung (Botschaft) der Russischen Sozialistischen Föderativen Sowjet-Republik in Deutschland," June 12, 1923, in PAAA, R 94575, and the complaint lodged with the Foreign Office about Aschberg's monopoly by the Handelskammer of Pforzheim, March 13, 1926, in PAAA, R 94426. On the "worker bonds," see Aschberg, "Wandering Jew," 62–63. On German gold shipped to Soviet Russia: French intelligence report from Kovno, April 20, 1926, in QOURSS 483, 31.

Epilogue: The Specter of Communism

1. The best study of NEP is Alan Ball, *Russia's Last Capitalists: The Nepmen*.

2. The actual recorded decline in population, on the territories of the Tsarist empire absorbed into the Soviet Union by 1924, was "only" 12.7 million, but this did not account for a projected demographic increase of 13 million extrapolated from birth figures. See Pipes, *Russia Under the Bolshevik Regime*, 508–509 and 509n.

3. See McMeekin, *History's Greatest Heist*, epilogue.

4. John Reed, *Ten Days That Shook the World*. One million rubles: cited in Pipes, *Russia Under the Bolshevik Regime*, 213n. On fellow travelers, the classic study is David Caute, *The Fellow-Travelers*.

5. "Lunatic asylum": Letter from the Director of the Russian & English Bank, Petrograd, January 24, 1918, in PRO, FO 371/3701. Churchill on sodomy/recognition: cited in McMeekin, *History's Greatest Heist*, 178.

6. Citations in Ball, *Russia's Last Capitalists*, 26–27.

Sources

Archives and Principal Collections Used

Arbetarrölsens Arkiv och Bibliotek (AAB), Stockholm, Sweden.
Olof Aschbergs Arkiv. 12 boxes.

Archives Nationales (AN), Paris, France.
BB 18/6727. Banque russo-asiatique.
F 7. Police générale.

Arkhiv Vneshnei Politiki Rossiiskoi Imperii (AVPRI). Moscow, Russia.
Fond 135. Osobyi politicheskii otdel.
Fond 138, opis 467. Sekretnyi arkhiv ministra.
Fond 149, opis 502b. Turetskii stol. Opis 502b. Miscellaneous.
Fond 151, opis 482. Politicheskii arkhiv.
Fond 187, opis 524. Posol'stvo v Parizhe.

Bundesarchiv Bern (BB), Bern, Switzerland.
E 21 "Polizeiwesen 1848–1930" files.

Bundesarchiv Militärabteilung (BA/MA). Freiburg, Germany.
RM 5/2596. The Imperial German Navy. Naval Staff, Section B. Matters of International Law. Russia: Agents' Reports on General Conditions, Trade, Army, and Navy Discipline, Progress of Revolution, Negotiations for Separate Peace. October 18, 1917, to December 8, 1917.
RM 5/4064. "Russland. Feb. 1918 to 31.12.18."
RM 5/4065. "Russland. 1 Jan 1918 to 31 March 1918."
RM 40-4. Sonderkommandos der Marine in der Türkei. Politische Nachrichten und allgemeine Nachrichten über den Kriegsverlauf.
RM 40/215. Nachrichten von der türk Armee (cont.), February 1918– October 1918.

Deutsches Bundesarchiv Berlin (DBB). Lichterfelde, Berlin, Germany.
R 901. Auswärtiges Amt.

Gosudarstvennyi Arkhiv Rossiiskoi Federatsii (GARF), Moscow, Russia.
Fond P1. Opis 1.
Delo 3. Prikazyi Moskovskogo i Zamoskvoretskogo raionnogo VRK [voenno-revolyuts. Komitetov] ob artilleriiskom obstrele Kremlya.
Fond P375. Voenno-Revolyutsionnyi Komitet pri Stavke Verkhovnogo Glavkomandyushchego. Mogilev.
Opis 1. VRK pri Stavke Verkhovnogo Glavkomanduyushchego. 1917–1918 gg.
Delo 5. Perepiska o pogromakh i drugikh besporyadakh, a takzhe i prinyatii mer k ustraneniyu pogromov besporyadkov. December 1 to 24, 1917.
Fond P1236. Voenno-Revolutsionnyii Komitet (Petrogradskii VRK, PVRK) pri vserossiiskom tsentral'nom ispolnitel'nom komitete.
Opis 1. Petrogradskii VRK. 1917–1918 gg.
Fond P1245. Opis 1.
Delo 1. Perepiska s Sovnarkom, VTsIK, Narodnyi komissariatom prodovol'stviya, NKPS I dr. uchrezhdeniyami po voprosu registratsii byivshikh ofitserov-sluzhashchikh sovetskikh uchrezhdenii. 1918.
Fond P6993. Opis 1.
Delo 1. Stenogramma zasedaniya s'ezda delegatov s fronta ot 24 aprelya 1917 g./bez okonchaniya.
Fond 529. Opis 1. "Byuro zaveduyushchego zagranichnoi agenturoi departmenta politsii v Konstantinopole." (Okhrana files). 1911–1914.
Fond 555. Opis 1. Guchkov, A. I. Lichnoe Delo.

Haus-, Hof- und Staatsarchiv (HHSA), Vienna, Austria.
Politisches Archiv X. Russland.
Karton 133. Berichte 1908 IX-XII. Weisungen, Varia 1908–1909.
Karton 134. Berichte 1909 I–IX.
Karton 149. Russland Liasse VIIIb, IX, X.

Hoover Institution Archives, Stanford University, Stanford, California.
Collection: Alekseev, Mikhail V.
Box 1. Manuscript "Tri Nedeli. (21 avgusta–14 sentyabrya 1917), n.d."
Folder 7. Kornilov, Lavr, Note concerning September 1, 1917.
Collection: Basily, Nicolas de. 11 boxes.
Collection: Girs (Mikhail N.).
Folder 1-1. Russian Diplomatic Representations (General), 1918–1919.
Folder 1-9. "Nekotoryie Zametki i Pis'ma posle moego otchisleniia

ot komandovaniia, 1918."

Folder 1-20. "Russia—General—History—Revolution and Civil War."

Folder 1-22. "Moscow, military and political situation, report on, by Colonel Novosil'tsev, June 1918."

Folder labeled "Telegrams. From March 14, 1919, to April 22, 1919."

Collection: Golder, Frank. Box 2, folder 2. Diaries, 1914–1923.

Collection: Kerensky, Alexander.

Folder 19. "Speeches and Writings."

Collection: Kesküla, Alexander.

Box 1.

Folder 1-2. "Keskuela's relations with the German govt., passports, university certificates issued to the name of Simon Pobitoff."

Folder 1-5. "1960." Kesküla interview/diary composed in Madrid.

Box 2. News Clippings.

"Sonntagsbeilage. National-Zeitung Basel, Nr 303, Sonntag, 5."

"Juli 1964": "Der schlafende Tiger. Erinnerungen an Aleksandr Kesküla. Von Prof. Adolf Gasser."

Collection: Larsons, M. J. (Max Laserson). 2 boxes.

Collection: Russia Shtab Verkhovnogo Glavno Komanduyushchego. ("Hoover Stavka"). 1 Box.

National Archives Annex (NAA), College Park, MD. USA.

State Department Reports on Russia, M 316, rolls 119–121.

National Archives of the United Kingdom (PRO). Kew Gardens, London, UK.

ADM (Admiralty Office Correspondence).

File 137/940. Russia. Black Sea Reports. September 1916–June 1917.

FO 371. Foreign Office Correspondence.

Boxes 2093–96. Russia correspondence, 1914.

Boxes 2445–50. Russia (War) correspondence.

Box 3000. Russia (War) correspondence, cont.

WO 33. War Office Correspondence

Box 731. Wartime correspondence, 1914–1918.

Politisches Archiv des Auswärtigen Amtes (PAAA), Berlin, Germany.

Akten betreffend. Allg. Angelegenheiten Russlands. (Russland 61.)

R 10066–80. January 1, 1908, to March 31, 1917.

Akten betreffend. Allg. Angelegenheiten Russlands. Russland 61 secr.

R 10136–38. January 1, 1888, to January 1920.

Akten betreffend: Eisenbahnen in Rußland.

R 11010–11. July 1, 1908, to December 31, 1914.

Akten betreffend: Finanzielle Beziehungen Russland zu Deutschland

Préfecture de Police, Paris, France.
Dossier "Aschberg, Olof."

Quai d'Orsay Archives (QO), Paris, France.

Angleterre, "Grande-Bretagne–Russie. Janv. 1921–Mai 1922" (folder 61)
URSS: debt (folder 421)
URSS: gold (folders 481–483).

Correspondence politique et commerciale dite "nouvelle série," 1896–1918. Russie.
File 4. Politique Intérieure. Dossier général. 1906–1914.
Files 8–11. Politique Intérieure. Pologne. 1896–1914.
Files 32–42. Politique Etrangère. Alliance franco-russe. 1896–1918.
File 50. Politique Etrangère. Relations avec Angleterre 1906–1914.

Riksarkivet Stockholm Utrikesdepartement (RSU). Stockholm, Sweden.
Rysslands handel med Sverige 1900–1918, and continuation (Handel med Sverige: 1918, dec. –1919, sept. etc., –1922)
Boxes 4456, 4466, 4466b, 4467, 4477, and HP 494–495.

Rossiiskii Gosudarstvennyi Arkhiv Ekonomiki (RGAE). Moscow, Russia.
Fond 413. Ministerstvo vneshnei torgovli SSSR (Minvneshtorg SSSR).
Opis 3. Foreign Trade, 1917–1920, especially with Scandinavia.
Opis 4. Founding documents of Narkomvneshtorg (NKVT), etc.
Opis 6. Red Army Procurement, 1917–1922 and beyond.
Fond 7632. Gosudarstvennoe khranilishche tsennostei (Gokhran) Narkomfina SSSR. 1920–1922. (2 opisi)
Fond 7733. Ministerstvo Finansov SSSR (Minfin SSSR). 1917–1991.
Opis 1. Narkomfin RSFSR, 1917–1923, especially the "Seifovaia komissiia" files.

Rossiisskii Gosudarstvennyi Arkhiv Sotsial-Politicheskii Istorii (RGASPI). Moscow, Russia.
Fond 2. Lenin.
Opis 4. Biograficheskie dokumentyi V. I. Lenina (1871–1923 gg.).
Delo 10. Denezhnyie dokumentyi V. I. Lenina, N. K. Krupskoi i M. I. Ul'yanovoi.
Opis 5. Pis'ma 1898–Nov. 1917. (Correspondence).
Fond 4. Opis 3. (Lenin).
Delo 39. "Delo Tsentral'nogo kontrrazvedyivatel'nogo otdeleniya Glavnogo upravleniya general'nogo shtaba za. No. 87,

t.P. (prodolzhenie) perlyustratsionnyie telegrammyi V. I. Lenina i dr. 10 (23) maya–11 (24) oktyabrya 1917 g.

Delo 40. Byuro razrabotki sekretnyikh arkhivov, deistvovavshe-go s iyunya 1917 g., sostavlennyie po agenturnyim doneseni-yam sekretnyikh sotrudnikov (provokatorov) dlya Komissii po obespecheniyu novogo stroya, ob organizationnoi, pro-pagandistskoi rabote "lenintsev," bol'shevikov-primerentsev (etc.).

Delo 41. Materialyi predvaritel'nogo sledstviya o vooruzhen-nom vyistuplenii v Petrograde 3(16)–5(18) iyulya 1917 goda. (Witness Depositions Taken After the July Days).

Delo 45. Telegramma nachal'nika Petrogradskoi militsii vsem komissaram o poluchenii ordera ot sudebnogo sledovatel-ya po osobo vazhnyim delam na arrest . . . V. I. Ul'yanova (Lenina), obvinyaemogo po delu o vooruzhennom vosstanii 3(16)–5(18) iyulya 1917 g.

Delo 48. Perepiska mezhdu Ministerstvom vnutrennyikh' del Avstro- Vengrii i Direktsiei politsii v Krakove po voprosu ob osvobozhdenii V. I. Lenina iz-pod aresta v Novom Targe. August 16 to September 11, 1914.

Delo 64. Telegrammyi generala L. G. Kornilova ministru pred-sedatelyu Vremennogo pravitel'stva A. F. Kerenskomu s tre-bovaniem predaniya voenno-revolyutsionnomu sudu V. I. Lenina i dr. lits. (July 23/August 5 to 12/25, 1917).

Fond 17. Politbiuro TsK RKP (b)—VKP (b).

Fond 464. Opis 1. Vserossiiskoe Byuro frontovyikh i tyilovyikh voenn-yikh organizatsii pri Ts.K. RSDRP/b.

Delo 1. Pis'ma, telegrammyi partiinyikh organizatsii, komite-tov, otdel'nyikh lits po povodu sozyiva Vserossiiskoi konfer-entsii voennyikh organizatsii fronta . . . April 22, 1917, to June 22, 1917.

Delo 4. Pis'ma, zayavleniya, zapiski o vyidache oruzhiya, parti-inyikh biletov Vserossiiskogo byuro voennyikh organizatsii o sozyive partiinogo sobraniya Petrogradskogo garnizona, o prieme v chlenyi partii i dr. voprosam. Avtografiya N. I. Podvoiskogo. May 31, 1917, to beginning of 1918.

Delo 5. Spisok zavodov s ukazaniem kolichestva rabochikh, krasnogvardeitsev, oruzhiya; chlenov Soveta "Krasnoi gvar-dii," svedeniya o Krasnoi gvardii i voinskikh chastyakh. April 20, 1917, to October 1917.

Delo 6. Protokol sobraniya Voennoi organizatsii pri TsK RSDRP (b) ot 26.XII.1917 g. s povestkoi dnya: 1. O sozdanii sotsialisticheskoi armii. 2. Tekuschie dela.

Delo 7. Protokolyi zasedanii Byuro I Ispolnitel'nogo kollektiva pri Byuro frontovyikh i tyilovyikh voennyikh organizatsii pri TsK RSDRP (b). January 14, 1918, to March 22, 1918.

Delo 15. Finansovyie dokumentyi: kvitantsii, raspiski. March 1917 to March 28, 1918.

Opis 3. Povestki dnia zasedanii. (Politburo Minutes, 1919–1923).

Fond 538. Opisi 1–3. Internationale Arbeiterhilfe (1921–1935).

Fond 670. Opis 1. Grigory Sokol'nikov (Lichnoe delo).

Rossiiskii Gosudarstvennyi Arkhiv Voenno-Morskogo Flota (RGAVMF). St. Petersburg, Russia.

Fond 11. Kolchak Aleksandr Vasil'evich, Admiral (1874–1920). (Lichnoe delo). Opis 1.

Delo 45. Pozdravitel'nyie telegrammyi v svyazi s naznachiem A. V. Kolchaka komanduyushchim flotom Chernogo morya i t.d. May 1916 to June 26, 1917.

Delo 57. Pis'ma raznikh' lits k A. V. Kolchaku, January 25, 1917, to July 21, 1917.

Fond 716. Morskoi shtab verkhovnogo glavnokomanduyushchego (stavka) 1914–1917. Opis 1.

Delo 267. Doklady komandovaniya Chernomorskogo flota o deistviyakh za ianvar'-avgust mesyatsyi 1917 g. Podlinniki. 31.1.1917 to 25.8.1917.

Delo 277. Gosudarstvennyi perevorot', February 24, 1917, to June 6, 1917.

Delo 278. Perepiska s' Genmorom, komanduyushchimi Balti-iskim i Chernomorskom flotami, komanduyushchimi fron-tami i dr. o revolyutsionnyikh' sobyityakh' v strane. Febru-ary 28, 1917, to March 20, 1917.

Delo 279. Continuation. March 11, 1917, to September 23, 1917.

Delo 280. Politicheskie voprosyi, July 5, 1917, to October 28, 1917.

Delo 283. Ministerstvo Morskoe Morskogo Shtaba. Verkhov-nago Glavnokomanduyushchago. Delo o lichnome sostave. January 1917 to July 10, 1917.

Delo 293. Telegrammyi o politicheskikh sobyityakh na Cher-nomorskom flote. June 25, 1917, to September 9, 1917.

Rossiiskii Gosudarstvennyi Istoricheskii Arkhiv (RGIA). St. Petersburg, Russia.

Fond 1276.

Opis 13. Council of Ministers (Protocols, Correspondence, etc.).

Opis 14. Provisional Government (Protocols, Correspondence, etc.).

Fond 1278.
Opis 10. State Duma (Protocols, Transcripts, Correspondence, etc.)
Delo 3. Gosudarstvennoi Dumyi. Delo Vremennago Komiteta Gosudarstvennoi Dumyi. Prikazyi Komiteta. 28 Fev. 1917 goda po 18 iyunya 1917 goda (Rodzianko's "Ghost Duma").
Delo 5. Telegrammyi predsedatelya vremennago komiteta Gos. Dumyi M. V. Rodzianko v Stavkkomom vsekh frontov o sverzhenii samoderzhaviya, sostave Vremennago pravitel'stva I priglashennii gen. Kornilova na post glavnokomanduyushchego Petrogradskim voennyim okrugom . . . 1 marta 1917 goda po 27 iunya 1917.
Delo 9. Prikazyi, rasporyazhanie i tsirkulyaryi vremennago pravitel'stva: ob otrechenii Nikolaya II ot prestola i obrazovanii Vremennago pravitel'stva. . . . 2 marta 1917 po 29 iunya 1917.
Delo 12. Vozzvanie Vremennago komiteta Gos. Dumyi k naselenyu, sodatyi i t.d . . . Obrashchenii k' naseleniyu i armii. March 7 to September 7, 1917.
Fond 1358. Opis 1.
Delo 1939. Peterburgskoe telegrafnoe Agenstvo. Neopublikovannyie telegrammyi/podlinnyie. S' 8ogo Yanvarya po 15 avgusta 1917 g.

Rossiiskii Gosudarstvennyi Voennyi Arkhiv (RGVA). Moscow, Russia.
Fond 1. Upravlenie delami Narkomata po voennyim delam. Opis' 1. Kantselariya. December 1917 to November 1918.

Rossiiskii Gosudarstvennyi Voenno-Istoricheskii Arkhiv (RGVIA). Moscow, Russia.
Fond 2000. Opis 1. Glavnoe upravlenie General'nago Shtaba. (Stavka).
Fond 2031. Opis 1. Shtab glavnokomanduyushchego armyami severnogo fronta (Northern Army).
Fond 2067. Opis 1. Shtaba glavnokomanduyushchago armiyami Yugo-zapadnago fronta (Southwestern Front).

Tsentral'nyi Gosudarstvennyi Istoricheskii Arkhiv Sankt-Peterburga (TsGIASPb). St. Petersburg, Russia.
Fond 1695. Opis 2.
Delo 1. O roste vliyaniya bol'shevikov. Prokuror. Petrogradskago Sudebnyoi Palatyi. Delo po obvinenyi soldat gvardim Moskovskikh' polka prinimayavshikh uchastii v vooruzhennim vyistu.
Delo 30. Uchastie v sobyyityakh' 3–5 iyulya 1917 g. Kronshtadtskogo garnizona.

Vincennes. Service Historique de la Défense (VSHD). Vincennes, Paris, France.

7 N 1538. Attachés militaires. Russie. 1902–1914.

Yivo Institute. Bund Archives. New York City, USA.

ME1-88/103. Bolshevik Military Organization. Pamphlets, 1906.

Document Collections

Adamov, E. A., ed. *Konstantinopol' i prolivyi*. 2 vols. Moscow: Izdanie Litizdata NKID, 1925–26.

———. *Razdel aziatskoi Turtsii. Po sekretnyim dokumentam b. Ministerstva inostrannyikh del*. Moscow: Izdanie Litizdata NKID, 1924.

Bunyan, James, ed. *Intervention, Communism, and Civil War in Russia, April–December 1918. Documents and Materials*. Baltimore, MD: Johns Hopkins Press, 1936.

Bunyan, James, and H. H. Fisher, eds. *The Bolshevik Revolution, 1917–1918. Documents and Materials*. Stanford, CA: Stanford University Press, 1961.

Degras, Jane. *The Communist International, 1919–1943: Documents*. 3 vols. New York: Oxford University Press, 1956–1965.

Emmons, Terence, and Bertrand M. Patenaude. *War, Revolution, and Peace in Russia: The Passages of Frank Golder*. Stanford, CA: Hoover Institution Press, 1992.

Galperina, B. D., and V. I. Startsev, eds. *Petrogradskii Sovet rabochikh i soldatskikh deputatov v 1917 godu*. 4 vols. Moscow: Rosspen, 2003.

Golder, Frank, ed. *Documents of Russian History 1914–1917*. Translated by Emanuel Aronsberg. New York/London: The Century Company, 1927.

Grave, B. B. *Burzhuaziia nakanune fevralskoi revoliutsii*. Moscow/Leningrad: Tsentrarkhiv, 1927.

Hahlweg, Werner, ed. *Lenins Rückkehr nach Russland, 1917: die deutschen Akten*. Leiden: E. J. Brill, 1957.

Kerensky, Alexander F., and Robert Paul Browder, eds. *The Russian Provisional Government 1917*. 3 vols. Stanford, CA: Stanford University Press, 1961.

Krasnyi Arkhiv. Istoricheskii zhurnal. 106 vols. Moscow: Gospolitizdat, 1922–1941.

Lyandres, Semion, ed. *The Fall of Tsarism: Untold Stories of the February 1917 Revolution*. Oxford: Oxford University Press, 2013.

Pipes, Richard, ed. *The Unknown Lenin: From the Secret Archive*. Translations by Catharine Fitzpatrick. New Haven, CT: Yale University Press, 1999.

Pokrovskii, M. N., ed. *Drei Konferenzen (zur Vorgeschichte des Krieges)*. Berlin: Arbeiterbuchhandlung, 1920.

————.*Internationale Beziehungen im Zeitalter des Imperialismus.* 8+ vols. Berlin: R. Hobbing, 1931–.

————. *Tsarskaia Rossiia v mirovoi voine.* Vol 1. Leningrad: 1926.

Polnoe sobranie zakonov Rossiiskoi Imperii. Third Series (1881–1931). 33 vols. Brill Microfilms (1990).

Shchegolev, P. E., ed. *Padenie tsarskogo rezhima: stenograficheskie otchetyi doprosov i pokazannie, dannyikh v. 1917 g. v. chrezvychainoi sledstvennoi komissii vremennago pravitel'stva.* 7 vols. Moscow: Gos. Izd., 1924–1927.

Sovetsko-Germanskie Otnosheniia ot peregovorov v Brest-Litovske do Podpisaniia Rapall'skogo Dogovora. Moscow: Izdatel'stvo Politicheskoi Literatury, 1971.

Yakhontov, A. N. *Soviet Ministrov Rossiiskoi Imperii v gody pervoi mirovoi voiny. Bumagi A. N. Yakhontova.* St. Petersburg, n.p. 1999.

Zeman, Z. A. B., ed. *Germany and the Revolution in Russia, 1915–1918. Documents from the Archives of the German Foreign Ministry.* London: Oxford University Press, 1958.

Published and Online Works Cited or Profitably Consulted, Including Memoirs

Abraham, Richard. *Alexander Kerensky. The First Love of the Revolution.* New York: Columbia University Press, 1987.

Agnew, Jeremy, and Kevin McDermott. *The Comintern. A History of International Communism from Lenin to Stalin.* London: Macmillan, 1996.

Airapetov, O. R., ed. "Na Vostochnom napravlenii. Sud'ba Bosforskoi ekspeditsii v pravlenie imperatora Nikolaia II." In *Posledniaia voina imperatorskoi Rossii: sbornik statei,* 158–252. Moscow: Tri kvadrata, 2002.

Akimov, F. I. "Bol'sheviki v bor'be za soldatskie massy Iugo-Zapadnogo fronta (1914–fevral' 1917 g.)." In *Voenno-istoricheskii zhurnal,* no. 2 (1977): 87–88.

Albertini, Luigi. *The Origins of the War of 1914.* 3 vols. New York: Oxford University Press, 1952–1957.

Allen, W. E. D., and Paul Muratoff. *Caucasian Battlefields. A History of the Wars on the Turco-Caucasian Border, 1828–1921.* Cambridge, UK: Cambridge University Press, 1953.

"L'armeé rouge approvisionnée par la contrebande." *Echo de Paris,* November 20, 1920.

Artizov, A. N. *Getman P. P. Skoropadskii Ukraina na perelome 1918 god.* Moscow: Rosspen, 2014.

Aschberg, Olof. "A Wandering Jew from Glasbruksgatan" (*Ein vandrande jude fran Glasbruksgatan*). Unpublished English-language typescript translation by Alan Blair, located in Olof Aschbergs Arkiv at the Arbetar-rölsens Arkiv och Bibliotek, Stockholm, Sweden.

Ascher, Abraham. *P. A. Stolypyin. The Search for Stability in Late Imperial Russia*. Stanford, CA: Stanford University Press, 2001.

Astashov, Aleksandr. *Russkii front v 1914–nachale 1917 goda: voennyi opyt I sovremennost'*. Moscow: Novyi Kronograf, 2014.

Baker, Mark. "War and Revolution in Ukraine: Kharkiv Province's Peasants' Experiences," in Sarah Badcock et al., *Russia's Home Front in War and Revolution*. Vol. 3, book 1. *Russia's Revolution in Regional Perspective*, 111–142. Bloomington, IN: Slavica, 2016.

Balabanoff, Angelica. *Impressions of Lenin*. Ann Arbor: University of Michigan Press, 1964.

Ball, Alan. *Russia's Last Capitalists: The Nepmen*. Berkeley: University of California Press, 1987.

Bark, Peter. Memoirs (PBM). Columbia University Rare Book & Manuscript Library. Columbia University, New York, USA.

Barthel, Max. *Kein Bedarf an Weltgeschichte*. Wiesbaden: Limes, 1950.

Bascomb, Neal. *Red Mutiny: Eleven Fateful Days on the Battleship Potemkin*. Boston: Houghton Mifflin, 2007.

Basily, Nicolas de (N. A. Bazili). *Nicolas de Basily, Diplomat of Imperial Russia*. Stanford, CA: Hoover Institution Press, 1973.

Baumgart, Winfried. *Deutsche Ostpolitik 1918. Von Brest-Litowsk bis zum Ende des Ersten Weltkrieges*. Vienna/Munich: Oldenbourg, 1966.

Bayer, Waltraud, ed. *Verkaufte Kultur. Die sowjetischen Kunst- und Antiquitätenexporte 1919–1938*. Frankfurt-am-Main: Peter Lang, 2001.

Beller, M., and A. Burovskii. *Grazhdanskaia Istoriia bezumnoi voiny*. Moscow: Astrel', 2010.

Blücher, Wipert von. *Deutschlands Weg nach Rapallo*. Wiesbaden: Limes, 1951.

Bobroff, Ronald Park. *Roads to Glory. Late Imperial Russia and the Turkish Straits*. London: I. B. Tauris, 2006.

Bodger, Alan. "Russia and the End of the Ottoman Empire." In *The Great Powers and the End of the Ottoman Empire*. London: Frank Cass, 1984.

Bonch-Bruevich, Vladimir Dmitrievich. *Na boevyikh postakh fevral'skoi i oktyabr'skoi Revoliutsii*. Moscow: Federatsiya, 1931.

Braunthal, Julius. *Geschichte der Internationale*. 3 vols. Berlin: Dietz, 1961–.

Brenton, Tony, ed. *Historically Inevitable? Turning Points of the Russian Revolution*. London: Profile Books, 2016.

———. "The Short Life and Early Death of Russian Democracy." In *Historically Inevitable?*, Tony Brenton, ed., 142–162.

Brovkin, Vladimir. *Behind the Front Lines of the Civil War. Political Parties and Social Movements in Russia, 1918–1922*. Princeton, NJ: Princeton University Press, 1994.

Buchanan, George, Sir. *My Mission to Russia, and Other Diplomatic Memories.* London: Cassell & Co., Ltd., 1923.

Budnitskii, Oleg. *Den'gi russkoi emigratsii: kolchakovskoe zoloto 1918–1957.* Moscow: Novoe literaturnoe obozrenie, 2008.

Budnitskii, Oleg. "Generaly i den'gi, ili 'Vrangelevskoe Serebro." *Diaspora* 6 (2004): 134–173.

———. "Kolchakovskoe zoloto." *Diaspora* 4 (2002): 457–508.

———. *Russian Jews Between the Reds and the Whites, 1917–1920.* Translated by Timothy Portice. Philadelphia: University of Pennsylvania Press, 2012.

"Bulygin Duma Statutes": http://novaonline.nvcc.edu/eli/evans/his242/doc uments/frus/bulyginduma.html.

Caute, David. *The Fellow-Travelers. A Postscript to the Enlightenment.* New York: Macmillan, 1973.

Chernov, V. M. *The Great Russian Revolution.* New York: Russell & Russell, 1966.

"Churches Resist Decree of Soviet." *New York Times*, April 14, 1922.

Clarke, William. *The Lost Fortune of the Tsars: The Search for the Fabulous Legacy of the Romanoffs.* London: Orion, 1996.

Clements, Barbara Evans. *Bolshevik Feminist. The Life of Alexandra Kollontai.* Bloomington: Indiana University Press, 1979.

Cook, Andrew. *Ace of Spies: The True Story of Sidney Reilly.* London: Tempus, 2004.

———. *To Kill Rasputin: The Life and Death of Gregori Rasputin.* Stroud, UK: Tempus, 2005.

Crawford, Donald. "The Last Tsar." In Brenton, ed., *Historically Inevitable? Turning Points of the Russian Revolution*, 66–90.

Crisp, Olga. *Studies in the Russian Economy Before 1914.* London: Macmillan, 1976.

Criss, Nur Bilge. *Istanbul Under Allied Occupation 1918–1923 (Ottoman Empire and Its Heritage).* Leiden: Brill, 1999.

Curtiss, John Shelton. *The Russian Church and the Soviet State 1917–1950.* Boston: Little, Brown, 1953.

Daly, Jonathan. "'Storming the Last Citadel': The Bolshevik Assault on the Church, 1922." In Brovkin, ed., *The Bolsheviks in Russian Society: The Revolution and the Civil Wars.* New Haven: Yale University Press, 1997.

Davis, Robert H. et al. *A Dark Mirror: Romanov and Imperial Palace Library Materials in the Holdings of the New York Public Library: A Checklist and Agenda for Research.* New York: Norman Ross, 2000.

Deutscher, Isaac. *The Prophet Armed: Trotsky, 1879–1921.* New York: Oxford University Press, 1954.

Devlin, F. Roger. "Solzhenitsyn on the Jews and Tsarist Russia." *Occidental Quarterly* 8, no. 3 (Fall 2008): 61–80.

Dieter-Müller, Rolf. *Das Tor Zur Weltmacht*. Boppard am Rhein: Harald Boldt, 1984.

Dobrorolski, Sergei. *Die Mobilmachung der russischen Armee 1914*. Berlin: Deutsche Verlagsgesellschaft für Politik und Geschichte, 1922.

Dowling, Timothy C. *The Brusilov Offensive*. Bloomington: Indiana University Press, 2008.

Dune, Edward. *Notes of a Red Guard*. Translated by Diane Koenker and S. A. Smith. Urbana: University of Illinois Press, 1993.

Durnov, P. N. Memorandum to Tsar Nicholas II, February 14, 1914. http://www2.stetson.edu/~psteeves/classes/durnovo.html.

"8 American Officers Reported Captured." *New York Times*, January 30, 1920.

Feldman, Robert S. "Russian General Staff and the June 1917 Offensive." *Soviet Studies* 19, no. 4 (April 1968): 526–543.

Figes, Orlando. "The Harmless Drunk." In Brenton, ed., *Historically Inevitable? Turning Points of the Russian Revolution*, 123–142.

———. *Peasant Russia, Civil War: The Volga Countryside in Revolution, 1917–1921*. New York: Oxford University Press, 1989.

———. *A People's Tragedy: The Russian Revolution: 1891–1924*. New York: Penguin, 1998.

Fischer, Fritz. *Germany's Aims in the First World War*. New York: W. W. Norton, 1967.

Fisher, Harold H. *The Famine in Soviet Russia 1919–1923: The Operations of the American Relief Administration*. New York: Macmillan, 1927.

Fitzpatrick, Sheila. *The Russian Revolution*. New York: Oxford University Press, 2008; orig. 1982.

"France to Propose Action by Allies." *New York Times*, April 21, 1922.

Freund, Gerald. *Unholy Alliance. Russian-German Relations from the Treaty of Brest-Litovsk to the Treaty of Berlin*. London: Chatto and Windus, 1957.

Fuhrmann, Joseph T. *Rasputin: The Untold Story*. Hoboken, NJ: John Wiley & Sons, 2013.

Fuller, William C, Jr. *Civil-Military Conflict in Imperial Russia, 1881–1914*. Princeton, NJ: Princeton University Press, 1985.

———. *The Foe Within: Fantasies of Treason and the End of Imperial Russia*. Ithaca, NY: Cornell University Press, 2006.

———. *Strategy and Power in Russia, 1600–1914*. New York: Free Press, 1992.

Futrell, Michael. *Northern Underground. Episodes of Russian Revolutionary Transport and Communications Through Scandinavia and Finland 1863–1917*. London: Faber & Faber, 1963.

Gatrell, Peter. *Government, Industry and Rearmament in Russia, 1900–1914*. Cambridge, UK: Cambridge University Press, 1994.

"Germans Astound Genoa Conference By Announcing Compact With Russia, Granting All That Allies Reject." *New York Times*, April 18, 1922.

Gerschenkron, Alexander. "Russia: Patterns and Problems of Economic Development, 1861–1958." In *Economic Backwardness in Historical*

Perspective. A Book of Essays. Cambridge, MA: Belknap Press of Harvard University, 1962.

Grebenkin, Igor Nikolaevich. *Russkii ofitser i gody. Mirovoi voiny i revoliutsii, 1914–1918 gg.* Riazan: Riazanskii gos. Un-t., 2010.

Greger, René. *Die Russische Flotte im Ersten Weltkrieg, 1914–1917.* Munich: J. F. Lehmann, 1970.

Gross, Babette. *Willi Münzenberg: Eine politische Biographie.* Stuttgart: Deutsche Verlags-Anstalt, 1967.

Guchkov, Alexander, and N. A. Bazili. *Aleksandr Ivanovich Guchkov rasskazyivaet.* Moscow: TOO Red. Zhurnal "Vopros istorii," 1993.

Gurko, Vladimir Iosifovich. *Features and Figures of the Past. Government and Opinion in the Reign of Nicholas II.* Translated by Laura Matveev. Stanford, CA: Stanford University Press, 1939.

Halpern, Paul G. *A Naval History of World War I.* Annapolis, MD: Naval Institute Press, 1995.

Hasegawa, Tsuyoshi. *The February Revolution: Petrograd, 1917.* Seattle: University of Washington Press, 1981.

Heywood, Anthony. *Engineer of Revolutionary Russia: Iurii V. Lomonosov (1876–1952) and the Railways.* Farnham: Ashgate, 2011.

———. *Modernising Lenin's Russia: Economic Reconstruction, Foreign Trade, and the Railways.* Cambridge, UK: Cambridge University Press, 1999.

Holquist, Peter. *Making War, Forging Revolution: Russia's Continuum of Crisis, 1914–1921.* Cambridge, MA: Harvard University Press, 2002.

Hosking, Geoffrey. *Russia and the Russians.* Cambridge, MA: Harvard University Press, 2001.

Hovannisian, Richard, "The Allies and Armenia, 1915–18." *Journal of Contemporary History* 3, no. 1 (January 1968): 145–168.

———. *The Republic of Armenia.* 4 vols. Berkeley: University of California Press, 1971–1996.

Icones Russes. Collection Olof Aschberg. Donation faite au Musée National. Stockholm: Kungl. Boktryckeriet. P.A. Norstedt & Söner, 1933.

Isarescu, Mugur, Cristian Paunescu, and Marian Stefan. *Tezaurul Bancii Nationale a Romaniei la Moscova—Documente.* Bucharest: Fundatiei Culturale Magazin Istoric, 1999.

Karpova, Rosa Federovna. *L. B. Krasin, sovetskii diplomat.* Moscow: Izd. Sotsialno-ekonom. Lit., 1962.

Katkov, George. *Russia 1917: The February Revolution.* New York: Harper & Row, 1967.

Katzenellenbaum, S. S. *Russian Currency and Banking 1914–1924.* London: P. S. King & Son, 1925.

Kazemzadeh, Firuz. *The Struggle for Transcaucasia, 1917–1921.* New York: Philosophical Library, 1951.

Kennan, George. *Soviet-American Relations, 1917–1920.* 2 vols. London: Faber & Faber, 1956 and 1958.

Kerensky, A. F. *The Catastrophe. Kerensky's Own Story of the Russian Revolution.* New York: D. Appleton and Co., 1927.

———. *The Crucifixion of Liberty.* New York: John Day Co., 1934.

Kettle, Michael. *Sidney Reilly. The True Story of the World's Greatest Spy.* New York: St. Martin's Press, 1983.

Kipp, Jacob. "Lenin and Clausewitz: The Militarization of Marxism, 1914–21." *Military Affairs* 49, no. 4 (October 1985): 184–191.

Kotkin, Stephen. *Stalin, Volume One: Paradoxes of Power, 1878–1928.* New York: Penguin Books, 2015.

Kovalenko, D. A. *Oboronnaia promyishlennost' sovetskoi rossii v 1918–1920 gg.* Moscow: Nauka, 1970.

Krasin, Leonid Borisovich. *Dela davno minuvshikh dnei (Vospominaniia).* Moscow: Molodaia gvardiia, 1931.

———. *O vneshnei torgovle i otnoshenii k nei russkoi kooperatsii.* Novgorod: Tipografiia Gubsoiuza, 1921.

———. *Voprosy vneshnei torgovli.* Moscow: Gosudarstvennoe izdatel'stvo, 1928.

Krassin, Lubov. *Leonid Krassin: His Life and Work.* London: Skeffington & Son, 1929.

Krivoshein, K. A. *A. V. Krivoshein (1857–1921 g.) Ego znachenie v istorii Rossii nachala XX veka.* Paris: 1973.

Krivova, Natalya Alexandrovna. *Vlast' i Tserkov' v 1922–1925 gg. Politbiuro i GPU v borb'e za tserkovnyie tsennosti I politicheskoe podchinenie dukhovenstva.* Moscow: Airo-XX, 1997.

Kukuruzova, N. V. *Wealthier Than the Romanovs? The Wealth of Princes Yusupov.* St. Petersburg: Yusupov Palace, 2006.

Laserson, Max (M. J. Larsons). *An Expert in the Service of the Soviet,* trans. Dr. Angelo S. Rappoport. London: Ernst Benn, 1929.

———. *Im Sowjet-Labyrinth. Episoden und Silhouetten.* Berlin: Transmare, 1931.

Lazitch, Branko. "Two Instruments of Control by the Comintern: The Emissaries of the ECCI and the Party Representatives in Moscow." In Milorad M. Drachkovitch and Branko Lazitch, eds., *The Comintern: Historical Highlights.* Stanford, CA: Hoover Institution Press, 1966.

Lebor, Adam. *Hitler's Secret Bankers: How Switzerland Profited from Nazi Genocide.* London: Simon & Schuster, 1999.

Lenin, V. I. *Collected Works.* 45 vols. Moscow: Progress Publishers, 1977.

———. *Selected Works.* 12 vols. New York: International Publishers, 1937.

———. *Sochineniia.* Edited by N. I. Bukharin et al. Leningrad: Gosudarstvennoe Sotsial'no Ekonomicheskoe Izdatel'stvo, 1931.

———. *Socialism and War. The Attitude of the Russian Social-Democratic Labor Party Towards the War.* Geneva: Sotsial-Democrat, 1915.

Liberman, Simon. *Building Lenin's Russia.* Chicago: University of Chicago Press, 1945.

Lieven, D. C. B. *Empire: The Russian Empire and its Rivals*. New Haven, CT: Yale University Press, 2002.

———. *Nicholas II: Emperor of all the Russias*. London: J. Murray, 1993.

———. *Russia & the Origins of the First World War*. New York: St. Martin's Press, 1983.

———. *Towards the Flame. The End of Tsarist Russia: The March to War and Revolution*. New York: Viking, 2015.

Lloyd, Nick. *Hundred Days. The Campaign that Ended World War I*. New York: Basic Books, 2014.

Lohr, Eric. *Nationalizing the Russian Empire: The Campaign Against Enemy Aliens during World War I*. Cambridge, MA: Harvard University Press, 2003.

———. "The Russian Army and the Jews: Mass Deportation, Hostages, and Violence During World War I." *Russian Review* 60 (July 2001): 404–419.

Lyandres, Semion. *The Bolsheviks' "German Gold" Revisited: An Inquiry into the 1917 Accusations*. Pittsburgh: Carl Beck Series, University of Pittsburgh, 1995.

Malia, Martin. *Alexander Herzen and the Birth of Russian Socialism*. New York: Grosset & Dunlap, 1965.

———. *The Soviet Tragedy. A History of Socialism in Russia, 1917–1991*. New York: Free Press, 1994.

Malle, Sylvana. *The Economic Organization of War Communism*. Cambridge, UK: Cambridge University Press, 1985.

Manifesto of 17 October 1905. Online at: https://community.dur.ac.uk/a.k.harrington/octmanif.html.

Marx, Karl. *Capital*, vol. 1, and *Manifesto of the Communist Party*. In Robert C. Tucker, ed., *The Marx-Engels Reader*. New York: W. W. Norton, 1972.

Massie, Robert K. *Nicholas and Alexandra*. New York: Atheneum, 1967.

Mawdsley, Evan. *The Russian Civil War*. Boston: Allen & Unwin, 1987.

———. *The Russian Revolution and the Baltic Fleet: War and Politics, February 1917 to April 1918*. New York: Barnes & Noble Books, 1978.

———. "Sea Change in the Civil War." In Brenton, ed., *Historically Inevitable? Turning Points of the Russian Revolution*, 200–217.

McDonald, David MacLaren. *United Government and Foreign Policy in Russia 1900–1914*. Cambridge, MA: Harvard University Press, 1992.

McMeekin, Sean. *History's Greatest Heist. The Bolshevik Looting of Russia*. New Haven, CT: Yale University Press, 2008.

———. *The Ottoman Endgame. War, Revolution, and the Making of the Modern Middle East, 1908–1923*. New York: Penguin Press, 2015.

———. *The Red Millionaire: A Political Biography of Willi Münzenberg, Moscow's Secret Propaganda Tsar in the West, 1917–1940*. New Haven, CT: Yale University Press, 2003.

———. *The Russian Origins of the First World War*. Cambridge, MA: Harvard University Press/Belknap, 2001.

Melgunov, Sergei. *Kak bol'sheviki zakhvatili vlast'. Oktiabr'skii perevorot 1917 goda*. Paris: La Renaissance, 1953.

———. *Krasnyi terror v' Rossii*. New York: Brandy, 1979.

———. *Martovskie Dni 1917 goda*. Paris, 1961.

———. *Zolotoi nemetskii kliuch' k bol'shevitskoi revolutsii*. Paris: Maison du livre étranger, 1940.

Menning, Bruce. *Bayonets Before Bullets. The Imperial Russian Army, 1861–1914*. Bloomington: Indiana University Press, 1992.

Miliukov, Paul. *Political Memoirs*. Translated by Carl Goldberg. Ann Arbor: University of Michigan Press, 1967.

———. *The Russian Revolution*. 3 vols. Gulf Breeze, FL: Academic International Press, 1978–.

Miller, Margaret. *The Economic Development of Russia 1905–1914, with Special Reference to Trade, Industry, and Finance*. New York: A. M. Kelly, 1967.

Mitrofanov, Georgii. *Istoriia russkoi pravoslavnoi tserkvi 1900–1927*. St. Petersburg: Satis, 2002.

Morley, James William. *The Japanese Thrust into Siberia, 1918*. New York: Columbia University Press, 1957.

Moynahan, Brian. *The Russian Century. A History of the Last Hundred Years*. New York: Random House, 1995.

Münzenberg, Willi. *Solidarität. Zehn Jahre Internationale Arbeiterhilfe, 1921–1931*. Berlin: Neuer Deutcher Verlag, 1931.

Mutlu, Dilek Kaya. "The Russian Monument at *Ayastefanos* (San Stefano): Between Defeat and Revenge, Remembering and Forgetting." *Middle Eastern Studies* 43, no. 1 (January 2007): 75–86.

Nation, R. Craig. *War on War: Lenin, the Zimmerwald Left, and the Origins of Communist Internationalism*. Durham, NC: Duke University Press, 1989.

Nechaev, Sergei. *The Catechism of a Revolutionary*. https://www.marxists.org/subject/anarchism/nechayev/catechism.htm.

Nikitin, B. V. *The Fatal Years: Fresh Revelations on a Chapter of Underground History*. Westport, CT: Hyperion Press, 1977.

———. *Rokovye gody: novyia pokazanie uchastnika*. Paris: Les Editeurs Reunis, 1937.

O'Connor, Timothy Edward. *The Engineer of Revolution. L. B. Krasin and the Bolsheviks, 1870–1926*. Boulder, CO: Westview, 1992.

Osipova, Taisia. "Peasant Rebellions: Origin, Scope, Dynamics, and Consequences." In Brovkin, *The Bolsheviks in Russian Society. The Revolution and the Civil Wars*.

Paléologue, Maurice. *An Ambassador's Memoirs*. Translated by. F. A. Holt. 3 vols. London: Hutchinson & Co., 1923–1925.

———. *La Russie des Tsars pendant la Grande Guerre*. 3 vols. Paris: Plon-Nourrit, 1921.

Pares, Bernard. *The Fall of the Russian Monarchy. A Study of the Evidence*. New York: Knopf, 1939.

Pasvolsky, Leo and Moulton, Harold G. *Russian Debts and Russian Reconstruction. A Study of the Relation of Russia's Foreign Debts to Her Economic Recovery*. New York: McGraw-Hill, 1924.

Patenaude, Bertrand. *The Big Show in Bololand. The American Relief Expedition to Soviet Russia in the Famine of 1921*. Stanford, CA: Stanford University Press, 2002.

———. *Trotsky: Downfall of a Revolutionary*. New York: Harper, 2009.

Pearson, Michael. *The Sealed Train*. New York: Putnam, 1975.

Petroff, Serge P. *Remembering a Forgotten War*. New York: Columbia University Press/Eastern European Monographs, 2000.

Pipes, Richard. *The Degaev Affair. Terror and Treason in Tsarist Russia*. New Haven, CT: Yale University Press, 2003.

———. *Russia Under the Bolshevik Regime*. New York: Vintage, 1995.

———. *The Russian Revolution*. New York: Alfred Knopf, 1990.

Pomiankowski, Joseph. *Der Zusammenbruch des Ottomanischen Reiches. Erinnerungen an die Türkei aus der Zeit des Weltkrieges*. Zurich: Amalthea, 1928.

Price, M. Philips. *Dispatches from the Revolution: Russia, 1915–1918*. Durham, NC: Duke University Press, 1998.

Rabinowitch, Alexander. *The Bolsheviks in Power: the First Year of Soviet Rule in Petrograd*. Bloomington: Indiana University Press, 2007.

Radkey, Oliver. *The Unknown Civil War in Soviet Russia. A Study of the Green Movement in Tambov Region, 1920–1921*. Stanford, CA: Stanford University Press, 1976.

Radzinsky, Edvard. *The Last Tsar. The Life and Death of Nicholas II*. Translated by Marian Schwartz. New York: Doubleday, 1992.

———. *The Rasputin File*. New York: Anchor Books, 2001.

———. "Rescuing the Tsar and His Family." In Brenton, ed., *Historically Inevitable? Turning Points of the Russian Revolution*, 163–177.

Rauchensteiner, Manfried. *Der Tod des Doppeladlers: Österreich-Ungarn und der Erste Weltkrieg*. Vienna Verlag Styria, 1993."

"Red Leaders Split on Robbing Churches." *New York Times*, April 7, 1922.

Reed, John. *Ten Days That Shook the World*. New York: St. Martin's Press, 1997.

Rendle, Matthew. "The Problem of the 'Local' in Revolutionary Russia: Moscow Province, 1914–22." In Badcock et al., eds., *Russia's Home Front in War and Revolution*, vol. 3, book 1, 19–44.

Reynolds, Michael A. *Shattering Empires: The Clash and Collapse of the Ottoman and Russian Empires*. New York: Cambridge University Press: 2011.

Rodzianko, Mikhail. *The Reign of Rasputin. An Empire's Collapse*. Translated by Catherine Zveginsvoff. London: A. M. Philpot Ltd., 1927.

Roslof, Edward E. *Red Priests. Renovationism, Russian Orthodoxy, and Revolution, 1905–1946*. Bloomington: Indiana University Press, 2002.

"Russia Must Respect Private Property, Powers Will Tell Her in Note Today." *New York Times*, April 29, 1922.

Sanborn, Joshua. "The Mobilization of 1914 and the Question of the Russian Nation: A Reexamination." *Slavic Review* 59, no. 2 (2000): 267–289.

Saul, Norman E. *Sailors in Revolt. The Baltic Fleet in 1917*. Lawrence, KS: Regents Press of Kansas, 1978.

———. *War and Revolution. The United States and Russia, 1914–1921*. Lawrence: University Press of Kansas, 2001.

Sazonov, S. D. *Fateful Years, 1909–1916: The Reminiscences of Serge Sazonov, Russia's Minister for Foreign Affairs: 1914*. London: J. Cape, 1928.

Scharlau, W. B., and Z. A. B. Zeman. *The Merchant of Revolution. The Life of Alexander Israel Helphand (Parvus), 1867–1924*. Oxford: Oxford University Press, 1965.

Schilling, M. F., Baron, ed. *How the War Began. Being the Diary of the Russian Foreign Office from the 3rd to the 20th (Old Style) of July, 1914*, trans. Major W. Cyprian Bridge. London: G. Allen & Unwyn, 1925.

Sebag Montefiore, Simon. *The Young Stalin*. New York: Vintage Reprint, 2008.

Seidt, Hans-Ulrich. *Berlin, Kabul, Moskau. Oskar Ritter von Niedermayer und Deutschlands Ostpolitik*. Munich: Universitas, 2002.

Senin, A. S. *Aleksandr Ivanovich Guchkov*. Moscow: Skriptorii, 1996.

Service, Robert. *Lenin: A Biography*. Harvard: Harvard/Belknap, 2000.

Shapiro, Leonard. *The Russian Revolutions of 1917: The Origins of Modern Communism*. New York: Basic Books, 1984.

Shkliarevsky, Gennady. *Labor in the Russian Revolution: Factory Committees and Trade Unions, 1917–1918*. New York: St. Martin's Press, 1993.

Shukman, H. "The Relations Between the Jewish Bund and the RSDRP, 1897–1903." Unpublished D. Phil Thesis, Oxford University, 1961.

Smith, C. Jay, Jr. *The Russian Struggle for Power, 1914–1917. A Study of Russian Foreign Policy During the First World War*. New York: Philosophical Library, Inc., 1956.

Smith, Douglas. "Grigory Rasputin and the Outbreak of the First World War." In Brenton, ed., *Historically Inevitable? Turning Points of the Russian Revolution*, 48–65.

Sokolov, Nicholas A. *The Sokolov Investigation of the Alleged Murder of the Russian Imperial Family*. Translated by John F. O'Connor. New York: Robert Speller & Sons, 1971.

Solomon, Georg. *Unter den Roten Machthabern. Was ich im Dienste der Sowjets persönlich sah und erlebte*. Berlin: Verlag für Kulturpolitik, 1930.

Solzhenitsyn, Alexander. *August 1914*. Translated by H. T. Willetts. New York: Farrar, Straus, and Giroux, 2014.

———. *Deux siècles ensemble, 1795–1995. Tome 1: Juifs et russes avant la Révolution*. Paris: Fayard, 2002.

Stanziani, Alessandro. *L'Economie en Révolution. Le cas russe 1870–1930*. Paris: Albin Michel, 1998.

Steinberg, John W. *All the Tsar's Men: Russia's General Staff and the Fate of Empire, 1898–1914*. Baltimore, MD: Johns Hopkins University Press, 2010.

Steinberg, Mark D., and Khrustalëv, Vladimir M. *The Fall of the Romanovs. Political Dreams and Personal Struggles in a Time of Revolution*. New Haven, CT: Yale University Press, 1995.

Stevenson, David. *Cataclysm: The First World War as Political Tragedy*. New York: Basic Books, 2004.

Stites, Richard. *Revolutionary Dreams. Utopian Vision and Experimental Life in the Russian Revolution*. New York: Oxford University Press, 1989.

Stone, David. *The Russian Army in the Great War: The Eastern Front, 1914–1917*. Lawrence: University Press of Kansas, 2015.

Stone, Norman. *The Eastern Front 1914–1917*. New York: Charles Scribner's Sons, 1975.

———. *Europe Transformed 1878–1919*. London: Wiley/Blackwell, 1999/1983.

Sukhanov, N. N. *The Russian Revolution 1917. A Personal Record*. Translated by Joel Carmichael. New York: Oxford University Press, 1955.

Suny, Ronald. *Armenia in the Twentieth Century*. Chico, CA: Scholars Press, 1983.

———. "Empire and Nation: Armenians, Turks and the End of the Ottoman Empire." *Armenian Forum* 1, no. 2 (1998): 17–51.

"Tell of Kolchak's Gold." *New York Times*, September 30, 1919.

Tolstoy, Leo. *The Cossacks*. New York: Tark Classic Fiction, 2008.

Tuchmann, Barbara W. *The Zimmermann Telegram*. New York: Viking, 1958.

Tunstall, Graydon. "Austria-Hungary and the Brusilov Offensive of 1916." *Historian* 70 (1) (Spring 2008) 30–53.

Ullman, Richard. *Anglo-Soviet Relations, 1917–1921, Volume 3: Anglo-Soviet Accord*. Princeton: Princeton University Press, 1961, 1968, and 1972.

Vasiliev-Iuzhin, Mikhail. "The October Revolution in Saratov." In Jonathan Daly and Leonid Trofimov, eds., *Russia in War and Revolution, 1914–1922: A Documentary History*. Indianapolis, IN: Hackett Publishing Company, 2009.

Volkogonov, Dmitri. *Lenin. A New Biography*. Translated by Harold Shukman. New York: The Free Press, 1994.

von Hagen, Mark. "The Great War and the Mobilization of Ethnicity in the Russian Empire." In *Post-Soviet Political Order. Conflict and State Building*. London: Routledge, 1998.

Wawro, Geoffrey. *A Mad Catastrophe. The Outbreak of World War I and the Collapse of the Habsburg Empire*. New York: Basic Books, 2015.

Werth, Nicolas. "The Iron Fist of the Dictatorship of the Proletariat," "The Red Terror," and "The Dirty War." In *The Black Book of Communism. Crimes, Terror, Repression*. Translated by Jonathan Murphy and Mark Kramer. Cambridge, MA: Harvard University Press, 1999.

Wheeler-Bennett, John W. *Brest-Litovsk. The Forgotten Peace, March 1918.* New York: St. Martin's Press, 1956.

Wildman, Allan K. *The End of the Russian Imperial Army*. 2 vols. Princeton, NJ: Princeton University Press, 1980/1987.

Williams, Robert C. *The Other Bolsheviks. Lenin and his Critics*. Bloomington: Indiana University Press, 1986.

———. *Russian Art and American Money, 1900–1940*. Cambridge, MA: Harvard University Press, 1980.

Willmott, H. P. *The Last Century of Sea Power. Volume One: From Port Arthur to Chanak, 1894–1922*. Bloomington: University of Indiana Press, 2009.

Zenkovsky, Alexander. *Stolypin: Russia's Last Great Reformer*. Translated by Margaret Patoski. Princeton, NJ: Kingston Press, 1986.

Zhirnov, Yevgenii. "Kak Zakalialsia Brend. O role 'Rolls-Roisa' v rossisskoi istorii," *Kommersant-Den'gi*, March 15, 2004.

PICTURE CREDITS

Index